'Splendid, wide-ranging photographs by Robert Vavra . . .
a remarkable book : I can think of nothing anywhere near
so thorough.'
SPECTATOR

'An intimate picture of the places, people and spirit of
the essential Spain, and the photographs contribute much,
seeking to capture the real character and daily concerns
of Spaniards rather than presenting postcard views.'

GEOGRAPHICAL MAGAZINE

'From the glories of the Prado to the loneliest stone
villages . . . here is Spain, castle of old dreams and new
realities.'
NEW YORK TIMES

*Volume Two contains chapters on Salamanca, Pamplona,
Barcelona, bull-fighting, Teruel, and Santiago de
Compostela.*

ALSO BY *James A. Michener*

IBERIA

VOLUME TWO

Spanish Travels and Reflections

JAMES A. MICHENER

PHOTOGRAPHS BY ROBERT VAVRA

CORGI BOOKS
TRANSWORLD PUBLISHERS LTD
A NATIONAL GENERAL COMPANY

IBERIA

VOLUME TWO

SPANISH TRAVELS AND REFLECTIONS

IBERIA VOLUME TWO

A CORGI BOOK o 552 98733 6

Originally published in Great Britain
by Secker & Warburg Ltd.

PRINTING HISTORY
Secker & Warburg edition published 1968
Secker & Warburg edition reprinted 1969
Corgi edition published 1971

Published by Transworld Publishers Ltd.,
Cavendish House, 57–59 Uxbridge Road, Ealing,
London, W.5.

Made and printed in Great Britain by
Fletcher & Son Ltd, Norwich

Contents

Acknowledgments appear in Volume One

SALAMANCA

VIII

The hand of Salamanca
has always extended a welcome.

OCEANO
ATLANTICO

MILES
0   100

La Coruña

Burgos

Valladolid
Toro   Tordesillas
Medina del Campo
Madrigal de las Altas Torres
Porto   Arévalo
Salamanca
Avila
Madrid

Barcelona

Guadalupe

Lisboa

Sevilla

MAR MEDITERRANEO

Salamanca's Plaza Mayor is the finest in Spain and one of the four best in the world. St. Mark's in Venice has a richer variety of architecture; the Zócalo in Mexico City is larger in expanse; and the barbaric Asian splendor of the Registan in Samarkand is without equal. But the Plaza Mayor is unique in that its spacious area is bordered on all four sides by what amounts to one continuous building, four stories high and graced with an unending arcade of great architectural beauty. It is the most harmonious plaza extant, with its repetitious balconies and windows providing just enough accent and its blending colors creating a vision of amber loveliness. On a sunny afternoon, with the sidewalk cafés filled and the parade of charming girls in progress, it has a human warmth that the other great plazas lack, and it is worth a considerable trip to see.

To sit lazily in the plaza and study the minor variations in the vast building which curls about you is delightful. On the north side and the west the balconies are continuous, but on the south and east they are broken in interesting patterns. Both the north and south façades are interrupted by two large gateways, but the east and west have only one. The plaza isn't quite a perfect square. One afternoon when I had nothing better to do I stepped it off in all directions, but I forget the results. And on the north face the continuous building elevates itself slightly to become a palace serving as the town hall.

The outstanding feature is the endless arcade; in heat of day café chairs are moved off the plaza and under the arcade, but at other times it forms a graceful promenade lined with fine stores. Between the arches of the arcade, medallions have been prepared for bas-reliefs showing the prominent figures of Spanish history; medallions along the north and west have remained empty, but the first in line along the east contains Generalísimo Franco, well sculpted and imperial of mien, followed by imposing figures like Alfonso XI, Fernando and Isabel, she most stalwart, and Juana la Loca and her collar-ad husband Felipe I, the tragic couple whom we met at Granada. A curious feature of the medallions, and one which must have been accidental, is the fact that the carving of Carlos the Bewitched has begun to crumble, so that his features have fallen away to leave a sense of idiocy. The once-proud Habsburg chin has vanished in the rain.

Along the south there are generals, too. El Cid looking like a knight of medieval Germany, and el Gran Capitán who conquered Italy, Pizarro from the plains of Extremadura, and a strange fellow with German mustaches labeled Don Xptova Colón, the one who discovered America. The permanent impression of the plaza is one of complete unity rigorously enforced and quiet beauty where human beings can rest. Day or night, it is a magnificent setting.

Salamanca is a very old city and the town fathers must have had courage to decide, as late as 1729, to build a new plaza whose four sides would be kept harmonious. The work of renovation took seven decades, and not one façade was left untouched. In recent years the city fathers have been less courageous; they have surrendered to the automobile. Salamanca is so laid out that the easiest solution to its traffic problem is to allow several main arteries to flow into the Plaza Mayor, which thus becomes a huge traffic circle, and one can no longer dawdle across the beautiful pavement for fear of being run down. Furthermore, as in most European cities, the politicians have been unable to withstand demands for parking space and have allowed this once-glorious spot to degenerate into a vast parking lot, while from its rooftops gleams a forest of television aerials.

When I sat in the plaza I was accompanied by a ghost from my childhood days, a man whose trail I was to follow through many different parts of Spain, a man of the most contradictory and perplexing character but one who had been important to me for half a century. I could close my eyes and visualize him in this plaza he had frequented and recall the first time I had met him. It was in the sixth grade in a small Pennsylvania school and our teacher, a tall, rather thin woman whom we liked, had finally found a subject she could get her teeth in, and she spoke with an intensity that I can still remember.

'Especially the boys in class should listen to what I'm going to say.' No one moved. 'In your life you must have some great man to whom you look up.' We looked up to the basketball captain, who was in high school. 'Not many are worthy of such respect, but the hero of our next poem was.' We slumped. Another sales talk on memorizing poetry. 'He was one of the bravest men in history and he did something I don't believe any boy in this class could have done.' We sat up again. 'Any of you could be brave in

A street lamp in the Plaza Mayor.

victory. When your side's ahead I've seen how brave you can be. But this man was brave in defeat. And that requires a real man.' This was new and we listened. 'Against odds so great that other men would have crumbled, he fought on. When his companions failed, he didn't. He was more heroic than the heroes of fairy tales. He was a man you must remember.' I often recalled this sentence. 'But what do you suppose happened to him? At the very moment of victory, when he had done all he set out to do, what happened?' I wanted to slump, because I was pretty sure this was where the girl came in. He married her no doubt. It always happened in poems, but something in the teacher's voice caused me to hesitate. 'At the moment for which all boys long, the moment when he had won, a cannonball killed him.' No previous poem had ended this way, and we sat silent. 'In a strange city, on a battlefield overlooking the ships he had been fighting to reach, he was killed.' Moved by her own eloquence and feeling kinship with the boys of her class, she sat down, opened her book and began to read those lines which, unknown to me at the time, she was engraving on my mind:

> 'Not a drum was heard, not a funeral note,
> As his corse to the ramparts we hurried.'

Books were then distributed, bearing not only the poem but the famous painting by Smith, and we read the history of Sir John Moore, the English general who in 1808 and 1809 led an invasion into Spain against Napoleon and without fighting one engagement turned around and retreated to the northern port of La Coruña, where at the moment of having brought his army into sight of the rescue flotilla, he was killed by a cannonball.

Whenever our class memorized a poem, we held a competitive recitation, and in the case of 'The Burial of Sir John Moore,' I won handily, which was not entirely fair because I *was* John Moore. I had read everything I could find on him, and traced his route from Lisboa into Spain and out again, and knew La Coruña rather better than I did my home town. It was the first time in my learning that a subject had completely overwhelmed me and I it.

Therefore, it was with a sense of acquaintanceship that I sat in Salamanca and reflected that a hundred and fifty-eight years earlier, on November 13, 1808, General Moore had arrived in this plaza to hear reports of a concentration of English defeats and Spanish confusion. Suddenly, what had begun as an invasion to consolidate English and Spanish forces against Napoleon had become a trap in which Moore's entire army, the best in the field, was about to be swallowed up. If Moore had lived he would have hated the memory of Salamanca, for here he heard nothing but news of the most disheartening sort. The allies were in a state of collapse and Napoleon was triumphant.

As a boy I had not yet learned about my hero certain facts which were probably not in the books at that time, namely, that from Salamanca he had sent off a most puzzling series of letters in which he showed no hesitancy in predicting his defeat. To his quasi-sweetheart, Lady Hester Stanhope, who imagined that she was engaged to him and survived him to become one of England's outstanding eccentrics, he wrote that her little brother James, for whom she sought a commission, 'must get the Commander-in-Chief's leave to come to Spain. He may join me then. He will, however, come too late; I shall already be beaten.' In his diary he wrote: 'We have no business being here.' In his dispatches, either to England or to his fellow commanders in Spain, he wrote constantly of the probable need for retreat rather than attack, and a palpable sense of gloom possessed him. In Salamanca, General Moore had hardly been the hero whose exploits I had memorized; in fact, he was something of a fuddy-duddy and the disasters he foresaw were brought on partly by his own indecision and fatalism.

On December 11 he evacuated Salamanca and headed for the north, uncertain whether he was advancing to battle or taking the first steps in what would degenerate into a forced retreat. Rarely has a more confused and undecided leader led his troops into unknown territory, and we shall leave him as he marches out of the city but we shall meet him again in the north.

If you quit the Plaza Mayor by its southwest exit and wander through a series of attractive narrow streets you will come eventually to an austere little plaza presided over by the statue of a professor in robes, Fray Luis de León, whose spirit guards this place, and enclosed on four sides by old brown walls on which students have used a mixture of hog fat and bull's blood to scrawl the dates of their doctor's degrees, for this is the noble University of Salamanca, once the world's preeminent center of learning.

In the academic year 1567–1568 its rolls showed seven thousand eight hundred students taking courses ranging from mathematics to medicine and another five thousand hanging around the city to audit lectures. Carlos V spoke the truth when he said, 'This university is the treasury from which I furnish justice and government to my people of Spain,' for the cachet of a Salamanca degree could not be equaled. Throughout Europe foreign kings and cardinals submitted disputes to this faculty for adjudication, and if a professor from this university approved a debatable point, that practically established it.

The scholars teaching here investigated all matters. It was a Salamanca economist who first pointed out the national danger involved in bringing so much gold into the country without increasing at the same time the production of consumer goods; he saw that ruinous inflation must

FOLLOWING FACING PAGES:
Shields at the University of Salamanca.
Observe the busts set within the cockleshell
of Santiago de Compostela.

follow. Far more than half the intelligence of Spain centered in this school, and the roster of graduates who attained fame is a roll call of Spanish power. The most daring intellects, I suppose, attended Cardinal Cisneros' university at Alcalá de Henares, but it had a relatively brief life, whereas Salamanca continued through the centuries as the heart and core of Spanish culture.

Bologna, Paris and Oxford, all founded in the twelfth century, were the only schools that could compete with it, and during its early life—it was founded about 1230–1243—it tended to be more liberal and introspective than the others. It was powerful in theology and often provided

*In the cloisters of the university
some of the foremost scholars
of the world assembled,
but there have also been periods
of darkness.*

opinions on which the Spanish kings based their defiance of the Roman popes, but its greater fame lay in mathematics and science, in which it was a beacon light far ahead of its competitors.

Not all students who came here prospered, and in fiction 'the student from Salamanca' became a stock figure. In the Duque de Rivas' tragedy, *Don Alvaro*, the younger son, who follows Alvaro's trail to Peru, is described in this way:

> My cousin, who has just arrived from Salamanca, has told me that Alfonso is the crazy man of the University, more swordsman than scholar, and that he has the student bullies flabbergasted.

413

In an earlier play by Lope de Vega the earthy dialogue catches the spirit of Salamanca as understood by the common people across Spain:

BARBILDO: How did you get on at Salamanca?
LEONELO: That's a long story.
BARDILDO: You must be a very learned man by now.
LEONELO: No, I'm not even a barber.
BARBILDO: At least you're a scholar.
LEONELO: Well, I've tried to learn things that are important.
BARBILDO: Anyone who's seen so many printed books is bound to think he's wise.
LEONELO: I admit that printing has saved many talented writers from oblivion. Printing circulates their books and makes them known. Gutenberg, a famous German from Mainz, is responsible. But many men who used to have a high reputation are no longer taken seriously, now that their works have been printed.

Today the old classrooms, the cloisters, the marvelous library and the chapels can be inspected in the dignified buildings that enclose the plaza, and here one can catch a sense of what it must have been like to attend a university in the late Renaissance when ideas were exploding at such a furious rate. Each component at Salamanca is perfect, as if time had frozen the old patterns.

As a matter of fact, that is precisely what happened. Under pressures which will be made clear in this chapter, this grand university, light of Europe, began to grope and fumble. First, any student suspected of Jewish blood was excluded. Then it became difficult for bright boys from untitled families to gain entrance; vacancies were reserved for the nobility, who used the university as a kind of gentlemen's finishing school. At the end of the sixteenth century Salamanca no longer taught mathematics in any form and fifty years later enrolled not a single student in medicine. The fine interchange of ideas that used to be carried on with Oxford and Bologna was halted, and the sharp debate that once characterized the intellectual life of the university was silenced. Registrations dropped from seven thousand eight hundred to a mere three hundred in 1824.

I know of no other educational institution in the world that started so high as Salamanca to fall so low. Its eclipse was one of the severest blows Spain ever suffered, for with its castration the spark of national vitality ebbed, and any nation today that wishes to attain similar results should start by closing down its equivalent of Salamanca. Of course, the university did not physically disappear; except for years of revolution and crisis it kept its doors open and admitted a few hundred students who mouthed cautious doctrine taught by frightened professors. During the heyday of the Spanish empire students from Mexico and South America came to

A feature of university life in Spain is the tuna,
a group of students dressed as medieval troubadours
who roam the streets playing guitars and tambourines
in which they collect contributions.

Salamanca so as to be able, when they returned to their colonial cities, to boast as scholars had for five hundred years, 'I am from Salamanca.' There was also an Irish College attached to the university, and here young Catholics who could not obtain an education at home studied for five or six years, a large proportion of them finally becoming priests, so that much of Ireland's intelligence over long periods of time was trained in Salamanca.

Today the university functions normally. It is neither the superior center it once was nor the fraud that followed. It is known within Spain as the school for lesser intellectuals of good family, and few enterprising businesses would hire a Salamanca man when they might get a sharp young fellow trained either at Madrid or Barcelona.

Halfway between the university and the Plaza Mayor, at the northeast corner of two narrow streets, stands a stalwart brown Renaissance building four stories high, built in the early 1500s in the shape of a fortress. In Salamanca one can find many such buildings but this one has captured the imagination of all, because its main façade is studded with sixteen rows of beautifully carved conch shells, with varying numbers of shells to the row; some contain as many as twenty-three, others only fourteen, but they mark the building with elegance. This is the famous Casa de las Conchas (House of Shells), whose owner was a member of the Order of Santiago, and it illustrates how a capricious artistic invention can sometimes convert an ordinary structure into something enchanting.

When I am in Salamanca, I like to go to La Casa de las Conchas at noon as the sun creeps into the Calle de Meléndez and begins to throw the shells into lovely patterns of light and shade. I sit for about an hour on the stoop of a shoemaker's shop cater-cornered to the shells and enjoy the sensation of seeing the tip of one shell after another emerge from shadow into sunlight until finally the whole shell glows. The carved shields that top the windows burst into sunlight; the eagle pecks at the rays as they slide past and soon his wings are golden.

From the nearby cathedral, a curious affair in which a very old cathedral about to fall down was propped up by building a new one alongside it, bells begin to toll the quarter-hour and enough sun reaches the wall so that the protruding shells cast long diagonal shadows. At half past twelve the shoemaker suggests we have a cold drink; the whole façade is now in sunlight and will stay so for some hours. I see that the stone wall is not entirely flat, for the building is old, and here and there its stones have bulged, but now the house can be seen at its best, glowing in sunlight, and I wonder at myself for finding so much pleasure in watching the metamorphosis of a building notable only because some crazy architect slapped a couple of hundred conch shells across its face. Still, if I returned to Salamanca tomorrow I'd perch myself once more on the shoemaker's stoop to watch this bewitching ballet of sun and stone.

The ways of tourists are strange, and one afternoon as I sat in the Plaza Mayor I heard some Frenchmen at the next table tearing America apart. To the first barrage of criticism I could not logically protest: Americans were uncultured, lacked historical sense, were concerned only with business, had no sensitivity and ought to stay home. The second echelon of abuse I did want to interrupt, because I felt that some of it was wide of the mark: Americans were all loud, had no manners, no education, no sense of proportion, and were offensively vulgar in dress, speech, eating habits and general comportment, but I restrained myself because, after all, this was the litany one heard throughout Europe, here expressed rather more succinctly than elsewhere. But when these Frenchmen added a third charge I had to intervene: Americans menace the world because they refuse to face reality.

I happened to have in my hand at that moment the official card distributed by the French government honoring the twentieth anniversary of the Allied landings at Normandy on June 6, 1944. It was a well-presented design, as such things are apt to be in France, and showed a heroic General de Gaulle leading ashore an army of French soldiers and being greeted by stalwart members of the underground who had already vanquished the Germans occupying France. Far in the distance and bringing up the rear were one American foot soldier and one English officer. I passed the card along to one of my French neighbors and asked, 'Is this reality?'

He took the card, looked at it, smiled and said, 'History is what wise men say it is.'

'Do you really believe it happened that way?'

He tapped the card, neither in approbation nor rejection, and said, 'This is what has been agreed upon.'

'Have the charges you've been making about Americans also been agreed upon?'

'Yes.'

'So they are now the truth?'

'In Europe, yes.'

'Very interesting,' I said, turning away from the noisy Frenchmen to ponder the curious fate of Americans in the world today. I was at the moment especially depressed by some English books I had been reading, in which sensible writers with university degrees said the most extraordinary things about American travelers whom they had met in Europe. The Americans were all stupid and objectionable and loud and uneducated; and I sat at my table and made a list of the Americans I had met in recent travels: three Nobel Prize winners; two of the world's finest playwrights; three good novelists much read in England and France; four nationally famous bankers who in their spare time serve on the boards of universities, opera houses and museums; a score of quiet-spoken professors; a woman who helps run the Cleveland art museum; the director of one of our great symphonies; and two very well behaved painters. These people were, by any standard, among the leaders of the world and certainly

*Along the Sierpes in Sevilla,
along the promenade in Badajoz
and even in the smallest Spanish city,
you will find the glass-fronted club
where old men sit lost in reflection.
This one happens to be in the
Plaza Mayor at Salamanca.*

among the best educated and most gently cultured. Not one spoke in a loud voice; in fact, I had had to lean forward to catch what Tennessee Williams said, and the Ashcrafts, whom we shall meet in Pamplona, speak so softly they practically whisper.

'Why does no European ever meet this kind of American?' I asked myself. In the three latest English travel books on Spain there was a constant procession of American boors and boobs, but the authors were well-versed men and must surely have come into contact somewhere with the kinds of Americans I knew. I concluded that English writers could not be charged with animosity, for this they did not intend; they were merely accepting blindly a kind of American Black Legend and compounding it monotonously. I cannot charge them with planned falsehood, but I can query their powers of observation and their fairness in recording what they see.

In my travels I have encountered some pretty horrible English men and women. There was the chinless wonder in Singapore who for business reasons wanted to take me into the exclusive Raffles Club and spent some forty minutes coaching me on how I must behave, forgetting that I had

spent two years at one of Britain's best universities. He was so asinine he was funny. At the Sevilla airport I watched two formidable English women, the type who seem to be in constant supply, demand in piercing voices where their luggage was. In clear Spanish the porter replied, 'Enter the building, turn left, ten minutes.' The women, irritated by now, shouted their question again at the poor man, both speaking at once, and he with gestures explained once more, 'Enter the building, turn left, ten minutes.' The women looked at him with contempt, brushed him aside, and one said to the other in a loud voice. 'Poor beast. He doesn't understand a word we're saying.'

And so on. The point is that although I have seen such behavior ad infinitum I have refrained from writing about it as if it were standard English deportment overseas, because I know it isn't. I have met too many English gentlemen to allow myself such error. I do not refrain from lampooning the English because I love them but because I have regard for fact.

Sitting as quietly as my French companions would permit, I tried to discover what my true feelings were in this matter of honest description.

In my travels I have never met any single American as noisy and crude as certain Germans, none so downright mean as one or two Frenchmen, none so ridiculous as an occasional Englishman, none so arrogant as some Swedes and certainly none so penurious as the Portuguese. For raw misbehavior no American could surpass a prime example from India or Egypt, and for the unfeeling, uncultured boob that I encounter so often in literature as representing the American, I suspect one would do better to look among the Russians.

But in each of the national examples cited I am speaking of only a few horrible specimens. If one compares all English tourists with all Americans, I would have to admit that taken in the large the American is worse. If some European wanted to argue that seventy percent of all American tourists are regrettable, I would agree. If he insisted on eighty percent, I'd go along. If he claimed ninety, I suppose I wouldn't argue too much. But when, like the Frenchmen to my left and the English writers under my arm, he states that one hundred percent are that way, then I must accuse him of being false to the facts.

Of all the countries in which to travel, I find that today the American is judged more honestly in Spain than elsewhere. He is not loved, but neither is he abused. The average Spaniard objects to having American military bases on Spanish soil, but he acknowledges the need for protection. He is suspicious of the large number of American Protestants who come to Spain and is sure they are up to no good. He is aggravated by the sight of American military personnel spending large and easy sums of money, but he is gratified that the Yanks behave as well as they do. Because Spain is a dictatorship it is obligated to decry democracy, and since America is a leader among the democracies, newspapers run a constant commentary on our failures, especially in handling the race problem. Reading Spanish newspapers, one would judge that the United States was about to collapse, but at the same time the impression is given that she is a resolute ally on whom Spain can depend. Because Spain is a Catholic country, her newspapers must decry American excesses in sex, education and family life, and a lurid picture is presented, but Americans are also presented as courageous, good sports and dependable.

Two points are amusing. Because Spain for many years was lacking in consumer goods, it was obligatory to prove that the United States had lost its soul in pursuit of such goods. Special contumely was heaped upon our system of time payments. 'Americans have the television set, but they never own it. It has been loaned to them on time payments, and to meet those payments they mortgage their souls.' The soul of Spain, these articles pointed out, was not corrupted by time payments. But with the arrival of television the initial cost of a set was so great that the average Spanish family could not advance the cash at one time. A system of time payments was obligatory and one was initiated, but if you ask a Spaniard about this he says, 'Yes, but the system we worked out doesn't corrupt the soul.'

If on almost every topic Spain is reasonably fair to America, on one it is not. Spain hates Yale University. I suppose that if the government called for volunteers tomorrow to invade Connecticut and raze Yale, it could have an expeditionary force by twilight; in a period of three months I read four assaults on Yale, some lamenting that a great university should have fallen so low, others threatening reprisals. The trouble stems from the announcement by a group of Yale professors in 1965 that they had found a map proving that Christopher Columbus was not the first to discover America in 1492 but that a Scandinavian had by 1118 and possibly as early as 1020. 'The lie was bad enough,' a Spanish scholar told me, 'but to have announced it on the eve of October 12, El día de la raza, when the world was preparing to honor our great Spanish explorer—that was too much. With that action Yale blackened its name.'

It is surprising to find that most Spaniards consider the Italian Columbus as one of them, just as they nationalize the Greek El Greco. At the same time they protest when the French government includes Pablo Picasso in a list of French painters. When I commented on this contradiction, a Spaniard pointed out, 'You Americans insist in your literature courses that Henry James and T.S. Eliot were Americans, even though they emigrated to England, but you also claim a painter like Lyonel Feininger and a scientist like Albert Einstein, even though they did most of their work in Germany.'

Apart from such natural chivvying, the American traveler meets a more congenial reception in Spain than in other European countries, but I suspect this will not be true much longer, for the signs are that with affluence Spain will go the way of France. In Salamanca I decided to take advantage of the favorable travel conditions and visit a cluster of five small towns to the northeast, for in them I would be able to trace out a network of lives that had helped make Spain what it is today.

Madrigal de las Altas Torres (Madrigal of the High Towers), could there be a more poetic name for a town, even though the derivation must have been from some prosaic word like madriguera (burrow or lair of animals)? And could any town so named be lovelier than this, nestling sun-baked within its circle of ruined towers? Today it looks almost as it must have in 1450, its walls forming a complete circle, not large in diameter, its narrow streets wandering beneath arches. The same notable buildings are there, and when the church bells ring they send their evening song out across the same fields of wheat.

Only the towers are not quite the same. They still stand, of course, but many have lost their tops through crumbling, and the once impregnable defenses are no longer so. In spite of all I had read about Madrigal, I had not visualized what an excellent monument it was, a gem of medieval life protected within its walls.

The town is very ancient, dating back perhaps to Roman times. When the Moors reached this far north Christians tried to halt them here, and the town was destroyed in a series of sieges and countersieges, but when the Moors triumphed it was rebuilt and given both the towers and the name it bears today. It was the walls that attracted the kings of Castilla, for once inside these battlements they were safe, and it was here that Juan II, the one who sponsored the Conde Alvaro de Luna, whose genuflecting statue we saw in Toledo, built a palace in the early 1400s. Later it was converted into an Augustinian convent where surplus females of the royal line were hidden away, and it was in this convent that I picked up the thread I was to follow through the five towns.

I first saw the convent from a distance, an ugly, low palace with miserly windows and little to commend it. Walls in the shape of a lozenge enclosed a large garden, and I judged the whole could accommodate about three hundred nuns, but their lives would presumably be rather hard, for the old convent seemed cold and forbidding. I went to what must have been the main entrance to the castle when kings lived here, but it was closed.

'You enter by the side,' a woman called from the street, and I walked along the bleak wall until I came to a corner, where I found the present entrance tucked away under three handsome stone arches that formed a small protected porch containing a device I had often read about but never seen. It was a torno (wheel), a large lazy Susan with sides about two feet tall and set into the wall in such a way that the nun inside the convent who turned it could not see the person who might have deposited a bundle on the other side. This was the way in which the unwed mothers of Spain had traditionally turned their unwanted babies over to a convent without being recognized. Many notable Spaniards had started life in the turning of some torno.

I rang the bell which hung beside the contraption, and after a moment the torno slowly revolved while a nun inside checked to see if I had abandoned a baby.

'What do you want?' an unseen voice asked.

'To see the cradle of Spanish history,' I said, repeating a phrase seen on posters advertising Madrigal.

'Wait.'

There was a long pause, then finally a door, far removed from the torno, opened and I was greeted by two of the shortest, oldest nuns I had ever seen. 'Come this way,' they said, leading me into the convent that had once been a palace.

It was a quiet spot, marked with rough dignity rather than formal beauty. The double-tiered cloisters were low and unadorned, but they stood in such stateliness around the enclosure that they seemed more attractive than ornate ones I had seen elsewhere. In the center stood a low octagonal well, again of deep simplicity, protected by a plain tiled roof.

The rooms followed the lead of the cloisters, for they too were square and unadorned. 'This is the old kitchen,' one of the Agustinas said, and when I commented on how large it was, she explained, 'Yes, for in those days we had hundreds here. Now we are but twenty. And they speak of closing us down.' I looked about me at the medieval spaciousness, and she said gloomily, 'I know. It is large and we are small.'

Whenever the two nuns led me to a new part of the convent they first rang a warning bell, and I could sometimes catch the flight of skirts as someone disappeared around a corner, but if I did meet a nun unexpectedly face to face, one who had not heard the warning, she was always very old. 'This is the hall where nobles were received on visits,' my guide said, and for the first time I saw that long chain of portraits, painted in heavy brown by some untalented artist centuries ago. They are not good art, but they awaken powerful memories and convey an excellent idea of why such royal convents were necessary in the old days.

This tall, thin-faced nun is Doña María, the illegitimate daughter of Fernando the Catholic. This pleasant round-faced nun holding a skull in her right hand is Doña María Esperanza, also an illegitimate daughter of Fernando. This curious portrait of a nun who looks half infant, half dowager portrays Doña Juana, illegitimate daughter of Carlos V, while this austere nun proudly holding a crown is Doña Ana María, illegitimate daughter of an illegitimate son of Felipe IV and the actress María Calderón. And here is the most memorable of all, a saucy-faced young woman whom we must remember, for we shall study her strange career in detail. She is a delightful-looking person with her coif awry; of all the royal nuns she alone shows a peek of hairdo. She also is alone in wearing jewelry and in her left arm she carries a cute little puppy, and her whole manner is so provocative that one could predict from seeing her that 'this one will come to no good.' As a matter of fact, she ended her life as Mother Superior of the most powerful convent in Spain, but her road to that eminence was rocky. She is Doña Ana, illegitimate daughter of Don Juan de Austria, the illegitimate son of Carlos V. He was the admiral whose blue battle flags from Lepanto we saw in the museum at Toledo.

There are other portraits in this powerful row, many of them the illegitimate daughters of royalty, and one begins to understand why the existence of these girls, if they were allowed to move freely in society, could have been a considerable embarrassment to the crown. Since they were illegitimate they could not be offered in marriage to other heads of state, which meant that any adventurer might pick them up, sire a few children and claim hereditary rights to the throne of Spain. Great care was taken to keep them safely locked up and their imprisonment began at age five or six. The legend attached to the portrait of Doña Juana, daughter of Carlos V, tells the whole story: 'Illegitimate daughter of the emperor, died a novice at the age of seven years.' A legend across the frame contains a rather neat play on words:

> Date a Dios en tierna edad;
> Vivirás eternidad.

(Give yourself to God at a tender age, you will live eternally.) Many of these little girls matured to become responsible leaders of their convents.

'And here is the chapel,' the old nun intoned, 'and the beautiful marble tomb of Doña María, natural daughter of Fernando, and here is the organ brought down from Germany to soothe the king with soft music.' She went to the keyboard while her partner pumped a huge bellows, and soft wheezing sounds came forth as they had done four centuries ago.

I was beginning to think that we would never come to the room which had lured me to Madrigal, but now we passed along the upper tier of the cloister while my guide rang her bell to disperse any nuns working there and we came to a window from which I could look down into the rather large garden of the convent, where four nuns were weeding. 'We eat what we grow,' my guide said, 'and we don't get fat.' And then there we were! A very ordinary anteroom containing two royal portraits, and an inner room with no window and only a big rough wooden door whose panels opened one by one so that servants outside could pass food into the room without being seen. 'This is it,' the nun said reverently.

And I was in the room where Isabel of Castilla was born, known to history as Isabel the Catholic, loyal wife of that Fernando who sired the impressive line of illegitimate offspring. The more one studies Spanish history, tracing out the actual sources and operations of power, the more highly he regards Isabel. In personality, devotion, intelligence, fortitude and above all in administrative power, she makes all other women of her age and most of the men seem puny. War, the presence of Muslims on her soil and the philosophical upheavals of the age confronted her, but one by one she triumphed over them, leaving when she died a kingdom on its way to solidity where before there had been only a hollow crown.

The representative fact about Isabel is that she bore five children, some of whom were to become notable in European history, and she gave birth to each in a different city, often after days and weeks in the saddle protecting her realm. She was a colossus of her age, a woman who supported Columbus in his discovery of a new world, and Anglo-Saxon scholars fail to do her justice. For example, one major encyclopedia allots her only sixty-four lines while giving her unimportant daughter Catalina two hundred and forty-five merely because she happened to be the first wife of Henry VIII. And Mary Queen of Scots, who accomplished nothing compared to Isabel, is accorded a staggering eleven hundred and eight. This is not only insular; it is ridiculous.

How did she happen to be born in Madrigal? When the Conde de Luna was running Castilla on behalf of the weak and widowed king Juan II, he engineered, if you remember, a marriage between Juan and Isabel of

LOS REYES CATOLICOS

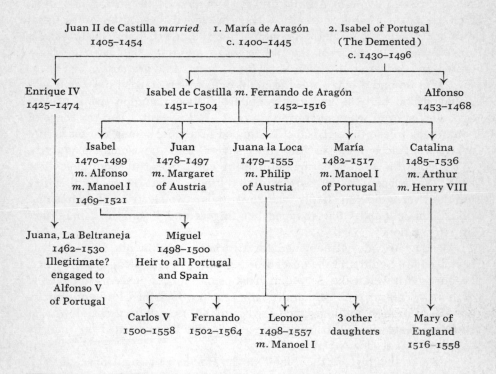

Juan II de Castilla *married* 1. María de Aragón 2. Isabel of Portugal
1405–1454   c. 1400–1445   (The Demented)
   c. 1430–1496

Enrique IV   Isabel de Castilla *m.* Fernando de Aragón   Alfonso
1425–1474   1451–1504   1452–1516   1453–1468

Isabel   Juan   Juana la Loca   María   Catalina
1470–1499   1478–1497   1479–1555   1482–1517   1485–1536
m. Alfonso   *m.* Margaret   *m.* Philip   *m.* Manoel I   *m.* Arthur
m. Manoel I   of Austria   of Austria   of Portugal   *m.* Henry VIII
1469–1521

Juana, La Beltraneja   Miguel
1462–1530   1498–1500
Illegitimate?   Heir to all Portugal
engaged to   and Spain
Alfonso V
of Portugal

Carlos V   Fernando   Leonor   3 other   Mary of
1500–1558   1502–1564   1498–1557   daughters   England
   m. Manoel I   1516–1558

Portugal, the lady who shortly thereafter caused Luna's head to be struck off and who later became demented. Juan already had one son, Enrique, who was first in line for the crown, and this Enrique would have a daughter Juana, who would be second in line. Isabel of Portugal would also present the king with a son, Alfonso, who would be third in line. Therefore, when in 1450 the queen announced that she was pregnant it caused little stir, for the crown was already protected with heirs, so while her husband in his feeble way watched over the government she hied herself to the family palace at Madrigal, not yet a convent, and there gave birth to a daughter, Isabel.

In the bare anteroom there was a portrait of her, and she looked to be a stocky, heavy-faced, powerful woman with large eyelids and a stunning air of command. Whether or not the portrait was physically accurate I did not know, but psychologically it was. No one ever reported her to be beautiful but many commented on the fact that she was a tender mother, a wise ruler and a woman of merciless determination.

While I had Isabel's character in mind, I wanted to see Arévalo, which represented the next step in her development, so I left Madrigal by the southern gate, picked up a small road which led to the east and after some twenty miles I came to Arévalo and its brooding castle among the ruins. The town was strange in many ways; through the centuries an unusual number of churches had been built and the town found itself with a surfeit. Sensibly, some of the unnecessary buildings had been deconsecrated and converted into mental asylums, others into granaries.

Arévalo had a plaza, not the main one, which startled me, for it was unpaved and had the low monotonous buildings common five centuries ago, so that even when men in modern dress crossed it, I had the sense of being back in the time of Isabel. I stopped in a store facing the plaza and asked what accounted for this timelessness, and the woman explained, 'We keep it this way so that motion picture companies can shoot their films here. We've been in the movies many times. Look! To make this five hundred years old you simply take down those two electric light wires and that Coca-Cola sign.' She snapped her fingers and I made the imaginary transformation.

Today Arévalo is renowned for two accomplishments. It makes the best bread in Spain and the best roast pig. Of the bread I can say only that I ate it as if it were cake. Served in crusty small loaves, it seems to be made of honey, cream, rock salt and coarse grain which has lost none of its goodness through milling. Once I was in the area with a friend who at each meal ate three loaves, by himself. When I commented on this, he asked, 'Why eat meat when this is here?'

As for the pig, at the Figón de la Pinilla (Eating House of Mrs. Pinilla), an old restaurant on the main plaza decorated with scenes from plays and movies, the dish is served each Tuesday, on all feast days and during the June feria. It is so well regarded in the region that Arévalo's poet laureate, Marolo Perotas, has cast the recipe into heroic blank verse:

> Everything is golden,
> Everything is aromatic,
> Everything is glistening
> Because of the lard and garlic.

If the verses are reduced to prose, which hardly seems appropriate for such a dish, the directions become simple: 'Select a fat little suckling pig twenty-one days old and barely nine pounds in weight, because if it is larger the result will be greasy, tough and coarse. Remove all the hair and slit the pig open from head to tail. Then in a rough black earthen casserole bake it at a temperature of 185°, and in a little more than an hour and a half it is ready to eat.' The result was so good that I had to fault the poet for having kept to himself the basting secrets. Suspecting that a good

Dressed in traditional black,
the women of Spain can be the most delightful,
robust and amusing in Europe.

many herbs went into the dressing, I slipped into the kitchen of the figón to interrogate the cook. 'Of course! Butter, onion, salt, lots of paprika, bay leaves, garlic, lemon, parsley, thyme and white vinegar.' I complimented him, and he added, 'Don't go easy on the paprika.' As he cooked it, the roast pig of Arévalo was a rich, greasy, succulent feast which Spaniards enjoy and foreigners approach with caution.

It was not for roast pig that Isabel of Portugal and her daughter Isabel, who was to be known as the Catholic, came to Arévalo, nor for the bread either. They came here to live in the castle, a large gloomy place but one that could be defended, while the king spent his last days in confusion and died. Young Isabel, still far removed from the succession, was of little importance, so mother and daughter stayed in the forbidding castle and slowly Isabel of Portugal went mad. She used to scream at her attendants and alternately love and berate her daughter. She beat her head against the wall on occasion, but for the most part she receded to quiescence and sat for days staring at the walls of her self-made prison. Her daughter was allowed little freedom, and her long stay at Arévalo could just as well have been spent in any other of the nearby towns, for they were monotonously alike.

Isabel's half brother, the infamous Enrique IV, ascended the throne and debauched the Spanish court to an extent that made him the worst king Spain ever had. Morals degenerated, sexual abuses became open, and it is generally believed that the austerity which characterized Isabel stemmed from her revulsion at her brother's behavior. She became personally involved when Enrique discovered that in her he had a pawn of value and started those tedious negotiations whereby he offered her in marriage to this or that impossible French or German or Portuguese royal personage. At one point he proposed a most decrepit Spanish nobleman and at another he conducted serious discussions over a possible marriage to the hunchback who later became Richard III of England, but Isabel shied away. It was degrading, to waste one's time cooped up with a near-mad mother and to be bandied about by a degenerate half brother, but that was the way Isabel passed her days in Arévalo.

By the time I picked her story up again at the little town of Toro, perched on a cliff overlooking the Río Duero, which crosses northern Spain to enter the Atlantic at Porto, her luck had changed dramatically. She had taken matters into her own hands and had found a husband for herself, the dynamic and gifted Fernando de Aragón, two years younger than she but a handsome, daring fellow who was to prove so adroit in manipulating Spanish interests in Italy that Niccolò Machiavelli would use him as the archetype of the cynical ruler in *The Prince*. It was a love match, at least on Isabel's part, but also a miraculous union of equals; Fernando was probably the best man in Europe for Isabel to have married and together they made a formidable team.

Never did Fernando look better, either to history or to his young wife, than at Toro, for here by his gallantry he ensured her crown. Her incompetent father, Juan II, had died. Her half brother, King Enrique IV, had also died. Her full brother, who might have inherited the throne, had died earlier; but this did not leave Isabel next, because Enrique had left a daughter Juana, who if she were legitimate would become queen. Juana was born in wedlock, of that there was no question, but nobles who sought to place Isabel on the throne pointed out that during Enrique's life he had been known openly as The Impotent, and a credible rumor was started: 'Juana is the daughter of the queen but not of the king.' Matters were complicated when the King of Portugal, seeing a good chance to meddle in Spanish affairs and perhaps win the throne for himself, announced his betrothal to Juana and his intention of using the Portuguese army to put her on the throne. This the nobles supporting Isabel could not permit and war became inescapable. After much jockeying back and forth, the two armies finally faced each other here at Toro in the year 1475.

I was fortunate in Toro in finding as guide—impromptu friend might be the better word—an old man some five feet tall and weighing about two hundred and twenty pounds. He was remarkable both for his information and for his trousers, which had to be ample to cover his girth but which also came nearly to his chin. He was encased in wool and his fly was at least twenty inches long. He was in love with Toro and its distinguished old buildings but his field of specialization was the Battle of Toro. 'It determined the course of Spanish history,' he said. 'If Portugal had won, no Isabel the Catholic. No Carlos Quinto. And Portugal would have won except for two Spanish heroes. You ever hear of Cardinal Mendoza of Toledo? Our warrior cardinal? His bravery helped save the day. But our hero was Fernando. How lucky Isabel was to have chosen such a man. What he did here at Toro will always be remembered.'

What my roly-poly guide told me next was so improbable that I did not believe him, convinced that he was repeating a legend, but later when I looked it up in histories I found that he had been telling the truth. In 1475 Fernando made this proposal to the King of Portugal: 'Since our armies cannot seem to reach a conclusion, let you and me duel in the old manner, the lady of the winner to become Queen of Spain.' At first the Portuguese agreed and plans were made for what would have been the last time in history when two sovereigns met in single combat to decide the inheritance of their nations, but at the last moment the King of Portugal withdrew, not surprisingly, since he was forty-three while Fernando was only twenty-three. Later in 1476, when battle between the armies could no longer be avoided, Cardinal Mendoza's firmness and Fernando's fine generalship gave victory to the Spaniards, and Juana, whom many modern historians accept as the rightful heiress to the throne, was driven from Spain. Isabel, by right of conquest, was Queen of Castilla, and as soon as the Moors could be driven out of Granada, would be Queen of Spain as well.

Standing on the cliff at Toro, looking down at the Duero below me, I listened as my fat guide with the amazing pants said, 'To think that the history of an entire peninsula should have been decided here . . . in a little town like this,' but when I questioned him on details, he had to admit that the battle hadn't occurred exactly at Toro. 'Farther down the river . . . toward Portugal . . . and if the truth were known, Queen Isabel wasn't here during the battle. She was back in Tordesillas, waiting, waiting. King Fernando rode down that road over there to take her the news, and when he reached her and assured her that she was to be queen, she wept. It was a very good marriage, that one.'

I was much taken with Toro, for it was an excellent town, far enough from the main road to receive few tourists yet so filled with memories that those who did come could see shadows of kings as they prepared for hand-to-hand combat. At dusk one night I crossed the river to travel out to the scene of battle, and I understood then how Fernando had utilized the river to advantage, and when I turned back, there was Toro atop its eroding red cliff, magnificent in outline against the dark sky of evening, its turrets jagged, its crumbling walls still defiant. Next morning I went on to Medina del Campo, coming in sight of this once-great city not long after dawn.

I stopped on a slight rise to imagine what it must have been like, in the sixteenth century, to be a merchant coming to Medina del Campo from Flanders. The journey across France and the Pyrenees had been difficult, but the fair at Medina was so important that one dared not miss it, for here the commerce of Europe was largely determined. From a hill like this, one would have seen a dozen informal caravans converging on Medina: Italians on horseback, Germans on foot, Frenchmen in a brotherly union of merchants and churchmen, all on their way to the fair. Off to the left, down from the upland plains of Castilla, there would be herdsmen coming in with huge flocks of sheep and to the right other herdsmen from Extremadura bringing cattle. As many as fifty thousand traders converged on Medina each year in its days of greatness.

But when I reached the city I could find no evidence of that glory. No restaurants were open, no bars, but I did find a bridge that crossed the Río Zapardiel, a stream I had often read about: 'From Antwerp and London came the merchants to set up their booths along the banks of the Zapardiel.' I had imagined a broad, flowing river. It was four feet wide, six inches deep and its banks were lined with rubbish, but at one end of the bridge there was a churro shop, and even though I knew I would be sick the rest of the day, I entered.

'Señor! You're a norteamericano but you know what's good, eh?' The speaker was a robust woman barely visible through clouds of smoke coming from deep pots in which boiling oil was being used to fry churros.

The smell was overpowering but it did have a certain enticing quality, as if to say, 'You know damned well churros are inedible, but don't they smell good?'

At a chrome-plated machine the woman was cranking a handle which extruded a flour paste about the diameter of a quarter, but with fluted edges. This she cut off in ten-inch lengths, twisting their ends together and plopping them into the crackling fat, where they fried for a few minutes to emerge an appetizing brown. She sprinkled them with a coarse sugar and set two before me.

'Chocolate?' I nodded, and into a small cup she poured a chocolate thicker than most soups and as delicious as it was aromatic.

Churros and chocolate! I suppose if one searched the restaurants of the world one could not find a worse breakfast nor one that tasted better. The churros were so greasy that I needed three paper napkins per churro, but they tasted better than doughnuts. The chocolate was completely indigestible, but much better than coffee. And the great gobs of unrefined sugar were chewy. Any nation that can eat churros and chocolate for breakfast is not required to demonstrate its courage in other ways.

I remember Medina del Campo as fifty-percent churro indigestion, fifty-percent frustration, for when the town was awake I went into the plaza and began asking people, 'Where is the old palace in which Queen Isabel died?'

'She died in the castle up there on the hill,' they all said, pointing to one of Spain's better-preserved fortresses, and it was appropriate to think that a girl who had lived so long in a similar castle at Arévalo had died in this enormous pile of rock, but I knew that this was only legend. Records proved that Isabel had died in a small palace somewhere inside the gates of Medina del Campo and I wanted to see where.

'Wait till the stores open,' the policeman said, so I wandered in the plaza and came upon something I had not expected, four low pillars not more than two feet high, connected by heavy chains, inside which stood two large ruined pillars and a plaque which read:

> DURING THE FIFTEENTH AND SIXTEENTH CENTURIES,
> WHICH MARKED THE APOGEE OF THE CLASSICAL FAIRS
> OF MEDINA DEL CAMPO, AT THIS POINT IN THE PLAZA
> MAYOR THE MONEYCHANGERS AND BANKERS OF THAT
> TIME INSTALLED THEIR BOOTHS OPEN TO ALL THE
> WORLD. MEDINA WAS, DURING THESE CENTURIES,
> COMMERCIALLY ECUMENICAL AND HERE THE LETTER OF
> EXCHANGE WAS CRYSTALLIZED IN ITS DEFINITIVE FORM.

More important than the cattle fair or the assembly of merchants had been this yearly meeting in Medina of bankers from all over Europe for the purpose of determining the relative values of national currencies and the clearing of loans against one another. For example, a merchant in Antwerp could promise a customer, 'I will pay your banker in London three hundred pieces of gold at the fair of Medina del Campo.' Or a banker in Naples could say, 'Three hundred coins, their value to be determined by the price of gold at Medina.' Here also were developed, as the signs said, the sophisticated instruments of international banking, for just as the university at Salamanca had constituted a kind of clearing house for ideas, so Medina had set standards for commercial dealings. While I was in Medina a conference of international bankers was being held in Madrid, but they did not take a side trip to Medina, where their profession began, and I thought that a pity.

When the stores opened, so did my confusion. 'Isabel's palace was over there,' I was told, but that was wrong. 'It's over there,' another said, but that was wrong too. Finally a friend had the good idea of inquiring at a bank, and by luck we hit the nephew of Medina del Campo's cronista— that is, the town's historian, poet, bibliographer and publicist—and the young man said, 'You won't believe what I'm going to show you, but it will be the palace in which Isabel died.'

'How can you be sure?' I asked.

'My uncle is the cronista. He knows everything.' And he led us to a crumbling building at one corner of the plaza, and no one could have guessed that this had once been a palace fit for the death of Europe's noblest queen. Inside the creaking door a temporary wooden booth had been erected for the sale of tickets to a comic bullfight: 'The Fireman Bullfighter! Estupendo! 75¢!' A fine old wooden stairway led to a second floor littered with all kinds of filth, and the rooms which once had housed the queen and her attendants were now barred, for a century ago the palace had been converted into a jail. Men who had stolen sheep or murdered tailors had spent their last days in the room which Isabel had used for her dying. With the coming of indoor toilets one closet had been redesigned, but it had degenerated into a state of filth. And so it went through all this historic site. It was ironic, I thought as I left the palace, that even the nearby church, which Isabel had done so much to save, was the ugliest I was to see in Spain, a true masterpiece of junk.

But her monument is not a broken-down palace in Medina del Campo nor an ugly provincial church nearby. Spain is her monument, united and Catholic, as she had determined it should be. Her administration was the best the country would know, for she kept little books in which she listed the names of all the capable men she met, so that when a vacancy occurred in any department she had an immediate replacement, who rarely proved unworthy. Militarily, financially and spiritually she left Spain a bulwark among nations, and I judge her to have been twice the ruler that her grandson Carlos V was and also better than her great-grandson Felipe II.

It was an Italian humanist, Pedro Mártir de Anglería, servant at the Spanish court since 1487, who wrote in a private letter the eulogy which most Spaniards accept as the final word on Isabel:

> The pen falls from my hand and my strength fails through grief: the world has lost its most precious ornament, and the loss should be mourned not only by the Spaniards, whom she has so long led along the road to glory, but by all the nations of Christendom, because she was the mirror of all virtues, the refuge of the innocent, and the scourge of the evil; I doubt that there has lived in the world a heroine, either in ancient or in modern times, who merits comparison with this peerless woman.

One must note, however, that much of what is popularly taught about Isabel is not true. She did not unify Spain, for when she died the nation once more divided. Fernando kept for himself the Kingdom of Aragón, but the Kingdom of Castilla went to Isabel's daughter Juana. Fernando, treated miserably by the nobles of Castilla, sought revenge by marrying, within a few months of Isabel's death, nineteen-year-old Germaine de Foix, niece of the French king. He did this for two reasons, to spite the Castilians and to sire an heir who would inherit his half of Spain.

Promptly, Germaine gave him a son, and in this way Fernando, in an act of revenge, threatened to destroy all that Isabel had accomplished, but the boy died shortly after birth, whereupon Fernando and his child bride tried desperately to have another, but the old man was not equal to the task, so Germaine instructed her apothecaries to concoct a brew of blood, herbs, magic elements and bull testicles, which she fed Fernando in such quantities that she undermined his health. He died without further issue and it was due solely to this lucky accident that Spain had another chance to unite.

Isabel's life with Fernando had never been easy, for while living with the queen he had fathered four bastard children, each by a different mother. The two girls we have met, tucked away at Isabel's command in the convent at Madrigal de las Altas Torres. One of the boys became a soldier, the other, at the age of six, Archbishop of Zaragoza. When Cardinal Mendoza died Fernando insisted that this youth, then only twenty-four, be made Archbishop of Toledo and thus primate of all Spain, but here Isabel put her foot down. She preferred naming an archbishop of her own choice and it was the best decision she ever made, for her candidate was Cisneros, and had he not taken charge when Fernando finally died, twelve years after Isabel, the breach between Castilla and Aragón would probably have become irreparable.

I left Medina del Campo and drove a few miles north to another cliff on the Río Duero, where in the town of Tordesillas the tragedy of Isabel came to an end, years after her own death. I had known of Tordesillas in other contexts without realizing that it was one of the principal theaters of the Isabel story. In 1493 Pope Alexander VI, seeking to obviate colonial quarrels between Catholic countries, had established a Line of Demarcation between Spanish and Portuguese claims. It ran one hundred leagues west of the Azores but was not entirely satisfactory, so in 1494 envoys of Portugal and Spain, supervised by representatives of the Papacy, convened here in Tordesillas to sign the treaty defining a new line two hundred and seventy leagues farther west. It was as a result of this treaty that a country like Peru became Spanish, whereas Brazil was Portuguese. But for the student of Spanish internal history, events of much greater significance occurred in Tordesillas and it was these that I wished to track down.

As the genealogical chart shows, Fernando and Isabel were blessed with numerous progeny, and one of the queen's notable accomplishments was her manipulation of their marriages. She married her oldest daughter, Isabel, to Alfonso, heir to the throne of Portugal, but he died suddenly, so the young widow was passed along to Manoel, the next in line; but the young Isabel said she would not marry him unless he agreed to expel all Jews from Portugal the way her mother had from Spain. This curious wedding present was granted and the marriage took place to the wailing of many Jews. Then it was Isabel who died, so her mother quickly arranged for her third daughter, young María, to marry the widower Manoel (when María died in 1517, Manoel took a third wife from the family, Queen Isabel's granddaughter Leonor!). When Isabel's youngest child, Catalina, reached the age of four she was promised in marriage to Arthur, Prince of Wales to the English throne, who was three, and when the girl was eleven the betrothal was formalized. At sixteen the marriage took place but Arthur was sickly and soon died, whereupon shrewd Isabel, in defiance of the Church's decree against such incestuous marriages, passed Catalina along to the dead man's brother, the new Prince of Wales, who was to become Henry VIII. Life with him was hell, but Catalina did escape the ax which ended the reigns of two of her successors, and she did give birth to Mary, who succeeded in restoring England to Catholicism, as her grandmother would have wished, even though the restoration was reversed by her successor, the Protestant Queen Elizabeth. It was with her son Juan and second daughter Juana that Isabel had her outstanding success, because for them she arranged a double wedding with the daughter and son of Maximilian, ruler of all Germany, Holy Roman Emperor and head of the house of Habsburg.

In Spain, Margaret of Austria, Maximilian's daughter, married Juan, heir to the Spanish throne, while in Flanders, Archduke Philip of Austria, son of Maximilian and heir to vast estates in the Low Countries and elsewhere, known in Spain as Felipe I, married Juana. It was in this manner that Spain became involved not only with the Habsburgs, who ultimately inherited the throne, but also with the Low Countries, which were to be a permanent thorn in Spanish flesh. Young Felipe was probably the most attractive prince of the century, a lustful, vain and somewhat stupid young man who set out to humiliate his dowdy Spanish wife and who with his infidelities drove her mad. (John Langdon-Davies, in his study of Carlos the Bewitched previously cited, argues that it was the other way around and that it was Juana's encroaching madness that almost drove Felipe out of his mind; but one must remember that the thesis of his book is that Juana was genetically insane, because of her inheritance from the demented Isabel of Portugal.) When this happened it was of no great consequence, because Juana, like her mother a generation earlier, was originally well removed from the throne. First in line was her brother Juan, who had married Felipe's sister. Second was her own sister Isabel, now Queen of Portugal; if her brother died she stood to be queen of two countries. And third was Isabel's son, heir to the Portuguese throne and putative heir to that of Spain as well, in which case the Iberian peninsula would again be united as it had sometimes been in the past. So for the present no one bothered much about Juana's trouble with her handsome husband; it was no worse than what Catalina had to put up with from Henry VIII. But once again, as in the case of the famous Isabel, miracles began to happen. Juan died suddenly. Isabel did the same. And to the horror of Portugal and Spain alike, young Miguel died at the age of two. Suddenly Juana la Loca, as she was being called behind her back, found herself heiress to the throne of Spain. If she could somehow control her husband and her mind she might look forward to a reign equaling her mother's in brilliance. With these prospects Juana and Felipe came to Spain to claim their inheritance, and we shall see them next wandering about the open countryside north of Tordesillas under conditions so gruesome as to form one of the weirdest chapters of history.

Before I started to trace the story of Juana, I wanted to see what modern Tordesillas was like, so early one morning I perched myself in the Plaza del Generalísimo Franco, where grass grew in the corners. Forty-four awkward stone pillars supported an arcade which in places threatened to collapse, while many of the houses fronting on the plaza showed walls that had to be propped up with poles. Several had been patched with a cheap stucco painted to simulate concrete block, and all needed painting. Such women as appeared tended to be dressed in black; they worked while their men in patched pants lounged in the shade. I noticed especially six brightly painted heraldic shields of Tordesillas being used as decorations around the plaza; they bore a set of flashy symbols consisting of keys, mountains, a river and three saddles. The last, I was to discover, were debatable additions, for there was much confusion as to what they signified. A bartender said, 'There was a big battle over there. Very crucial. Everything depended on what the volunteers from this town did. But like always they messed things up. They were late in their saddles [tarde en sillas] and after the battle was lost we were stuck with the name.'

A customer said, 'Wrong again. One of the old kings was hunting here and he had a fine afternoon, so he named the town Tarde en sillas, which means Afternoon in the saddles.' Another said, 'The name of the town comes from a word. Tardecillo, a little late. Has nothing to do with saddles.' I said that must be wrong because three saddles appeared on the town shield, and he laughed. 'A friend of mine painted those shields last year. To please tourists'; whereupon a fourth man growled, 'They all don't know anything. This town was named by the Romans before Spanish was a language. The name has no meaning.'

The only things in the plaza that reminded me I was in this century were two signs splashed in dripping letters: 'Viva Franco' and 'Gibraltar Is Spanish.' The latter brought me back to Queen Isabel, for on her deathbed she had added a codicil to her will instructing her people never to surrender Gibraltar; with much effort she had won it back from a noble family that had usurped it for private use, and she foresaw its importance.

I doubt that she could have foreseen the important role that Tordesillas was to play in the history of her family. It began ominously. On September 25, 1506, Felipe I, who ruled jointly with Juana, died at Burgos in the north. The queen was understandably distraught over losing the man who had bewitched her, and unluckily at this moment she fell under the control of a Carthusian monk, who consoled her: 'With sufficient prayers your husband the king will revive. I know a case in which a king who had been dead for fourteen years rose to rule again.'

These words helped launch Juana on a course without parallel. Keeping her husband's casket beside her, she moved to various towns and monasteries in northern Spain, seeking some area which might inspire Felipe to return. On the night of November 1 in the monastery at Miraflores she commanded the casket to be opened to assure herself that the king was with her. Either on Christmas night or a few days prior, having moved to a new area, she opened the casket again, and one of her companions reported, 'All had calcified into a solid mass and it did not have the odor of perfume.'

In April, under the stars of an open sky, she inspected the remains once more, and this incident has formed the subject for several fine historical paintings. In July she was settled at Hornillos, where she gave birth to a posthumous child, and in the church she again tried to communicate with the sadly decomposed body, and for a fifth time in her room nearby. Finally, in February of 1509, after nearly three years of such wandering, she came to rest at Tordesillas, where she reluctantly consented to have her husband buried in the local monastery. Then, so as not to be parted from him lest he should, as the Carthusian promised, rise from the dead to resume his reign, she immured herself in a nearby palace, where she was to spend the next forty-six years of her life.

How did the body of Felipe find its way ultimately to the grandiose tomb in Granada? After Juana had been locked up for two years her mind wandered so badly that she forgot the casket which had haunted her, she forgot the handsome young husband who had treated her so poorly, where-upon officials quietly disinterred the body for the last time and shipped it off to the royal pantheon in Granada, which had been Felipe's choice in the first place.

She posed quite a problem for the Spanish government. She was clearly the Queen of Castilla with claims to Aragón as well, and if sane should be ruling in Madrid; but if she was, as seemed likely, insane, she should be kept locked up and her son Carlos V should rule on her behalf. When Carlos arrived to assume the crown he visited his mother; he could speak Flemish, French, German and Italian but no Spanish, and in his brief conversation with her satisfied himself that she was indeed insane. It was under his instructions, therefore, that she was kept locked up, to become a constant source of scandal in the other courts of Europe. Ambassadors paid large sums for rumors of the queen. One reported that she urinated almost constantly, another that she was more animal than human, another that he understood she was quite sane. When a revolution broke out against Carlos, the revolutionists naturally sped for Tordesillas, where after an interview with Juana they pronounced her sane. To this day debate continues. All we know is that for nearly half a century she was kept imprisoned in a ratty old building which no longer stands.

From its windows she could look below to see the Río Duero idling past the cliffs as if it were a lake. Trees filled the distance, and flat fields on which wheat and grapes had grown as long as men could remember. She could also see the road to Medina del Campo and must often have watched with vacant eyes as various messengers rode up that road with instructions from the king. When the sky was cloudless she could see the battlements of the castle at Medina, and on moonlit nights the scene must have been beautiful. In winter her palace was bitter cold, in summer stifling.

We know what life was like in the prison at Tordesillas because Carlos V kept close tabs on his mother lest she escape and embarrass him; a wealth of documents exists, none more interesting than the list of persons in attendance on the queen which Amarie Dennis found in the archives of the National Library when doing research for her biography of Isabel:

The governing staff within the palace was composed of the Marqués of Denia and his wife; the Count of Lerma, Francisco de Rojas, and his wife; Fernando de Tovar and his wife; Luis de Cepeda, majordomo; Doctor Santa Cara; Ana Enríquez de Rojas, a nun; Magdalena de Rojas, Countess of Castro; Francisca de Rojas, Countess of Paredes; Margarita de Rojas; and Beatriz de Bobadilla, an elderly servant who had accompanied Juana to Flanders in 1496. The rest of the staff, whose names are all listed, was comprised of seven yeomen, two overseers, a food provisioner and seven assistants, a librarian, a bailiff, three cooks, three assistant cooks, a tailor and his helper, a cupbearer and his aide, an apothecary, a shoemaker, a furrier, a man to attend the braziers, a watercarrier, a carpenter, a poulterer, a sweeper, a hunter of partridges, six servants to take care of the silverware, fourteen lackeys, six butlers, twelve chambermaids, one seamstress, four laundresses, five serving maids, one wardrobe keeper, one carver, two gate-keepers, three footmen, twenty-four *montero* [huntsman] guards, and five bodyguards. To serve in the royal chapel, there were fourteen chaplains, two altar boys and three sacristans. Aside from these, there were the wives and the children of a large proportion of the servants of the household.

In other words, a hundred and fifty-five people to look after one addle-brained old woman.

Juana la Loca constitutes one of the mysteries of Spanish history. I find it difficult to believe that she was sane, but on the other hand I find in European history several monarchs who ruled more or less successfully while no more. sane than she. I suppose that with a council to guide her she could have governed moderately well; however, her son Carlos V was doubtless far more capable, though I am far from satisfied the he was as good for Spain as she would have been. Juana, completely Spanish, would at least have focused on Spanish problems rather than dissipate her kingdom in an attempt to dominate Europe, and it is tantalizing to reflect that a sane son destroyed Spain whereas an insane mother might have saved it.

There is one spot in Spain that everyone should see, for it pertains to the character of the country yet is so inconvenient to visit that there is no rational point from which one can say, 'Let's visit the Shrine of Guadalupe now. We may never have a better opportunity.'

It hides in a remote corner of Extremadura and could be visited from Badajoz, but the road is poor. It stands not too far from Trujillo, but when I was in that city I was told the route was so inconvenient that I ought to by-pass the shrine. Religiously it is governed from Toledo, and once years ago I intended to set out from Toledo to see it, but friends refused to let me risk the miserable road. At the monastery of Yuste, I was almost due north of Guadalupe, but there was no direct communication. Now, from a totally ridiculous point of departure, I was determined to see the shrine, so one morning I set out from Salamanca, kept Yuste to the east and dropped down through Trujillo to try the ferocious road that appeared on the map with the proud title Route C-401. The scenery was exciting, with low mountains, long vistas and here and there small villages where life progressed much as it had four hundred years ago, but the road was so twisting, with eight or ten right-angle turns to the half-mile, that the couple riding in the back seat of our car got seasick and the driver complained that his arms were wearing out.

But even if one had no concern with religion, the drive to Guadalupe would be worth the effort, for just as it seemed that all of us had had enough, the road climbed a sharp hill and below us we saw one of the

She must also have seen the magpie flying to Medina del Campo.

choice sights in Spain: a compact monastery, so beautiful in all aspects that it is an architectural treasure, set down in a rustic small village surrounded by handsome olive groves that fill the valley. The road stops. There is no economic life, no transportation, no rich farming. In fact, if it were not for what happened here around 1325 there would be no reason for the village to exist.

One day a cowherd whose name is remembered, Gil Cordero (Giles of the Lamb), was looking for a strayed cow that had been grazing along the banks of a turbulent river which came out of these unpopulated mountains, and as he did so he saw projecting from the soil the brown and weathered statue of a Virgin, later to be known as the Virgin of Guadalupe (River of the Wolf, according to some; Hidden River to others). As her history was uncovered, it was seen that she was no ordinary Virgin.

The last work of art done by St. Luke, the painter-physician-evangelist, was this carving of the Virgin, for which she posed on the Greek island of Patmos just prior to her death in Turkey. The statue was buried at the city that later became Constantinople, whence it passed to Rome. Around A.D. 600 Pope Gregory the Great ordered that St. Luke's Virgin be paraded through Rome in an effort to end the plague, which she did. The statue was then sent to Spain, but when the Muslims overran the country devout followers carried the Virgin to the banks of this remote hidden river and buried her, where she slept undisturbed for more than six hundred years, until Gil Cordero found her.

Her fame spread over Spain and was responsible for several victories over Muslim armies. As the Virgin of Extremadura she sponsored the settlement of the New World, where, after appearing personally to the Mexican peasant Juan Diego in 1531, she became even more popular than she was in Spain. From all parts of the world riches flowed into this remote shrine, until it became the wealthiest religious foundation in Christendom. The official historian of that period affirms that more than one hundred and twenty lamps of pure gold or silver burned at her shrine, that she had countless vestments heavy with jewels, and that the Hieronymite friars who tended the shrine had so much money that they ordered from Toledo cleaning buckets and broom handles of solid silver.

It became traditional for rulers of Spain to come to Guadalupe to pay homage to the Virgin, and large buildings had to be erected to lodge the royal visitors whose names form an index to Spanish history; therefore, it was not unexpected when in 1928 King Alfonso XIII came here to supervise the canonical coronation of the Virgin of Guadalupe; henceforth, she would be one of the official Virgin Queens of Spain.

There are three reasons why one should visit Guadalupe: to see the Virgin, to see her robes, and to see the Zurbaráns, and in the company of Don Pedro Rivas, the practical-minded mayor of the village, I proceeded to do so. Don Pedro was a different kind of mayor, a farmer with a rough-and-ready approach to his position and a manifest delight in the dark Virgin of Guadalupe. 'To approach her with due reverence,' he said, 'we must pause here in the anteroom. Look at those marvelous paintings! By Luca Giordano, who must have been an Italian. Aren't they glorious? And big? Look at that dear little angel with the bare bottom who leads Mary's donkey on the flight to Egypt. And the angels flying overhead with flowers. Isn't that a fine presentation of the Virgin protecting her child?'

I found the Giordanos (1632–1705) overpowering—nine huge canvases—but the eight polychromed statues of 'the strong women of the Old Testament' were delightful. They were carved in the fashion of eighteenth-century Versailles and showed shepherdesses with crucifixes, jewels, straw hats and those lovely flouncy skirts and aprons which milkmaids were supposed to wear at court revels. Ruth, Jael and Esther were especially charming, the first with wide black eyes and porcelain skin and under her arm a sheaf of gleanings from the fields of Boaz.

'But this is the room!' Don Pedro said with visible excitement as he led me to the shrine itself. How disappointed I was. There really wasn't much to see, just a wealth of gold and jewels and ornate carving. The Virgin, apparently, was not visible to ordinary eyes, and I must have

Even in the north, where one is not accustomed to the relics of the Moorish occupation, figures like this appear at the crèche to remind one that even cities like Salamanca were under Moorish rule for centuries.

shrugged my shoulders as if to say, 'Well, that's that,' when the mayor signaled two young friars, who slowly turned a revolving pedestal. As they did so, the Virgin came mysteriously into view, and she was so resplendent that no amount of previous reading could have prepared me for what I now saw. In a niche with wings, each inch of which was covered with either gold or enamel scenes from the Bible, stood a relatively small Virgin, an adorable figure, with dark mottled face and black right hand which held a scepter. She looked as if she had lain in earth for six hundred years, but her charm derived from the tradition of dressing her in a gown and cape made of luminous cloth of gold encrusted with jewels. Her robes flared out, hanging straight across at the bottom and tapering upward to her crown and halo of precious stones, forming a delicate, bejeweled triangle.

441

'¿Estupenda, eh?' the mayor asked. She was. It was the only word which applied, for visually she was one of the most appealing religious figures I have ever seen. I doubt if the leading prelates of Spain, sitting in conclave, could have come up with a more appropriate figure to epitomize their country's attitude toward religion.

'Do you like the Jesus?' Don Pedro asked. I looked about for a statue of Jesus and it was some moments before I discovered that in her left arm, which was of course invisible, the Virgin held a precious little doll-like figure of Jesus, also scarred in the face, also dressed in robes which duplicated the triangle formed by those of his mother. He too was crowned, but far less gloriously. As I looked at the two figures I reflected that it was at about the time when this series of buried Virgins was being uncovered in various parts of Spain that the country began to dedicate itself to Mary, long before the movement became common in other parts of the world, and I concluded that some two hundred years from now Spanish religion may well focus exclusively on the Virgin, with Christ having receded to a background position somewhat like that enjoyed by the Holy Ghost in Protestantism half a century ago. Already a Virgin like this adorable one of Guadalupe seems much closer to the heart of Spain than does a remote figure like Jesus.

I am not one to waste time marveling at the routine tapestries held in the usual monastery treasury, but at Guadalupe I was stunned when Don Pedro and the friars showed me where the robes for their Virgin were stored. One large shallow drawer after another was pulled out to display the many alternate sets of vestments. 'This one filled with flowers woven in silver,' explained the mayor, 'was sent here from the Netherlands in 1629. This one laden with diamonds and gold was made in the time of Carlos Quinto. And this one, well, who can describe it? The most costly piece of fabric in the world. A hundred and fifty thousand pearls, handfuls of diamonds, gold so heavy the cloth can scarcely be lifted. We have loved our Virgin and we have wanted her to dress well.'

'How many complete sets of robes has she?' I asked.

'These are just the precious ones,' and he indicated some thirty drawers. 'The lesser ones are over here. Peru, Chile, these three from Mexico with Mexican gold, Poland. She has many robes.' I had stopped looking at the robes, for I felt smothered in pearls and gold; instead I tried to imagine how a large meeting room nearby must have looked on that fateful first of January in 1577, when King Felipe II of Spain entered by this door and his nephew, King Sebastián of Portugal, entered by that to conduct the meeting which started the curious story that I shall be speaking of at the end of this chapter. It must have been an extraordinary scene and I wondered how kings could have covered the journey from Madrid and Lisboa to such a spot.

Finally, in the vestry of the monastery Don Pedro showed me that row of eight masterpieces painted by Francisco Zurbarán; if one does not see his work in this room one misses his talent. His commission was one of those ordinary jobs which have defeated so many good painters: 'Portraits of the leading friars in the history of this monastery.' The Hieronymites chosen were all of advanced age and position, mostly bald, and of monotonous history, but what Zurbarán accomplished with them is well-nigh miraculous, for the tall, powerful paintings unfold with a richness of style and imagination that one would never expect if he knew only Zurbarán's lesser work. The fine series impressed me as something that might have been done by Domenico Ghirlandaio, for though Zurbarán lived from 1598 to 1664, he painted with the style of an earlier age.

For me, the apex of the series was the third picture on the left-hand wall; it showed Zurbarán at his best. It was a portrait of Father Illescas, a political priest who ruled Guadalupe and later Córdoba. His cluttered desk provided an opportunity for one of Zurbarán's great still lifes; the figure of the Hieronymite became the occasion for a splendid hard-edge portrait of uncompromising intensity; the De Hooch-like scene beyond the pillars shows the entrance to the monastery with a friar at the door dispensing alms to beggars in a style recalling the best work of Giovanni Bellini. If this magnificent work were housed where large numbers of people visited, it would be an acknowledged masterpiece. It excels its seven companions only in the excellence of its parts and the variation shown therein. As a straight piece of painting I rather preferred the simpler picture of Father Yáñez, founder of the monastery, as he kneels before King Enrique III, who bestows upon him the biretta of Bishop of Toledo. It is uncluttered, direct and powerful. Spanish critics are amused by the fact that King Enrique, who ruled 1390–1406, is dressed in the costume of King Felipe III, who ruled 1598–1621. The courtier who looks out from the background is supposed to be a self-portrait of Zurbarán, and I wish this work were located in some capital city where I might see it more often.

One of the reasons why it is so rewarding to see the Zurbaráns in Guadalupe is that the vestry where they hang is a magnificent room well suited to the display of tall canvases. The walls are white and gold; the richly ornamented ceiling is studded with windows that admit good light; and the altarpiece of an attached chapel has a heavy ornateness that glistens. It is sometimes difficult for a foreigner to believe old accounts of how wealthy the religious buildings of Spain once were, but a visit to Guadalupe corrects that.

'But the thing to remember about this room,' says the mayor as we leave, 'is that lamp suspended from the ceiling.' He points to a huge bronze brazier of Oriental design, suspended on a fine chain. 'It was brought here,' the mayor explains, 'by Don Juan of Austria after the Virgin gave him victory at the Battle of Lepanto. Captured from a Turkish galleon. The point is, we Spaniards fought to attain buildings like this . . . rooms like this.'

From Guadalupe I went north over the Gredos Mountains to the walled city of Avila, judged by most people to be the finest medieval remnant in Spain. From any approach it is a handsome sight, perched on a hill with a river nearby and massive walls enclosing it. The gates of Avila look as if horsemen might clatter out through the portcullis, and I was fortunate on my first visit to enter the city along with a wedding party that had engaged a band. It was lunchtime and we were headed for the same restaurant near the walls of the city. It was very old, with low-ceilinged rooms and open rafters, and the food was heavy. The wedding party sang, and by the time everyone was half-drunk I could not tell what century this group belonged to. In 1300 they would have looked much the same, and in 1500, too. They were the perennial farmers of Spain come to town for a celebration, and it was a noisy, delightful day. I was invited to toast the bride in a harsh red wine that went well with the roast pig we were eating, and when I left I was given a boisterous farewell. Down in the streets of Avila the noise of the celebration followed me and I could imagine a watchman of some previous age clomping along and crying to the inn, 'Ho, there! Silence! Honest men want to sleep.' It was going to be some time before there was silence.

Most visitors who come to Avila do so to pay homage to a remarkable woman whose piety made the city famous; almost none come to seek out the musician whose genius I had discovered by accident and who now meant so much to me. The woman was Santa Teresa de Avila (1515–1582), foremost of the Spanish mystics and a writer of distinction. She was born of a good family and at the age of eighteen unexpectedly announced her intention of joining a convent, where she led a prosaic life marked mainly by a lively social life which she maintained with the leading families in the area, but at the age of forty she chanced to see a statue of Christ that had been left accidentally in her path and in a moment of divine inspiration she saw through to the reality of God. From that time on she became increasingly concerned with the mystical path to religious insight, retaining, however, the hard practicality of her upbringing. She sought Papal permission to reform the lax order of which she was a member and launched the Discalced (Shoeless; that is, they wore sandals) Carmelites as opposed to the traditional Calced Carmelites, who wore shoes. Her practical mind made her an excellent administrator, and before long she established branches of her reformed order in different parts of Spain, including two monasteries for men, but at the same time her spiritual life intensified, enabling her to write a series of books which constitute the classic statement of mysticism.

When she was fifty-two she met in Medina del Campo a young priest with whom her spiritual life would henceforth be linked, and their relationship forms one of the gentlest episodes of Spanish history. Juan de Yepis y Alvarez (1542–1591), twenty-seven years younger than Teresa, was the son of very poor parents. His father died early and his widowed mother took her brood to Arévalo and then to Medina, where Juan served as male nurse in a paupers' hospital. His close contact with misery bred two results: he took vows as a Carmelite and he entertained those first mystical visions which were to characterize his life. Like other great Spaniards he attended the University of Salamanca, where at the age of twenty-five he was ordained a priest. After brief service he met for the first time Teresa de Avila, whose fame filled the countryside. Judging from externals, no one could have predicted that this fashionable, witty nun from a fine family would find in Juan de Yepis, a retiring young priest from an underprivileged family, a bond of identity, but that is what happened. The English religious expert, F. Trueman Dicken, calls their friendship 'one of the most fecund of all Christian relationships since the time of the Apostles.' In Teresa's fight to defend her Discalced Carmelites, Juan became a bold champion, and as a result spent a long confinement in a Toledo jail, where his exceptional gift for poetry manifested itself. When he left the prison he was a major poet, a lyricist of the darker moods of the spirit; the title of one of his outcries has become almost a theme song of modern confusion, 'The Dark Night of the Soul':

> On a dark night,
> inflamed with love's desires,
> oh sweet happiness,
> I went forth unnoticed
> when my house was already asleep.

In the dark night Juan found the beginning of his mystical understanding, which drew him even closer to Teresa. During one five-year period he served as confessor to the convent in Avila, headed by Teresa, and for three of those years she was in residence, so that the two mystics were able to conduct long discussions which deepened the spiritual life of each. It was this period of shared ideas that led to the richest literary results; of her experience with Juan's sharp mind Teresa said, 'He is my little Seneca.'

Teresa lived to be sixty-seven; Juan died at forty-nine, as if he felt it unprofitable to continue without the presence of his mentor. Together they bore the moves made against them by the Church and the persecutions initiated by monasteries and convents that did not want to be reformed. Each suffered severe discipline and even the threat of investigation by the Inquisition, but when they were dead, persons who knew them began to realize that in Teresa of Avila and Juan de Yepis, now known as Juan de la Cruz, this wall-girt town had produced two saints whose miracles stemmed from their close acquaintanceship with God. Teresa attained sainthood first, in 1622, Juan in 1726, and they live today as the twin glories of Avila. In the fall of 1967 Pope Paul VI announced that henceforth Santa Teresa would be considered as one of the doctors of the Church. Prior to this, there had been no woman so honored.

To Spain mysticism is as natural as the olive tree, but here it avoids both the mysterious excess and the delirious rapture of eastern mysticism.

It is a practical, one might almost say realistic, method for attaining a realization of God. It requires no trauma, is far removed from catatonic trance and avoids special vocabularies and recondite ritual; it is a very special brand of mysticism and the principal theological gift of Spain to the world at large. No better exemplars could be found than this curiously assorted pair of Avila; they were hard-headed realists when it came to the management of religious societies and self-disciplined intellects when it came to rationalizing and reporting their religious experiences. They insisted, however, upon the reality of their approach to God and defended it in pure and simple prose, none better than these sentences from the opening of Teresa's *Interior Castle:*

> Few tasks which I have been ordered to undertake have been so diffi-
> cult as this present one of writing about prayer because I do not feel that
> the Lord has given me the spirituality for it, and because for the last three
> months I have been suffering from such noises in the head that I find it dif-
> ficult to write even about ordinary things. . . . But I began to think of the
> soul as a castle made of diamond or very clear crystal in which there are
> many rooms, just as in heaven there are many mansions. . . . For if we
> consider the matter, the soul of the righteous is but a paradise in which, as
> God tells us, He takes delight. . . . Let us then consider the many mansions
> of this castle, some up high, others lower down, still others along the sides,
> and in the very center of all the principal one, where takes place the most
> secret intercourse between God and the soul.

They are children bathed in sunlight, Teresa and Juan, and they illuminated Avila and all Spain.

It is obvious that to an organized Church the mysticism expressed in the above quotation from Teresa poses a threat, for it runs the risk of degenerating into the Quaker heresy of 'each man his own priest,' because if by the mystical process one can attain direct contact with God, the intercession of Church and prelate is no longer essential, although it may for social reasons continue to be convenient. It was this potentiality in the preaching of Teresa and Juan that kept them hovering between sainthood and heresy, and much of the opposition they encountered during their working lives originated in an honest fear on the part of the Church that they were encouraging in others, if not practicing themselves, a separatism which must end in apostasy.

After their deaths that is what happened. The Illuminati, those who found God for themselves through the mystical illumination of their own souls, became quite a plague to the Church in Spain; they were considered no better than Protestants and had to be eliminated. The Inquisition was especially harsh in dealing with them, and those who were not burned were exiled, so that one sees in Avila not only the glory of Teresa and Juan but also the degeneration of their ideas in the practices of the Illuminati.

I had not come to Avila, which I remember as a uniformly evocative town, to recall Santa Teresa; I came to pay homage to one of the finest artists Spain has produced, the equal in his field to Cervantes in the novel or Velázquez in painting. I had found him for myself in one of the tardiest discoveries on record. When I was a student the music of Palestrina struck me with force; it was exactly what I had been looking for and I have never since tired of listening to *The Mass of Pope Marcellus*, which must be one of the finest pieces of choral music. But once in Germany when I bought a Polydor record of some Palestrina music, I found that the second side had been filled out with a short composition by another Italian composer, Tommaso Lodovico da Vittoria, of whom I had not heard. It was an 'Ave Maria' of such exquisite construction that I found myself playing it eight times for every once that I played Palestrina. Of all the musical settings for this prayer, and I am not forgetting Bach and Schubert, I found Vittoria's the finest, and when I looked about for other compositions by this minor Italian, I found other pieces which seemed to me about as good as choral music could be, and I began to wonder why Palestrina was so well known and his countryman so little.

I am ashamed to say that ten or fifteen years passed before I discovered that my Tommaso Lodovico da Vittoria was not an Italian at all but a Spaniard from Avila named Tomás Luis de Victoria (1548–1611), who customarily added Abulensis (of Avila) to his name, and that he had written a dozen great works which stand with the best of his age, or of any age for that matter. In time I acquired recordings of his *Officium Defunctorum* (Mass for the Dead, 1603), which critics usually select as his masterpiece, his motets and especially his *Responsories for Tenebrae* (1585), those deeply moving evening prayers. The *Officium Defunctorum* has additional interest for anyone who has visited Avila; Victoria wrote it for the funeral of the Empress María, daughter of Carlos V and sister of Felipe II, and its first performance occurred in the convent where Victoria served as chaplain, that of the Descalzas Reales, first of the Teresan convents in Madrid.

As Victoria becomes better known, the grandeur of his production is increasingly recognized. He was the equal of Palestrina in all except homophony, and this he seems to have avoided consciously. The richness of his construction and the dramatic manner in which he interweaves as many as six threads of sound, uniting them occasionally in majestic chords, form one of the joys of sixteenth-century music and I would suppose that for many who know music generally, the discovery of Victoria will be one of the few remaining delights. There could be no better approach than a recording of his majestic Christmas responsory 'O Magnum Mysterium' (O Great Mystery, 1572), which is divided into three contrasting parts: the animals observe Christ lying in their manger; peo-

FOLLOWING FACING PAGES:
*The demureness of the Spanish woman
and the arrogance of the Spanish man begin early.*

ple voice their astonishment at a virgin birth; and all explode into one of the finest hallelujahs ever written. Because of its variety and power, the 'Mysterium' is a favorite of professional singers and numerous good recordings exist.

As I walked through the narrow streets of Avila, listening to the voices of Victoria's choirs as they sang the music I had come to know so well, I reflected on the curious fate that had overtaken Spanish music. Victoria died in 1611, on August 27, a day held in reverence by mystics throughout the world as the anniversary of Santa Teresa's vision of being struck in the heart by a lance of fire held by an angel. He left Spanish music the equal of any being composed in Europe; each basic building block required for future construction had been fashioned and there was no structural reason why Spanish music should not have matured as did Italian and German and every reason why it should have surpassed French and English, but in the decades that followed, it retreated slowly, step by step, from its capable beginnings until it foundered in trivia. Even its failures lacked reach; the inheritors of Victoria produced no great masses, no soaring affirmations of belief, no operas, no symphonies, no string quartets, so that one can only ask, 'What happened?'

I spent three nights in Avila wrestling with this problem, for although the focus of my question was music, it applied equally to drama, painting, poetry and to a lesser extent the novel, and if I could find a reasonable answer to the problem of music, I might discover what had happened to the other arts. After such favorable starts, why had there come decline?

I liked Spanish music. I had studied most of the work done by Falla, Albéniz, Granados (1867–1916) and Turina (1882–1949) and had an understanding of at least the first and last of that Big Four. I judged Falla's work to be as inspired thematically as any then produced in Europe; *El sombrero de tres picos* and *El amor brujo* are gold mines of invention and are equaled only by the best work of Richard Strauss. As for Turina, his *Sinfonía sevillana,* which one can hear only on records and then with difficulty, seems a fine lament for lost opportunities; it cannot be called a great symphony in the class of the best writing done by French and English composers, let alone the German, but it is a rich tapestry and one that I have always liked.

But the more I listened to Spanish music the more I began to suspect that it failed because it lacked inherent seriousness; it did not direct itself to the major themes of life and thereby condemned itself to a secondary accomplishment. It could produce zarzuelas but not operas or symphonies. The fault could not lie with the composers, for they give ample evidence of their competence; it must have lain with the society in which they worked. Something quite stifling happened to Spanish intellectual life following the death of Victoria and it is reflected in the decline of Spanish music, as it would have to be. The melodies remain, the rhythms, the technical competence and the brilliant orchestration, but the heart has gone dry.

I once asked an international conductor about this, and he said, 'I love to conduct Falla. So colorful, so inventive. But whenever I touch his music he reminds me that what Spain needed in his day was not Spanish themes but the full explosion of world ideas. Falla of course understood this, for he had worked in Paris, but his audiences did not, and they would not have supported a composer of international stature. When you cut a nation off from world intercourse dreadful things happen.' He had recently conducted in four Spanish cities and was disturbed to find that even in 1966 Spain did not import or know the work that was being done by contemporary composers. 'It's a closed society. Falla and Albéniz, Mozart and Beethoven.'

Why had silence replaced the song? It was not any aridity in Spain as such, for her daily life provided a lyricism used to good effect by alien composers as diverse as Mozart, Verdi, Bizet and Rossini. Of course, they wrote opera, which is a complex form that may or may not be congenial to a given group of composers, but even in simpler forms Spanish musicians had at their disposal thematic material much richer than that used by Brahms, Smetana and Bartók, but they did little with it, abandoning their subject matter to foreigners like Strauss, Rimski-Korsakov, Chabrier, Ravel and Lalo. Now, we know that Spanish composers had the training and the technique, so their failure to create must have been caused by some force outside themselves. And the more I contemplated this problem, the more I was driven to that central question of Spanish intellectual history: Was it the Inquisition that crushed Spain's creative life?

The Black Legend would have us think so. It says that the Inquisition so terrorized Spanish society that anyone with an inquiring mind was silenced, that science and invention were impeded and that the speculation which is necessary alike for progress and great works of art was impossible. Much evidence of philosophers imprisoned and theologians burned can be cited to support these charges, and years ago when I first studied the matter there was no adequate rebuttal.

In recent decades, however, Spanish intellectuals have begun to fight back and some of the arguments they have developed have been startling. For me the most representative came in a book where I did not expect them, César Silió Cortés' *Isabel the Catholic, Founder of Spain*, printed in 1954. Dr. Silió, a member of the Royal Academy of Moral and Political Sciences, finds in writing his biography that he must deal frontally with this matter of the Inquisition, since it was Queen Isabel who sponsored the institution. If the Inquisition were judged to be as bad as anti-Spanish writers have charged, its evil would reflect upon the patron Queen of Spain; but if it were seen to be otherwise, then whatever glory pertains to it would also pertain to Isabel.

Dr. Silió's arguments are unequivocal. 1. The Inquisition was not a Spanish invention but was of Italian origin, was centuries old and was introduced into Spain rather later than elsewhere. 2. It was not introduced by Isabel, for it had operated in Spain under her predecessors as early as 1232. 3. Compared to the earlier versions, the Isabel Inquisition was only one-fifth as harsh in the number of persons condemned to death. 4. It actually saved lives, for because of it the religious wars which seared the rest of Europe were avoided. 5. Far from inhibiting Spanish intellectual life, it in a sense encouraged it; on the Spanish Index one can find not a single book of philosophical merit, whether written by a foreigner or by a Spaniard. 6. Nor did it deter science, for it never proscribed a single line of Copernicus, Galileo or Newton. 7. The punishments it did administer were far less severe in kind and number than those exercised in other countries at the same time, a fact conspicuously true when one considers the large number of half-mad people who were burned as witches in Germany and England, a practice which the Inquisition did not tolerate, because only a brief questioning by the Inquisitors was needed to prove that the accused was mentally incompetent.

Silió makes three additional defenses which must be considered in further detail. 8. He points out that the period of Spain's greatest intellectual achievement coincided with the apex of Inquisition power, and no inhibition deterred the artists, writers and musicians. Cervantes wrote *Don Quixote* when the Inquisition was strongest. Calderón de la Barca wrote his soaring dramas in the same climate and so did Lope de Vega. Victoria composed his great music under the Inquisition. Poets, essayists and historians flourished in this period, and none seemed to suffer. Books were printed at a rate which exceeded that in other countries and philosophy and sciences prospered. This was the age of the university, when Salamanca and Alcalá de Henares were at their apex in both number of students and vitality of thought. If one wants to insist that the Inquisition hampered intellectual life, he has the Golden Age to contend with.

9. Furthermore, the Inquisition was necessary because Jews had infiltrated national life and had to be eradicated. In fact, the ordinary people of Spain were more insistent upon this than were the rulers, for as Silió says, 'The massacres of Jews were the work of popular wrath, of people faced by the infiltration of a tenacious race, astute and industrious, who, even though they suffered death and cruel exploitation, bent before the hurricanes in order to surge forth anew, like some evil weed, monopolizing the riches, exploiting usury and gathering together everything.' Silió also points out that it was impossible to accept Jews within the society because they stole little Christian children and crucified them, thus making a mockery of Good Friday. In proof of this charge he cites the case of Yucé Franco, who during the last days of June, 1490, assembled a group of Jews to perform just such a crucifixion. Franco, whose name was typically Jewish, was captured on July 1, 1490, and it was not until sixteen months later, after the most careful legal investigations by the Inquisition, that he was condemned. Even then all evidence was turned over to the university faculty at Salamanca for them to assure themselves that the trial had been

properly conducted, and when Salamanca approved, the dossier was for-
warded to a jury of educated men here in Avila, and they too concurred.
The public burning took place in this city on November 16, 1491, as a
result of which wild popular riots broke out against all Jews, even though
Fernando and Isabel had forbidden such outbursts. Silió contends that it
was only this hideous Jewish crime, one of many, that forced the Spanish
sovereigns to decree the general expulsion of Jews from Spain. Silió points
out that the facts of the Yucé Franco case and the justice of the decision
cannot be questioned, even though there was no visual proof of the crime,
because the investigation was carried out under the personal supervision
of a wise and just judge, Tomás de Torquemada, who is proved to have
been a humble man, lacking ostentation, desiring only justice, and far
from the 'new Nero' that popular writers have tried to make him. When
the old lies against the inquisitor general are removed one by one, Torquemada stands forth as 'an agreeable, lovable, hard-working, able and modest man whose only ambition was to imitate Jesus Christ.' Such a man,
Silió argues, would never have let the Inquisition get out of hand.

Silió's final point is brief and powerful: 'The Spanish Inquisition as
established by the Catholic Kings was adequate to its time and necessary
in that time.'

Some years ago I was obliged to read everything in print in the
languages I could handle regarding the Spanish Inquisition, and I reached
these conclusions, which in certain limited areas coincide with Silió's. 1. In
the beginning Spain's Inquisition was no more cruel than similar inquisito-
rial bodies operating in other European countries. 2. The number of
persons executed in Spain at the height of the European movement, say
from 1492–1550, did not exceed records established in other countries. 3.
The operation of the Spanish Index in proscribing books was more lenient
than the Italian. 4. No one can deny that Spanish culture achieved its
Golden Age coincident with the Inquisition. 5. So far as I was able to
ascertain, no Jew was ever executed by the Inquisition. If a man under
investigation could say simply, 'Yes, I'm a Jew and have never been
otherwise,' his gold and silver were confiscated and he was banished from
Spain, but he was in no way subject to the Inquisition and certainly he was
never burned. 6. The Jews who did suffer, and in the thousands, were
those who had at one time been baptized as Catholics, had been legal
Catholics and had committed apostasy by reverting to Jewish practices.
These were rooted out with great severity, but when they were burned, it
was as Catholics, not as Jews. 7. Particularly sad were the cases of
shipwrecked English sailors in the middle years of the sixteenth century,
for if they swam to Spanish soil they were in real danger of being burned.
The Inquisition maintained that any Englishman who was then a Protestant must have been born and baptized a Catholic and was ipso facto a
heretic deserving death. The frequency with which such sailors were
condemned on this theological technicality was appalling. 8. The persecu-

tion of Protestants in Spain, more especially the hated Lutherans, may have been more severe in numbers than the similar persecution of Catholics in Protestant countries, but it was not more vicious. The falsity of the Black Legend was obvious. 9. But the more I studied this problem the more apparent it became that something fundamental had happened in Spain that had not happened in the rest of Europe, and I began to think that the differential must be this: That whereas all European nations had originally sponsored some form of Inquisition, with Spain's less cruel than others, it was only in Spain that the institution lingered on, so that the last public burning occurred in 1781, when an old woman was hauled to the stake after witnesses had sworn that 'she had conducted carnal converse with the Devil, after which she laid eggs with prophecies written on them.' On February 22, 1813, the Cortes abolished the Inquisition by a vote of ninety to sixty, but on July 21 of the following year, King Fernando VII having regained the throne, it was restored. In 1820, when the nation turned more liberal, the king again had to order the abolishment of the Inquisition, but as soon as he felt himself strong enough to do so, he revoked his decree. It was not until July 15, 1834, that the tribunal was finally suppressed, its properties being applied to a reduction of the national debt, but even then strong movements arose throughout Spain demanding 'the restoration of our beloved Inquisition,' and for years the issue remained lively. The last public execution which could be charged against the spirit of the Inquisition took place on June 26, 1826, in Valencia, the victim being a schoolteacher whose crime was that in public prayer he used 'Praise be to God' rather than 'Ave Maria.' It was the terrible prolongation that constituted the difference, as if Spain had found in this bizarre social weapon a ritual that satisfied some deep national appetite. I therefore answered my rhetorical question affirmatively: The Inquisition, through its persistence, had been the cause of Spain's decline.

Then in 1965, when I had finished my study, a book called *The Spanish Inquisition* appeared and I discovered with a certain wryness that its author, Henry Kamen, who teaches history at the University of Edinburgh, had done my work for me, but about four years too late. He had summarized in unhysterical form our knowledge of the Inquisition, and I commend his book to anyone who wishes to pursue the matter. It is true that he relies on old standard works like Juan Antonio Llorente's *Historic Memoir Regarding Spanish National Opinion on the Inquisition* (circulated in manuscript in 1811; later developed into the four-volume *Histoire critique de l'Inquisition d'Espagne,* Paris, 1818) and Henry Charles Lea's *A History of the Inquisition of Spain* (1906–1908), but he also looks into collateral problems, and it is this aspect of his work that is most rewarding.

On basic facts about the Inquisition he differs little from Silió, except of course regarding the Yucé Franco ritual murder, which modern scholars know to have been an invention, and he also confirms my conclusions with an important exception, which I shall note in the next paragraph. The facts he cites are sometimes startling. 'The total number of so-called witches executed in the seventeenth century in Germany alone has been put as high as a hundred thousand, a figure which is probably four times as great as the number of people burned by the Spanish Inquisition in all its history.' The Bishop of Bamberg during the period 1622–1633 caused six hundred witches to be burned and in the same period the Bishop of Würzburg nine hundred.

Kamen reaches three main conclusions. The ordinary people of Spain applauded the Inquisition and did not think of it as oppressive. My argument, that the Inquisition caused Spain's decline, he holds to be inaccurate, in that he finds no substantial evidence to support it. He believes that the real tragedy of the Inquisition was that it helped create a closed society from which alien elements were expelled and into which no new ideas were allowed to enter. It is in the analysis of this third proposition that he provides much new material.

He contends that although the Inquisition may have begun as a solution to a religious problem, it quickly became an instrument for enforcing a pernicious theory regarding 'purity of blood,' which meant that any family whose ancestors had been either Moorish or Jewish was contaminated. Since Moors had married in Spain for seven hundred years and Jews for eleven hundred, and since there had been forced conversions of both, there had to be much impure blood in Spain, and its eradication provided a chance for informers to appropriate jobs, money and titles now belonging to the impure. Researchers who hoped to overthrow great families drew up a black list entitled *The Green Book of Aragón,* which identified families in that kingdom having impure blood, involving hundreds in catastrophe. It was so successful that in 1560 a disgruntled cardinal, irritated because two relatives had been refused admittance to a military order, compiled *Blot on the Nobility of Spain,* identifying by name those families with impure blood.

It is difficult to imagine what such a charge entailed. The family could have been practicing Christians for three hundred years and without blemish so far as their Catholicism was concerned, but merely because they had a touch of Moorish or Jewish blood they could not send their sons to a university, or work in certain jobs, or hold office in a cathedral, or become officers in the army, or dignitaries in the Church. Military orders like that of Santiago had strict requirements of racial purity and became instruments of reaction and oppression. All Spanish life was corrupted by this mania and thousands were drawn into the net of the Inquisition principally because friends reported that they had hidden their Jewishness. Before a man could apply for any important job he had to present a genealogy going back numerous generations, and the compiling of such records provided a fruitful source of bribery and blackmail. Incredible as it seems, laws policing purity of blood continued in force until January 31,

455

1835; in the army the application of the principle continued to 1859 and in the obtaining of marriage licenses to 1865.

It was this continuing battle for conformity that punished Spain so severely; although the role played by the Inquisition in religion could be matched in other countries, its part in eradicating those social variations which interact to build strong nations was here unique. Spain was driven by a mania for homogeneity, not realizing that no one group of people can generate all the concepts necessary for its survival. The country insisted upon a closed society and succeeded in getting it, but what it excluded was more significant than what it enclosed.

In 1770 the University of Salamanca forbade Descartes to be taught because he was dangerous to Catholic principles, Thomas Hobbes because he was too compendious and John Locke because he was obscure and must be read with extreme care. As late as 1645 a university professor in Logroño was sentenced to four years' imprisonment and perpetual deprivation of the right to teach because he had referred to the contents of a prohibited book. At one point the Inquisition of a northern city issued the blanket directive that no university should teach from any book that had been published within forty years. Even the great professors who had worked at Alcalá de Henares with Cardinal Cisneros building the *Poliglota* were intimidated and efforts were made to prohibit the study of Greek on grounds that devout men knew that the true Bible existed only in Latin. For me the insanity is best exemplified in the case of a man who was overheard wagering his word against God's nose. A learned gloss was issued proving that such a statement identified the blasphemer as a member of the Badian heresy, which treated God as a corporeal being with human attributes, and for believing this a man should be burned. Word crept across Spain that it was prudent to remain silent, and speculation ceased, but as Kamen points out, it was not the Inquisition that should be blamed but the total drift of society.

However, we must not explain away too much. There is today in Spain a strong spirit of revisionism in historical scholarship which says, 'Since the excesses charged against Spain by the Black Legend have been proved false, their contraries must be true. Thus Felipe II was a king without blemish. The Inquisition was good rather than bad. Tómas de Torquemada was a gentle Christian. And, as a matter of fact, Spain never suffered a decline.' A frontal attack is also mounted against any criticism of contemporary Spain, however mild, by charging that the author is once more purveying the errors of the Black Legend. In recent reading I have collected eighteen examples of newspaper articles attacking books, plays, paintings, motion pictures and general news stories as contaminated by the Black Legend. Honest and fair comment supported by historical re-

Born workers on a farm, Don Alipio Pérez-Tabernero Sanchón and his brother accumulated wealth and became masters of four of the greatest bull farms in Spain.

search on the one hand or by contemporary observation on the other is thus condemned, and it is even popular to deny that Spain ever suffered post-Golden Age reversals, but to refute this tempting thesis one needs only quote the experts. Sometime around 1640, when Spain ached from defeats in all fields, King Felipe IV said, 'These evil events have been caused by your sins and mine in particular . . . I believe that God our Lord is angry and irate with me and my realms on account of many sins and particularly on account of mine.' In 1957 Generalísimo Franco said of a later period, 'While other world powers were able to marshal their strength, Spain sank into a hundred-year sleep.'

The decline was real and I believe, in spite of Kamen's argument to the contrary, that the Inquisition was largely to blame. For almost four centuries it enforced an intellectual conformity and rejected all minorities. The Moors, the Jews, the Illuminati, the Jesuits and the Protestants were expelled and their ideas with them. Spain thus became the next nation in a tragic series who decided to fence out new ideas rather than welcome them and she suffered the inescapable penalty. An oyster can live to itself, but without grains of sand for agitation it cannot produce pearls.

Walking one night along the ramparts of Avila, I reasoned, 'If Spain had kept her Moors, her agriculture and manufacturing would have prospered. If she had kept her Jews, her commercial management would have kept pace with England's. If she had retained a few inquiring Protestant professors, her universities might have remained vital. And if she had held onto her Illuminati, her spiritual life would have been renewed.' But then I had to face the greater reality. 'If she had done these things, she'd now be a better Spain. But she wouldn't be Spain.'

After my wide excursions afield—to the fair at Medina del Campo, to the dark Virgin of Guadalupe, to the Avila of Victoria—I returned to Salamanca to visit for the last time those two rooms at the university, almost side by side, which were converted into shrines by the heroism of two philosopher-poets. The first was a stone-arched classroom left pretty much as it must have been on that day in December, 1578, when Fray Luis de León returned after an absence of some years. The rude benches without backs remain the same and the small windows in the outer walls. The lectern with its canopy is the same as the one at which the professor stood that eventful day. The room was crowded, not only because Fray Luis was the most famous of the Salamanca lecturers, a wise, gentle elderly man of sweet understanding and compassion, but because he had accomplished something that few men of his day could parallel.

In 1572, at the height of a brilliant career as Spain's leading theologian and humanist, he was attacked by jealous persons in the university, who whispered to the Inquisition, 'We all know that Fray Luis is half Jewish, so he's suspect to begin with. But he has now translated King Solomon's Song of Songs into the vernacular. He invites even the most ordinary man in Salamanca to read it. And that is heresy.' Especially serious was the additional charge that often, after studying the original Hebrew version of the Bible, he would question the accuracy of the Latin. Fray Luis was apprehended and for several months was under interrogation, after which he was thrown into jail at Valladolid, where he heard only silence. At the end of a year he pleaded to be told what the charges against him were and who his accusers, but he heard nothing. His trial was intermittent and clandestine; all he knew was that he had committed some serious crime bordering on heresy, but its definition he never knew. Finally, after nearly five years of this, he was set free and, what was the more miraculous, allowed to return to his post in Salamanca. Of his experience in jail he wrote:

> Here envy and lies   have kept me imprisoned.
> Happy the humble state   of the wise man who retires
> from this nefarious world,   and with meager table and house
> in the pleasant countryside   passes his life alone;
> he serves only God,   neither envied nor envious.

This was the morning of his reappearance, and notable persons came to the university to hear his reaction to his long persecution. As he made his way from his rooms, his gown slightly askew in his usual careless manner, the university plaza was crowded with silent students. Fray Luis walked with eyes straight forward, not daring to acknowledge the furtive glances of approbation which greeted him. As he entered the cloisters and elbowed his way through the crowd he came at last to the room in which he had taught for so many years, and when he saw its familiar outlines, with his friends perched on the narrow benches, and when he knew that among them must be those whose rumors had caused his imprisonment and who would surrender him again to the Inquisition within a few years (he was to die in disgrace at Madrigal de las Altas Torres), he must have wanted to lash out against the injustice he had suffered and would continue to suffer as a Jew and a humanist. Instead he stepped to the rostrum, took his place behind the lectern, grasped the lapels of his robe and smiled at the crowd with the compassion that marked all he did, and said in a low, clear voice, 'As we were saying yesterday . . .' And he resumed his lecture at the precise point of its interruption five years before.

Down the cloister from Fray Luis' austere classroom is another of much different character, the Lecture Hall, dating from the fifteenth century. Its principal adornment is a group of four handsome stone arches that support the ceiling and a grisaille of Fernando and Isabel done sometime in the eighteenth century. Lists of men who have brought honor to Salamanca appear, but one of the greatest is missing and will probably remain so until the passions of this age are past, after which he will occupy the place of honor. To understand why, we must see this hall as it was on October 12, 1936, the Day of the Race.

At one end of the hall rose a three-stepped dais, done in red carpeting.

It was lighted by two intricate chandeliers and ornamented with a large portrait of Francisco Franco. The dais contained ten long old-fashioned benches on which sat the dignitaries of the university and seven high-backed red-plush chairs occupied by the rector, the local bishop, generals from the victorious Franco army which had recently captured Salamanca and an extraordinary fire-eater type of man so common in Spanish history and so incomprehensible to outsiders. He was General José Millán Astray, leader of the Foreign Legion and the only hero to come out of Spain's disastrous military adventures in Africa. He was a psychotic man, preternaturally thin, blind in one eye, lacking one arm and scarred across his entire body with mementos of defeat in desert battles. A major reason why he was a popular hero was the battle cry he had sponsored, 'Long live Death!' What this meant no one understood, but it had a rich fifteenth-century ring, and Spain echoed Millán Astray's challenge, 'Long live Death!'

On this day the general had the pleasure of addressing a university gathering, and universities had long been his anathema because scholars were alien to his Legion and learning refuted his cry of 'Long live Death!' So with choice, sardonic words the mad general ripped into Salamancan life, excoriated people who bothered with books, cursed regional areas like Cataluña and the Basque country, and promised that when Fascism triumphed, all such aberrations would be cauterized with a flaming sword. Fascists planted in the audience cheered. Intelligence was condemned and students were summoned to an unending war of extermination. The cadaverous general sat down and the crowd roared its approval of the new world a-coming.

Then the rector of the university rose, the distinguished philosopher-poet Miguel de Unamuno (1864–1936), author of the widely read *The Tragic Sense of Life,* and, with José Ortega y Gasset (1883–1955), Spain's leading intellectual. He knew that he ought not let this nihilistic challenge go unanswered, but he was an old man; police forces of the new Spain surrounded him; and in the chair to his right sat Franco's wife. If ever silence could have been condoned, this was the time, but Unamuno adjusted his robes of office, like Fray Luis before him, and began speaking in a soft voice: 'I, as you know, am a Basque, born in Bilbao. And the bishop, whether he likes it or not, is a Catalan, born in Barcelona.' He said that to speak of liquidating such men was silly. He then turned his attention to General Millán Astray and said a few simple things that some, at least, in the audience had been thinking but which fear had kept muffled. He said that the emaciated general was a cripple, a heroic one to be sure, but a cripple in both body and mind, and that because of his own withered nature he was determined to enforce on healthy Spain his sickly philosophy. Specifically, Unamuno said, there could be no sense in a rallying cry such as 'Long live Death.' Exactly the opposite spirit was required.

General Millán Astray, accustomed to total obedience in his Legion, could not tolerate opposition and especially not from a college professor. He leaped to his feet, waved his one arm and screamed, 'Down with intelligence! Long live Death!'

At this moment the mad general and the poet stood facing each other and neither would give way. 'Long live Death!' the general bellowed. 'No,' the poet replied. 'Long live intelligence.' Like the permanent contrasting forces of Spain the two men stood, and because the hall was filled with blue-shirted Fascists, the general won. When Franco heard reports of the meeting and of how Spain's leading intellect had challenged the spirit of the new regime, he is reported to have ordered, 'If necessary, shoot him.'

It was not necessary. Unamuno was already stricken and died shortly thereafter, leaving behind one of the most glowing memories of contemporary Spain, that of the philosopher-poet who defended the permanent values of Spain at the risk of his own life.

(Just as the telephone conversation between Colonel Moscardó and his supposedly sixteen-year-old son has been proved to be largely apocryphal, thus destroying a legend favorable to Franco, so doubts have been cast on the authenticity of some of the details of the Millán Astray–Unamuno confrontation. The original account came from a journalist, Luis Portillo, and was accepted by Hugh Thomas and many other serious writers. José María Pemán, one of the scheduled speakers that day and member of the Royal Academy, has denied that it took place, but Emilio Salcedo, in his life of Unamuno [1964], says that during the formal addresses relating to Spain's role in the New World, Unamuno was inspired to take notes on a piece of paper which has come down to us. At the conclusion of the set speeches he rose to make a few observations based on his notes but was interrupted by the general, whereupon something like the scene I have described took place, though not in the highly dramatic form suggested by Portillo. I have discussed this matter with a fair cross section of Spaniards and they believe that an intellectual scuffle, pretty much as described by Salcedo, did occur.)

Today in the hall which his bravery consecrated there is no mention of Unamuno's name and surely no bust or portrait, but often visitors sit in silence, their eyes closed, thinking of this courageous man and of his poem to Salamanca, where so much of his creative life had been spent.

> Forest of stones that history tore
> from the bowels of mother earth,
> refuge of quietude, I bless thee,
> my Salamanca.

> In the depths of my heart I cherish
> thy robust spirit; when I shall die,
> cherish thou, my golden Salamanca,
> my memory.

THE DEMON PASTRY COOK

For some two hundred years the kings of Spain had been trying to trick Portugal into surrendering its independence and becoming a province of Spain. This was not unnatural, because under the Romans, Visigoths and Muslims, Portugal had been an undifferentiated part of Spain and all prudent Spaniards hoped for the day when that would be the case again.

In 1576, when Felipe II sat on the throne of Spain, prospects for union began to brighten, for Sebastián (in Portuguese Sebastião), the twenty-two-year-old King of Portugal, was a moody, headstrong ascetic who loved only horses and refused to marry, even though he realized that if he died childless his throne would pass, ridiculous as it seems, to his granduncle Henrique, a childless cardinal in his dotage, whose principal pleasure was supervising the Portuguese Inquisition. If the young king died childless and the old cardinal did the same, the crown of Portugal would then pass into the hands of Felipe, who was Sebastián's uncle, and the peninsula would once more be united.

Spies brought unbelievable news to Madrid. 'Sebastián refuses to marry. He has epileptic fits and is afraid he's impotent.' And 'His Jesuit advisors have convinced him that he has been chosen by God to lead a great crusade into Africa and rescue it from Islam.' And 'Poor Sebastián is so excited about his crusade that he can think of nothing else. Portugal is falling into ruin while he seeks only to make himself physically fit to captain his armies. Each day he trains, sleeps on the ground, rides horseback for miles and will speak to no one of government.' And 'He insists that every noble family in Portugal send at least one of its sons to fight in Africa against Islam.' And 'Portugal is bankrupt. King Sebastián constantly demands new taxes and no one can call him from his folly.' And 'The only persons who can gain the king's ear are his Jesuit advisors, and they keep telling him, "March to Africa." '

In December of that year Felipe II proved that he was a just and honorable king. He summoned his Portuguese nephew to the remote monastery of Guadalupe to caution him against the folly of such a crusade, and when they met there on January 1, 1577, Felipe pointed out how slim were the chances of success, how imprudent it would be to strip Portugal of her wealth, her army and her sons, and how important it was for Sebastián to raise up a strong line of future kings. In other words, Felipe argued against his own interests, for he had only to encourage Sebastián to make a fool of himself and die in battle, and the throne of Portugal would come to Felipe. 'Don't go to Africa,' he pleaded.

Sebastián, considering his Spanish uncle uninformed and cautious, said bluntly that he would go and he demanded Spanish help, reminding

Felipe that only eighty-four years ago this same enemy had occupied part of Spain. Such an appeal Felipe could not refuse. He promised Sebastián a fleet and an army. Then the two kings worshiped at the shrine of the Virgin of Guadalupe and prayed for a Christian victory.

Sebastián hurried back to Portugal. 'We shall save Africa!' he announced, but in assembling his reluctant army he was so tardy, and his plans changed so swiftly, that in the end Uncle Felipe had to say, 'You have wasted too much time. I have changed my mind and shall not send the fleet and army that I promised.' With this stroke he ensured the failure of the enterprise, and some of Sebastián's lay advisors tried to warn him of this fact, but his Jesuit counselors insisted that the crusade go forward.

How bombastic was the armada that sailed from Lisboa in June, 1578, eight hundred vessels under chaotic leadership. How ridiculous was the military adventure once Africa was reached, a young king who knew nothing of arms determined to seek out the enemy personally and destroy him. The adventure was a disaster, the worst item of which was the fact that when Sebastián finally died under an enemy onslaught, no one saw where he was killed or how. There was no witness to his death and his body was not then recovered, if indeed it ever was. He vanished from history as ineptly as he had appeared, a strange, quixotic youth who succeeded in nothing, not even in dying properly.

But he was dead and the precarious crown of Portugal passed into the hands of Cardinal Henrique, sixty-seven years old, childless, tubercular and even more bumbling than Sebastián had been. It seemed only a matter of time before Felipe II would inherit the throne and unite the two kingdoms. However, King Henrique showed unexpected spirit and decided to petition the Pope for special permission to marry the thirteen-year-old daughter of a duchess under the extravagant impression that he could sire a son before he died. Alas, the plan was tardy; the petition could not be acted upon by the Pope, and the old cardinal died without legal issue. Portugal became once more a part of Spain and would presumably remain that way forever.

That was in 1580. But as the years passed, Portuguese patriotism did not diminish and an understandable rumor began to circulate through the peninsula. 'Suppose King Sebastião did not really die in Africa! Suppose he was so ashamed of his defeat that he crept from the battlefield and took an assumed name! Suppose he should suddenly reappear! Why, he'd be the legal King of Portugal! The Spaniards would have to get out! And that would be the last we'd see of Felipe II!' It was an enticing possibility. In the year 1592, when the rumor began to gain its greatest credence, how old would King Sebastián, the one in hiding, be? Only thirty-eight. He'd be heavier now, of course, but he'd have the same general appearance. Tall, with a slight impairment in the left side of his body, a superb horseman, daring, hot-tempered, regal in manner, blond. Yes, he would be noticeably blond, with sharp blue eyes and fair skin. Where could he be hiding, this lost king who would save all?

Especially persuasive was the Portuguese explanation as to why Sebastián had gone into hiding. 'It's all very simple, if you think of it. Why did King Sebastião get into trouble in Africa in the first place? Because his uncle, King Felipe, offered him an army and navy and then took them away. Don't you see? Felipe wanted Sebastião to be killed by the Moors, and if they hadn't done the job he would have. Poor Sebastião had to hide. He's gathering another army in secret. And soon he'll reappear. Watch.' Supporters of this theory had to explain away one stubborn fact. Some years after the disaster in Africa, King Felipe, always studious to protect his claim to the throne of Portugal, dispatched envoys who discovered Sebastián's corpse, which they brought back to a well-publicized funeral in Lisboa. To this the Portuguese developed a persuasive argument: 'I grant that a funeral was held. I attended it myself. But when was it held? In 1582. And when does Felipe claim that Sebastião died? In 1578. How could anyone identify a body four years dead? Felipe tricked you with a false corpse. You listen to me. Our king never died. Right now he's wandering somewhere in Europe and I for one expect to see him any day.'

When these rumors reached Felipe in El Escorial he told his aides, 'We must keep an eye out for this make-believe Sebastián.' The absent king, if he returned, could cause much trouble. For one thing, he would tear Portugal away from the empire, and this King Felipe did not intend to permit. 'Watch for Sebastián,' was the command passed to the king's officials.

It is not surprising that the Iberian peninsula should have become preoccupied with such a bizarre problem as late as 1592, because in Russia at this time much the same thing was happening. There in 1591 the acknowledged heir to the throne, Prince Dmitri, had died, perhaps at the hand of Boris Godunov, who assumed the crown and whose reign was plagued by rumors that Prince Dmitri had not actually died but was merely hiding until it was safe for him to appear. At embarrassing moments a series of Dmitris did step forward, or persons claiming to be Dmitri, and Russia was threatened with civil war. If it could happen in Russia, it could happen in Spain, and the agents of King Felipe took extra precautions.

Madrigal de las Altas Torres! Could one find in all Spain a town more suited for swift intrigue and high romance? It lay in a gentle plain of considerable beauty and was completely surrounded by a high wall marked by many towers. Its small streets ran under poetic arches and its plazas were dignified by sturdy ancient buildings. It was particularly noted for its convent, because in one of its cells the great Queen of Spain, Isabel the Catholic, had been born, and here many fine ladies from renowned families lived as nuns, helping the poor and keeping out of the way of their richer relatives.

In 1594 the convent housed one beautiful nun who was to become famous in history, Doña Ana de Austria, twenty-six years old and the granddaughter of Carlos V. She took her name from her father, who had been the savior of Spain, Don Juan de Austria, half brother to Felipe, which made her niece to the king. This would be important.

Doña Ana was in the convent for a reason common to that age. She was without question the daughter of the great Don Juan, but her father had never bothered to marry her mother, so the child was put in the convent to expiate her father's sin. She was gracious, well educated and tender in spirit. She was also romantic and often wondered what her life might have been if she were not illegitimate. Finally, she was dreadfully uninformed about life in the world at large, for like all female bastards of the royal line she had been stuck away in the convent at the age of six and had known only uneducated country girls who were taking orders and who were required to address her as 'Your Excellency.' Oh yes, Doña Ana also had a collection of jewels, some of them so stamped as to indicate that they were part of the crown treasure, and this too would be important.

The only man whom Doña Ana saw regularly was her confessor, Fray Miguel de los Santos, an Augustinian monk who had once served as royal courier from the court of Portugal to Rome and twice as provincial of his order. He had an intensity of spirit that Doña Ana liked and a willingness to talk with her for extended periods following her confession. He told her that he supposed he was the most saintly of all living men in that he prayed most of each night, disciplined himself three times each week and gave all his money to the needy. Then he told her something which must have excited her profoundly. 'I believe God has selected me for some special task, because each day of my life, when I come to the most solemn part of the Mass, I see in the heavens a giant crucifix, and beside it dressed in kingly armor with a baton of gold and flag of green silk a blond young man whose face I cannot see.' 'Who might the young king be?' Doña Ana asked. 'I wouldn't know,' her confessor replied. 'When God wants us to know who he is, we'll see his face.' What no one in Madrigal seemed to know was that Fray Miguel had once been preacher to the royal family of Portugal.

In the spring of 1593, before any overt acts had occurred in Madrigal, Fray Miguel began having a new set of visions, and these, too, he communicated to Doña Ana, as was only natural since she appeared in them. 'I saw a vision of Jerusalem,' he told her, 'and it was groaning under the heel of Islam, but at the right side of the city I saw you standing to bring deliverance and on the left side the handsome young man who now wore the crown of a king.' When Doña Ana asked what this signified, her confessor replied, 'I suppose it means that you are destined to save Jerusalem.' And the young man? It was someone Fray Miguel had seen before but he could not remember exactly who he was.

He next had a vision of Jesus Christ being crucified, with Doña Ana on his right side and the same fair king on the left. This signified, he said, that Doña Ana and the king were to work together for Jesus, as man and wife.

Hard on this exciting vision came one which spelled out the future in specific terms. The young king was her cousin, Sebastián of Portugal. He was alive and God intended Doña Ana to be his wife and queen. For the rest of that year the monk continued to ensnare the nun with a kaleidoscope of visions in which she appeared as the bride of King Sebastián, and he hammered at how much more pleasant it would be to rule as queen with a handsome man at her side than to wither away as a nun in a cell. 'Where is the king?' she asked. 'We have only to wait,' Fray Miguel assured her. 'If it is God's intention that you marry the king, God will bring him to you.' So the beautiful nun waited.

Everything I have told you so far is a matter of history, well recorded in documents, because what happened in Madrigal beginning in June of 1594 shook Spain, and many self-serving reports were filed in the royal archives by participants in the drama. What happened in the next four months, however, cannot be accurately determined and has been the subject of much speculation. The best historical summary is found in *A King for Portugal,* published in 1964, by the student of Portuguese history, Mary Elizabeth Brooks. The best dramatic account appeared on the Madrid stage in 1849 and often thereafter, *Unconfessed Traitor and Martyr,* the work that José Zorrilla, who also wrote *Don Juan Tenorio,* considered his masterpiece. And recently, at a date I have not been able to determine, Alonso de Encinas, a native of Madrigal, published an enchanting little essay titled 'The Pastry Cook of Madrigal.' The Zorrilla play is pure invention and I shall not borrow from it. The Encinas essay purports to be fact but is at variance with Dr. Brooks, so I shall use it sparingly. I shall, however, rely for the next few pages upon fact and legend as I heard it in Madrigal.

A major point of difference between history and legend centers upon the person of Don Rodrigo de Santillán. Legend says that he was the leading citizen of Madrigal, and a man who took seriously his role of alcalde and confidential agent of King Felipe. A petty noble, pompous, suspicious and easily swayed by the merest whisper from the king, he kept an eye on all that happened in Madrigal and dispensed an honest justice in any matter that did not impinge upon the crown. That is, if two farmers quarreled over a pig, Don Rodrigo could be depended upon to ferret out the facts and render a just decision. But if the pig happened to belong to the king . . . well, that was quite another matter. That demanded looking into, and when Don Rodrigo looked into something where the king's interest was at stake, there was apt to be a hanging.

On this point history is clear-cut and firm. Don Rodrigo de Santillán was not the mayor of Madrigal; he was a senior and respected judge of the Chancillería de Valladolid (High Tribunal of Justice) and so far as can be ascertained had no personal connection with Madrigal. The Royal Archives

THE PORTUGUESE SUCCESSION

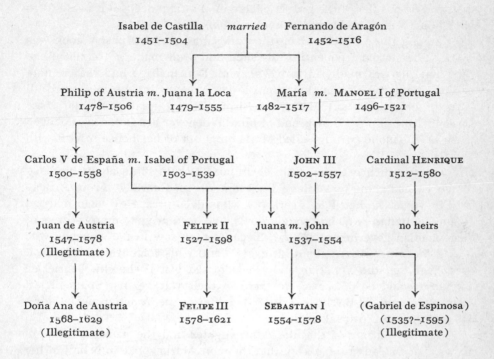

at Simancas contain literally a thousand pages of reports written by Judge Santillán and these show him to have been a perspicacious gentleman, jealous of his prerogatives and determined to do the king's will. Legend required him to be the alcalde of Madrigal so that his daughter María, a quiet girl, reserved and lovely, could play a major role in developments. When the events began to unfold she had not yet given signs of being interested in any of the young men in nearby towns who would normally have married her, and villagers began to wonder what was going to happen to her.

They liked her and their speculations were without rancor. They were therefore pleased when a tall stranger, who seemed to be about forty years old, accompanied by a fair-haired girl of two and a maidservant, appeared in town to open a pastry shop. He announced that his name was Gabriel de Espinosa and he posed only as an honest workman who baked good pastry and looked after his little girl, but his bearing was so noble, his speech so refined and his accidental references to past deeds in which he had

467

participated so convincing, that the citizens of Madrigal were satisfied that
he must be an important man in hiding.

'The younger son of some noble family,' was the general judgment.
'Got into trouble with the daughter of a duque or something. The mother
died and he has their little girl. He's here in Madrigal only till it's safe to go
back home and claim his inheritance. And his titles.'

Among those bedazzled by the handsome, taciturn pastry cook was
María. She started frequenting his shop and soon made no secret of the
fact that she was madly in love with him. Don Rodrigo had rather more
exalted plans for his daughter than a pastry cook, and he interposed all
sorts of objections, but María was firm. 'He's a great gentleman,' she
insisted. 'One day you'll be proud of him.' Whenever her father was obliged
to be in Valladolid, strong-willed María crept out of her house to visit with
Gabriel.

On one such occasion Gabriel dropped certain hints about his past.
When he had come to Venice . . . 'From where, Gabriel?' 'From Africa.'
And in Venice he had had a series of wild adventures. He'd been married
to a noble Italian lady, had fought duels, had been privy to many secrets of
the Venetian government. 'Why?' 'Because they saw in me someone who
. . .' Whenever pressed about his exact identity his voice trailed off. But it
was clear that the Venetian state had devised plans whereby Gabriel de
Espinosa could be of service to them in their war against Spain. 'I left
Venice,' he said. 'Is the little girl the daughter of the Venetian noble lady?'
He preferred not to speak of that.

The love affair of the alcalde's daughter and the pastry cook went
forward at a steady rate, except that the more María spoke in behalf of her
lover, the more the mayor objected. 'He's a tricky one,' Don Rodrigo said.
Sometimes he would leave his office in one of the towers and stand looking
at the pastry shop, and when he had about decided that this Espinosa was
a fraud, the cook would greet a customer in such grandeur that even Don
Rodrigo had to acknowledge that here was a most unusual man. Most
unusual.

Don Rodrigo's problem was about to be resolved in a way he could not
have anticipated. As soon as Gabriel de Espinosa arrived in Madrigal, Fray
Miguel, still serving as confessor to Doña Ana, doubled his visits to her
cell and warned her that the hour of decision was at hand. 'I had a vision.
God appeared and told me that he was about to bring King Sebastián into
our presence. Are you prepared?' She said she was ready for whatever God
required of her, but how could she marry Sebastián, since she was
already a nun? Her confessor reasoned, 'You were thrown into this convent at a tender age and against your will. When you took your vows to
become a nun, did you do so willingly?' Doña Ana said she had never
wanted to become a nun, and Fray Miguel cried, 'See! Your vows are void
and you are free to marry.'

When this was settled, Fray Miguel had a further vision telling him that the long-absent king was about to arrive in Madrigal. 'How will we know him?' Doña Ana asked, and the friar said, 'When I was preacher to the kings of Portugal I knew Sebastián well. He was tall and gracious, bold and daring, a superb horseman and blond. I would know him.'

Finally, one day Fray Miguel arrived in a state of agitation. In his vision the night before he had seen God's finger pointing at a handsome man whom he had seen earlier standing with Doña Ana at Jerusalem and at the Crucifixion. 'He is King Sebastián and he lives,' said the voice of God. What was more, he was hiding right here in Madrigal until the day came to disclose himself. And what was best of all, he was now in the anteroom. Fray Miguel kept Doña Ana from fainting, and when she had composed herself he kicked open the door and there stood the king, waiting to claim her as his bride.

It was not long before the pastry cook was sleeping at the convent. (Many historians, especially those of the Church, deny that the affair reached this point; however, much evidence suggests that it did. At any rate, oral tradition in Madrigal insists that it did.) At the trial several nuns were convicted of having connived at slipping Gabriel into the convent, and the conspiracy was probably greater than the testimony admitted to public record showed. The whole convent seems to have been enchanted at the prospect that one of their members might become Queen of Portugal.

Espinosa had no trouble in convincing Doña Ana of his royal claims. He had indeed fled Africa in disguise, as Fray Miguel had guessed, and he had been wandering the earth looking for a queen exactly like Doña Ana. All auguries were now good for his recovery of the throne, and if she would stand by him in the months ahead . . . She wanted to know exactly what this meant, and he said there was the matter of expenses. 'I have these jewels,' she said, and he thought they would just about cover the cost of regaining the crown.

At the same time, however, he was not neglecting his duties with the alcalde's daughter, 'because,' as an old gentleman at Madrigal suggested, 'he wasn't at all sure he could get Doña Ana out of the convent.'

In October, 1594, events came to a climax and Fray Miguel prevailed upon Doña Ana, who was hopelessly in love with the pastry cook, whom she habitually called 'Your Majesty,' to give him her jewels to pay for a clandestine trip to France. 'There are in that country,' Fray Miguel said, 'thousands of loyal men waiting to rise on your husband's behalf.' The friar had fallen in the habit of speaking to Doña Ana as if she were already married to the king. 'It will be a simple matter,' he assured her, 'to explain to the Pope that you were made a nun against your will. He'll permit you to marry the king.' The passionately involved nun gave Espinosa her jewels, but at the last moment she either enclosed or mailed him two love letters as well, and in so doing condemned him to a dreadful death.

So much for the blend of legend and fact. From here on, each item of the story is historically founded and based on existing documents except as specifically noted. On October 7, 1594, Gabriel de Espinosa, on his way to consult with a group of supporters in France, left Madrigal and journeyed to Valladolid, where at an inn he fell in with a pretty country girl, whom he sought to impress by showing her the jewels he was carrying. He looked forward to spending a pleasant evening with the girl and offered her a drink from a cup carved from what he assured her was the horn of a unicorn. But she was no fool. She knew that unicorns were so rare that if a man of apparently modest means had such a cup he must have come by it evilly. She slipped out of the inn to inform upon him and by sheer coincidence came upon Judge Rodrigo de Santillán, making his nightly snooping rounds, for, as he later boasted in a letter to King Felipe,

> You have undoubtedly understood and noticed, sir, throughout my life, how lacking I have been in greed and how much more I esteem honor than wealth, and I seek this by patrolling by night and laboring by day as everyone knows.

Don Rodrigo listened to the girl's story and agreed with her that it sounded suspicious. He accompanied her to the inn and found there the mysterious pastry cook of Madrigal. Here was the chance he had been awaiting and he summoned the guard to arrest the man. When he searched Gabriel's belongings he found a cache of jewels, some of which were so marked as to make him think they belonged to Her Excellency Doña Ana de Austria, the nun at the convent in Madrigal.

'We have caught a thief,' Don Rodrigo announced, and after clapping Espinosa into jail, he returned to his quarters and at midnight wrote two letters which speak well for his sagacity in dealing with matters touching upon the royal family. The first was to Doña Ana and was couched in deferential terms, as befitted a letter addressed to the king's niece.

> Señora Doña Ana de Austria,
>
> Most Excellent Lady: Tonight I have personally arrested, at an inn of Valladolid, a certain Gabriel Espinosa, who claims to be a pastry-maker in the town of Madrigal, in whose possession I have found some valuable jewels which seem to belong to Your Excellency, and he says that he has been commissioned by Your Excellency to come to Valladolid to sell them. I humbly beg Your Excellency to inform me if what this Gabriel Espinosa has claimed is true, and, in the meantime, he remains in jail and the jewels in my possession, at the disposal of Your Excellency. May God keep Your Excellency many years as is the wish of this humble servant of Your Excellency, who kisses your hands. From Valladolid, September 28, 1594.
>
> The Judge, Don Rodrigo de Santillán

As soon as this was dispatched to Madrigal, Don Rodrigo sent a much different type of directive to Don Luis Portocarrero, Alcalde de la Real Chancillería de Valladolid.

My esteemed and respected friend:

Upon receipt of this letter, I ask you, the better to serve Our Lord the King, to go to the house of the pastry-maker Gabriel Espinosa in Madrigal and take possession of everything you find in it, and to arrest those who normally live in the house, except for any guests who might be there, whom you will order to find other lodgings unless they seem suspicious to you, for in that case you will arrest them also; search the house and, if you find documents, make a packet of them and send them to me as safely and rapidly as you can. This is all that I need to tell you, Don Luis, and I reiterate my friendship for you and bid you farewell. May God keep you. From Valladolid, September 28, 1594.

The Judge, Don Rodrigo de Santillán

The second of these two letters and the one that follows shortly are not reported in the archives but are of ancient tradition. For what happened next we have documentary evidence from Judge Santillán himself. Next morning, September 28, when Espinosa was already in jail as a thief, Don Rodrigo happened upon the two love letters from Doña Ana and in them found the words, several times repeated, 'Your Majesty.' On the evidence of these letters it was clear that the pastry cook had been passing himself off as the vanished King of Portugal, and this was quite a different matter. This was treason.

Don Rodrigo, recognizing that he had come upon something monstrous, immediately reported his conclusions to King Felipe at El Escorial. A full-scale investigation was launched, and then a trial, and in each, Judge Santillán conducted himself with dignity, if not impartiality. From the first he was determined to accomplish two ends: he would hang the pastry cook, and he would protect his own relationship with the king, to whom he wrote: 'Since, according to the indications given by the beginning of this affair, it seems that it might offer me some profit, I beg you not to let me be deprived of it now by those who used to sleep and wench while I was patrolling and working.' He was ambitious, but to accomplish his aims he did not pervert justice and at his hands the accused received fair trials. The daughter María, which legend gives him, does not appear in the official records as pleading for the life of her lover, but on this matter Madrigal tradition is unequivocal. She never wavered in her affection for the pastry cook nor in her belief in his innocence. She remained convinced that he was the younger son of a noble family and that he had behaved with pundonor.

In the lengthy investigation conducted by Don Rodrigo there were four principal witnesses: Gabriel Espinosa, the servant girl who had appeared with him in Madrigal, Fray Miguel and Doña Ana. A special ecclesiastical judge was brought in to try Fray Miguel and the nuns, and torture of the most severe sort was applied to all but the latter. One innocent bystander who was questioned was sentenced to four years in the galleys, but this was rescinded when the judge found that in his questioning, the man had been so severely tortured, he would never again be able to use his arms.

The charge was treason. Fray Miguel and Gabriel de Espinosa, whoever the latter might be, had cooked up a scheme whereby Portugal would be detached from the throne of Spain, where it rightfully belonged. In addition, a convent had been violated, a royal nun had been seduced and jewels pertaining to the royal family had been stolen. The outcome of the trial was known before it started. Don Rodrigo had found a way to ingratiate himself with the king and nothing would prevent him from pursuing his advantage. What the trial really came down to was a fourfold mystery. Who was Espinosa? Was he widely supported in Portugal? And to what extent was Doña Ana de Austria involved? In particular, King Felipe insisted upon knowing whether the little girl was Doña Ana's daughter by the pastry cook, for if so she was a member of the royal family and Felipe felt that this changed everything.

The process against Gabriel continued for more than nine months: questions, torture, compare the answers, questions again, torture again, compare again and repeat the cycle. A particularly obnoxious aspect of the trial, if it should be called such, was that on the surface it was an ordinary trial for treason, conducted honorably, but at each step Don Rodrigo sent King Felipe a summary of what was happening and sought from the king advice as to what to do next. It was therefore the king who conducted the trial, and always he wanted to know, 'Who is that little girl?' A good deal of the torture was an attempt to find a satisfactory answer to that gnawing question.

If Doña Ana was not put to the torture she received little consideration otherwise. Early in the process she felt herself so abused that she wrote a strong letter of protest to her uncle, King Felipe, which we have, and his response, better than anything else in the case, shows how Spain was governed at the time.

My dear niece:

I have received with surprise your complaint against Don Rodrigo de Santillán and I regret that this judge has become involved in a dispute with you that I wish could have been entirely avoided. You are a person who, because of dedication and piety, lives withdrawn from the world and has no knowledge of administrators of justice, whose great severity must be tolerated and even applauded, first, because they act in Our name and know how to see that it is respected, and, second, because with their harsh severity they keep evil people cautious and fearful of punishment, thus preventing many crimes. For the common good it is better that they be harsh than lenient, because leniency is not understood by such people as mercy, but rather weakness, and they take advantage of it, multiplying their crimes and doing great injury to those who lead good and honest lives. Don Rodrigo de Santillán is perhaps more severe than he needs to be, but this is owing to the zeal with which he serves Us and has served Us all his life. As for disrespect, if there should be any such as may be to the detriment of Our dignity (since you are so close a relative of Ours, the daughter of Our most dear brother), We should not hesitate to punish Don Rodrigo most severely if there were good reason for it; but if the disrespect is perhaps more apparent than real, it is wise of princes not to allow anyone to understand that it is even possible for a vassal to show them disrespect. It is better to leave well enough alone. The two persons whom you sent to me with your recommendation that the one be made a corregidor in the Indies and the other provisioner of Our armies in Flanders have been taken care of, but We beg you, Our dear child, not to be so soft-hearted with office-seekers, because they will eat Us out of house and home. I know that certain people are going to Madrigal to see you so that you may serve as intercessor with me in the affairs of Portugal. The Duque de Coimbra and two other important gentlemen of that kingdom, who have spent some days in the Capital, have told everyone that they would not seek an audience with me until they can present themselves with your letters of recommendation for me. This affair is very serious and I wish you to proceed with great prudence and slowly, and to inform me of everything secretly, to which end I have ordered relays of post-horses to be stationed along the highway, so that your letters can reach me within twenty-four hours. Receive these people, listen to them, communicate to me immediately what they say to you, and do not again receive them, under pretext of illness or with some other clever excuse, until I shall have written to you, counseling you as to what you should tell them, because in these affairs of Portugal it is necessary to proceed very alertly, and you can discover more than I could if I were seeing them, because with you they will not be so much on their guard. May God keep you many years, my very dear child, and do not forget in your prayers to plead with God for your uncle.

The King Don Felipe

Finally the judges handed down the sentences, first having received initialed authorizations from the king. Doña Ana was deprived of all privileges due her as a member of the royal family; for four years she would live in solitary confinement; she would be allowed to attend Mass only on feast days; on Fridays she could eat nothing but bread; and for the rest of her life she could have contacts only with the least-educated members of her order. The nuns who helped slip the pastry cook into her quarters were given harsher sentences.

Espinosa's serving girl, having confessed under torture that the child was hers and not the daughter of Doña Ana or some other noble lady, was given two hundred lashes, which must have nearly killed her, and was then banished.

Fray Miguel presented a special problem. As a friar he could not be condemned by lay authority, yet clearly he had been the manipulator of the whole plot. In Lisboa he had observed the Portuguese royal family at intimate quarters and had known how to find someone who looked like the king and then coach him in his role. He had done a great job. Many

Portuguese nobles were convinced that Espinosa was their lost king. Fray Miguel paid dearly for his fling but could not be hanged because as a priest his person was inviolate, even to the wrath of the king. However, Judge Santillán, after conducting scrupulous investigations into his background, developed the interesting theory that since Miguel's parents had come from Jerez de los Caballeros, where we found Balboa's birthplace, he must be a secret Jew because Jerez was known to contain many such, and as Santillán pointed out to the king, 'never has there been an evil of any importance or a crime of any seriousness where a converted Jew hasn't played a part.' At any rate, a weak-willed Spanish archbishop was finally found who was willing to strip the friar of his ecclesiastical privileges, whereupon the lay arm of the government grabbed him, led him through the streets of Madrid with chains about his neck, then dragged him back for public humiliation in Madrigal, after which he was hanged.

That left a problem. Who was this pastry cook? The strange thing is that no one ever knew. One fantastic rumor, which I both heard in Madrigal from people who swore it to be true and found in the Encinas book, is reflected in the genealogical chart on page 467, but kept within parentheses since it can only be legend. King Sebastián's father was John of Portugal, who failed to attain the throne because he died prematurely in 1554, eighteen days before Sebastián was born. When a mere youth he had married Princess Juana, daughter of Carlos V, and when the young couple were living in Valladolid, John of Portugal fell in love with the very beautiful daughter of a pastry cook who worked in Madrigal, and by her he had an illegitimate son who was given the name Gabriel de Espinosa. Later, by Carlos V's daughter, he had a legitimate son, Sebastián. Gabriel and Sebastián were thus half brothers, which accounted for the unquestioned similarity between them and also for the fact that when Gabriel returned to Madrigal he had a pastry shop waiting for him.

A second rumor was thoroughly explored during the trial and came to be the one generally accepted by members of the government. According to this, Gabriel was a child who had been abandoned in the torno of a Toledo convent and had grown up reckless and willing for any adventure. The turmoil in Portugal attendant on King Sebastián's crusade attracted him and he may or may not have gone to Africa with the king. On subsequent travels through Europe he learned German and French, but how he fell into the hands of Fray Miguel was not known. Furthermore, the very fact that he had been abandoned secretly in a torno added fuel to the suspicion that he was the offspring, legitimate or otherwise, of some noble family.

The third rumor was the one that Espinosa himself had used when wooing María, the alcalde's daughter. He was the acknowledged son of a noble family and for some reason wished to travel incognito for the time being.

And, finally, there were many in both Portugal and Spain who believed that he was indeed the lost King Sebastián, and that King Felipe knew it. Just as Felipe had tried in 1578 to cause his nephew's death by denying him the army and navy he needed, so he now in 1594 ordered his horrible execution.

At Felipe's direction Gabriel de Espinosa, whoever he might be, was taken back to Madrigal de las Altas Torres and was there paraded through the streets in a wicker basket. His tour ended at a gallows, where a discalced priest jammed a crucifix into his mouth every time he sought to address the crowd. He was hanged, cut down, beheaded and hacked into quarters, which were nailed to trees on four different roads leading out of Madrigal. The head was exhibited in an iron cage hung from the tip of a pike in the town itself as a deterrent to the next man who might want to challenge the right of Felipe II to rule Portugal.

Fray Miguel, when he faced death, recanted prior confessions made under torture and insisted that Espinosa was King Sebastián. On the gallows, Espinosa conducted himself like a true king and convinced many. It seems to me that the most damning evidence against him was twofold: when he was locked in his cell, without recourse to the dye pots of an apothecary, his hair grew in almost white, so that he looked more nearly sixty than the forty that Sebastián would have been; but as an old man in Madrigal pointed out to me, 'Think a minute! He was under such torture that his hair turned white.' And, as Judge Santillán skillfully brought out, he could not speak Portuguese.

Especially ironic was the fact that even if Espinosa had escaped hanging by Felipe, even if the plot had worked, he was doomed, because under torture Fray Miguel confessed that he intended using Espinosa only until Portugal gained its independence. Then Fray Miguel would have denounced Espinosa as an impostor. He would have been executed and a real member of the Portuguese royal family called to the throne. As for Doña Ana, she was a giddy nun and was expendable. As a matter of fact, such deviousness was not necessary, for in 1640, by what might be termed natural processes not requiring the existence of a King Sebastián, Portugal regained her independence from Spain.

Long after the executions of Fray Miguel and Espinosa, long after bitter Felipe II was dead, the dismal affair at Madrigal ended on a note of gracia. Felipe III, who had already reigned for twelve years, relented at the thought of his cousin Doña Ana de Austria's being immured in a cell and appointed her, when she was forty-two years old, abbess of the largest and most important convent in Spain, Las Huelgas, and there she ruled for many years, firm, able and disposed to listen sympathetically when young nuns came to her with emotional problems.

FOLLOWING PAGE:
Strings of garlic.

IX

PAMPLONA

OCEANO
ATLANTICO

MILES
0   100

Santillana del Mar
Azpeitia   Roncesvalles
Santiago   Pamplona
de Compostela
Tudela
Barcelona
Porto

Madrid

Sintra   Elvas
Lisboa

Faro   Sevilla

MAR MEDITERRANE

Word had circulated through Europe and America that the mob was gathering in July for the feria of San Fermín at Pamplona. The two British bullfight experts Angus Macnab and Kenneth Tynan were to be there. The American aficionados Darryl Zanuck, Orson Welles, and Conrad Janis had reservations. Hemingway's mentor Juanito Quintana had assured us that he was coming, and although the queen of bullfight fans, the stately Tigre from London, couldn't make it, she was sending as deputy her son Oliver, a most attractive young man fresh out of Eton with a penchant for running a few inches in front of the largest bulls. The ineffable Matt Carney, whom I had not met, was coming down from his bizarre occupation in Paris, and I looked forward to making his acquaintance, and Bob Daley, who had just published a good book on the bulls, would be there, but what was most attractive to me, Robert Vavra, in charge of illustrations for this book, was to be on hand, as would be the American matador John Fulton, who was flying in from Mexico. I wanted to talk to both of them. So with a good deal of cabling for reservations and renting of cars, the mob set out for Pamplona.

My reasons for going were fourfold and none was connected with bullfighting, much as I enjoyed it. First I wanted to see the Navarrese city of Tudela; then I wanted to talk about music with Don Luis Morondo; next I wanted to study Pamplona's curious cathedral; and finally I wanted to picnic once more in the enchanted Pass of Roncesvalles. I would have traveled a considerable distance to do any one of these things, and the happy prospect of doing them all and in conjunction with the celebration of San Fermín was enticing.

Tudela is a small city on the right bank of the Río Ebro and has little to commend it except a public square with some fine arches and a few

479

church buildings that might concern an architect but which had no inter-est·for me. I was drawn to Tudela by a crowded district which huddled along the river's edge; eight hundred years ago this area had been a warren of narrow streets from which a great man had fled to adventures so preposterous as to make him one of the major travelers of history, and it was to him that I wanted to pay homage, for I was indebted to his work.

He was known simply as Benjamin of Tudela and probably he had no other name, for he was a poor Jew who lived in the local ghetto, but in 1165 he decided to see something of the world, and long before I had ever seen the city of Tudela, I had imagined him saying goodbye to the misera-ble Jewish quarter and sailing down the Ebro to some port city that gave him access to the Mediterranean and the known world of that time.

Now, seeing the Ebro as it passed Tudela, I doubted that he could have sailed it. He must have walked, perhaps to Zaragoza and then over to Barcelona, where he entered upon the Mediterranean. At any rate, in the years following 1165 Benjamin wandered through the Near East, trading and listening and making notes. He visited more than three hundred places, and wherever he went he asked about the condition of Jews in the region and compiled a census of all families known to be Jewish, so that today it is from Benjamin that we know about the Jewry of that time. He was especially careful to note conditions in the Holy Land, where the Crusades had pretty well eliminated Jews in 1099. But when he reached these supposedly destitute lands he discovered several enclaves in which Jewish families had persisted for a hundred generations.

Benjamin was an indefatigable traveler and apparently a man of courage, for he penetrated to areas that other Europeans had not seen, and if his report, existing only in manuscript till 1543, lacked the literary quality of Marco Polo's narrative, it surpassed the Venetian's account in factual matters and antedated it by more than a century. I owed Benjamin of Tudela much, for from his tight and cautious writing I learned things that I required to know in writing one of my novels, and now as I stood in his native city, looking at the narrow streets that he must have known and from which he had fled, I felt very close to him, for he had traveled the lands that I had traveled, and he had written of things I had written about, but he had done it when to do so required both imagination and courage. I wish I had known this doughty old Jew; I wish I could have sat with him on the shores of Lake Galilee when he noted in his journal that fourteen Jewish families had now crept back to this village or that, where all had been expelled or murdered half a century before. I found in Benjamin a great resilience of spirit and it was gratifying to walk the streets he had walked.

There was another reason why I wanted to see Tudela: here I would catch my first glimpse of the Río Ebro, to which the title of this book is related. In pre-Roman times this river was known as the Iberus and those who lived along it as Iberes. To the Greeks the eastern half of Spain was

Iberia, and thus the word entered classical history. The French writer Jean Descola in his *A History of Spain* (1962) offers quite a different derivation:

> At about this time the country acquired a name. The Hebrews called it Sepharad, 'border' or 'edge.' The Greeks christened it Hesperia, 'the Occident,' or He Spania, 'the sparse.' More significant, however, was the term 'Iberia,' which derived from the Celtic word *aber,* 'harbor' or 'river.' And indeed, the first known inhabitants of the peninsula were precisely the Iberians who came from the valley of the Ebro.

Since no authority I have consulted supports this theory, I do not know what to make of Descola's claim that the word *Iberian* is of Celtic origin.

To the Romans, of course, the name Iberia referred to that region of the Caucasus now known as Georgia, and it is surprising to find that a respected authority like William Smith in his *Classical Dictionary* (1881) limits his definition of Iberia to the Asian area, ending with the aside, 'No connection can be traced between the Iberians of Asia and those of Spain.' (Strictly speaking, therefore, the most notorious Iberian of history was Josef Stalin.) The more authoritative *Harper's Dictionary of Classical Literature and Antiquities* (1965) also defines Iberia as Georgia but does add a second definition: 'One of the ancient names of Spain, derived from the river Iberus.'

The Oxford English Dictionary cites Henry Cockeram's *The English Dictionary, or an Interpretation of Hard English Words* (1623) as reflecting general European usage in its simple definition of Iberians: 'Spaniards.' It was in this tradition, which I follow, that Isaac Albéniz in the years 1906–1909 composed his delightful suite *Iberia,* originally for the piano; six typical section titles are Sevilla, Ronda, Almería, Triana, Málaga and Jerez. For him and for all others who are mindful of the classical past, Iberia serves as a synonym for ancient Spain, and for the most evocative of modern Spain.

In general usage, of course, the word has come to indicate the entire peninsula, including both Spain and Portugal. The first recorded example of this usage in English came no earlier than 1611, but today *Lippincott's Gazetteer* (1952) says briefly: 'The Iberian peninsula comprises Spain and Portugal,' while *The Random House Dictionary of the English Language* (1966) relegates the traditional definition of Georgia to second place, defining the word primarily as 'a peninsula in SW Europe, comprising Spain and Portugal.'

Even though I am following the older definition, a chapter of this book could legitimately have dealt with Portugal, because in the years when I was visiting Spain, I grabbed at every opportunity to wander in Portugal; one of the most relaxed vacations I ever experienced came when a group of us rented a historic quinta (country seat) at Sintra, the exquisite hill town near Lisboa in which Lord Byron composed much of his heroic poem *Don*

Juan. For more than a month I tramped over the hills he had known and down those tight and twisted lanes that he had loved. The Portuguese spoke of him with enormous affection, as if he had been with them only a few tourist seasons ago; his demonic presence hovered about me as I worked at my typewriter, because at some earlier date someone had told the Englishman who owned our quinta that he looked exactly like Lord Byron, and this had had a bad effect upon the man. The study I was using was literally lined with volumes on the poet. Apparently my Englishman had a standing order with booksellers in London and New York: 'Send me anything printed about Lord Byron.' He also had copies of several of the more romantic portraits of the poet, which proved that Byron did resemble the owner of the quinta, or the other way around.

Wherever I wandered in Portugal, I discovered quiet Englishmen who had lived for decades in quiet crannies of this hospitable country. Portugal has always held a fascination for the English, who term it 'our oldest ally and one of the world's most civilized spots.' I often suspected that these Englishmen were engaged in a conspiracy of silence, and one afternoon a group of them begged me, 'For God's sake, Michener, don't tell anyone, and certainly not the rich Americans, how heavenly this place is.' It was Europe's most economical retirement spot; it had the best servants, the best wine, some of the best food, and a host of small localities from Porto in the north to Faro in the south to which an educated Englishman could retire in dignity.

I am often asked to compare Portugal and Spain, and the simple truth seems to be that whichever of these two countries one visits first continues as his preference. No one can be more energetic in defense of a new-found land than the Englishman, Frenchman or American who has visited Portugal first and then moved on to Spain: he loves the first and is never easy in the second. I discovered this when I traveled westward across Spain with an American couple who had worked for some years at our embassy in Lisboa, for it was touching to watch how apprehensive they were of all things Spanish and how their spirits revived the closer they got to their beloved Portugal. 'We wouldn't feel safe drinking Spanish water, thank you. We've been all through Portugal and we've never seen villages as dirty as those in Spain. Doesn't anyone have paint in this country? The fact is, we feel safe in Portugal but in Spain you never know. Our police are so much better.' As we approached the western border of Spain it became a question of whether we should take our lunch in Spanish Badajoz, which I preferred because of the great seafood zarzuela I knew was waiting, or press on to Portuguese Elvas, which lay just across the border. 'Oh,' my embassy friends said, 'we'd never want to eat in a Spanish restaurant if a clean Portuguese one were nearby.'

Well, the first of the two countries that I saw was Spain and my affection has always rested there. It was not until my trip with the Lisboa couple that I saw the peninsula through Portuguese eyes, and when I did this I had to admit that of the two countries Portugal was the cleaner, the better organized, the better controlled; it was not illogical that the knowing English had elected this small country as their choice of Europe. But I also found that it lacked the culture of Spain; there was no Portuguese Velázquez, no Victoria, no García Lorca, no Santa Teresa, and of course no Seneca. The genius of the Iberian peninsula seemed to have resided principally in the more easterly regions, and it was for this reason that I preferred Spain.

On two different occasions after long stays in Portugal, I crossed into Spain and each time those of us in the automobile felt a surge of joy, an expansion of the spirit and a sense of growing nobility as we entered Spain. Once the driver of our car dismounted, rubbed his hands in Spanish soil and exulted in being home again. My joining him irritated my wife, who like many women preferred Portugal. 'You're being silly and unfair,' she protested. 'Portugal is much finer than you admit it to be.' The driver, who had been disappointed in Portuguese girls, replied, 'There's one thing I'll admit. It's the only country in the world where a man's mistress is apt to be uglier than his wife.'

There was a final reason for choosing *Iberia* as a title for this book: the word is unusual in that it is just as beautiful in its English pronunciation (Eye-beer-ee-ya) as in its Spanish (Ee-bare-ya), a fact recognized by Matthew Arnold when he inscrted the word in the closing lines of "The Scholar-Gipsy," one of the stateliest passages of English poetry:

> To where the Atlantic raves
> Outside the Western Straits, and unbent sails·
> There, where down cloudy cliffs, through sheets of foam,
> Shy traffickers, the dark Iberians come;
> And on the beach undid his corded bales.

The short drive from Tudela to Pamplona ran due north through the handsome country of lower Navarra, climbing as it went, for I was approaching the Pyrenees, and although it was now early July, the air was brisk and I could sense the vigor that characterizes northern Spain. Then, as the car turned a corner, I saw before me the smokestacks and factory walls of a prosaic industrial city that might be termed the Youngstown of Spain, and I thought how disappointed must be those foreigners nurtured on Ernest Hemingway's vision of Pamplona as it existed in the late 1920s, when they saw this drab profile. Judging by first appearances, Pamplona was no romantic center for expatriates but rather a commercial hub more concerned about labor unions than fiestas.

My first explorations of the city through its southern gateway confirmed this judgment: I saw dozens of garages where knowledgeable young men were tearing down Ford and Citroën engines and rebuilding them. I saw glass factories and cordage shops and lumber yards and carpenters' benches. But when I entered the wide avenue leading to the central square I entered a new world, for now I found myself surrounded by a hornets' nest of small cars from all over Europe filled with some of the most attractive young people I had seen in years: blondes from Sweden, handsome dark-haired men from Italy, students in leather pants from Germany and a substantial quota of Americans under the age of twenty-five. There was noise and excitement. The heart of Pamplona was apparently going to be much different from the environs.

The first specific proof I had that a feria was about to begin came when I saw Spanish men parading with long strings of garlic about their necks, wearing them as women do pearls. I was to ask many times what these strands of garlic reaching down to the knees signified, but no one could tell me; doubtless it had something to do either with ancient fertility rites or with charms to banish ghosts during feria.

When I came to the public square it was as if I had entered another city, one belonging to the nineteenth century. In the center among scattered trees stood an old-style bandstand featuring iron grillwork; about the edges of the square sprawled a dozen cafés, their chairs and tables covering the pavement from door to gutter; above the cafés rose several ancient hotels with tall French windows that didn't close; and everywhere there were hordes of young people determined to have a good time.

I was supposed to meet Vavra at the Bar Txoco, but when I got there all tables were filled with students from South Africa, Germany, Sweden and Great Britain. They were a riotous lot, some with necklaces of garlic, most stone-drunk at five in the afternoon, with the feria not yet begun. Unable to find a chair, I was about to leave when I heard a loud, insinuating 'Psssst,' and I turned to face the man who would symbolize Pamplona for me.

He was in his late forties, a disreputable, baggy-kneed, bleary-eyed, gap-toothed, fumbling, stumbling waiter from a nearby café who made his living by luring customers away from the Bar Txoco to his flea-infested joint and exacting from them, for his pains, a shot or two of whiskey. He was the most debauched Spaniard I had ever seen, a disreputable Sancho Panza, and as he offered me a chair he whispered, 'You want to meet a refined Spanish girl? Speaks English.' When I ordered wine he made a new proposition: 'Can I pour a shot for myself?' The duplicity with which he dispatched his drink without being detected by the owner of the café was ingratiating, and as he placed my wine on the table he asked, 'You interested in marijuana?' I was to see a great deal of this one-man vice ring in the eight days ahead, for he seemed to work all hours without sleep, fortifying himself with cadged drinks and lurching about his corner of the plaza in a kind of Renaissance debauchery. 'Look!' he whispered admiringly as I sipped my wine. 'Ernest Hemingway. And our lousy newspapers tried to tell us he was dead.'

I looked to where he pointed, and my jaw dropped. There, entering the plaza behind the wheel of a small, trim Karmann-Ghia, came Ernest Hemingway, dead these five years. He wore his famous hunting cap with the short brim, and field jacket. His white beard looked exactly as it had during the last years of his life, and his portly figure was the same. Even the features of his expressive face were unchanged, and after he had parked his car in the space reverently saved for him by the police, he stepped into the plaza exactly as he had done forty years before when gathering the impressions that later served as the foundation for *The Sun Also Rises*.

'Adiós, Hemingway!' several Spaniards called, and a warm smile diffused the bloated face of my degenerate waiter as he cried, 'Don Ernesto! Welcome back to Pamplona.'

With much ceremony Hemingway was offered the table next to me, and two Spaniards asked for his autograph. Taking from an inner pocket of his field jacket a stack of printed calling cards, one face of which contained his photograph, he signed two and handed them graciously to the petitioners, who then withdrew.

'Are you Vanderford?' I asked across the tables.

'I am,' he said, and I was about to ask him for one of his famous cards when I was interrupted by two Pamplona newspapermen whom I had known some years before when making a pilgrimage to Santiago de Compostela. They wanted to know which bullfighter appearing in the feria had lured me back to San Fermín, or which parties at which café, and they were not prepared when I explained that I had come primarily in hope of meeting with Don Luis Morondo. The reporters hesitated a moment, as if they did not know the name of the man who is probably the most famous Pamplonan alive today. I thought it would be egregious of me to describe him any further, and I was pleased when one finally smiled and said, 'Oh, you mean Morondo the musician!'

I did indeed. For some years I had owned a fine phonograph record produced by Morondo and his chamber-music group from Pamplona, and I was so impressed by it—a collection of fifteenth- and sixteenth-century music sung a cappella—that I had made inquiries in musical circles in New York and London and found that among those who knew choral singing, Morondo's Pamplona group was considered one of the most polished ensembles. 'Can you arrange for me to meet him?' I asked the newspapermen.

'Perhaps,' they said, and I left them to attend a concert which Morondo was giving to honor the opening of San Fermín. On stage came sixteen singers, eight good-looking young women in evening dresses backed up by seven young men and one older man in tuxedos. Each man stood on a box of a different height, so that all seemed to be equally tall. Each singer wore the traditional red scarf of San Fermín. The group made a stunning appearance, but was its singing to be as good as I had heard on the record?

Then Morondo appeared, tall, slim, well groomed. He could have been a Spanish grandee in his fifties. With a minimum of gesture he launched his singers into a program which began with fifteenth-century church music and ended with 'Old Black Joe,' in honor of the Americans who had crowded into Pamplona. The Stephen Foster was sung in clear English and made an amusing effect, but the highlight of the performance was a work that fitted precisely the spirit of the feria, García Lorca's 'Lament for Ignacio Sánchez Mejías' arranged for choral group. At the repeated phrase, 'At five in the afternoon,' one could sense the beginning of the tragedy that would end in the death of this fine matador.

The group could sing. The individual pyrotechnics of the singers were less conspicuous than those of similar groups trained in London or Paris and there seemed to be less variation in attack and emphasis, but the ensemble singing, which is what such a group must master if it is to achieve a good reputation, was as good as any I had ever heard. There was less exhibitionism, less dramatic effect for effect's sake, than in a comparable American group, but a much nobler end result. If one demanded exciting solo work from either individual singers or the various choirs, he would not find it here, but if one sought a powerful and authentic total effect, here it was. The voices were wonderfully modulated, finely matched and superbly disciplined. It was obvious from the first note that Dr. Morondo had his group under control and that they sang pretty much as he wanted them to sing. I left the theater, thinking, It was worth the trip north to hear such music.

Next day I met Morondo, and close up he was even more impressive than he had been on the podium. He was taller than I had thought, had very blue eyes, a quiet voice and a most infectious smile. He wore an attractive jacket with no lapels and reminded me of a younger Toscanini. It was painful to discover that his life had been that of nearly every creative figure in Spain, an endless duplication of demanding jobs which taken together had barely paid enough wages for him to live and do the work of which he was capable. A pupil of a pupil of the Frenchman Dukas, Morondo had in recent years simplified his life: he now served as professor at the normal school, professor at the consistory, director of the orchestra, director of the choral group, lecturer at the university, plus teacher, advisor, consultant and friend to all young musicians in the area. In spite of this deluge he maintained a youthful appearance and a lively humor.

I began, 'Maestro, I've come to Pamplona to see you because in Avila I found myself perplexed about the problem of Spanish music.'

'I am too,' he replied.

'I've always heard of Felipe Pedrell [1841–1922] as the patron saint of modern Spanish music . . .'

I was not allowed to finish, for at the name of that great musicologist whose theories had inspired Albéniz, Granados, Turina and Falla, Morondo's face lit up and he cried, 'He was the master of us all.'

'But what actually did he accomplish?'

'He sent us back to Spanish themes, to the great work done by unknown Spanish song writers of the fifteenth and sixteenth centuries. You might say that all we've done has been built upon the bones of Pedrell.'

'Two problems confuse me.' I said. 'First, Pedrell in Spanish music seems to me like Squarcione in north Italian painting. Each was a notable teacher, but neither left much of his own work for us to hear or see. For twenty years I've been interested in Pedrell and I've yet to hear a note he wrote.'

'That can be corrected. I'll bring you his songbooks tomorrow.'

'Are there any recordings of his songs?'

'Actual recordings? No. But you hear Pedrell in all Spanish music. His songs live in all of us.' (During the rest of my stay in Spain I was not to hear a single note that Pedrell wrote, nor have I yet, but I sensed him to be a more important musician than many whose names and works I knew well.)

'Second problem. The individual themes that Pedrell brought to the attention of his group . . . Let's say the ones I hear in the four composers we named . . . They're some of the greatest themes in contemporary music. Better I'd say than similar national themes I find in Brahms, Dvořák, Smetana or Bartók.'

'I'd agree. They are supreme musical notations.' Morondo nodded. For eighteen years he had served as director of Spain's oldest symphony, the one Camille Saint-Saëns used to conduct, and he knew well the music I was speaking of.

'But Brahms and the others from the rest of Europe took poorer themes and made of them great symphonies and concertos and quartets. Why . . .'

Dr. Morondo interrupted me. 'You want to know why Spanish composers haven't done the same?'

'It seems to me they've abused the great material Pedrell handed them. They've utilized it on a lower level than was necessary.'

To this criticism Dr. Morondo preferred to make no comment, but some weeks later in Barcelona a more critical Spanish musician commented on the problems I had raised in Avila: 'When you demand that Falla and Albéniz take Spanish themes and build from them what Brahms and Dvořák built from theirs, you're out of your mind. Germany and Austria of that day had orchestras and opera companies and string ensembles that needed the music these men were writing. Spain did not. One small orchestra here, another there, a visiting opera company from Milan, and an audience who wanted to hear only *Carmen* and *La Bohème*. The

Spanish audience still doesn't want a symphony or an opera featuring a large ensemble and a complicated structure. It wants a short, individualized work and that's what the Spanish composer learned to supply. Zarzuela, not opera. Because symphonies and operas are not within our pattern. Besides, the material that Pedrell resurrected for these men was ideally suited to individual types of presentation. In criticizing Falla and Albéniz for not having produced in the grand manner, you are criticizing not the composers but the Spanish people, and you are betraying your own lack of understanding.'

'But do you agree,' I asked this Barcelona expert, 'that the themes themselves, those soaring, passionate Spanish groups of statements we find in Granados and Falla . . . They're better than what Brahms and Dvořák had to work with, aren't they?'

'Much better. But if you ask me next, "Then why didn't Spanish composers build better with those building blocks?" I'll have to repeat that your question makes no sense. It just doesn't relate to the facts in Spain.'

Back with Dr. Morondo, I changed the subject. 'The main reason I wanted to see you was to ask whether I'm correct in judging Victoria to be Spain's foremost composer?'

A look of joy suffused Morondo's agile face, and after nodding his dark head back and forth he said, 'There was the great one.'

'I'd hoped you'd have something of his on the concert yesterday.'

'A little too profound for opening a bullfight.'

I told him of my embarrassing experience in thinking for so many years that Victoria was an Italian, and he laughed. 'Many people still do. It's Italy's revenge for our stealing Colón.' I then explained how Victoria's 'Ave Maria' had come to mean so much to me, and Morondo began to hum the opening notes of this composition, those marvelous sequences broken in rhythm and emphasis. He conducted as he sang and I joined him in this haunting masterpiece, but when we came to the 'Ora pro nobis' with its majestic theme and timeless devotion he threw up his hands, halted his unseen choir and cried, 'What dramatic use of words and music. Victoria could do what none of us have been able to do since.' He then asked me if I knew Victoria's *Officium Hebdomadae Sanctae* (The Offices of Holy Week, 1585), and when I said no he promised to bring me a score to study, and this he did and to my pleasure I discovered that the nine *Responsories for Tenebrae* which I liked so much were part of this noble work. The *Officium* has not yet been recorded in its entirety, so I have not heard it, but from the fragments I have been able to acquire here and there I judge Morondo to have been correct in calling it Victoria's masterpiece.

Before I left America, André Kostelanetz had advised me, when in Pamplona, to visit the Pablo de Sarasate museum containing mementos of the violinist who began in Pamplona and startled the world with his virtuoso playing, and as I looked at the old programs with their florid fruit-flower embellishments, I recalled a dictum I had read years before: 'Spanish music has always been designed for the individual.' If this is true then some of the flamboyant compositions of Sarasate are closer to the essential spirit of Spain than the symphonic work of Turina, which I like. In praising Turina, I am perhaps being obstinate; but even though Spaniards insist that the symphony is not suited to their cast of mind, I prefer the reasoned symphony of Turina to the brilliant incidental pieces of Albéniz and Granados; in fact, I have begun to suspect that Pedrell was the evil genius of Spanish music. Had he not come along to draw his followers into the bypaths of antique themes, wonderful as they are, might not Spanish music have matured into major forms as did the music of Hungary, Austria and Czechoslovakia?

About the Pamplona cathedral I had no hesitation. It is the ugliest beautiful church in existence, and to study it carefully over repeated hours is an experience in art that proves invaluable to people like dress designers and poets. The beauty is provided by the cloisters, which cannot be equaled in northern Spain for graciousness and intricate Gothic poetry; critics have praised them in terms which I do not find excessive. The interior, with six fine arches running down each side of the nave, with spacious aisle and lovely chapels, is also a handsome creation, and when the especially strong transept is added, with soaring stone arches where it crosses the nave, one has a noble place of worship, not particularly spiritual, perhaps, but clean and hard as befits the north. I have always liked the beautifully carved tombs of King Carlos III of Navarra and his Queen Leonora as they stand exposed before the altar, for in them one sees carving of a high order, and they lend both royalty and somberness to the soaring interior.

It is the façade which provides the ugliness. Originally it seems to have been a perfectly good Gothic work suited to the cloister and the spacious interior, but at the end of the eighteenth century the architect Ventura Rodríguez, who had acquired a national reputation as the man who could be trusted to improve old churches, which he had done in other parts of Spain, was invited to try his luck on Pamplona. He proceeded to tear down the existing Gothic façade and to erect in its place a Greco-Roman horror that makes the once-gracious building look like the courthouse of Deaf Smith County, Texas. It is so bad it must be seen to be believed. I had very much hoped Robert Vavra would choose to photograph it for this book, but he said, 'It's so ugly that no film can do it justice.'

The tall Gothic towers have become blunt and squat, one a rigid duplicate of the other. Each is composed of many disparate elements that add up to miserable failure. Eight rather good Corinthian columns fail to convey any sense of loftiness because they are capped by a pediment totally lacking in inspiration. The main feature is a pair of horrible plaster angels in exaggerated poses between two senseless urns. Over the main door leading to the nave an Assumption of the Virgin of no discernible style whatever was added in 1956, while on the right tower a sundial has been placed, which because of the orientation of the church can tell time for only a few hours in the late afternoon. Finally, as if the twentieth century sought to help the eighteenth in the job of destroying a beautiful building, atop the whole is a huge and glaring neon cross.

I think a protracted study of the Pamplona cathedral should be obligatory for anyone who plans to revise the work of others who have gone before him. A composer who plans to update Victoria's 'Ave Maria' should see what happened when Rodríguez updated a Gothic cathedral. A film director about to improve on Molière should remind himself of the disaster that sometimes overtakes such ventures. If a whole work falls out of style, as can well happen, the fall will be mitigated by a certain inherent grace, whereas if one refurbishes a Gothic cathedral with a Greco-Roman façade, a couple of plaster angels and a neon cross, only confusion can result. I was reminded of something Ernest Hemingway said of motion pictures that had been made from his works: 'I attend each one with a trusted friend and a quart of gin and I haven't been able to last through any of them yet.'

There could be no locale more appropriate for recalling Hemingway than Pamplona during San Fermín and no year more suitable than this, for that morning in formal ceremony at the town hall the alcalde had conferred on Hemingway posthumously the distinction of the honorary red scarf of San Fermín, and the crowd had nostalgically approved; so in the evening I invited to the Caballo Blanco (White Horse), perched on the city walls, four devotees of Hemingway who had known him in the final years. I promised them mixed salad, a copious menestra and conversation, and I was gratified when they appeared: Juanito Quintana, who had served as prototype for Montoya in *The Sun Also Rises;* Kenneth Vanderford, that strange Ph.D. from Indiana whom I had met in the plaza; John Fulton, whom Hemingway had befriended in the last years; and Robert Vavra, to whom Hemingway had been especially kind.

When we took our seats in the handsome tavern—recently assembled on this spot, using stones and floor plans borrowed from various Renaissance ruins that were about to be torn down in other parts of Pamplona —the two women who ran the place brought bowls of mixed salad heavy with onion, olive oil and sharp vinegar, and we remarked how fortunate the timing of San Fermín was: it arrived just as the crisp lettuce, the red tomatoes and the strong onions ripen, so that all during feria one can eat this astringent dish. Tonight there would also be my favorite of northern Spain, menestra. In hot olive oil cloves of garlic are browned; vegetables of all kinds, including especially artichokes, are added until a soup is formed, then shellfish previously cooked, plus a boiled chicken. The whole is put in

Some handsome things of great age
should be left as they are

the oven until properly blended, then served with onion bread and grated cheese.

When the menestra was finished and the flan was being served, cold and shimmering and golden, the conversation began, and I would like to report exactly what was said, retaining the contradictions and false starts as they occurred that night.

Michener: I've been reading Hotchner's book on Hemingway and I've asked you here to help on one point. Hotchner claims that in that last year when we saw Hemingway, he'd already begun to fall apart inside and was contemplating suicide. Did you catch any glimpse of that?

Quintana: I was close to him at that time. He never gave a hint that he might commit suicide.

Vavra: I certainly saw nothing. What impressed me was his willingness to help Fulton. At the Miramar Hotel in Málaga he took me aside and said, 'Fulton has guts and I know you kids are having it tough in this ambiente. I'd like to help.' Well, a lot of people said that in those days but nothing ever happened. And like all the rest, Hemingway left without doing anything. But about a week later, when I thought he had forgotten his promise, he very quietly slipped me a hundred-dollar traveler's check. For weeks we didn't cash it. Just sat looking at it.

Michener: You notice anything strange about him, John?

Fulton: One important thing. I'd read about his love for Maera, who was one of the great old bullfighters, a real man, and I simply couldn't comprehend his sudden affection for Ordóñez and Dominguín, they simply weren't in Maera's class as rugged men.

Vavra: At Málaga I heard Hemingway say, 'Poor boys, Ordóñez and Dominguín. They're really having it tough. Fight in the north one day, have to fly all the way to the south that night, then fight again next day.'

Fulton: Maera used to make such trips by car. And old cars, at that. And arrive shaken up and without sleep. And go out and fight Miuras. I never understood Hemingway's sudden debasement of his critical values.

Michener: Did he know much about bullfighting?

Vanderford: He knew a great deal. But the Spaniards love to put him down. They ridicule his knowledge of the bulls.

Vavra: But they ridiculed him only after his article criticizing Manolete, the article in which he put Manolete down for the very things that Spanish writers had been criticizing for years.

Vanderford: Yes, especially then, but I don't believe Spanish bullfight critics have ever taken Hemingway very seriously, or any Anglo-Saxon expert on the bulls. To show you how Spaniards reacted to Hemingway's remarks on Manolete, K-Hito, one of the best critics, wrote an indignant article which he concluded by stating that in the future, of the two Hemingways, I was to be known as 'Hemingway el Bueno,' meaning that the real one was a bum.

Vavra: Strange that he was so Madrid-oriented. Andalucía, the cradle of bullfighting, never much interested him, nor did Mexico.

Quintana: I met Ernesto when he first came to Spain. He stayed in my father's hotel, Hotel Quintana, on the square where the Bar Brasil now is. And he knew almost nothing about the bulls. Couldn't speak any Spanish either. I was a great admirer of Maera and I introduced Hemingway to him. I was amazed at how quickly this man could learn. He had a fantastic identification with the drama of the ring and caught on immediately. By the time he left Spain he knew bullfighting as well as any of us.

Michener: How did he treat you?

Quintana: Always a marvelous friend. Once he said, 'Juanito, you're never to worry about money. You've been my constant friend and I'm going to take care of you.'

Michener: Did he?

Quintana: No.

Michener: The Hotchner book says he kept you on his payroll. Sent you money regularly from the States.

Quintana: That book has done me much harm. If you want the facts, as a friend I can trust, here they are. Ernesto paid me faithfully every peseta he ever owed me, but only what he owed. Never sent me a penny from America. Only for services I performed in Spain. As a guide, that is. Since his death, people who were connected with him send me letters all the time asking for copies of this paper or that, so I get the photocopies made and send them to the States, but no one ever sends me expenses for the work. Nor even thank-you letters for my time and money.

Michener: The book says Hemingway was fed up with you. For having failed to get tickets for the bullfights in Pamplona.

Quintana: Señor Hotchner wasn't even with Hemingway when this was supposed to have happened. He hadn't asked me to get any tickets. In those days tickets were easy to come by. You could buy your own. I remember when I first met Hotchner. Little town called Aranda de Duero. Hemingway treated him with indifference. Certainly the great friendship Hotchner speaks of wasn't visible to me . . . or to any of the rest of us.

Michener: I take it you didn't like the book.

Quintana: Much was truthful and very sweet in its picture of Ernesto. But the bad things about me . . . I remember the day I introduced Hemingway to Ordóñez, here in Pamplona. It's not good to be made fun of.

Vanderford: You keep asking questions, Michener. What did you think about Hemingway?

Michener: One of the things I'm proudest of in my life is that when I was in the trenches in Korea, *Life* magazine sent me the galleys of Hemingway's *The Old Man and the Sea.* Wanted me to make a statement to sort of back them up in their venture of publishing the whole thing in one issue. So there I sat, absolutely cold turkey, knowing nothing about the book and remembering the debacle of *Across the River and into the Trees,* and how the critics had slaughtered him, and I was praying that this one would be good so that he could regain his reputation. So I read it by lantern light with the Chinese popping at us from across the valley, and a great lump came in my throat, and when I finished I wrote something about feeling good when the daddy of us all won back the heavyweight crown. I was the first to read it. And stick my neck out. It was used in full-page ads across the country. One of the best things I ever did.

Vavra: Did he ever say anything about it?

Michener: I met him only once. For about twenty minutes. I was working in New York, and Leonard Lyons, who was a close friend of Hemingway's, called at lunchtime and said, 'Papa's in town. He's having lunch at Toots Shor's. You want to meet him?' I did, very much, but couldn't get away. About four in the afternoon I was walking down Fifty-first Street to my hotel, and as I passed Shor's I thought, Hemingway may still be in there. So I went inside. Lyons was gone but Hemingway was in a corner surrounded by men I didn't know. Only one I knew was Toots Shor. After a while I introduced myself and Hemingway was embarrassed and I was embarrassed. He knew what I'd written about *The Old Man,* but we were both embarrassed. So he did all the talking, and I remember two things he said. That the time came when a man didn't want to be known locally as a distinguished Philadelphia novelist but wanted to put his work up against the best in the world. He had put his up against Pío Baroja and Flaubert, and any man who was satisfied to be idolized locally was a crapper. He also said he couldn't stand what the movies had done to his things.

Quintana: When he saw *The Sun Also Rises* he was very angry, and I asked, 'Where are you going?' and he said, 'To have a fistfight with Darryl Zanuck.' He asked me what I thought of the picture, and I said, 'Terrible. They made me short, with a ruddy face and very large cheeks. And they used a Mexican actor to play me . . . a Spaniard!' Ernesto laughed.

Fulton: He was always concerned with how he looked. You might even say

intana, friend of Ernest Hemingway;
nderford, the poor man's Hemingway;
d the Conde de la Corte, famous bull breeder.

495

he was vain. Arjona, the photographer from Sevilla, took a shot of him on a cold blustery day. Came out very bad. Reluctantly Hemingway signed a copy for me, 'To John Fulton, with best wishes from his paisano, Ernest Hemingway.'

Vavra: But when I pushed my copy of the same picture under his nose, he groaned, 'I'll be damned if I'll sign that one again,' so he drew a cartoonist's balloon out from his mouth and inside wrote the word 'Mierda,' and that's all he would do.

Fulton: Tell about the bullfight articles you'd written?

Vavra: I showed him some criticisms I'd written for a magazine in the States, and he read them carefully, put them down and said, 'It's easy for a critic to make wisecracks. It's easy to be clever. But its god-damned hard to be truthful. Now you sit down and write half a dozen more and I'll go over them with you. And we'll cut out the cheap cracks. Because a real critic is after the truth which the writer or the matador doesn't see for himself. Cheap cracks are the concern of vaudeville.'

Michener: In these last years what was he like as a man?

Vanderford: Class all the way. And with me he was a gentleman, too. He must have been irritated that I looked so much like him. Baseball cap and everything. But I'd had my beard long before I tangled with Hemingway. Anyway, he could have raised hell about me but he didn't. I remember when someone showed him one of his novels I had autographed: 'All that glitters is not gold nor is every man with a white beard named . . . Ernest Hemingway.' He looked at it, laughed and told reporters, 'I don't care what the sonofabitch signs so long as it isn't my checks or my contracts.' He showed class.

Fulton: He seemed anxious to help me and other Americans. Asked me, 'What can I do to help?' I said, 'For instance, you can ask Ordóñez to let me serve in one of his fights as sobresaliente [understudy].' He said, 'You're an American and I'm an American. If I can help I will.' Two days later he told me Ordóñez had said, 'Sobresaliente is for boys who are down and out.' But Hemingway said, 'This is a good fighter,' so Ordóñez agreed, 'I'll set it up for Ciudad Real.' I waited and the Ciudad Real date came and went. Then I had a letter from Hemingway's secretary telling me that Hotchner, who had never faced a bull, had got the job as sobresaliente. That fight was important to me . . . could have been very important in my career. It was disgusting to learn that such a mockery had been made of bullfighting.

Quintana: In the last year Ernesto was the prisoner of the people around him. But he still behaved with gracia. The people of Pamplona loved him.

Vanderford: But Hemingway could be ungracious too. Back in 1929 a little old lady . . . A retired schoolteacher, I'd guess. She approached him and said, 'Mr. Hemingway, I saw my first bullfight this afternoon and frankly I didn't like it as well as I thought I would from reading your description.' He could easily have replied, 'Well, there's no accounting for tastes,' or something neutral like that. But he asked, 'How much did you pay for your ticket?' She said, 'Three hundred pesetas.' He pulled some bills from his pocket, thrust them at her and said, 'Here's your money.' She wouldn't accept it.

Quintana: On the other hand, people who were jealous of him were always trying to make scenes. They didn't know him, so they said he was a drunk and a fighter.

Vavra: I found that out when I tried to track down the truth about the famous incident with Matt Carney. In a bar I heard some guy saying, 'Matt Carney tried to drink a toast with Hemingway, but the old man grabbed the bota, threw it a mile and cursed Matt vilely.' This didn't sound like the Hemingway I knew, so I asked around to get the true story. Seems Hemingway was giving a party and Matt tried to barge in. He was drunk and abusive, but Hemingway treated him gently and said, 'I can't drink with you now.' It was Carney who used the foul language, not Hemingway. Matter of fact, Hemingway tried to ease him away so the cops wouldn't arrest him. That's how they slander Hemingway in Spanish bars.

Vanderford: Michener still hasn't said what he thinks about the Hotchner book.

Michener: In our family it caused a brouhaha. Mari, as the wife of a writer, sided with Mary Hemingway. She thought the book was an unwarranted and inaccurate invasion of privacy and she wanted the courts to forbid its publication, even though it was our own publisher, Random House, who was defending the right to publish. Mari told Bennett Cerf, 'I side with the enemy.' I felt the opposite. Hemingway was a public figure and relevant facts about him should not be held from the public. I take my attitude on such matters from the Supreme Court decision in the case where some jerk called Senator Joe Clark a Communist. Clark sued for libel, and the Court held that when Clark entered the race for the Senate he offered himself as a public figure, which made him fair game for anything anyone wanted to say against him, so long as it wasn't part of a malicious conspiracy.

Vanderford: How does this apply to Hemingway?

Michener: Hemingway went to great lengths to constitute himself a public figure and Hotchner had every right to comment about the operation.

Vanderford: Even about the suicide?

Michener: Especially the suicide. Hemingway's whole public life was dedicated to the creation of a legend. And a legend with certain implications. Therefore, the suicide must not be seen as the act of a casual individual but as the culmination of a carefully prepared legend. Now, either the final act was in conformity with legend or it wasn't.

Vanderford: What do you think?

Michener: I've told you I wanted it printed.

Vavra: But when it was printed? What then? Because of its errors it's a betrayal of friendship. On the part of a guy who, it seems to me, had never really understood or known Hemingway. If you're going to do something like that you have to do it right. Tell the whole story and be honest about it.

Michener: Maybe that's why I liked it. It was a legend about a legend. As I read it I said, 'Hotchner gives me a picture of Hemingway the brawler, the boaster, the race-track tout, the Cuban exile. But he doesn't give me one glimpse of the man who wrote the great books.'

Vavra: How can you say that's good?

Michener: Because I think the lives of writers are like that. I think that now and then the public should see the terrifying contradictions. I can't get out of my mind an interview that *Time* magazine carried with Hemingway. They played it up like the word of God, and one part especially they carried in a box . . . for effect . . . Hemingway saying that as long as man's juices were running he was in good shape . . . and boasted to the world that his were still running. Very sexy. Very tough. But at the end of the Hotchner book we are shown a pitiful man who confesses that his juices have stopped running . . . nothing in life . . . no sex . . . no fun . . . so he blows his brains out. I've got to compare him with men like Verdi and Michelangelo and Hokusai, who never talked tough but who did their best work when they were old, old men. To them there was something superior to the running of juices.

Quintana: You're wrong when you say he committed suicide. I don't believe that. Not long before he died I had a wire from Ketchum, Idaho. From Ernesto, saying he wanted the best seats at Pamplona. He planned to be with us, that I know. Of course, he'd been drinking too much and had been told to stop. But not suicide. That wasn't in his mind.

Fulton: On the day the news came over the wire I went out to see Juan Belmonte and told him, 'Don Ernesto just committed suicide,' and Belmonte said, very slowly and very clearly, 'Well done.' In Belmonte's autobiography there's a long passage about how Belmonte had wavered about committing suicide in 1915. Had an obsession about it, and Hemingway knew this. Anyway, a little while later Belmonte, the greatest of them all . . . Well, he shot himself the same way. Right through the head.

Quintana: And you, Michener, what did you think?

Michener: I think he acted properly. He had built himself into a legend and when it showed signs of blowing up in his face he ended it with distinction. An act in harmony with the legend. He proved he was as tough as he had claimed to be.

Vavra: Then you knew it was suicide?

Michener: How could it have been anything else? Remember that time Hemingway came through Madrid incognito? Insisted he wanted no publicity. Big beard. Baseball cap. Hunting jacket. Wherever he went those six or eight bodyguards clearing the way for him. It was the most conspicuous literary disguise since Leo Tolstoy used to go around in his muzhik's costume. And you could see he loved every phony minute of it. But such performances run the risk of blowing up. And when his threatened to do so, he had the gracia to end the legend with a splendid gesture. The best thing about the suicide was that it was artistically right. And I'm damned sure he realized it.

I left the dinner party and wandered back to the square, where by purest chance someone said, 'That's Matt Carney over there. You want to get the straight dope about his fight with Hemingway?'

It was in this way that I met the legendary Carney, a forty-year-old California Irishman who, his friends are convinced, will become a first-rate novelist. Many years ago he came to Europe to finish a book but as he was knocking about Paris he was spotted by an agent whose job it was to find male models for advertising. Carney had the rugged New World look of a Mississippi gambler, and French advertisers flocked to him in such numbers that he earned a great deal of money. He was conned into posing for high-fashion ads and soon found himself the pin-up boy of Paris. For the past seven years he had been working on a novel, *Run Out of Time*, but had been somewhat sidetracked by the purchase of a bar in Torremolinos. He loved Spain and spoke like a drunken angel, with fiery Irish eloquence, and as he approached my table I saw that his handsome features were marked by a colossal black eye, which made him doubly Irish and doubly handsome.

'Who hung the mouse on you?' I asked.

'A Basque woodchopper with a right hand of phenomenal speed. But as I went down I had the presence of mind to kick him in the balls and when he doubled up I knocked out one of his front teeth. So now he's a Basque woodchopper with a phenomenal right and one missing tooth.'

A habitué of the bar ran up with a set of photographs from that morning's running of the bulls, and the photographers had caught Matt in regulation Pamplona costume of white shirt, white pants, red scarf and sash and rope-soled shoes, running about six inches in front of the horns of a massive bull. Later pictures in the sequence showed him flat on his face, with bulls, oxen and people running over him. A final shot showed him up and grinning, with his fantastic black eye.

'A very fine run,' he said as he studied the photographs, but in his opinion it did not equal the one which some photographer had caught four

years ago in color film. Matt had a copy of the postcard which was now sold in Pamplona souvenir shops. It showed him sprinting for life ahead of a bewildered bull whose left horn was about to toss him far and wide.

'He gave me a neat six-inch scratch which wasn't particularly dangerous, but could have been.' I suggested that judging from the photographs, he must carry quite a few horn wounds on his hungry-looking body. 'Nope. I've been lucky. But I do have this one to muzzle those clowns in Paris who sit around cafés explaining how to run the bulls at Pamplona.'

'How many years you been coming here?'

'This is my fourteenth. The running this morning was fine. Not great. Bulls couldn't catch up with the runners. But it would have to be graded fine.'

'Would you tell me what happened with Hemingway?'

'Will you treat it with respect?'

'In your words.'

He ordered a beer, sat back, fingered the edge of his eye and said, 'I revere Hemingway. And years ago I revered him even more. So this evening at San Fermín, I was sitting here, where you are, and he was over there, where Orson Welles is sitting now. He was with the elite of the feria, everyone important, and I looked like a real bum. Drunker than I am now. He had done some of the good writing of our generation. I'd done nothing more permanent than a popcorn fart in a typhoon. So I grabbed my bota, staggered over to his table and shouted, "Hemingway, you old bastard, have a drink with me." Mary Hemingway said, "Please don't. He's drunk." So I shouted, "Drunk or sober, Hemingway, have a drink with me," so he grabbed the bota, wound up and threw it as far as he could. It landed on a truck in the street, and I announced in a loud clear voice, "Mr. Ernest Hemingway, fuck you!" At this he brushed Mary away, leaped to his feet and began cursing me. He lunged at me and I was going to break him in half, fat old man that he was, but two Swedes dragged me away, and that night when I got back to my room I wrote a letter to him and said, "Mr. Hemingway, I revere you as one of the fine writers of my generation and I am overcome with remorse that I should have behaved in such a way. Please forgive me." I gave the letter to Peter Buckley, who did that great book on bulls in Spain, and he delivered it to Hemingway, but Big Dave, who was there at the time, told me that Hemingway took one look at the letter, sneered and tore it up. He was real big talking about brawls and that, but when he had one in his lap he didn't know what to do nor how to end it. To me Ernest Hemingway is a crock of shit.'

The one good eye that I could see was steely blue and the craggy face was resolute. The sandy hair, with a few streaks of gray, was tousled and the faded red scarf was pinned at the neck with the diagonal shields of San Fermín. At the edge of his shirt a jagged horn scar showed across his chest.

'The scar? How'd you get it?'

Matt Carney.

'I have this crazy thing. All year long, when I'm working in Paris, I keep thinking of Pamplona. San Fermín. To run, to touch, to feel the horn tips edging closer.'

'Is it something mystical?' I asked.

Matt looked at me as if I were out of my mind. 'Christ, you miss the whole flaming point. It's fun! It's joy!' He showed me a photograph from the morning paper and I suppose that in years to come this shot will often be seen in books, for there was Matt galloping a few inches ahead of the steers and bulls, alone and laughing his Irish head off. It was as lovely a portrait of man's inherent nonsense as I had ever seen. 'I run the bulls for joy, which is the chief ingredient in generosity. In this way I prove that I have the capacity to give myself whole hog to some activity.'

'Do you run to prove your bravery?' I asked, for in recent years the most courageous acts at Pamplona had been Matt's.

'To stand in the street before the run begins . . . to visualize the bulls coming at you . . . to sense what might happen . . . yes, that takes courage. But when those rockets go off and the black shapes come tumbling at you . . . Hell, you've already made your commitment and all it takes now is a sense of joy . . . to be part of the stampede.'

'Yet you think that Hemingway was a crock of crap?'

'I must. He glorified this sort of thing, but when it came to him, face to face with a bota of red wine, he didn't know how to handle it. No gracia. No understanding. A good writer. Not the greatest man. But a good writer.'

In this book I have tried to keep the focus on Spain and Spaniards rather than upon the experiences and opinions of foreign visitors. I have filed away those diverting accounts of what happened to a German in Córdoba or to an Englishman in Badajoz, but in this material on Pamplona during San Fermín, I must speak of foreigners, because the city is crammed with them and it is what happens to them that makes the festival intriguing. If three beautiful Swedish girls of nineteen can find no place to sleep but in the street, one cannot ignore them, nor can he close his eyes to a sports car filled with six handsome juniors from the University of California, three girls, three boys, who sleep sitting in their car near a main intersection.

I am not, however, going to deal with the young punks who have come here for a sexual holiday; what with the shortage of beds in Pamplona they could do better elsewhere. Nor am I concerned about the various groups who look at one running of the bulls, attend one bullfight and spend the rest of their time at LSD and marijuana parties. What I am involved with are those lineal descendants of Ernest Hemingway and his fictional characters who four decades ago discovered the high hilarity of San Fermín, which through the years has not diminished.

To understand the magic of Pamplona one must follow the passage of

Once a year, and once only, the citizens of Pamplona are not limited in the amount they drink or where they drink it or where they sleep it off.

a typical day. The feria, which regularly starts on July 7, San Fermín Day, is billed throughout Spain as the festival of the bulls, signifying that for once in the mean and ugly world of bullfighting the animal himself, known as the only element in the fight that has not been corrupted, is meant to be king. And in a sense he is.

Shortly before midnight, in the darkened streets of the lower part of town where barricades have been erected to form a runway, the bulls for the next day's fight are turned loose from the reception pens known as the Corrales de Gas, run across the river on a narrow bridge, then up the steep hill to the temporary corral at the bottom of the Calle Santo Domingo, where they will spend the rest of the night. It is an eerie thing to see the hurrying bulls loom through the darkness and rush past on almost silent hoofs. They are frightened by the dash across the bridge and uncertain about the rush up the hill, so they run with concentrated purpose, like ghosts who have little time for their night journey. A rush, the rattle of hoofs on paving stones, an echo of panting, the clean, lingering smell of animals on the night air and they are gone, mysteriously and with a sense of great drama.

From midnight, with the bulls now safely in their corral, until six o'clock in the morning, when the bands begin to play in all parts of town, Pamplona is a dream city. At the Bar Txoco on the square, customers from Scandinavia and Germany, delighted to be again where there is warmth, sit all night at small tables drinking beer. At the next bar my degenerate waiter whispers, 'Shift over to this table, and I can serve you.' With every order the Swedes give him, he pours one for himself, and for the whole eight days he will be drunk. In cars parked throughout the city, boys from Harvard and girls from Wellesley sleep on back seats, wrapped in blankets. Bank lobbies have been thrown open by the police, and college students from Oxford and the Sorbonne sleep on the marble, boy-girl, boy-girl, boy-girl, right up to the teller's cage. Others, not lucky enough to get into the banks, sleep on the sidewalks; and in the public square by the bandstand, hundreds lie on benches or on the grass. The town is a vast open-air dormitory, and each sleeper has about his throat the red scarf of San Fermín and in his hand a bota of red wine.

At a quarter to six bands playing the music of Navarra start circulating through all parts of the city, wakening both those who slept in beds and those who did not. If the sleeper is fortunate he is awakened not by a brass band but by one of the three-man groups consisting of two playing antique oboes and one beating a drum, for if there is sweeter music on earth I have not heard it. The sound that comes from these old oboes is like the whispering of a thousand birds at dawn; it is the fairy music that elves dance to; it is the Middle Ages captured in haunting notes; and long after all else in Pamplona has been forgotten, these delicious sounds will echo in the memories of men and women in small towns in Norway and Peru, those who were wakened at Pamplona by the oboes. I once had a record of them on their morning rounds, and at a house party in southern Spain I would occasionally play it on the gramophone, and those in the audience who had not known the music at San Fermín would ask, 'What's that wailing?' But those who had wakened to it during the feria would have tears in their eyes.

By six o'clock the streets of Pamplona are jammed with twenty or thirty thousand people, from boys of five to old couples of eighty, for to lie late abed during San Fermín would be insanity. Some fourteen thousand of these early risers are heading toward the bullring, and now one begins to understand why Pamplona is such an ideal spot for an all-out feria like this. The bullring is practically in the center of town, a couple of short blocks from the central square, so that life moves alternately from the ring to the square.

At the bullring, people pay sixty cents for entrance to what will become a major part of the feria. The real fun won't start till seven, but shortly after six a band, led by a zany conductor with a magisterial sense of comedy, entertains the crowd with songs of Navarra and nonsense of a high order. It's a bright, lovely part of the day and time passes swiftly.

Meanwhile, along a course nine hundred yards long and leading through the very heart of the city, temporary barricades have been erected in such manner that later on they can be dismantled in about ten minutes and stored along the sidewalk for use next morning. When in place, and it takes a goodly number of men to gear them properly, these barricades form a continuous runway from the Santo Domingo corrals, up to the colorful town hall, along Doña Blanca de Navarra (formerly known as Mercaderes), then up the historic Estafeta, an extremely narrow street, through an open square and into the tightly barricaded chute that will throw the stampeding animals into the bullring itself.

At half past six this narrow course has attracted young men from all parts of Europe, and some not so young. Matt Carney is running for the eighty-fourth morning. Tigre's tall son is running for his fourth; already he's been on the tips of the bulls' horns, but without incident. John Fulton and several Spanish matadors will run for the fun of it, and because they inherently love the bulls and enjoy being with them in any circumstances. Even Kenneth Vanderford, in his Hemingway cap, will be running, and he will by no means be the oldest participant, for yesterday a man of seventy-five was pegged by the bulls and is now in the hospital. It is a madness, this running with the bulls, and it never leaves a man's blood.

Promptly at seven a powerful rocket flies into the air and explodes aloft to signify that the gates to the corral have been opened. As soon as all the startled animals have dashed into the street, a second rocket explodes to warn everyone that they are on their way, six bulls and six large oxen pounding ahead at a full gallop up Santo Domingo, past the military hospital and into the square before the town hall. They run extremely fast, and as they go men run ahead of them, seeming to fly along the narrow streets. But since the bulls can run much faster than the men, the animals catch up with the speeding humans and sometimes knock them down or one man trips over another and there is a pile-up. When you first see a batch of runners stumble and fall into a heap, with enraged bulls bearing down upon them, you think, My God! They'll be killed.

But the forward motion of the bulls is such that they prefer to surge onward with the oxen rather than lag behind to fight with fallen men. I have seen incredible accumulations in which several dozen men have formed a mad pile in front of the flying animals, but the latter have plunged ahead, fighting to get over the human barricade, and whereas they have bruised some with their heavy hoofs they have not bothered any with their horns. If a man falls and can roll into the gutter and lie motionless, there's a good chance he will escape.

It is when a bull becomes detached from the herd and finds himself alone that he panics. Then he starts slashing out with his horns and darting with savage speed at whatever confuses him. It is then that young men, no matter how adept at dodging, go to the hospital. Over the years, of a hundred men wounded by horns at Pamplona, fully ninety-five have been

In the last century only butchers and those
who worked with cattle ran in the streets
before the bulls. Today any adventurer
from Vienna or Pasadena
is entitled to do so.

In ancient Greece and Rome and especially on the
island of Crete valor was proved by a man's
willingness to touch his fingers to the horns
of a wild bull. In Pamplona today the same ritual
persists unconsciously. Honor and virility are
believed to be bestowed by proximity to the bull.

wounded by solitary bulls who have been isolated as they rush toward the arena. But even if a man does get trapped by a lone bull, and even if the horns are two inches from his gut, there's always the likelihood that some other runner will attract the bull's attention at the last fragment of a second, and the horn will miss. When this happens people say, 'San Fermín came down to make the save.' San Fermín protects a lot of lives.

It takes the animals about two minutes to gallop the nine hundred yards, and now they thunder into the bullring, where some thousand runners have preceded them, and again the animals stay bunched and drive like lemmings for the exit that will take them to the corrals behind the stands. But again, if one bull gets detached he will drive and hook at anything that comes his way until he is lured by capes into the exit. One morning I had proof of this. Because I could not run with the bulls, the city authorities had granted me a pass permitting me to perch atop the barricade at the chute, and after the bulls were well past and safely in their pens I walked fat and happy into the arena in what I judged was complete safety, only to find that a huge red bull had become detached from the oxen and was running in a great circle about the arena on a course which brought him almost face to face with me as I stepped into the sunlight. I practically fainted with astonishment, to see that huge, horned face looming so close to mine, but he was intent on finding his mates and San Fermín led him on.

Rules for running with bulls are not haphazard. A local ordinance governs, and copies are widely distributed. The crucial rule, and one that could not be known intuitively, is that no runner may in any way attract the attention of the bulls by waving his arms or anything else. To do so might attract the bull not to himself but to someone farther on who is unaware of what is being done and is therefore unprotected. Also, once the bulls have caught up with a runner and passed him, he may not run at their heels, lest they sense him there and turn back into the crowd. Women may not run, nor drunks, nor men with unusual costumes that might attract the bulls in their direction. The governing concept is that once the bulls are started on their course, clearly marked by fences, they will keep going unless someone radically diverts their attention and lures them into masses of unsuspecting people. I have seen six bulls run right over a pile of twenty or thirty fallen bodies, so intent were they in plunging ahead. Had anyone at that moment sidetracked their herding instinct, someone would surely have been hurt.

When all the bulls are safely inside the bullring corrals a final rocket is fired to announce that all is well. If it goes off in less than three minutes, listeners know that the bulls made a good run without any having been detached from the herd, but if the final rocket is much delayed, apprehension grows. A bull may have become separated and young men from Norway and Holland may be pinned against the improvised barriers at the town hall or against some shop door in Estafeta.

Now that the bulls are out of the ring and it remains filled with young men in white trousers and red sashes, a different gate is thrown open and into the crowd catapults a heifer, the tips of her horns covered with leather. Year for year and pound for pound, the female of the fighting strain is as brave and rough as the male, a fact which she proceeds to demonstrate by slashing into the men and knocking them over as if they were tenpins. The audience roars its approval as the heifer sweeps the arena. She is like a charge of compressed dynamite, for her energy seems tireless and her aim unerring. She runs like this for eight or ten minutes, dispensing contusions as if they were kisses, but there is one group of men who bewilder her, and these she damages but does not disperse.

Among college students it is considered gallant to take up a position directly in front of the gate from which the vigorous heifer emerges into the arena. There they form a pile of some sixty or seventy students, several bodies high, and in this uncomfortable formation they wait the charge of the animal. I've seen heifers hit this pile of humanity like thunderbolts, bore into it with horns slashing and feet pumping, only to be defeated by the sheer bulk of the bodies. The students protect their heads, but their backs and bottoms sometimes take serious punishment. Yet there they are, piled up and waiting as each heifer emerges. They are the stars of the morning.

Each day some five or six heifers are thrown into the arena, occasionally two at the same time, and the havoc is hilarious. The band plays, people cheer, students limp off to the hospital, teeth are loosened, but the only real brawl I ever saw came when a bulldogger from Texas started to wrestle a heifer to the ground. Everyone in the arena who could lay a hand on the Texan beat the bejeezus out of him, knocking him flat and bruising him rather badly. It is forbidden to grab the heifer in any way or to strike her with anything but a rolled-up newspaper; she has all the privileges and that way the fun is better.

It is now eight o'clock, when the all-nighters drift off for a few hours' sleep. Others wander back to the central square, where the waiter whispers, 'Pssst, move over here!' Hot coffee and croissants are the order, and in many languages people discuss the events of the morning. At eleven, enterprising photographers appear with their postcards recording that day's excitement, and one shows Matt Carney, wild grin on his face, going down before a stray bull, while Tigre's son and John Fulton can be seen artfully dodging the pack as it sweeps by. A lot of astonished people in America and Scandinavia are going to receive these cards in a few days, showing their neighbors in extraordinary predicaments.

At high noon Don Luis Morondo will lead his a cappella group in a concert of sixteenth-century motets and at three a company of comedians from Madrid will perform in *La tía de Carlos* (*Charley's Aunt*), which is as funny in Spanish as it was in the Brandon Thomas original.

At four-thirty parades start to form in various parts of the city, the

best one originating at the town hall, where the morning's barriers have been expertly removed and stacked. A brass band of about a dozen pieces, all playing fortissimo, lines up behind the members of a drinking club whose banners, brightly painted in comic-strip style, proclaim their faith in Navarra, good wine and predilected bullfighters. Huge leather botas of wine appear on many shoulders, plus bottles of beer and gin. At five a group of picadors on their way to the bullring appear on horseback and the parade sets forth, a noisy, raucous wonderful gang of men who won't be sober for six days. They march through the streets at a leisurely pace, shouting the songs of San Fermín and alerting the populace to the fact that the bullfight is about to begin.

In 1966 the theme song was the first two lines of Verdi's splendid aria from *Rigoletto*, in which Gilda realizes that she is in love with the duke who masquerades as a student:

510

*Six Spanish women at a table
in the plaza during San Fermín.*

Caro nome che il mio cor,
Festi primo palpitar . . .

For eight days I was to hear this melody chanted twenty-four hours a day, never more than the two first lines, never less. It became the haunting leitmotiv of the feria, the half-mad cry of happiness. I am sure the incessant repetition has permanently ruined *Rigoletto* for me and that if I were tomorrow in an opera house where Joan Sutherland started 'Caro nome che il mio cor,' I would rise and bellow, 'Viva San Fermín.' I am sure that whenever I hear this theme again I shall smell Pamplona and taste the flow of red wine from the botas. Never has a musical theme so swamped a city.

Now from everywhere appear pairs of men lugging plastic buckets, and even tubs, loaded with bottles. They converge on the Calle Estafeta, where an ice company is ready to fill their buckets with ice, so that the beer will remain cold during the fight. If Pamplona provides an excess of music, it also provides an abundance of beer and wine, and there is no bullring in Spain where so much is consumed during the fights. The result is that the public, especially the part occupying the cheaper seats in the sun, is always ready to protest violently the less fortunate performances in the ring, even to showering seat cushions and chunks of bread on the hapless bullfighters. This tense atmosphere means that the actual bull-fights at San Fermín are apt to be mediocre, and some of the best matadors prefer not to show themselves in this rowdy city. Others, because of the hostile *ambiente*, quickly lose whatever enthusiasm they may have brought to the fight. Many people blame the mediocrity of the fights on the early-morning running of the bulls, believing that the pounding of their hoofs on the hard stone paving blocks weakens their legs and that the presence of thousands of runners frays their nerves. Since Pamplona's is the only major fair in which the bulls are run through the streets, it is easy but perhaps not accurate to blame any deficiency in the condition of the bulls on this circumstance.

Take the fifth day of the feria in 1966, when everything went wrong. On July 11 three matadors of excellent reputation, Ordóñez, Murillo and Fuentes, were to face bulls from one of the better ranches, that of Don Alvaro Domecq. As the drinking clubs marched into their sunny-side seats, accompanied by their bands, they were excited, because this promised to be a great afternoon. It is difficult for one who has not been to Pamplona to imagine what that half-hour prior to the fight was like, because in the tightly packed stands seven different full-sized bands blared away, each attending to its own tunes, and the noise passed comprehension. From it there was no retreat, only surrender to the deafening salvos of raw sound.

Well, when the first bull appeared he looked wonderful, and since he was to be fought by Ordóñez, a recognized master, it looked as if the promise of the day might be fulfilled. The bands exploded with joy, but before Ordóñez had made even one pass, a peon had the misfortune of luring the bull against a post in such a way that it suffered a concussion and had to be destroyed in the arena. The crowd broke out in an angry demonstration, partly against Ordóñez and his unlucky peon, partly because this was the fourth such accident of the fair, and partly because it was not yet apparent whether the judge would allow a substitute bull. The substitute was granted, Ordóñez made a few passes, the bull fell down because of weak knees, and Ordóñez dispatched it with unseemly haste and with a sneaky, low-blow sword thrust, whereupon the crowd's protests were renewed.

The second animal proved difficult and Murillo could do little with it, so he killed it quickly to a chorus of protests. The third bull looked pretty good, but once more, as a peon was putting it through its first passes, it grazed a horn against the wall and snapped it off at the base. According to bullfight regulations, bulls injured after they are fairly in the arena are not to be replaced, but the judges frequently do allow such substitution, in part to avoid the public's wrath. A tremendous protest now broke out, which was increased when the judge, having ignored the regulations in the case of the first bull and having allowed a substitute, now decided to enforce them; he refused to grant a substitute. When a matador fights a bull that has lost one horn, honor requires that he never pass it on the side of the broken horn, but this afternoon the public was unwilling for Fuentes to pass this one on either side and insisted that he kill it forthwith, which he did.

As for the fourth bull, it remains in my memory as the worst-fought animal I have ever seen, for it was a fine-looking bull and brave with the horses. But Ordóñez, sick of the afternoon and the Pamplona mob, gave a few trial passes, noted that the bull had a slight tendency to hook to the right, and said the hell with it; and the audience had to sit in the stands and watch this fine bull wasted. To show his contempt for the crowd, Ordóñez deliberately killed in the most disgraceful manner, with a running, sideways swipe of the sword, a punctured lung, the breathing-out of the bull's blood through its nostrils. The protests began as soon as his intentions became apparent and finally became so clamorous that I feared a riot must ensue. It was a shame-filled conclusion to a shameful performance.

On the fifth bull it was clear that Murillo, a man noted for his pundonor, hoped for a triumph. He did a competent faena, during which the band played, but on the whole it was a lackluster performance that didn't get through to the public, with the result that he killed the bull perfunctorily, to a moderate chorus of protests. And this was a real pity, because some of us in the stands knew that Murillo, from the neighboring region of Aragón, had always been looked upon with a certain favor by the natives of Pamplona, and this was his farewell performance in the city, since he was to retire at the close of the season.

The sixth bull came weak to the fight, and poor Fuentes, a young matador who could not afford the luxury of a shameless performance like that of Ordóñez, tried his level best to make up for the disappointment of not having been able to fight his one-horned bull. And he did accomplish a few good passes, because the band played for his faena. But he tried so hard and so long that, running into unexpected difficulty on the kill, he heard the humiliating trumpets sound a warning. And so ended a representative, but nevertheless interesting, Pamplona bullfight.

Fights in this city have a unique feature, the singing of the audience.

'Navarra, Navarra, número uno!
Como Navarra no hay ninguno.'

(Navarra, number one. Like Navarra there is no other.) When a matador is doing poorly, through lack of pundonor, one row of chanting people starts swaying to the left, the ones above and below to the right, so that the whole plaza seems to be in motion, and if you look at the alternately

swaying figures you become dizzy, and all the while the swaying figures are bellowing a song whose shouted refrain consists of the phrase 'Todos queremos más.' (We all want something more.) At the fight when Antonio Ordóñez refused to try, the stands bellowed:

'Ordóñez, Ordóñez, sinvergüenza!
Ordóñez, Ordóñez, paga la prensa.'

(Ordóñez, shameless one. Ordóñez, pays the newspapers.)

The drabness of the Pamplona fights was underscored by the arrival that afternoon of Brewster Cross, an American architect, who during his years of work in Spain had learned to take such fine color photographs of bullfighting that they appeared on the covers of bullfight journals. For the past six years he had been seeing an average of ninety fights a year and during that time had turned down numerous promotions to work in other countries because, as he said, 'I've discovered an ambiente I love and I'd be nuts to lose it so long as I can make a living here.' He was delayed in coming to Pamplona, he told us, by a bullfight in Madrid. 'I've been waiting through more than two hundred fights to see that one special thing. That afternoon which the Spaniards describe as culminating. Each time you enter the gates you say, "I hope this is going to be it." But always you're disappointed. The other day, however, Curro Romero was on the program, and although I'd never seen him in top form, I knew he had the capability. If the right bull came along. On his first bull, nothing. But on his last animal, the greatest single performance in the world of art I've ever seen, and I've seen people like Horowitz and Menuhin. It was the most evocative, the most elegant, the most artistic. When he finished with that noble animal, my palms were wet with tension and Aristotelian catharsis.'

The fights had been bad that afternoon, but there are compensations. After the last bull the mob wandered slowly over to the square to drink beer and consume vast plates of expensive breaded shrimp. A gang of college kids from California, on marijuana and LSD, sprawled at a table served by the debauched waiter, who looked no worse than they, and Orson Welles, very handsome with slightly grayed hair, conducted an interview with Kenneth Tynan for the benefit of television cameras. Matt Carney surveyed the scene with bleary eyes and condemned it all as bad, while a group of Scandinavians, who had skimped to buy their tickets for the disastrous fight, sat glumly in a land from which the sun had vanished.

But by ten-thirty all had changed. From the public square a rocket ripped into the night air and exploded with a huge bang to initiate a half-hour of fireworks which festooned the sky with fiery banners. This night they were under the supervision of Pirotecnica Vicente Caballer of Valencia, the Vatican of fireworks, so they were bound to be good. There

olonel Tom Nickalls, father of Oliver
nd one of England's top experts on horses,
the bullring in Pamplona.

were colored rockets and noisy ones and flowered ones, and at the end two powerful shots which signified that the display was over.

Now it was midnight again, and from the Corrales de Gas six more dark shapes emerged to run quietly across the bridge and up the hill to the temporary corrals, from which they would erupt next morning at seven to chase brave young men through the streets.

If I have not spoken in this account of orderly sleeping and eating it is because one does not worry much about such matters during San Fermín. The most gracious thing you can do for someone you meet in the plaza is to say, 'I have a bath at my place. You look as if you need one. Come along.' The invitee has been sleeping in a bank lobby for six nights and needs a wash. As for food, it is available if you can elbow your way to the counter.

The true heroes of San Fermín are not those who run with the bulls, nor the amateurs who dodge with the heifers, nor even the matadors who do the fighting, but the police of the city. With an unruly mob of many thousands on their hands, and most of them young people of high spirit from foreign lands, the quiet police steel themselves to show courtesy, tact, humor and a benevolent indulgence. To do so is not easy, for a young man who has just run before six Miura bulls is not apt to be frightened by a policeman, but at five o'clock one morning as I sat in the square I witnessed the following incidents, none of which unnerved the two stolid policemen who were keeping order. A sports car flying the flag of the American Confederacy roared past with two buglers playing their mangled version of the rebel yell. Three Swedish girls, who had slept in the streets, were playfully molested from four sides, to their delight. An impromptu band of six instruments played three different pieces of music, accompanied by revelers dancing in the streets and over the tables. An Englishman insulted two Spaniards, who quickly took care of him, but his place was taken by a Chinese student who came out flailing karate chops and elbow jabs; him the two policemen watched admiringly. Two drunken newspaper vendors sat in the middle of the street assuring each other in brotherhood, 'I'll sell your papers and you sell mine.' A French car banged through the square sideswiping two parked cars at different corners, then steamed off at top speed.

The imperturbable police did nothing, but what I didn't know until later was that at two that morning, when things had quietened down a bit, these same policemen had walked slowly through the sidewalk bars and had arbitrarily arrested the six or seven worst-looking hell-raisers, and these we would not see again for some days.

During San Fermín the government distributes thousands of copies of a pamphlet in Spanish, French and English warning against unacceptable behavior: 'Any act uncivil or offensive to common decency, such as a lack of respect to women, will be severely punished. All behavior that offends the moral sensibility of the people will be absolutely repressed.' This high-sounding dictum is enforced in a curious way. A French girl in our group nearly fainted when a Spanish man ran his hand so far inside her dress that he reached her navel. The police smiled. An English girl was astounded when another Spaniard slipped his hand deep inside her sweater. The police laughed. But at the bullring, when a deluge interrupted the fight one day, a Swedish boy happened to take off his shirt to wring it out, and the same policeman grabbed him, roughed him up and hauled him off to jail on grounds that his behavior had 'offended the moral sensibility of the public.'

I wander back to my hotel to read briefly in Pedrell's collection of old songs and to think how inappropriate to Pamplona is the famous one attributed to Juan del Encina (1469–1529). It is a mournful chant dating from around 1505 and probably referring to some royal death, perhaps that of Felipe I in 1506. In recent years certain pessimists have proposed it as an appropriate lament for the passing of Spain's age of greatness:

> Sad and hapless Spain,
> all should weep for thee,
> bereft of joy
> now and forevermore.

I have never felt that Spain deserved such a lament; her Golden Age vanished, to be sure, but there are many signs that she is capable of creating another, on altered terms. There is an enormous natural vitality in this country which, properly channeled, could produce a new age of literature, art, philosophy and even government.

Certainly the national sadness referred to in the chant is nowhere evident during San Fermín, so I turn to another of Pedrell's recoveries, a song which probably could not be sung publicly in Spain today. It is numbered 79 and the words were written about 1555 by some unknown poet and set to music by an irreverent troubadour named Juan Navarro (fl. 1540–1565) of Sevilla. Pedrell entitled it 'The Nun's Song' and in it are reflected the anti-religious feelings which are always cropping up in Spain at unexpected places:

> Alas for hapless me!
> What a hard life within these walls!
> What a close jail these bars make,
> Annoying, gloomy prison!
> Cruel convent, vexatious, avaricious, scornful:
> Would that I might see you burning in bright flame.
>
> Oh, what a harsh rule,
> Dismal and irksome choir!
> Why should one have beauty and grace
> If they cannot be seen or enjoyed?
> Life without hope!
> What a great injustice, what fate so hard,
> that only death should free us!

517

San Fermín provides a constant kaleidoscope of visual imagery. The parades vary; papier-mâché giants fifteen feet tall wander through the streets; sometimes additional bullfights are offered at eleven in the morning; and on Thursday morning the bullring is occupied by a weird exhibition of Basque sports featuring two events that defy reason. In the first, four huge men in rope sandals, white trousers and T-shirts march forth, each bearing two long-handled axes whose heads are protected by leather sheaths. The men divide into teams of two each and stand at attention before the wood they must chop: two rows of logs laid out on the ground, each row consisting of eight logs about eighteen inches in diameter.

Referee and timers appear and the contestants untie the leather sheaths; then you see how carefully the cutting edges have been honed. A whistle blows, and the lesser man on each team leaps onto the first log of his row and begins cutting a wide V into it, sending the chips flying as he swings the ax with fierce energy against the wood. When he has the V well defined and about half cut, he leaps down and his more skilled partner takes over, swinging with even greater force, and he completes the V halfway through the log, which is rather difficult, for as the cut grows deeper, wood grips the ax and lets go only when the man gives a powerful upward jerk.

At this point the first man takes over and starts the V on the opposite side, and when it is half cut, the second man jumps onto the log and hammers home a series of tremendous cuts until the log falls in two. Now the first man starts on the next log, and for some twenty minutes the two men alternate in chopping their way through the eight big logs, and remember that since they are standing on the log, to chop it they must bend forward so that the ax strikes below their feet, putting a severe strain on the stomach.

I was relieved when the leading team finally chopped its eighth log in two, for my stomach was hurting in sympathy, but to my surprise the two men ran from the row they had been chopping and across to those which their opponents had been cutting. It became apparent that both teams would chop through all sixteen logs with a combined thickness of at least twenty-four feet. Without pausing in the broiling sun, the superbly muscled men continued this extraordinary feat for some forty minutes and finished less than a minute apart. I could understand how the Basque in the bar had given Matt Carney the black eye.

What followed was for me even more memorable. Two Basque shepherds brought into the arena rams from the Pyrenees and allowed them to smell one another, whereupon the animals, each aware that a rival had come into its terrain, quietly withdrew to a distance of about twenty feet, dug their feet in and leaped forward, butting heads in the middle of the ring with shattering force. I expected them to have broken necks, but

This Basque woodchopp
has just won the national championship at San Ferm
He is as great a local hero as any matad

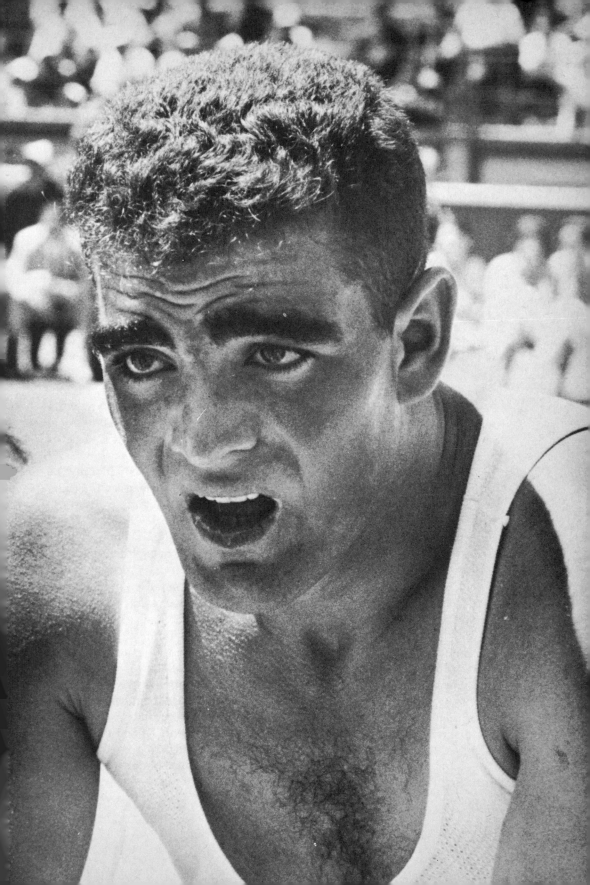

instead each blinked his eyes, shook himself and went back to his starting position, from which he leaped forward again, striking his opponent with unbelievable force, forehead to forehead. You could hear the impact a hundred yards away.

This continued, methodically but with deadly intent, for some twenty or thirty butts until you would think the horns must drop off. Occasionally one would feint cleverly and the other would fly over his head, to receive a sharp butt from below as he went past, but usually the two beasts met head-on, and the blows became sharper as the fight continued. What surprised me was that when at the start of a round the two rams considered themselves too close for maximum effect, they would back off so that the blows would be more shattering.

Finally the judge declared the contest a draw, and I asked a Basque sitting next to me what would have happened otherwise, and he said, 'They'd go right on till sundown. Or till one of them is killed.'

In view of the richness provided by San Fermín it seems captious to say that I arranged three excursions into the countryside, but there were places as important to me as Pamplona, so one morning, after no sleep, Vavra and Fulton and I set out for the little Basque town of Azpeitia, where I wished to pay my respects to a Basque who had played a significant role in history, Don Iñigo López de Recalde. The journey to Azpeitia was a delightful jaunt through the countryside of Navarra and Guipúzcoa. North of Irurzun we slipped through the Pass of the Two Sisters, a defile that reminded me much of the Iron Gates on the Danube but even more of the Cilician Gates in southern Turkey. From its northern exit it threw us into a fine hill country with alternate views across deep valleys and shrouds of fog which slowed us down to less than a walk. Finally, descending from a high plateau, we came upon Azpeitia, and it was exactly as I had imagined: a trivial place of no consequence, with an ordinary village church that one would not remember long and townspeople who greeted any stranger in French, for they stood close to the French border.

I got out of the car and started to walk to the small church, when a blacksmith at his forge, now converted into a garage, said, 'It's not here that you pay your respects but up the road a little farther.' I had expected little in the town to remind me of Don Iñigo and I found little, so I was willing to proceed in the direction the blacksmith had indicated, and after driving for a mile or two I received one of my major shocks in Spain.

For we came not to some small church memorializing a great man, but to a vast establishment centering upon a huge eighteenth-century basilica built of the finest marble. This was the memorial to Don Iñigo, better known as St. Ignatius of Loyola, the man who founded the Society of Jesus. His army was given Papal approval by Paul III on September 27, 1540, and the powerful work of the order stems from that date.

Before the basilica we found more than a hundred autobuses from all parts of Europe, for unexpectedly we had stumbled into a jubilee celebration of the order, and when we entered the basilica we found prostrate on the floor twenty-five young Jesuits about to be ordained as priests. Faces to the stone, dressed in white and gold, the candidates lay with their arms and heads covered by squares of gold cloth while a cardinal intoned a lengthy prayer over them while standing before a magnificent altar set among entwined Solomonic columns of gray-brown stone heavily ornamented in black and white and highly polished. Above the prostrate figures rose a statue of Ignatius Loyola, the young roustabout from Azpeitia who in 1521 at the age of thirty, while fighting for the king at Pamplona, had been severely wounded in the leg. During his convalescence, in a house that now stands encased as a shrine within the heart of the basilica, the young hellion had undergone conversion, and his years of travel and study had ensued, including a stay at Salamanca and a perilous brush with the Inquisition, which almost nipped his career at the start. He had persevered in his new-found devotion and had inspired others, Italians and Germans mostly, to an equal commitment, and with them had founded the order which was to shore up the Church at a time when it was beset by enemies from within and without. If Martin Luther was the scourge of the Catholic Church, then St. Ignatius was the scourge of Lutherans, and it was his movement in defense of Catholicism that helped establish a balance in Europe. He is my favorite Spanish saint, for I find Santo Domingo, founder of the Dominican order, too bloodthirsty for my liking—I cannot forget his persecution of the Albigenses—and Santa Teresa too nebulous. But Ignatius, the stubborn, worldly Basque who came to God late and then with such fury—him I can understand and him I regard with personal identification.

The history of the Jesuit Order in Spain has rarely been peaceful, but the lead in repressing the movement has usually come from neighboring countries. In 1759 Portugal decided that it must expel the Jesuits from both the mother country and the colonies. In 1764 France reached the same conclusion. So in 1767 King Carlos III of Spain announced the expulsion of the Jesuits from Spain and the New World alike, but later they crept back. In 1835, with the inauguration of reforms in government, they were expelled again, but again they returned; and in 1932, with the launching of the republic, they were ousted once more, but with Generalísimo Franco they reappeared. The loss involved in these expulsions was Spain's, for even though the Jesuits might be difficult to manage, it was they who were mainly responsible for what education Spain offered, and they were usually expelled at the precise time when the nation needed the international insights which they offered.

Now, as the twenty-five young Jesuits lie prostrate, the order seems secure in Spain, and as the priest prays he uses appropriately the Basque tongue:

'Ogi zerutik etorria
zu zera gure poz guztia
Bildots santua ara emen . . .

From the basilica of Loyola, whose magnificence had astonished us, we pushed on to Santillana del Mar, site of the Caves of Altamira, where in 1869 the world's first concentration of prehistoric art was discovered by accident. When first I heard John Fulton's reasons for wanting to visit Altamira, I must confess I could not express much enthusiasm for what he had in mind. He said, 'I want to see how cave men drew their bulls and how they colored them, because I have in mind to publish a book with a series of bull pictures done as these early men did them.'

'On rock?' I asked.

'No. With bull's blood and a mixture of oil and ochre.'

I said to myself, 'If that's what a young man wants to do, why should I argue?'

For more than a thousand years before that day in 1869 when the Caves of Altamira were discovered as a major glory of western art, the small town of Santillana had been well regarded as an exceptionally fine village. Here three or four country lanes intersect and each is lined with rare old houses and churches that date back at least to the year 870. In Santillana it was a custom for proud families to emblazon their homes with heraldic shields, so that today the town could well be set aside as a museum showing what happens when everyone tries 'to keep up with the Barredas,' for one house is finer than the next and this family shield larger than that, until finally the Villa family offers an escutcheon so tremendously big that the human figures on it are known locally as giants. The guidebook warns: 'This shield is so close to the spectator that the effect is perhaps a little pompous.' On the other hand, the Collegiate church is an unpretentious gem of Romanesque architecture, and even the emblazoned houses have an unusual charm in that their ground floors are given over to the stabling of cattle, whose aromas permeate the village, making it doubly attractive and homelike.

In other words, when the caves that lay below the village fields were about to be discovered, which would bring millions of visitors to Santillana, the town was already a poetic, pastoral museum; today it is a national treasure in which the Barreda palace has been converted to a handsome parador where one can obtain good meals and from which he can study the shields and explore the caves. There are few small towns in Europe more worth a visit than this.

The caves, at first sight, were merely a repetition of what I had come to know along tourist routes, whether in the Shenandoah Valley or along the rivers of Europe. Compared to the Carlsbad Caverns of New Mexico they are trivial in size, but they are clean and well lighted and their small rooms give a sense of underground living.

One area led to another of no conspicuous interest, but at the end of the trip I came to a low-ceilinged room about fifty feet long by thirty wide—as big as a motion picture house in a small village—and when my eyes had adjusted to the restrained light and when I looked upward I saw something so much grander than I had been led to expect that I can describe it only as one of the major surprises of my adventures in art. I had known the art was there. I could visualize what the wild bulls looked like. I knew what colors had been used to outline them, and I even knew how particular animals stood. But knowing all this, I knew nothing about the impact of this silent, hidden room upon the imagination.

For example, I had always believed that the great bulls of Altamira ranged along the walls of the cave. They are all on the ceiling. I had supposed I would find no more than a dozen good specimens. There are about thirty, each one a major work of art. I had supposed the colors to be faded, as they are in other prehistoric caves, and the bulls mere outlines which the mind fills in with pigment. Instead they are as bold and fresh in their color as if they had been painted last week. To stand at either the high end of the cave or the low and to look across the expanse of ceiling and see the animals rising and falling mysteriously along the rocky surface is to see not a prehistoric drawing but a field of bulls the way artists some seventeen thousand years ago must have seen them on the seacoast plains bordering the Bay of Biscay.

The thing that surprised me most, as I recall this amazing room, was the series of bulls constructed around rocky protuberances which jutted down from the ceiling. Mostly these extrusions are elliptical, but some are circular; they project eight or ten inches or perhaps even a foot, forming kinds of rocky hummocks standing forth from the rocky pasture lands. On these humps the ancient artists, using a trickery not surpassed by Salvador Dali, drew sleeping animals, wonderfully curled, with their feet tucked under them and their heads resting on their forelegs. The sense of reality thus created is magical; the bulls look as if at any moment they might rise from their slumber. One of the first French scholars to study Altamira summed it up in a phrase that has not been equaled: 'This cave is the Sistine Chapel of prehistoric art.'

John Fulton, studying the manner in which the pigment had been applied, pointed out something that I had not seen for myself: 'Nowhere in the cave is there a hunter, or any weapon used in hunting. The men who drew these animals must have loved them.' I've since seen a study which claims that the circular animals painted on the protruding rocks are wounded and about to die, but I saw no evidence of this and I suppose Fulton was closer to the truth. These are drawings done by men who studied animals and who loved them, the way the farmers of present-day Santillana love their beasts and share their houses with them, even though in the end they must live off them.

The cave was enhanced by a poetically enthusiastic guide four feet eight inches tall who spoke with swift impartiality a blend of French, Spanish and English, intermixing his words in such a way as to create the impression that he was speaking some ancient language that might have been used by the cave men: 'Regardez les animaux qui suivent el campo, comiendo, pensando, corriendo and lying down on their sides.' I found that if I could catch only a few words in each language I was able to build up a picture of the cave as it must have existed when men spoke with similarly fragmented thoughts.

One of the most interesting aspects of Altamira is a museum some distance from the entrance to the caves, for it contains a collection of the artifacts found on the site. The caves were discovered when a huntsman's dog fell into them one afternoon. The dog was pulled out and the incident forgotten until six years later, in 1875, when another in Spain's long line of amateur enthusiasts, this time Marcelino Sanz de Sautuola, heard of the cave and went exploring. It is interesting to note that it was only after four years of intensive work that the small cave containing the paintings was found by Don Marcelino's daughter María, who stumbled upon the scene where bulls wandered across the ceiling. In 1880 Don Marcelino published his findings, only to be branded a fraud. It was years before the authenticity and significance of the find were recognized.

In the building of which I speak, a small exhibition has been put together of the things Don Marcelino found and meticulously catalogued. Here are the stone axes, the wedges, the arrow points and the thin bones pierced to serve as needles, vestiges of a complex civilization. Especially attractive to anyone interested in art is a considerable group of sea shells, each containing the dried-out remnants of paint used by the prehistoric artists: red, black, gray, yellow, brown, white. Many of the pigments are the same as those employed by artists today, particularly a raw ochre which Fulton found in rock form on the beach nearby. If these dried colors were ground in a pestle and mixed with oil, they could be used now, and it is moving to think that in them we have the specific materials utilized in making the oldest surviving paintings in the history of art.

When I saw the shells I did not at first understand why they affected me as they did. Then I remembered. In the atelier of the American painter Karl Knaths at Provincetown on Cape Cod, I had seen exactly this type of shell, used precisely in this way and containing exactly these colors. In seventeen thousand years some of the ways of art had not changed, and at last I understood why Fulton wanted to paint his series of pictures using bull's blood, red ochre and native oils, for that was the way the whole exciting business had begun.

I was profoundly affected by Santillana: the houses with their arrogant shields, the good smell of cattle, the beautiful Romanesque church, the timeless bulls wandering across the roof-land meadows, and the sea-shell palette with its dried-up paints. I wanted time to think about this concentration of experience, so I walked slowly out of town and up the steep Camino Comillas to the fork where a secondary road branches off to Suances, and there sitting on a stone wall I had a splendid view of the region. Low mountains hemmed in the village and meandering stone fences outlined the fields. Red roofs marked the houses I had enjoyed and huge barns proved that the land was profitably farmed. This was northern Spain at its best, heavy with trees and richness, and I wondered if it were possible that the prehistoric men had lived above ground, reserving the caves as religious sites or refuges in time of war. If they lived on this particular bit of land they knew beauty at first hand, and it was this natural beauty that had characterized their art. I took a few steps backward, and I had crossed the watershed. Santillana had vanished and I was looking down at the Bay of Biscay, where rolling hills dropped to the sea, taking with them lonely, weather-beaten trees and a very old church that seemed about to plunge into the waves. Sunset was coming on and men were leaving the fields and heading for homes I could not see. They had been tending corn, which grows abundantly in these parts but is eaten only by animals.

It was night and I returned to Santillana, where the only argument that Vavra and Fulton and I were to have in five months of delightful travel ensued. There was a chirping sound, and Vavra said, 'Oh, it's owls.'

Without thinking that I was contradicting a professional naturalist, I blurted out, 'More likely frogs.'

'Couldn't be frogs up there.'

'Tree frogs.'

Vavra ridiculed this supposition and we agreed to lay our disagreement before Fulton, who said that to his uneducated ear it was neither frogs nor owls, so we turned to local experts. The first five farmers, who had lived all their lives in the presence of this sound, gave such radically different answers that I will merely repeat them.

'It comes from squeaking machinery.'

'It's a kind of fish that lives in the ditches.'

'An insect. Very bothersome.'

'It's made by the swallows going to bed.'

'Snails. It's the mating call of snails.'

Now, obviously the sound came from either an owl or a tree frog, and to have five local experts fail even to include these animals in their suggestions was unnerving, but Fulton came up with the first practical observation: 'Whatever it is, is singing down there in that sewer.'

Vavra refused to accept what seemed to me conclusive evidence that the singers were frogs; he claimed that what Fulton was hearing was an echo coming from the sewer, and we left Santillana not knowing what was responsible for the twilight serenade, but some days later Vavra, who takes these matters seriously, reflected, 'It would be extraordinary for an owl to live in a sewer.'

Excellent as Santillana was, it was our third excursion that remains most vivid in my mind. I have never bothered much about whether or not people will remember me when I am dead; but I am sure that as long as my generation lives, in various parts of the world someone will pause now and then to reflect, 'Wasn't that a great picnic we had that day with Michener?' I have lured my friends into some extraordinary picnics, for I hold with the French that to eat out of doors in congenial surroundings is sensible: in Afghanistan we ate high on a hill outside Kabul and watched as tribesmen moved in to attack the city; at Edfu along the Nile we spread our blankets inside that most serene of Egypt's temples; in Bali we picnicked on the terraces and in Tahiti by the waterfalls; and if tomorrow someone were to suggest that we picnic in a snowstorm, I'd go along, for of this world one never sees enough and to dine in harmony with nature is one of the gentlest and loveliest things we can do. Picnics are the apex of sensible living and the traveler who does not so explore the land through which he travels ought better to stay at home.

One of my happiest experiences in Spain was the discovery, many years ago, of a remarkable American woman who loved picnics almost as much as I did. Patter Ashcraft, in her late thirties, the descendant of a distinguished Cleveland family, had been early in life inoculated with bull fever. When I first knew her she had a monstrous Buick convertible, in which we drove like demented Spaniards, but now she had a more sedate Volkswagen, in which she followed the ferias up and down Spain, spreading hilarity wherever she struck. She was known to her friends as L'Incomparable, and she spoke in such a low whisper that her husband Edwin, a Princeton CIA type, had to be constantly reminding, 'Darling, turn up the volume control.'

It was during the Sevilla feria one year that we discovered our mutual interest in picnics; we organized repeated forays into Las Marismas, and in subsequent years we had cajoled our friends into the countryside at Salamanca, along the western rivers of Spain, in the rural areas near Madrid, and at the spot from which El Greco painted his famous view of Toledo.

Patter and I disagreed on only one detail: she thought a picnic should be composed only of items that could be bought in stores, like a round of cheese, a slab of ham, six bottles of wine, whereas the best picnic I had ever attended prior to Pamplona had consisted of ramekins of lima beans baked with traces of baked ham, garlic and blackstrap molasses, a green salad with a good dressing and ice-cold éclairs, three to a customer. In other words, Patter was of the American school; I of the French—and the latter is obviously superior.

On this day Patter's theory was to prevail, and her car was loaded with choice cans and bottles when we set out to a picnic ground which I had selected years before; I had spotted it on my pilgrimage to Santiago de Compostela. We were eight as we left Pamplona after the morning running of the bulls: Patter and her husband; Bob Daley, long-time European sportswriter for the *New York Times,* and his French wife, both with a good sense of what makes a picnic; Vavra and Fulton; the Hemingway double and I. We were headed north, toward the Pass of Roncesvalles, that historic and mystery-laden route through the Pyrenees which Charlemagne had used in 778 for his retreat through the mists and where he had failed to hear the battle horn of his dying Roland.

The success of our picnic was assured by the fine tins Patter had bought and by the rare site I had selected, but insurance was taken out when Bob Daley, fearing that we didn't have enough food, stopped in the town of Espinal, and while we seven studied the fine modernistic church, quite radical in its architecture, he bought an extra loaf of bread, and in doing so, acquired a culinary masterpiece: it was round and flat, about the size of a large chair cushion and not more than two inches thick, so that it was practically all crust, and better crust was never baked.

We drove to the statue of a pilgrim which marks the southern end of the pass, and thought with what relief the religious wanderers of the medieval period must have reached this spot and given thanks at the statue for having escaped the robbers that infested the dark woods of the area. Farther on, at the lonely monastery, the gates of which had rescued thousands and fed millions in the long years of its existence, the others studied the stalwart and well-carved church, but I wandered through the network of stables and barns from which the small fields in the pass had been farmed for twelve centuries. Everything was low and compact, to fight against the winter winds that tormented the area, and all things had a sense of past ages, so that one stood surrounded by history, whether in the barn or in the transept.

I had in mind a spot well beyond the monastery of Roncesvalles, a spot where a small stream came out of a woods, but Patter was by now in the lead car and she caught sight of a meadow far below the road where seven rivulets converged, their banks lined with moss-covered trees, and when I saw it I had to acknowledge that her choice was best. We lugged our tins and bottles and Bob Daley's marvelous chunk of bread down to the seven streams, and there in a glade so quiet, so softly green that it seemed as if defeated knights might have slept in it the evening before, we spread our blankets and prepared the meal.

It was not a picnic we had but a kind of dedication. We were in a pass where significant events had occurred, where the legend of Roland had been created to give meaning to Christianity's fight against Islam, and before we had been in the silent place for a dozen minutes it had possessed us and made us a part of history. 'If there ever were dryads,' Vanderford said, 'they must have lived here.'

For some hours we wandered along the rivulets and talked of the feria at Pamplona. One group of trees had strange knees that protruded to make

fine chairs, and in them we sat as we discussed the bullfighters, the disappointments they had caused and the near-tragedies that had occurred at the running of the bulls. As we ate, and relished the bread from Espinal, John Fulton told of the American military personnel in Spain who had planeloads of American bread, white, gooey, lacking in everything except chemicals, flown across the Atlantic to the PX's 'so that our children can grow up knowing what real bread is.' The idea was so fascinating that no one could think of any comment.

And then the mysterious thing happened that made of this picnic with Charlemagne a thing of haunting beauty, so strange and memorable that all who participated would afterward say, 'Remember that picnic in the Pass of Roncesvalles,' except that Peggy Daley, being French, would call it 'Roncevaux.' A fog rolled in and blotted out the sun. It was not a cold fog, but it was heavy, and soon we were immersed not in a woods cut by rivulets but in a dream through which strange figures moved and horns echoed. We could barely see from one to the other and the trees on which we had been sitting became vague shapes, but no one thought to leave, for a curious light pervaded and voices seemed unusually clear, though echoes were no more.

The voices said strange things. Bob Vavra surprised us by announcing that he was a gypsy, a real gypsy with roots in Bohemia in Czechoslovakia. 'You ought to see my father in California. In his seventies and as bronzed and lean as a hickory limb.' We recalled that unbelievable day, May 23, 1435, when through these passes came the Original Band of gypsies to burst upon an unsuspecting Spain. They were led by that engaging rascal, Thomas, self-proclaimed Earl of Little Egypt. The gypsies had learned that then as now Europeans were easy targets if one announced himself an earl or a duke or a count, so Earl Thomas brought along a couple of each. The gypsies had also learned that Christian Europe was much concerned about the advance of Islam, so Thomas explained that his band had been forced to flee from Little Egypt because they were Christians and their kingdom had been overrun by the infidel. Thomas said he could stay in Europe only a little while, collecting funds for the recapture of his native land. Then, at the head of a mighty crusade, he would lead his victorious Christians back to Little Egypt and win new laurels for the faith. Who had made him an earl? He was vague about that. Where was Little Egypt? He was vague about that, too. When would the crusade start? Any day now. In the meantime, money must be collected, and for a whole hilarious decade Earl Thomas and his brazen band hoodwinked Spain and gathered funds. 'Spaniards have ever since held gypsies in low regard,' Vavra reflected. 'Up to a few years ago they could have no passports, were not inducted into the army and suffered all sorts of restraint. You'd be surprised how many Spaniards stop cold dead when I say innocently, "But I'm a gypsy." ' What was at first held most strongly against them was the fact that after

529

be mists at Roncesvalles.

gathering all that money from Christian Spain, they made no effort to recapture Little Egypt, nor would they even divulge where it was.

Matador Fulton told an equally strange tale. He was born in Philadelphia, Fulton John Sciocchetti, to a conservative middle-class Italian-Hungarian family who changed their last name to Short, so his name was legally Fulton John Short, but in the ring he was known as John Fulton. As an art student at the Philadelphia Museum School he gained high marks, but reading Hemingway's *Death in the Afternoon* alerted him to the romance of the bullring, and when his military duty took him to camps along the Mexican border he began to train as a bullfighter, and once he did this, he was lost. He kept us chuckling in the mists as he recounted one after another of the misadventures which seem to overtake all bullfighters: 'I was fighting this time in Tijuana and there was this dippy dame from some society or other in southern California who conceived a passion for bullfighters, one after another, and this week it was "our heroic American matador, John Fulton." As the fight was about to begin she leaned down out of the stands, grabbed at my hand and told her husband, "I have fallen madly in love with this young man and I warn you that if the bull wounds him I shall leave you sitting here, because my place will be in the ring with the wounded hero." Her husband looked at her, looked at me, then put his hands to his mouth and bellowed, "Come on, bull!" '

Vanderford astonished me by having in his pocket the details of that first bullfight I had seen in Valencia so many years ago. Working in his patient way through the newspapers of the period on file in Madrid, he had found answers to my questions: The fight had occurred on the Sunday after Easter, April 3, 1932, in the plaza at Valencia. The bulls were from the ranch of Don Manuel Comacho of Sevilla, and the matadors appear to have been regular, no more. Marcial Lalanda, so-so. Domingo Ortega, details. El Estudiante, details. He continued with his deflating analysis of the fight which I had remembered as something rather more than regular. But there the record was: 'The bulls were mansotes y sosos' (cowardly and dull). Then he stunned me by saying, 'And the second fight, which you recall as having been held on Monday, actually took place on Tuesday, because on Monday there was a comic bullfight.' This I couldn't believe. I knew it was Monday, for I could recall every incident after the first fight and how I had got my ticket for the second and the conversations with the cuadrillas. If I was certain about anything in the past, it was the day on which this second memorable fight occurred, yet there the record was. Tuesday, bulls of no consequence, three novilleros of limited ability who never progressed to full matador. To me they had been good; the bulls had been brave; and the fight had taken place on Monday. I suppose much memory is like that.

Vavra coaxed Bob Daley to tell us how he had got married, and Daley said that as a fledgling foreign correspondent about to sail for Europe for the *New York Times* he had acquired from a chance acquaintance the name of a girl in Nice whom the acquaintance had seen once and had considered 'the most beautiful girl in Europe.' When his ship docked, Daley had headed straight for Nice, had searched for the girl and had married her on the spot. 'Everybody should be so lucky,' Vavra said, for all agreed that Daley had got himself a gem. In what spare minutes I could find during San Fermín, I was reading the manuscript of Daley's forthcoming novel, *The Whole Truth*, which dealt with a fledgling correspondent covering Europe for New York's major newspaper, not named, and at last I understood where Daley had got his idea for the central love story in which his young reporter goes to a setting like Nice to marry a girl like Peggy. I was finding Daley's account of newspaper life overseas faithful to what I had observed in Tokyo, Vienna and Paris but I feared that it would get an adverse review in the *New York Times* when it appeared, and it did.

Then someone asked why Roland had sounded his horn at this gloomy spot, and I explained that three events, one historical, two legendary, had been telescoped here, but that no one was required to believe either of the legendary versions. 'Young Charlemagne crossed the Pyrenees in 778 not to aid the Christians of Spain against the Moors but to subdue the fractious Basques. He failed, and on his return a rabble of Basques overtook his rearguard at Roncesvalles and killed some two dozen men, and Charlemagne was unable to do anything about it, for after their victory the Basques vanished. That much is history. Many years later a legend grew up, claiming that when Charlemagne invaded Spain he was an old man dedicated to helping Christians expel Moors. In his entourage rode his nephew Roland, the fairest knight who ever was, and Archbishop Turpin, as good a swordsman as he was a cleric. At Roncesvalles, when four hundred thousand Moors attacked, the archbishop slew four hundred but in the end was killed. Last of the defenders was Roland, who with his sword Durandal propped himself against the kind of tree we've been sitting on today and sounded his horn Olifant to summon his uncle back to the fight, but in vain. Turning his face to Spain, so that Charlemagne would know he had died confronting the enemy, Roland perished somewhere near here. That was the first legend. Centuries later another legend appeared, supposed to have been written by Archbishop Turpin, who did not die at the pass but escaped, and this account claims that the reason Charlemagne came into Spain was neither to punish Basques nor to brawl with Saracens but to go on pilgrimage to Santiago de Compostela. It was on his return that the Battle of Roncesvalles occurred, when Roland and his thousand knights perished at the hands of the infidel. I make no choice among the versions.'

The mists thickened and a kind of darkness covered the valley, up whose steep sides we could hear the whispering of birds; it took no imagination to believe that it was in such surroundings that Roland had sounded his horn Olifant, and one could understand how the notes had been absorbed, so that Charlemagne could not hear them. It was a pass, as we saw it then, where brave men had fought and where heroes had died. In the mists the members of our party looked like the ghosts of those heroes, looming now into view, retreating again into the mists, and we lingered on, barely making it back to Pamplona in time for the bullfight.

It was lucky for me that we were not delayed, for as we entered the patio de caballos, that part of the ring in which the picadors exercise their horses and where the cuadrillas meet to pray in the chapel before the fight, I recognized two figures whose presence in Pamplona could not have been more happily arranged. The first was one of the handsomest toreros, a lithe square-jawed man in his late fifties, with a heavy head of gray hair, who looked as if he might, with a little training, step forth to meet the bulls once more. Only a few years earlier he had appeared in that excellent motion picture *Tarde de toros* (Afternoon of Bulls), in which he had given a fine performance in the bullring. In the history of bullfighting he was an authentic master, Domingo Ortega, of whose fight in 1932 I had just been speaking with Vanderford.

Beside him was a taller man who might have been a few years younger, also handsomely preserved and with hair equally gray. He had the lean, aquiline face of a professor of philosophy at Madrid University and the clear eyes of a man who had served long as a matador. He leaned forward when he spoke, and his voice was soft, controlled. When he smiled it was with the inborn reserve that had characterized his fighting, for this was Luis Gómez, El Estudiante, the third fighter on the bill that day in 1932.

What happened next surprised me, even though I have often moved in the world of bullfighting and have known the idiosyncrasies of the professionals. I introduced myself to the matadors and they, accustomed to such interruptions whenever they wandered into the patio de caballos, nodded indifferently; but then I said, 'The first fight I ever saw was in Valencia early one spring when Marcial Lalanda and you and you fought, and I have never forgotten it.'

Ortega's deeply lined face broke into a wide smile. 'I remember exactly. It was in 1932. A great afternoon for me.'

'April 3, 1932.' El Estudiante nodded. 'One of my first fights as a full matador.'

Apparently the afternoon had meant as much to them as it had to me, for they recalled the scene and Lalanda's role and the fight the bulls gave; it was later that I learned how close Ortega had been to retiring from the ring before he got started.

In his first fights he had been desultory, 'Nada,' as the Spaniards say, and critics recommended that he quit. It was not until this fight in Valencia at the beginning of the 1932 season that he had demonstrated a classic quality which was to make him immortal: a dry, controlled, ascetic style which was the despair of those who loved flamboyance and the delight of those who respected art.

When Vavra suggested a photograph, Ortega was no longer indifferent. Smiling broadly, he looked at me and said, 'It's remarkable that you should remember.' It would have been remarkable had I forgot.

Any man who attends the feria of San Fermín must decide whether or not he will run with the bulls, and since thousands of men run each day for seven days and only a few go to the hospital, with not more than one fatality every eight or ten years, the chances are obviously favorable; yet there is that negative possibility, and on those days when I was not perched on the fence at the chute I had had the bad luck to be stationed opposite the military hospital on the Calle Santo Domingo, into which some of the damaged were hauled on stretchers, and seeing a rather lively trade, I decided not to run. There were also in 1966 special reasons which would excuse me from participating, in addition to which I was practically sixty years old, and runners of that age were not frequent.

However, on the next-to-last morning when the bulls were run I happened to be at a spot where few foreigners go, and as the dispatching rocket exploded at the corrals I happened to look down the street from which the bulls would appear, and there waiting for them was Hemingway's tutor, Juanito Quintana! He must have been in his seventies, yet there he was in the street, waiting for the bulls, with no friends around to applaud or no necessity to prove his manhood. The crazy idiot was there for the sheer hell of it, and as the bulls of the Conde de la Corte thundered up the hill, Quintana ran briefly before them, then ducked into a doorway. I think he would have been embarrassed had he known that I had seen him, for this was the action of a foolhardy man acting completely on his own.

It was also the action of a man who loved bulls, and the sight of him in the street haunted me all that day. I said to myself, 'You've loved the bulls as much as Quintana ever did. In Mexico and Spain you followed them as a young man. You may never be in Pamplona again, and tomorrow is the last running. You belong on the street.'

I scouted Santo Domingo, for if I were to be anywhere I wanted to be there where the bulls first meet the flying men, and since for extraneous reasons I was not able to run, I wanted to find some doorway in which I could take a relatively safe position. But when next morning I had taken my position, two unnerving things occurred at about two minutes of seven. A friend read me a passage from a recent book: ' "Sometimes, when a man knows the bulls are gaining on him, he falls flat on his face and lies still and the bulls go past; or he may do something that can be most perilous, he can step into a doorway and keep still; but there is a chance that a bull will stop and gore him." ' More disturbing was a wild-eyed man who took a position near me with a transistorized tape recorder strapped to his belly. The machine played church hymns nonstop and the man wore a doleful look as if he expected this to be his last morning with the bulls. But seven o'clock was at hand and I could not retreat.

The first rocket fired and the gates swung open. The second rocket fired, the oxen led the bulls galloping into the street and huge numbers of men began surging up Santo Domingo. Just as the main body reached where I was waiting, a young man fell in the street and others piled over him. One onrushing bull, distracted by the accident, lunged at the fallen man, missed, trampled him and came on toward my doorway. At the last moment the bull swerved back to join the herd and I vaguely remember a wild pounding of hooves as the animals raced past. It had all happened in a few seconds and somehow the fallen man at my feet had been uninjured, but as I lingered in the doorway talking with him, a stretcher came down Santo Domingo bearing a young man whose face had been crushed by the flat side of a horn; it looked as if he would lose his eye.

I have written favorably of two ferias, those of Sevilla and Pamplona, and the reader who finds himself with time to attend only one may wish a comparison.

Ambiente. The surroundings of the two are so radically different as to permit no comparison. Sevilla represents the soul of Andalucía; Pamplona is the heart of Navarra. If I were a first-time tourist and could see only one, I suppose I would learn more from seeing Andalucía; if I knew Spain reasonably well, I would want to see Navarra.

Setting. Sevilla is more interesting architecturally and culturally than Pamplona, but the physical accouterments of the Sevilla feria cannot compare with that charming proximity of bullring and central square in Pamplona. One can get swallowed up in Sevilla, and without money he can miss the feeling of the feria; but in Pamplona, if one can stagger he can find his way to the square, and there the action is.

Parades. The wild parades of Pamplona, lasting all day and night, with the giants, the big-headed dwarfs and the tipsy revelers, cannot be taken lightly; they are some of the best fun in Europe, and with a red scarf and a bota of wine anyone can participate in the street dancing. As a Frenchman told me in Pamplona: 'It's wrong to say there is dancing in the streets. It's the streets themselves that are dancing.' But the religious processions in Sevilla are incomparably greater. So, too, are the daily exhibitions of horsemanship in the park and along the casetas, for they are essentially Spanish and imbued with a grace that one does not often witness.

Music. The only folk instruments in the world that I have ever heard which approach the unearthly oboes of Pamplona are the rhythm drums of Afghanistan, and even against those wild instruments the oboes win by a mile. No matter how sorry the bullfight, when the oboes play during the

At dawn each year many foreigners dance in the street
reaching for a sun that once ros
but will not rise again

placing of banderillas one finds three minutes of exquisite beauty. They stand without competition. Yet I cannot forget the soft midnight clapping of hands in Sevilla. Perhaps one should not make comparisons where pure beauty is concerned, as in the case of the oboes and the hands.

Food. During feria in Sevilla it is quite impossible to get a decent meal; even in fine hotels the food thrown at the customers is disgraceful. In Pamplona I had delicious plates at four places: mixed salad and menestra at the White Horse Tavern; bacalao at Marcelino's, where Hemingway used to eat; stewed veal at Casa Mauleón, near the bullring, where prices are reasonable; and delicious garlic snails at Olaverri's at the southern end of town. It is true that I spoke well of El Mesón in Sevilla, but that was only in comparison with the other restaurants in that city; compared with the best in Pamplona it was no more than average.

Bullring. A friend of mine partial to Sevilla once said, 'To compare the noble Maestranza of Sevilla with that dump in Pamplona is like comparing Yankee Stadium with the Little League park in Akron, Ohio.' So far as the interiors of the two rings are concerned, this is not an extravagant judgment, for the Maestranza is incomparable whereas the 1967 additions to the Pamplona ring, augmenting its seats by some six thousand, have only increased its lack of architectural beauty, but when one considers the whole setting, things are different. From the outside, the Sevilla ring cannot be seen; houses and stores encroach on every inch and the outer walls are actually not visible, so that the apparent ring, even though it sits beside a river, consists merely of a pair of undistinguished doors. But in Pamplona the ring sits within a lovely park of trees in one of the most congenial settings in Spain. Broad areas surround it, and fine walks. The architecture is pleasing and the ambiente is total. Inside the ring, during a fight, if one looks off to the southeast he sees high in the air the white marble tower of a neighboring church; the ramparts are filled with priests in black robes, taking in the fight with binoculars. In Pamplona this tower is known as 'the crow's nest.'

The bullfights. In Sevilla one has stately bullfights conducted in classic manner and with a noble restraint. In Pamplona one has lively exhibitions in which bulls play an honored role, but often a secondary one to the riotousness of the crowd.

The running with the bulls. Here Pamplona is so far ahead that it is embarrassing even to mention Sevilla. There is nothing in Europe, or America or Asia either, to equal these early-morning gallops with death, and if one is young and adventurous, even one morning running with the bulls might be worth two weeks of Sevilla.

Flamenco. Pamplona, on the other hand, has nothing to match the flamenco shows of the casetas in Sevilla, which is to be expected, since Pamplona lies outside the flamenco zone.

Circus. The circus area in Pamplona is scattered and ineffectual and the circuses that frequent it are small. The area in Sevilla is concentrated and the circuses are delightful. When the carnival area of Sevilla is added, the advantage is all Sevilla's.

Picnics. I have already spoken of the pass at Roncesvalles, but I am not forgetting the fine picnics in Las Marismas, and for the average visitor not concerned with Charlemagne and Roland, I suspect a picnic in the Sevilla area might be preferred.

Acceptance. This is a subtle point that might weigh heavily with younger people, although it is no longer of much importance to me. To be accepted in Pamplona one needs only a white shirt, tennis shoes, a red scarf, a red sash and a bota of wine. With this equipment the town and the square and the bullring are available, and the fellowship continues for eight long days. To be accepted in Sevilla . . . the phrase is a misnomer. One is never accepted in Sevilla. I have spent much time in that city, during feria and otherwise, and I have rarely received either hospitality or courtesy. I thought perhaps that this was because I didn't ride, but a distinguished horseman told me, 'If you ride you're treated even worse. If your jacket is an inch too short, the Sevillanos ask, "You hunting for frogs?" If your hat is not cocked at precisely the right angle, they say, "You boor." And if your horse is not obviously the most expensive, they jeer, "You cheapo." ' To wangle an invitation into a caseta is almost impossible, and I once sat for an entire feria in the Aero Club without once being spoken to, not even by waiters. Some of the loneliest and unhappiest people I have ever met have been Europeans, not Americans, trying to make a go of it in Sevilla. But I have reached the age at which I neither expect nor demand acceptance; all I require is that the local citizens not throw bottles at me, so my preference between the two ferias remains with Sevilla. The privilege of seeing the Holy Week procession before the feria starts, and the daily parade in the park, and the casetas, and the horse fair, plus the superb bullfights in the best of rings is an opportunity I would not surrender, not even when the people who organize these matters are so inhospitable.

All ferias end, but few so mournfully as Pamplona's. At nightfall after the last bullfight is over, the bands that were once so gay pass slowly through the plaza and the narrow streets playing dirges, and when they reach the mournful wail which concludes their requiem, those marching throw themselves prostrate in the street, and with their foreheads beating the stones, cry in the night,

> 'Poor me, poor me! How sad am I.
> Now the Feria of San Fermín
> Has ended. Woe is me.'

A city is in lamentation, and well it should be, for there are not many things like San Fermín.

FOLLOWING PAGE:
Intellectual Spain.

BARCELONA

OCEANO
ATLANTICO

MAR MEDITERRANE

0   MILES   100

Vich
Montserrat
Barcelona
Sitges

Teruel
Castellón de la Plana
Burriana
Valencia

Palma

Madrid

Lisboa

San Juan de Alicante
Elche
Benidorm

Guadix
Sevilla
Granada

Torremolinos
Gibraltar

To travel across Spain and finally to reach Barcelona is like drinking a respectable red wine and finishing up with a bottle of champagne. For Barcelona is an exhilarating city, replete with challenging aspects. It is not only the political capital of the north, where one can best evaluate the problem of regional separatism in Spain, especially Catalan, but it is also the intellectual capital of the country, with a fascinating collection of museums. It is a world almost to itself, a unique metropolis bound more to the Mediterranean than to the mountains, more to France than to Africa.

I approached Barcelona in a leisurely and almost ideal way. One morning I awoke in the Parador de San Francisco inside Granada's Alhambra. This is generally held to be Spain's choicest parador if one is concerned with history and architecture, for it is very old and its cloistered patio is exceptional. After a farewell visit to the tinsel-and-stucco buildings of the Alhambra and a final look at Manuel de Falla's carmen, my wife and I drove out past the Torre Bermeja and up onto the plateau that would lead us eastward to the Mediterranean. At the last curve we looked back at the beautiful Muslim city and at the cathedral where my four kings lay, Fernando, Isabel, Felipe, Juana, and like the Moor we saw no more.

It was autumn as we drove north and harvesting was under way. Golden grain, russet fruits, red grapes and crimson peppers were being gathered and this part of Andalucía looked positively rich, so rich that I remembered the explanation as to why Granada produced poor wine: 'Her grapes have not suffered enough.' In the good fields we saw that morning there had been little suffering.

Before long I was surprised to come upon the famous village of Guadix, for I had supposed that it lay farther south. During the final siege of Granada in 1491 a crucial victory had been gained here by the Christians, but memory of it has pretty much been submerged by the fame of the town's cave dwellings, and these are something to see. Set in a lunar landscape of bleak hills and rocky pinnacles the houses of Guadix are dug into the faces of the hills, and when chimneys are piped up through the solid rock so that fires can be lit, are quite comfortable. This style of architecture has been adopted in many different countries, most notably in central Turkey, but at Guadix there is a difference, because the doorways into the caves have been handsomely plastered and decorated with red tiles, so that they look like the entrances to churches or villas of some importance. They have been rewhitewashed once or twice a year for six or seven centuries, so that like the house of Núñez de Balboa in Jerez de los Caballeros, they are now encrusted in a kind of man-made rock of soft and delicate outline. To see Guadix in the afternoon sun, with its pinnacles dark brown like burnished gold and its cave entrances stark white, is to see a dream village more appropriate for goblins and giants than for human beings.

The reason I wanted to see Guadix had nothing to do with its architecture, handsome though that was. This was the pueblo in which Alarcón had located his short novel *El sombrero de tres picos*, and as I looked at the miserable economic level at which the villagers lived, I could hear the music which Falla had composed for this work and I could visualize the four leading actors in the rustic comedy. This was the house of the hard-working miller and over there was the fly-stained office of the lecherous corregidor (one who corrects, hence magistrate) who had conceived an evil passion for the miller's wife. This grapevine could be the one from which she plucked the grapes used for bedeviling the corregidor, and that little stream is probably the one into which he tumbled while pursuing her. And the biggest of the houses, not attached to any cave, would pretty surely have been the corregidor's, where the miller went to enjoy himself with the corregidor's wife while the latter was having no luck with the miller's wife. Seeing the supposed setting of the ballet gave me a better understanding of Falla's music, for he caught the color and sound of a Spanish village. Two orchestral suites have been excerpted from the ballet. The first summarizes the dance of the miller's wife, the magistrate and the episode of the grapes, and is not outstanding; the second gives us the dance of the neighbors, the miller's farruca and the final dance, and is probably the best work Falla ever did. I have never been able to account for the discrepancy in the quality between the two suites, but I have come to prize the second as fit to stand beside Stravinsky's *Petrouchka* or Prokofiev's *Love for Three Oranges*.

Beyond Guadix we came to that series of Andalusian villages perched on the sides of hills where life is as bleak and unrewarding as anywhere in Europe. The bulk of the people are illiterate and are intended to be kept that way by their landed masters. Life is even more miserable than in the villages of Extremadura, because here there is less hope. The earthen floor, the solitary garment with patch upon patch upon patch, the early marriage and the early death, these are the marks of rural Andalucía. It is no wonder that whole villages have emigrated. Where do they go? Listen to the litany of rural Spain as I heard it from an Andalusian.

'A good many men from this village . . . Germany. When they go they promise, "We'll come back. I won't forget you, Prudencia." But we never see them again.'

'Do they find Catholic girls? In Germany?'

'They come back to Spain. But not to this dump.'

'Where do they go?'

'Where would any sensible man go? Barcelona.'

Whenever a man from Andalucía, fed up with his miserable lot, pronounced the word Barcelona it was as if he were uttering a benediction. 'That whole village beyond the hill, they all went to Barcelona. You can plow the main street and plant your grapes, because they won't be back.'

'Is life in Barcelona that good?' I asked.

'No. It's very hard. But it's a life.' Here the Andalusian made the gestures which I had seen before. He rubbed the cloth of his shirt to signify that in Barcelona men could afford clothing. And with his fingers he put imaginary food in his mouth, and this required no interpretation. Wherever I went in rural Andalucía, I encountered these signs.

I sought out an intellectual from the area, living of course in a different part of the country, and he said, 'My region is the heart and soul of Spain. Everything good comes from Andalucía, and believe me when I say that all of us who live in exile do so with a sigh. Just as our hard fields make great fighting bulls, so they make fighting men. If I thought I'd never again see Andalucía, I don't think I could live.'

'Then why do so many leave?'

'Two harsh reasons. The landed families own Andalucía and they've sworn that nothing down there will ever change. For them the system is good, and for them it will continue. The second reason, the Church. In this city you've met liberal priests. In Barcelona they have tremendous priests, willing to fight even the police on behalf of students and ordinary people. But in Andalucía the Church has one last stronghold of the old system, when peasants behaved and listened to their betters. So down there the Church is an agency of repression. It preaches a kind of life that flourished five hundred years ago . . . when things were supposed to be good.'

My informant paused and said, 'Actually, a thousand years ago when Moors occupied the region life was probably better than it is now. A thousand years and there's been no progress. Have you ever seen a true back-of-the-mountain Andalusian village?'

'I've seen Guadix.'

To residents of Andalucía who might have an adventurous or inquiring mind, Barcelona is as foreign and as exciting as France.

He laughed. 'That's a metropolis. They have buses and a cinema. They have no money but they do have spirit. No, I mean the really forlorn Andalucía. You haven't seen it and you can't know.'

I said, 'I went into the Sierra Nevada south of Granada. Well back. I've seen.'

He reflected on this for a moment and said, 'Even that's the good part. I'm speaking of the truly bleak areas over toward Murcia. Spend a week in one of those villages, as I have, and you'll understand why people from Andalucía flock to Barcelona.'

'Why not Madrid?'

'That's a subtle problem. In the minds of these people Madrid is merely an extension of what they already have. Landed power. The Church. Feudalism intensified. But Barcelona, with its nearness to France and its fronting on the Mediterranean, is a complete break. In Madrid

544

there's not much hope for an Andalusian peasant. In Barcelona all things are possible. And when you get to Barcelona and see the tremendous number of Andalusians who have emigrated there, look at how poorly they live. Really, until they get established they live like swine. But not one ever leaves to return home. Because in Barcelona there is hope.'

I asked what would happen to Andalucía if the exodus continued, and he said, 'The landed families and the Church will win their battle. They'll keep it just as it was five hundred years ago. Unless . . . '

As so often happens in conversations with Spaniards, he hesitated, considered his words carefully, then plunged ahead. 'If at Franco's death there is trouble, everyone expects it to come in Madrid and Barcelona, especially the latter. It won't. Well, in a way it will. There'll be some rioting and temporary disturbances, but they'll be easily handled. But if the atheistic peasants of Andalucía rise, watch out. Because they will not be easily put down.'

He suggested that when the turnover came I forget Madrid and Barcelona, for they would provide only flashy headlines. 'Keep your eye on what happens in Andalucía, for that will be the powder keg. If it can be controlled, all will be controlled.'

I asked, 'But haven't the more durable spirits gone off to Germany and Barcelona?'

'They have. That's why the powers in control down there have never tried to halt emigration. They want the bolder men to get out. But conditions are so poor that even the not-so-bold may feel they have to do something. Watch Andalucía.'

At Guadix, I had faced two major decisions and with a lack of courage had in each case chosen the easier way out. Repeatedly I had been told, 'You cannot understand modern Spain unless you look into the Gibraltar Question. And you must see what's happening in Torremolinos.' Had I intended doing either, my last chance would have been to head south at Guadix, but I ignored the turnoff and continued due east. Concerning the Gibraltar Question, which monopolized Spanish newspapers during my last three visits, I did not feel qualified to judge. In 1704 the English had occupied the rock during a war in which Spain performed poorly. On July 13, 1713, a provision of the Treaty of Utrecht confirmed English possession. Since then the promontory had constituted a key link in the life line that bound England to Egypt, India and Australia. The Treaty of Utrecht contained many provisions, two of which England had apparently broken during the years when Spain was in no condition to challenge her: According to the treaty, England was allowed to occupy only the area immediately adjacent to the rock and was obligated to respect a demilitarized zone established between English and Spanish holdings, which was easy to comply with in an age of ships, but which could not be respected in an age of aviation when British forces stationed at Gibraltar required landing fields that could be built only in the demilitarized zone; in this respect the Treaty of Utrecht was unquestionably violated. Out of respect for Spanish sensibilities, England also undertook never to bring into Gibraltar any Jews or Muslims, but during the years of indolence she had allowed several Jews to take up residence and many Muslims, and had thus once more violated the treaty.

It was interesting to see how Spain enlisted support from jurists in all parts of the world, especially Latin America, to condemn England for having unilaterally abrogated a treaty 253 years old; but in addition to this legalistic approach there was the more persuasive one that colonialism as represented by England's holding on to Gibraltar when Spain wanted it back was outmoded. Again a storm of support was whipped up in the Latin countries, and barely a day went by without my reading in the papers some statement from a dignitary in Lima or Caracas condemning Great Britain as a colonial tyrant. This argument was somewhat blunted by the fact that Spain herself held tightly to a chain of colonies in Africa, and I was often amazed at the prospect of Spain's lambasting Great Britain for doing only what Spain was doing; but just before I left the peninsula for the last time, the Spanish government cut that moral Gordian knot: 'We will give all our colonies self-government as soon as they are ready for it.'

This question of self-government is a tricky one, because if a plebiscite were held in Gibraltar, which the Spanish often call El Peñon (the Large Rock), there is good reason to believe that at least seventy percent of the residents would elect to remain under some kind of British rule. To the Spanish this is an infuriating statistic, but I never felt that it was determinative. In the long run Gibraltar ought to be Spanish and to keep it in any other status is anachronistic. I suppose that most sensible Britons feel the same way and that in time some kind of modus vivendi will be worked out, perhaps fifteen or twenty years hence, when tempers have cooled a bit. In the meantime, two factors operate to keep Spain from pressing the matter as diligently as she seems entitled to. First, an open breach with Great Britain would necessitate an interruption of the profitable sherry trade with London, which would quickly throw Andalucía into bankruptcy. Second, Spain as a newly baptized tourist country could not afford a belligerency which would frighten away even one season's flow of tourist income. As a matter of fact, I thought that both Spain and Great Britain were behaving well. One day the Spanish press, in obedience to government orders, stirred up such a frenzy of attack against London that minor anti-British riots broke out in several cities, with the stoning of British automobiles and the menacing of British consulates. Later I learned that the Spanish government had been frightened by the implications, and during the next week the press carried no more inflammatory nonsense. Instead there was a warm article about England's queen, Isabel II, and a laudatory review of a London football team.

(When the plebiscite was held, on September 10, 1967, those living in Gibraltar voted as follows:

Citizens eligible to vote	12,672
Number who actually voted	12,247
Spoiled ballots	65
Number preferring to return to Spain	44
Number preferring staying with Great Britain	12,138
Percentage favoring Great Britain	99.6)

The Gibraltar Question has produced an accidental side effect that is unfortunate. Spain is one of the few nations in the world which has refused to recognize the State of Israel. Three reasons have been given: the government's reluctance to exacerbate Muslim feeling since Spain's colonies contain mostly Muslim inhabitants; the understandable desire of a Catholic country to have the holy city of Jerusalem governed by an international commission to which the Pope would appoint a large proportion of the representatives, rather than to have it as it long was, half in Muslim hands, half in Jewish; and the inconsistency that would result if Spain were to recognize a Jewish state while invoking against England the anti-Jewish terms of the Treaty of Utrecht. I suppose the last reason is the operative one. It is ironic that Spain should refuse this gesture to the Jews, because Generalísimo Franco is highly regarded by Jews; during the worst days of World War II, when pressures from Hitler were at their heaviest, Franco refused to issue anti-Jewish edicts and instead provided a sanctuary, never violated, for Jews who managed to make it to Spain. Many thousands of Jews owe their lives to Franco, and this is not forgotten.

On the other hand, it is not uncommon to find in unexpected quarters stubborn anti-Jewish propaganda. For example, Agustín Serrano de Haro's *Yo soy español* (I am a Spaniard), a text in primary history, was written by a government inspector of primary education, endorsed by Church and lay authorities, and widely used since publication in 1944. One of its chapters dealt with still another case of supposed ritual murder by Jews of a Christian child, this time seven-year-old Domingo del Val de Zaragoza, who in the thirteenth century was supposed to have been crucified, thus attaining local sainthood. Serrano's inflammatory text was accompanied by three horrendous illustrations, the last of which showed the hideous Jews catching the child's blood in goblets. When I first saw the book the chapter ended with this tag line, 'So now you know, children, what Jews are like.' After disenchantment with Nazi Germany set in, this line was dropped, and when in the spring of 1967 I saw the twenty-sixth edition of the text, I found that the whole chapter had been eliminated.

As for Torremolinos, I was visited in Pamplona by a delightful Californian who runs a bar in the beach town, and he said, 'Michener, you would be false to every canon of good reporting if you chickened out on

547

Torremolinos. It's the living most . . . the capital de gustibus . . . the new wave . . . the perpetual party. It's Sweden-on-the-Sand. It's the Lourdes of LSD. It's the only spot in Spain where the Guardia Civil doesn't run things, and you must see it.'

Several other advisors had recommended Torremolinos, in somewhat similar phrases; it had become the international capital of the Mediterranean, superior to Positano, more fun than Nice and less expensive than either. I heard some great stories about the goings-on in the marijuana belt, but I judged that here was a town that merited a younger man than I to record its frivolity, and with some regret I headed north.

Just before we hit the Mediterranean coast we came to Elche, where we saw a sign saying, 'See the Dama de Elche,' and I stopped quickly at a garage: 'Has the famous statue of Elche been brought down here from the Prado?'

'Yes. You can see it in town.'

I thought how fine it would be to see this famous work on the site of its discovery seventy years ago, but when I had parked near the building where it was on display, a policeman said, 'Never heard of it. What is it?' and I supposed that I was once more in an area where citizens were unacquainted with their town's principal treasure, but in a bookstore the clerk smiled warmly and said, 'Señor, what a pity! The great statue was here. For our two-thousandth birthday. But it's now back in Madrid.' I was disappointed, but she took a paper and drew a map. 'If you've already seen the statue, why not go out to the farm where it was discovered? You'd find it most interesting.'

So we sought a small country road and traveled through the once-great date plantations of Elche; in Muslim days there had been over a million date palms here and their fruit was famous as far as Egypt. Now the vast plantation has diminished to a mere fraction of its former size, and many have adduced this as proof of how Spain suffered when the Moors were expelled. I think a truer interpretation would be that tastes have changed and that non-Muslims simply do not eat as many dates; where the palms used to grow I found almond trees, one of the most poetic of the fruit family and as gracefully restrained as a solitary guitar playing at night. While I was marveling at the beauty of the almond trees, my wife pointed to a spot at which five fields came to a point, producing something I had not previously seen: growing side by side were dates, almonds, olives, oranges and pomegranates. As much as anything I saw in Spain, this curious juxtaposition demonstrated how rich the Mediterranean littoral had always been, whether under Roman, Visigoth, Muslim or Spanish rule; we were in a garden that stretched for hundreds of miles.

The farm where the Dama de Elche was found, if indeed she was a dama, had assembled a small, miserably arranged museum of artifacts found within its boundaries. In it we found griffons dating back to 400

B.C., lintels from Roman temples, Visigothic sherds and a wealth of urns, jewelry, lions and mosaic floors. The very helter-skelter of the place lent it a kind of historical integrity: this was how things were dug up at such a site; and when we explored the fields themselves we could see the roots of the buildings: this had been a temple which at some period had served as a synagogue and later as a mosque. Elche must have been enormously wealthy in its great days, for these buildings were rich; beyond them lay the field where the statue had been found and here I experienced the same sense of frustration that had overtaken the scholars who first studied the work. Judging from the site, the statue could have been lost there as late as Renaissance times, but if someone had told me, 'You can see that it might have been laid down long before the Romans came,' I would have had to agree to that too. I think it appropriate that this splendid work remain a mystery. Man or woman, Iberian or Roman, priest or warrior, the thing stands nobly by itself, a perpetual challenge to the imagination.

I had heard of Alicante, one of the big seaports on the coast, and I knew that like all the littoral it had experienced considerable growth in recent years, so I was not entirely surprised when I saw its dozens upon dozens of new high-rise apartment houses, occupied principally by newcomers from Scandinavia and Germany; but I had never heard of San Juan de Alicante, a trivial little seaside village four miles to the north. I suppose, looking back on it, that this was one of the biggest shocks I experienced in Spain for as we came around a bend in the road following the sea, I found myself facing a resort settlement which three years ago had been barren ground and which now sprouted some three dozen fourteen- and eighteen-story spanking-new apartment buildings done in the most advanced modern style. They looked like mushrooms that rise on a forest floor after a storm, and the storm that called them forth was a mighty one which has swept the entire Spanish seacoast. From the French border south to Gibraltar a score of San Juan de Alicantes have risen in the past five years, and for the remainder of our trip north to Barcelona we would never be out of sight of this forest of new apartment buildings . . . not clusters of two or three but literally hundreds at a time and many thousands in all. I doubt if there is another area in the world that even comes close to the explosion that has overtaken this coast.

Who built the apartment houses? Spanish gamblers who have put together a little capital, borrowed heavily from banks and sold off their product to tourists before the first floor was finished. Who owns them now? Mostly Germans, some Swedes, some Dutch, a good many French. Some entrepreneurs from those countries buy entire apartment houses, which they rent out by the season; more often the floors are sold off singly to individual families on a cooperative basis. In one area of San Juan de Alicante all signs were in German; in another, French. One has to travel this coast to appreciate how unimportant to modern Spain are the

English-speaking tourists, for I did not come upon any district in which the signs were in that language.

I suspect my description of San Juan has failed to convey to the reader what has actually happened; how can he picture that jungle of concrete that has risen so swiftly from bare land? How can he visualize these very tall apartments, with no gardens, no ambiente, except that each room has an exquisite view of the sea? How can he understand that in Spain there has suddenly appeared this alien city, most of whose inhabitants speak northern European languages, frequent Nordic bars with Nordic bands, and when the season is over, board up their apartments and go back to Berlin and Stockholm? It is a revolution of considerable magnitude, but the best place to acquaint oneself with it is at Benidorm, a charming village a few miles farther up the coast.

Here the activity has multiplied about one hundred times within five years! Where there were three dozen towering apartments to startle me at San Juan, there must have been several hundred at Benidorm. It has a spacious beach, mountains inland and an unruly sort of charm. It is preponderantly German, and while I was staying there it gained notoriety because a mad German described as the Werewolf of the Autobahn was supposed to have fled to Benidorm after having slain several girls near Berlin. He was said to be hiding out in some kind of disguise that would not attract attention, but the Spanish police nabbed him. He had been riding up and down the beach at Benidorm, dressed head to toe in a white silk suit and driving a flaming red Mercedes convertible while accompanied by four blondes. Reporters pointed out that such a disguise was scarcely calculated to avoid attention, but the police said, 'Reverse thinking on the part of a born criminal.' Later when the reporters discovered that the suspect's passport showed that he had been in Benidorm at the time of the murders and had indeed been registered with the local police, the latter said, 'That's a technicality we haven't discussed yet.' That afternoon the suspect was discharged and held a press conference at which he announced that an Italian movie company was going to star him in a picture to be called *The Werewolf of the Autobahn*. He thought that maybe the four blondes would get parts, too.

Benidorm is like that. Looking at the real estate explosion of which it is merely a part, one asks, 'What good has it done the Spaniards?' and the answer is problematic. The building gamblers who have underwrittten the initial costs of the apartment houses have used their small funds to exert a favorable leverage, and since they know how to avoid taxes they have often ended up millionaires. Laborers' wages have been kept low, and although some of the new bars and stores have fallen into Spanish hands, most are owned by foreigners. What seems to have happened is that the low cost of Spanish construction has subsidized good housing for Germans and Swedes with minimum rewards to Spaniards. Thus the precedent set by the conquistadors, who operated a good thing for themselves and for Peru but who benefited Extremadura in no way, is once more being honored. And just as the Extremaduran emigrant builds up Germany in return for a little gold exchange, so the Mediterranean builder erects homes for northerners. What profits do accrue do not benefit the countryside, except for the service jobs created by the new developments. Furthermore, any threat of war over Gibraltar or any upheaval attendant upon the passing of Franco could evaporate the tourist industry overnight and leave these vast buildings vacant. If this were to happen for even a season, with the resultant defaulting on mortgages and the loss of income to stores, the Spanish economy would be seriously compromised. Morally there is also the problem of allowing impoverished Spaniards to see that their government, which cannot build them houses or schools, is able to construct luxury housing for aliens. Few Spaniards, of course, can afford these beach-side palaces.

On the other hand, in several good sites back from the beach in locations like Alicante and Benidorm, Spaniards are beginning to build high-rise apartments for themselves. An official in the Health Administration explains how this works: 'I can't afford to put up the money for a beach house. Nor can the other fellows in my division. So the government has come to us and said, "We won't lend you the money to build an apartment at Alicante, because you're not a good risk. But there will always be someone like you employed by the Health Administration, so we'll lend the money to the Ministry so that they can put up housing at the beach, and it will belong to you as long as you work there." ' In this manner, even though they own no equities, a few of the benefits of the enormous building boom trickle down to Spaniards, but it should be noted that their buildings are not on the beach; those sites are reserved for foreigners because they have the money, and Spaniards, from their long association with the landed families, are habituated to seeing the best of everything remain in the hands of the few.

Wherever I looked along the coast I found evidence of its being converted into an endless ribbon of vacation land. New paradors of clean design were being located at the spots where tourists driving down from France in sports cars would want to spend the night on their way to Torremolinos. Good private hotels were frequent. The narrow road was being widened into one uninterrupted boulevard that would stretch for seven hundred miles. The beach areas had been given fine-sounding names which reverberated with overtones of sun and fun: Costa Brava, Costa Dorada, Costa del Azahar (Orange Blossom), Costa Blanca, Costa del Sol, and beyond Gibraltar on the Atlantic, Costa de la Luz. By this simple device Spain has enhanced the charm of its playlands manyfold. I am told that throughout northern Europe one gains cachet if he says, 'I'm spending my vacation on the Costa del Sol.'

North of Valencia on the Costa del Azahar, I began to experience a sense of excitement, for I was returning to familiar ground. To the left ran the small railroad leading through the mountains to Teruel, and I remembered my exploration years ago; next a road cut off to the right, and as I drove down it I could smell the orange blossoms which had lived in my memory with such persistence, for this was Burriana, that little shipping center where I had first landed in Spain. Could this be the waterfront where the oxen had lugged the heavy barges into the sea? It was now a spacious, jetty-girt harbor with orange boats from Denmark and Germany tied to its piers. Handsome port buildings had been erected to house officials, and almost at the spot where I had first come ashore a high-rise apartment was going up. Not a single item that I remembered still existed, except the Mediterranean, and it had been so pushed around that I scarcely recognized it. Little Burriana, a modern shipping center! Empty, bleak Burriana with its straining oxen, now a location for apartment houses. No transformation then under way in Spain represented so much personal drama as this, and once I had seen it I required no further explanation of what the Spaniards call 'The Miracle of the Mediterranean.'

Once we had passed Castellón de la Plana my wife took over, for we were now approaching that provocative region called Cataluña, which I had never seen but which she had visited some years before, to her intense pleasure. If I said, 'Madrid's an exciting city,' she said, 'But wait till you see Barcelona!' If I liked the park in Sevilla, she said, 'Wait till you see Montjuich in Barcelona.' And no matter what street in Spain I spoke favorably of, she always said, 'It's pleasant, but wait till you see Las Ramblas.'

As we approached the city she asked the driver to keep to the beach road, and there we saw that lovely chain of seaside villages which not even modern builders have been able to spoil, especially Sitges, where we spread a picnic at the farthest point of the pier so that we could look back at the low houses and the village square. 'Three parts of Cataluña are superb,' my wife explained as we finished our first meal in the region. 'Seacoast towns like Sitges, mountain towns like Vich, and Barcelona. You're going to love this part of Spain.'

Her enthusiasm began to infect me, and as we crossed the river with the beautiful name, Llobregat, she pointed to a small mountain on our right, standing with its feet in the sea. 'Montjuich,' she said. 'We'll spend a lot of time here.' When I asked why, she said, 'Half a dozen museums plus a village like none you've seen before.'

She directed the driver to make a series of tricky turns and within a few minutes we found ourselves at the foot of that tall and florid column which dominates the harbor area of the city and which carries at its top a monument to Christopher Columbus. 'When he returned from the New World,' my wife explained, 'he reported to Fernando and Isabel here. Barcelona was the first city in Europe to hear the official account.'

After we paid our respects to Columbus she began to chuckle with delight, clapping her hands and whispering, 'This is what I've been telling you about. Las Ramblas.' It was a wide boulevard consisting of two outer streets for traffic and a spacious central mall for pedestrians, the latter containing newspaper kiosks and many flower stalls. 'Look! There's the woman who sells roses. Over there's the old man who made me my bouquets. Have you ever seen so many flowers?' That day Las Ramblas was indeed a garden, for it was laden with blooms, but I had little time to study them, for now my wife tugged at my arm. 'Look! Look! The bird stalls.' At home we have many birds, wild ones of course, who feed at our window like insatiable gluttons, and we had missed them. Now we were to have, in our front yard as it were, the wonderful bird stalls of Barcelona, and although I shall not be referring to them again, the reader should know that each morning when I started out to explore the city I stopped first to visit with the birds—hundreds of them from all parts of the world—in small, clean cages, well fed and cared for. One can grow to like a city which gives its morning greeting in such a manner.

Las Ramblas proved to be as rewarding as my wife had predicted. It is a heavenly promenade, probably the best I know, and on it I spent many hours. A rambla is a ravine, and this one served as a drainage ditch in time of heavy rain. It is referred to in the plural because it is composed of different sections: La Rambla de los Capuchinos, La Rambla de los Estudios, plus at least three others. It's the center of Barcelona life: here stands the splendid opera house, so plain on the outside, so luxurious inside; here are the theaters, many of the good restaurants, some of the big hotels, and at the inland end, the central Plaza de Cataluña, where the trains and subways focus. At the seashore end, near the Columbus monument, stand the tattoo parlors and the cheap movies. The kaleidoscope is never-ending, for even at four in the morning, when the rest of Spain is asleep, sailors are prowling Las Ramblas and the late restaurants are doing good business.

What seemed to me particularly appealing was that quite close to the boulevard were the city's most varied sights. Off to this side the red light district, where contraceptives, ostensibly forbidden to be sold in Spain, are available in shops which display them in the window. Over here the vast market, one of the best I had seen, close to our hotel and selling a huge variety of fruit and seafood. One stall carried twenty-nine different kinds of olives, large gray-green ones bitter to the taste, sweet ones pitted and stuffed with blanched almonds, tiny black ones which my wife preferred. On the opposite side were the narrow streets which ran to the Gothic quarter, whose concentration of antique buildings alone would attract any visitor, and farther along were the streets leading to this museum or that.

FOLLOWING FACING PAGES: *Most travelers believe that Barcelona's Las Ramblas is the most beautiful street of the north.*

Not the least of the treasures were the bars where dozens of tapas were lined up twenty-four hours a day, including some of the best seafood one could wish. To spend a week in a room facing Las Ramblas, visiting the museums or the Gothic quarter, taking one's meals in the fine restaurants nearby and at night listening to the music of Barcelona, would be an introduction to Spain that might spoil one for what was to come later.

My introduction, following a stroll along Las Ramblas, buying newspapers from London, Paris and New York that I hadn't seen for weeks, was as appropriate as one could have devised. My wife had a letter of introduction to Dr. William Frauenfelder, the Swiss-born director of the Institute of North American Studies in Barcelona, a learned man who knew the city and had a special affection for it. He met us at our hotel and said, 'If you like music there's a concert tonight that will tell you much about Cataluña. Care to attend?' I asked what the program was, and he said, 'That's what makes it so significant. A choral group singing Haydn's *The Seasons.* You've heard the saying? One Catalan starts a business. Two Catalans organize a corporation. Three Catalans form a choral society. In this city music's important.' We said we'd join him, whereupon his manner changed and he became apprehensive. 'I must warn you about one thing. The building in which you'll hear the music is . . . it's unusual. You must prepare yourself for it.' I wondered how one prepared himself for a building, and he explained: 'When you go in, please, please, Mr. and Mrs. Michener, don't gasp or raise your voices. And above all,' here he took us by the hands, 'above all, dear friends, don't laugh. You would destroy your whole effectiveness in Barcelona if you laughed.'

Such a challenge I had not met before. Not long ago my wife and I had been present when Chagall's ceiling at the Paris Opéra was unveiled; we had sat right in front of André Malraux and had behaved rather well, craning our necks back till we were staring into Malraux's face, and shortly thereafter we had attended an opening at Lincoln Center and had not hooted, but apparently the music building in Barcelona was another matter. 'What you had better do,' Dr. Frauenfelder suggested, 'is simply go into the building and allow it to absorb you. Don't say anything. Just look.' We agreed to do this, and at a late hour that night we appeared at the Palau (Palacio) de la Música and one look at the bewildering façade satisfied me that no amount of previous warning from Frauenfelder could have prepared us. The Palau had been erected in 1900 when architects in many parts of the world were getting fed up with old formalisms and fake Greek temples, but the Barcelona architects had had the courage to do something about it. They cast aside balance and austerity and above all they avoided standard types of pillars and capitals. They invented new kinds of pillars, big and small. They devised capitals that looked like turbans and others resembling mushrooms. They tacked on balconies, offset windows, and in one area added a statue of Richard Wagner in his well-known beret. On one shelf someone who looked like Joan of Arc came striding out of a sculptural group, but she was wearing a beard. And wherever I looked I saw not stone or concrete but a mixture of colored ceramic and brick, delightful to the eye, since light played across the surface unevenly, here reflecting as if from a mirror, there deadened by the rough surface of the brick. It was an extraordinary façade, appropriate for the illustration to a Gothic fairy tale, and my wife whispered, 'What must the inside be?'

Gritting my teeth, for I had never before entered such a building except at an amusement park, I followed Dr. Frauenfelder inside, and at the door he whispered, 'Remember, let it flow over you.'

We entered a large auditorium each square inch of which seemed to be covered with florid decoration consisting of pillars covered with broken pieces of ceramic, gigantic sculptural groups featuring flying horses, and colored stones set at odd angles. The effect was that of crawling into an overwhelming grotto, but before I could embarrass Dr. Frauenfelder by laughing, I glanced at the empty stage and saw that its two side walls were covered with eighteen of the strangest statues I had ever seen. They were larger than life size and showed women in medieval costume playing a variety of unfamiliar instruments. They had been carved in a way that was new to me: everything from the waist down was painted flat on the wall in a stylized manner, using pieces of mosaic glass for effect; everything above the waist was carved in stone naturalistically and stood out from the wall like an ordinary statue. The union created an effect that was completely charming, bearing no relationship to reality but a great deal to art.

It was these curious stone women who won me over. They seemed exactly right for the stage of a music hall, and once they established the tone, all the other bizarre phenomena fell into place. Why not have the angle where the proscenium joins the roof covered by rearing horses flying through space? No other symphony hall had such horses, and when I looked closer I saw that Valkyries were riding them. Why not? If this is a place where you come to hear music, why not have a gigantic bust of Beethoven on the right of the stage and someone who looked like Josef Stalin on the left? Dr. Frauenfelder had given me good advice: 'Let it flow over you.' I sat down and did just that, and slowly the wonderful harmony of the place asserted itself; in Rome and Chicago and Tel Aviv I had been in dozens of concert halls, and they'd all been alike and quite uninspiring, but nothing else on earth was like Barcelona's Palau de la Música, and when the chorus of Catalan singers came out and stood on the stage, surrounded by the eighteen stone maidens playing their antique instruments, it was astonishing how the living and the dead united to form one majestic whole.

I fell in love with this crazy hall. I went to it night after night, and no matter what the style of music, the hall seemed to accommodate itself, and what was the more surprising, the stone girls adjusted their manner of playing, too. I heard Illinois Jacquet and Bud Freeman give a jazz concert, and the girls played jazz. I heard a tenor soloist, and they accompanied him. Best of all, I heard one of the Madrid symphonies play a Wagner program, and during the 'Ride of the Valkyries' not only did the eighteen girls join in the music, but high on the ceiling I heard stone horses neighing and warrior maidens shouting, 'Ho-yo-to-ho.'

On the left wall of the stage, as one faces it, the eighth girl plays a drum and wears a high Chinese-type hat beneath which appear long Saxon braids. She has a determined face, with distinct ridges at the corners of her mouth, and her head is twisted in an enchanting manner. She is completely adorable in a resolute, stubborn sort of way, and after the Dama de Elche she is my favorite statue in Spain, for she symbolizes for me the Catalan temperament, and often as I sat in her palace, listening to music, I stared at her and thought not of Haydn or Wagner but of Cataluña.

Next morning I had the good luck to meet José Porter, who runs a bookstore not far from the cathedral and who is a dedicated Catalan. For some time I had been searching for a book relating to one of the greatest Spaniards, Ramón Llull, and I asked Señor Porter to help, but this day he was inflamed over a fact which exacerbates all Spanish intellectuals: the United States had once more used Columbus Day as an excuse for honoring Italians.

'My God!' Porter cried in his jumbled office, his round face getting red with the indignity he was suffering. 'Only a fool believes in the face of modern research that Colón was an Italian. Don't Americans ever read books?'

I pointed out that the best extant biography of Columbus was by an American, Samuel Eliot Morison, and that he had accepted him as an Italian. To this, Porter, whose name was Catalan with French overtones, exploded, 'Nonsense. Do you know nothing of Armand Bernardini-Sjoesedt?' I shook my head, and he said with blistering contempt, 'It's time his works were known in America.'

Porter was a short man with the pugnacious appearance of a prize fighter, and now with a jabbing forefinger he proceeded to give me ten reasons why Columbus was not Italian. 'First, even the standard biographies which claim he is Italian admit that he came to Spain when he was already a middle-aged man, yet not once do we find even a shred of his writing to be in Italian. Second, those who claim he was Italian never agree as to where he was born. Third, some time ago I was invited to address a learned society in the United States, Cleveland I think it was, and the chairman, knowing my research, took me aside and said, "Señor Porter, we're proud to have you with us, but I must insist that in your speech you make no mention of the fact that Colón was not Italian. All of us who are scholars know that to be a fact, but it would be suicide to say so in this country. The Italian politicians are too strong and they'd cut off our funds." So in what you like to call the freest country in the world, the truth was muzzled. Fourth, it was a Jew of Barcelona, Luis de Santángel, who put up the money to finance Colón's trip of discovery, and we in this city believe he did so because of reasons which I will develop as we go along. Fifth, it seems to me significant that when Colón returned to Spain he reported not to Sevilla or Madrid but to Barcelona.' Here I said that this could have been because Fernando and Isabel were here at the time, but he was already into his sixth point. 'When Colón reached this city he handed Luís de Santángel a letter of appreciation for his money, and it was written in Catalan. Seventh, no existe in todo el mundo ninguna carta firmada Colombo [there does not exist in the entire world one letter signed Colombo] but only those signed Colón, which is Catalan for pigeon; in other words, he never wrote in Italian or signed his name that way, but he did write in Catalan and he used a Catalan signature. Eighth, the first missionary to accompany Colón to the New World was a Catalan, Bernard Boyl. Ninth, the foremost soldier to accompany him was also a Catalan, Pere Margarit. Tenth, none of his portraits look Italian, but they do look Catalan.'

Triumphantly Señor Porter threw his arms wide, rose from his desk and ran to stand over me. 'It seems completely clear to me that Cristóbal Colón was a Catalan. Look it up in Bernardini-Sjoesedt.'

It was that afternoon when my wife and I discovered the full flavor of Catalan patriotism. We were taken by subway beneath the boulevard which runs northwest from the Plaza de Cataluña, and at the terminus we climbed out to board a dinky little blue-and-white trolley, which deposited us at the bottom end of a funicular railway. This lifted us to the top of a very steep hill, crowned by a Catholic shrine of some importance, which was surrounded cheek-by-jowl with a rowdy amusement park. 'This is El Tibidabo,' our Catalan guide said, 'the place where the devil tempted Jesus.'

'How did it get that name?'

'Tibi, Latin meaning: To thee. Dabo, Latin for: I give. It was to this spot that the devil brought Jesus when he tempted him with the pleasures of earth.'

'Wait a minute!' I protested. 'The Bible says that . . .'

'My friend, if the devil had taken Jesus to the top of some arid hill in Palestine and Jesus had rejected a hunk of desert, would that have had spiritual significance? But if the devil brought him here, and if Jesus turned down something as glorious as Cataluña, wouldn't that signify? From the top of El Tibidabo he pointed out the glories of his land. 'Down there the seacoast, the best in Spain. Back here the sacred mountain of Cataluña, Montserrat. There the Llobregat coming out of the hills. And before us at our feet Barcelona, like a carpet of beauty. This spot . . . right here on El Tibidabo . . . ' He was overcome with emotion, but with his right hand inscribed a complete circle, encompassing one of the loveliest views in Spain. Later he said, 'If Our Lord was not tempted by what he saw on El Tibidabo, he was beyond temptation.'

Succeeding days were filled with trips illustrating many different aspects of Catalan life, and although it would be instructive to report the richness we found, it will be wiser to concentrate on our experiences with the intellectual activity of the region, because Barcelona specializes in this, and the reader may be surprised to discover how fine its quality is. That evening Dr. Frauenfelder arranged a visit to the home of a prominent hostess, where I had the good luck to sit with a spirited Catalan, José María Poal, a medical doctor eager to get me started right in his city. Approvingly he said, 'Last night I saw you at the Palau de la Música, listening to Haydn being sung in Catalan. A proper introduction.' Dr. Poal was a short man, as most Catalans are, with very dark hair, a beard but no mustache, and heavy glasses. Like many men from this region he was a brilliant talker and commanded three or four languages; ideas were a challenge to him, and when I asked a question, he would cry, 'Ah, yes! I was thinking about that the other day,' and he took pleasure in explaining his thought processes, or those of the typical Catalan, as if I were a student, which indeed I was. 'Yes! What is a Catalan? I was pondering this only yesterday and came to the conclusion that we must be understood as the diametric opposite of the Hungarian, who came out of Asia and maintained himself as an enclave in the midst of surrounding European peoples. We're the perfect mixture, a fusion of Celt-Iberian, Phoenician, Greek, Roman, French, Aragonese, Catalan, with a sprinkling of Visigoth, Mussulman and Jew. Better than any other group in Spain, we're able to see the world as a whole . . . especially Europe.'

I asked Dr. Poal to identify the salient characteristics of the Catalan, and without referring to past contemplation he cried, 'Not art. Not architecture. Not writing, although we've had some great ones. Music. Pinch a man on the streets of Barcelona and if he doesn't cry out in pitch, he's not a Catalan. Three years ago the choral group you heard last night was in financial trouble. Had to have ten million pesetas or go out of business. A group of us went quietly through the streets of this city, telling our friends, "The voice of Cataluña is about to be silenced. The chorus that inspired your father and mine in the dark days is broke . . . busted . . . the strings on the lute are torn." Within twenty-four hours we had the ten million pesetas, for a Catalan would rather miss a meal than his music.'

Dr. Poal reminded me of one fact which Americans tend to forget. 'The influence of France on Spain has been considerable, and usually positive. Much of our best thinking has been inspired by French precept, and this is particularly true of Cataluña. In this room tonight I would suppose that better than fifty percent speak French and more than that read it. At many stages of history we were part of France, and if one were to carve out a linguistic Cataluña, much of it would be found over the Pyrenees in France. A man like myself . . . I feel a tremendous pull toward the Pyrenees. They exert a kind of fascination on the Catalan mind. Always keep your eye out for the French influence in Spain. It's usually constructive.'

What Dr. Poal overlooked telling me was something I already knew, that France did not reciprocate the warm feeling of Spaniards like Poal. Agitation for a separate Catalan state, or for a separate Basque, arose in northern Spain but involved substantial areas of southern France, for there were about as many Catalans and Basques living in France as there were in Spain. Therefore, this area of Spain was something of a headache to France. Contemptuously, French thinkers repeated the aphorism 'Africa begins just south of the Pyrenees,' and most Frenchmen dismissed Spain as something so exotic that no rationalist could comprehend her. In French regions adjacent to Cataluña the feeling was exacerbated in 1939, when hundreds of thousands of Spanish patriots fled through the mountains to take up what they considered temporary residence in France; they remained for more than a quarter of a century. Finally, during many periods of history, Cataluña formed a part of France and was governed by Frenchmen, so that it can be considered a defected province but one that France was well rid of.

I thought it best not to raise such questions but I did pose two others. First, what was the future of Cataluña? 'Ah yes! I've been thinking about this a great deal and I know of no one in my acquaintance who dreams any longer of Cataluña as a separate state. At one time it could have been free . . . like Switzerland . . . or maybe a union of Basques and Navarrese of Spain and France . . . a rough confederation of some kind . . . but those days are gone. Everyone knows it. We must integrate fully with Spain, and everyone I know is eager to do so. But I would lie if I did not say that I feel more Catalan than anyone else in this room or perhaps in all Barcelona. My heart throbs to the rhythm of this land. I write poetry in Catalan. I should. It was my grandfather who compiled the Catalan grammar. Montserrat, Vich . . . these places are part of me and I would die rather than betray Cataluña. But politically our future rests in being a creative part of Spain. God, how the rest of Spain needs us!'

Second, with the continued influx of immigrants from Extremadura and Andalucía, would not the spirit of Cataluña be watered down until it vanished? 'Now, now! I've just been reading a fine book on that very subject. You've got to read it. Francisco Candel's *Los otros catalanes* [The Other Catalans]. It's a probing analysis of this very problem, and Señor Candel claims that it works the other way. The Andalusian comes up here, sees the wonder of Cataluña . . . the schools, the hospitals, yes, and the big factories where men earn a decent wage. Señor Michener, in five years he's a better Catalan than I am.' I said I doubted this because my experience in other nations had been contrary, to which Dr. Poal replied, 'Other nations, yes. But Cataluña is special. Because we are so mixed in our heritage we are not narrow-minded little provincials. We have a bigness of spirit . . . a singing of the heart. This communicates itself, especially to people like the Andalusians, who've lived in a bitter, narrow world.'

As a result of my talk with Dr. Poal, I acquired a typed copy of Dr. Salustiano del Campo's research paper, 'On the Assimilation of Immigrants in Cataluña,' completed only a few weeks earlier. To me its statistics were interesting, because I had already witnessed in other parts of Spain the passion with which poverty-stricken families had said, 'He's lucky. He moved to Barcelona.' Here was a study reporting the results of these moves.

'Why did you immigrate to Barcelona?' Nearly half replied, 'Because I wanted to find a better life,' but many made the tragic confession, 'In my village I was unable to earn a living.'

'Has the move worked out well?' More than half replied that it had exceeded the hopes they had had when they left their villages. Only ten percent said they had been disappointed.

'What kind of effect has the immigration had on Cataluña?' Among those moving in, more than half believed that Cataluña had been lucky to get them; among the Catalans who had to make places for the immigrants, only a third thought the influx had been beneficial. About half doubted that the move was for the best.

'Are the immigrants learning to speak Catalan?' The testimony of both the immigrants and the native Catalans among whom they worked was unequivocal: very few learn Catalan. This is probably for the good of Cataluña, since it will make assimilation with the rest of Spain easier, but it must create apprehensions in the minds of fervid Catalans like Dr. Poal.

Then followed a series of tables which I found fascinating. They reported on Dr. del Campo's attempt to identify the 'social distance' which separated the various groups of newcomers. People from twelve regions of Spain, such as Extremadurans and Andalusians, were listed, accompanied by people from twelve foreign countries, such as Frenchmen and North Americans. A variety of questions was then put to Catalans and immigrants alike, with the results shown in the table on page 563.

It is interesting but not surprising that in the choice of marriage partner both Catalan and immigrant preferred mates from any part of Spain, even ill-regarded Murcia, to foreigners; religion had much to do with this, because if one chose a Spaniard, no matter how lowly, he was at least sure of catching a Catholic. In all columns the social distance between the Murcian and the highest-ranking foreigner was considerable.

I concluded from my reading of Dr. del Campo's study that the dilution of Cataluña was inescapable. Immigration into the area is more massive than I have been able to convey; word has gone out to the other

As a Catalan, which region's people do you like best?	As an immigrant, which region's people do you like best?	If you were to marry, from which would you choose?
1 Cataluña	1 Aragón	1 Cataluña
2 Valencia	2 Cataluña	2 Valencia
3 Baleares	3 Navarra	3 Baleares
4 Basque region	4 Castilla	4 Basque region
5 Navarra	5 Valencia	5 Navarra
6 Aragón	6 Asturias	6 Aragón
7 Asturias	7 Basque region	7 Asturias
8 Castilla	8 Extremadura	8 Castilla
9 Extremadura	9 Andalucía	9 Extremadura
10 Galicia	10 Baleares	10 Andalucía
11 Andalucía	11 Galicia	11 Galicia
12 Murcia	12 Murcia	12 Murcia
13 France	13 Mexico	13 Mexico
14 Mexico	14 France	14 France
15 Italy	15 Brazil	15 Brazil
16 Brazil	16 North America	16 Italy
17 Germany	17 Italy	17 North America
18 England	18 Germany	18 Germany
19 Sweden	19 England	19 Sweden
20 North America	20 Sweden	20 England
21 Argentina	21 Morocco	21 Argentina
22 Venezuela	22 Argentina	22 Venezuela
23 Morocco	23 Venezuela	23 Norway
24 Norway	24 Norway	24 Morocco

parts of Spain that here is the good place to live and that for generations to come there will be jobs along the Catalan coast. I would expect the immigration to increase rather than diminish, for if I were a young Spanish laborer in some backward Extremaduran or Andalusian village I would cut out for Barcelona tomorrow. I would be homesick, to be sure, and I might long for the intimacy and love of my native pueblo, but it would see me no more. I would not subject myself to its humiliation when I could live in the freedom of Barcelona.

Since my earliest days in Spain I had wanted to see how the publishing business operated, for I bought many books and knew a few writers, but always I had been advised, 'Hold that till you reach Barcelona. It's the publishing capital of Spain.' So one morning I reported to Ediciones Destino, whose president, Señor José Vergés Matas, proved generous with his time. He was an unusually handsome man who looked to be about forty-two, with prematurely white hair and a large mobile face featuring even teeth and a modern type of eyeglass. 'The old firms die out,' he said gravely. 'You won't believe it, but I founded this company. Yes. First we published magazines and made a big success. This one here,' and he showed me his firm's leader, a magazine of opinion and news, 'sells about sixty thousand copies a week.' I looked at the cover and saw that it was in its thirtieth year.

'Did you say you founded this?'

'Yes. Thirty years ago.' He was obviously somewhat older than the forty-two I had guessed. Then he added. 'I was quite young at the time, believe me. Today I wouldn't have the courage. Well, when the magazines made money we turned to books, and in Spain that's an adventure because in this country we don't have many readers. In North America you have two hundred million people.' I was constantly being surprised at how much educated Spaniards knew about my country and how little we know about theirs. 'Some good books in your country can hope to sell a hundred thousand copies. In Spain we have one-sixth as many people, about thirty-four million, so we should expect to sell one-sixth as many books, or sixteen thousand. How many do you suppose we do sell?'

I knew that Spanish readers bought fewer books than Americans did, just as Americans bought fewer than English or Japanese, but I had no idea that the editions of important books were so minute. Señor Matas said, 'We're lucky if we sell three thousand copies. We print that number, hopefully, and we keep our costs so low that we break even if we sell twelve hundred. We put only fifteen hundred in covers. We bind the rest only if we sell our first effort. If not, and this is usually the case, we throw away the second fifteen hundred sets of sheets.

'We pay about the same royalties to authors that you do. On the first eight thousand copies, ten percent. On the next two thousand, twelve percent. Above ten thousand copies, fifteen percent. But not many writers can live off what they earn publishing books in Spain.'

I had noticed on the shelves lining his office a series of what looked like novels, all published in the same format and stretching for some distance around the room. When I asked what they were, his wide face broke into a smile of satisfaction. 'One of the best ideas I ever had. The Premio Eugenio Nadal. He was an editor of ours. We've given this prize each year since 1944, and we've found some sensationally fine books. All novels. In 1947 Miguel Delibes' *The Shadows of the Cypresses Lengthen,* in 1959 Ana María Matute's *Earliest Memories.* And of course this one in 1946, José María Gironella's *A Man.* Because we've held our standards so high, and partly because of luck, we can assure the author who wins this prize a sale of at least twenty thousand. He earns some real money if he wins the Premio Nadal. Maybe four hundred manuscripts will be submitted.'

Señor Vergés told me that of all the books published in Spain, ninety percent are handled by Barcelona firms, and of books of high quality, about ninety-eight percent. Much of the actual printing, however, is done on big presses in cities like Bilbao. 'What we're finding profitable is joint publication with houses in Italy, Berlin, Geneva and Amsterdam. We bring out expensive books in color, like the paintings of Goya or *Life in Prehistoric Times.* We print all the editions, regardless of language, in Switzerland and especially Italy, which seems to have the best color presses in the world these days, and this enables us to keep costs so low that we all make money. But here is something we do that you don't do any longer in America, and our authors appreciate it.'

He pointed to a shelf on which rested thirty volumes, bound in leather and most handsomely designed, representing the complete works of a novelist held in much esteem locally, *The Complete Works of Josep Pla.* 'They sell for six dollars and forty cents a copy and large numbers of people feel that they must have the complete set.'

'When did Pla die?' I asked.

'He's still alive. We do this for our living authors,' and he pointed to four or five other such series.

I picked up one of Señor Vergés' books and saw that it was not in Spanish but in Catalan. 'There's a problem for you!' he said. 'Of our thirty-four million population, thirty-one million read Spanish and they will buy three thousand copies of a book. Only three million read Catalan, but they will also buy three thousand copies of a book published in Catalan. Therefore, it's just as profitable for us to publish in Catalan as it is in Spanish.' I could not believe this, but Señor Vergés referred to two editions of Truman Capote's *In Cold Blood,* one in Spanish, one in Catalan. 'The publisher will sell about the same number of each,' he said. 'Catalans read. They're the Bostonians of Spain.'

Recalling the way in which English and American authors jump from one publisher to another, I pointed to the Premio Nadal novels and asked, 'When you give a man the prize, are you able to hold on to him for his subsequent books?'

Apparently this was as touchy a point in Barcelona as it was in New York, for Señor Vergés frowned and said, 'Alas, the prize is often the nudge they need to go off to some other publisher. Look at him.' He pointed at José María Gironella's novel, the winner in 1946. 'He left us, and you know what happened with his later books.'

Friends had arranged for me to meet Gironella, Spain's phenomenal success. His last three books, dealing with the Civil War, had been tremendously read, *The Cypresses Believe in God*, *A Million Dead* and the one currently in the windows of every bookstore, *Peace Has Broken Out*. Within a few weeks of publication the last had sold a hundred and fifty thousand copies, fifty times normal expectations, which would be comparable to the unheard-of figure of five million for the United States. In other words, Gironella was the man who broke the restraints of Spanish publishing.

I found him in a neat, book-crowded apartment, with a group of unexpected works lying handy to his desk: a life of Franklin D. Roosevelt, a critical study of Lenin, biographies of Gandhi, Stalin, De Gaulle. William Shirer's *Rise and Fall of the Third Reich* was prominent and on a table by the davenport Capote's *En sangre fría*.

Gironella was a slim, tense man in his late forties, I judged, although my experience with the publisher had somewhat unnerved me where guessing ages was concerned. He smiled easily and said, 'I'm surprised a norteamericano writer would want to speak with me. When my first book was published in America, Spanish Marxists living abroad crucified it and charged me with being a Fascist lackey. The publisher, I won't bore you with his name, wrote and told me he wouldn't be taking any more of my books because he couldn't afford to have a Fascist on his list. Later somebody told me that the real reason he cut me off was that my book didn't sell very well. I'd cut an author off too, if he was a disappointment financially as well as politically.

'Actually, I doubt that the tag "Fascist lackey" applies to me. At home I'm accused of being a dangerous liberal. I believe the fact is that I have described the war pretty much as it occurred, and to do this would enrage norteamericanos who saw it otherwise and Spaniards who had their own version.'

Gironella, who in appearance reminded me of Arthur Miller, had traveled widely throughout Europe. 'Almost all the countries. Communist too. I understand you've been to Asia. I found it wildly exciting. Japan, India, Egypt. This year I want to see Israel. I don't understand how a serious writer these days can judge his own terrain if he knows no other.'

I asked him why he continued to live in Cataluña, and he grinned. 'I grew up in a town near Gerona [Catalan, Girona]. I suppose that's where my family got its name. Gironella. The Girl from Girona. It's a grand region. The other day this fellow heard a lecture on the glories of Castilian literature, and which writers did the speaker refer to? Valle Inclán, a Galician. Pardo Bazán, another Galician. Ibáñez, a Valencian. Pío Baroja, a Basque. Unamuno, a Basque. Lorca, an Andalusian. Jiménez, another Andalusian. And at the end of the list he referred to me. a Catalan. I love the regions of Spain.'

I asked whether he thought the influx of Andalusians would modify

Flower seller on Las Ramblas

Cataluña. 'For the better. In my little town they've opened a night club. Stiff, suspicious Catalans go there, listen to the guitars till midnight, then raise their right forefinger, whisper one reserved "Ole" and go home satisfied that they've participated in the glories of Old Spain.'

I saw a good deal of the book business in Spain and constantly had the feeling that it stood about where it had in the United States fifty years ago. There was much peddling of illustrated Bibles on street corners, where fast-talking men in overcoats spread their big volumes on collapsible tables and buttonholed people as they climbed out of the subway or left the cinema. The Bibles seemed poorly put together and were far below the quality of similar ventures in Italy or Germany.

What to me was wholly incomprehensible was the hawking of complete sets of authors like Honoré de Balzac and Victor Hugo in poor translation encased in cheap impermanent binding. Some of these sets, whose authors I cannot now remember, were truly grotesque; the average Spanish family had no conceivable need for the collected works of Bret Harte, for such books could not possibly relate to their needs. There seemed to be two reasons for this phenomenon. Spain did not encourage or at times even allow honest discussion of contemporary problems, so it was understandable that publishers would look to foreign literatures for sets of books which might sell because of clandestine reputations. Certainly the ideas of Balzac and Hugo were at odds with those of Generalísimo Franco's Spain, but they were French ideas and therefore to be discounted. For example, one could not possibly publish in Spain the kind of book attacking Franco that one publishes in the United States attacking whoever is President at the time, nor would one publish a novel on any significant contemporary issue, so for first-rate treatment of the human condition one must look abroad. The second reason we have already uncovered. Spanish families love to buy sets of books, whether they read them or not, and since Balzac wrote many books, he produces an impressive set.

This accounts, too, for the sale of encyclopedias, often wretched in scholarship. One finds sets of volumes on almost anything, not as banal perhaps as the comparable volumes now being peddled in the United States on our history, the nature of science or great moments of discovery, but still pretty bad. From time to time I consulted these miserable works in search of rudimentary data and they had nothing to offer, yet they appear proudly in many homes, gathering a dust of respectability that is rarely disturbed and never with profit.

On the other hand, Spain has produced one of the world's outstanding encyclopedias, the great *Espasa-Calpe* in some ninety volumes, publication of which began in the 1920s. It is a reputable work, unbalanced perhaps in its emphasis on Spanish history and thought, but with a mature coverage that makes one wonder how Spain, with so few readers, could have produced such a work, whereas the United States, with infinitely greater resources, has not. Of course, the *Espasa-Calpe* is not found in many private homes, but Señor Porter, the bookseller, had one in his, and I was surprised in other homes I visited to see the endless rows of this extraordinary work. It was the exhibition set nonpareil, but it was also a gold mine of material in which to prospect. For example, the article on *Don Quijote* covered pages 1117–1214 of Volume 48, and like several other such entries, was a book in itself, for the pages of *Espasa-Calpe* are quite large. Experts told me that in coverage of topics the Spanish encyclopedia surpassed Mussolini's distinguished *Enciclopedia Italiana* and in thoroughness of treating those topics, the *Britannica*. It was, however, less distinguished in scholarship than the famous Eleventh Edition of the *Britannica*, but not inferior to the later editions.

This matter of Spanish scholarship baffled me. Repeatedly I bought books whose titles led me to expect an orderly development of an idea, as for example, *History of Spanish Colonization in Africa*, only to find that the accurate title should have been *Some Casual Reflections on Random Aspects of a Gentleman's Travels in Our African Colonies and Elsewhere*, in which the first chapter dealt with a trip the author once made to Kenya, the second with a hippopotamus hunt in the Congo, the third with a hortatory essay on the need for more Catholic missions, and the fourth with God knows what. I doubt if there is another country in the world, except Japan, in which books are so poorly organized and so dependent upon the personal whims of the writer. Especially aggravating is the fact that few Spanish books contain indexes, at least none of the hundreds I have bought, and some which pretend to scholarly completeness, such as the history of the zarzuela which I have before me as I write, lack both index and table of contents, even though they are the kind of book one consults for particular items rather than reading seriatim. Can one take seriously the scholarship of a man who fails to provide even a table of contents?

On the other hand, if, as I sometimes think, the measure of a contemporary society is whether it can support poets, Spain is far ahead of the United States, for poetry is published in Spain, as it is in Russia and Israel, and it is not much published, with honorable exceptions, in the United States. A man in Spain can build an enviable reputation from a few volumes of poems and is then held in an esteem which knows no parallel in America, for poets like Lorca and Jiménez are worshiped in Spain.

I met many Spanish writers and studied the lives of more, and concluded that there is no nation in the world where it is so good to be a dead writer. Wherever I went I saw placards announcing grand assemblies of Homenaje a (Homage to) Benito Pérez Galdós (1843–1920) or Vicente Blasco Ibáñez (1867–1928) or Pío Baroja (1872–1956). I attended three such homenajes to writers, and they were moving affairs at which men rose to give orations the like of which I had not heard for fifty years. All aspects of the life and writings of the man in question were reviewed and true homage was paid him as a continuing cultural force. In the parks I found statues to these writers and in the newspapers a constant series of essays on their significance. Subjected to such a continuing barrage, I began to believe that Pedro Antonio de Alarcón, the author of the story from which Falla's *El sombrero de tres picos* was adapted, was a much greater writer than Walt Whitman, because I had never heard of anyone in Camden holding a Homage to Walt Whitman. He was dead, so forget him because in life he had been troublesome.

The case of Pío Baroja is interesting. This acidulous Basque wrote strongly anti-clerical novels, as did Blasco Ibáñez, and during their life-times they were anathema, but now that they are dead they are the subject of frequent homenajes and their accomplishments are praised as having brought real honor to Spain. I was present when the tenth anniversary of Baroja's death was observed, and the enmity which the state had held against him as an anti-clerical radical was forgiven and he was ushered into the pantheon with editorials and homenajes that would have been impossible even five years before. In a way, the same thing has happened to Hemingway; he was a foe of the Franco government and while he lived was more or less persona non grata, but now his greatness is being acknowledged: 'A few days before the death of Baroja, he was visited by Hemingway, who wished to tell the old man that the Nobel Prize for Literature which the norteamericano had won belonged really to Baroja. Hemingway, who was a gallant man, spoke only the truth and we are proud that he had the elegance to proclaim it when others of less pundonor would have remained silent.'

No American writer that I know is going to have in death the kind of immortality that Spain confers on her authors; I was present when Dr. Gregorio Marañón died, a kind of Charles Beard plus André Maurois, and one would have thought that the king had died. Indeed, it was a kingly role that Marañón played, that of a great medical man who wrote essays on Spain's periods of ascendancy. But when I dug deeper I found again and again that mournful refrain, 'Pío Baroja lived poorly on his meager in-come,' or, 'After a life of complete privation he died miserably,' and when I began to question not one person in the creative fields but many, I found that whereas it was wonderful in Spain to be a dead writer, to be a living one was something else. The Premio Nadal, which Señor Vergés' company awards each year, brings the author only $3,333, and few can logically hope to win it. Most struggle a lifetime in near-poverty, abused by society and held in contempt by its rulers. If they write honestly they run the risk of being thrown into jail; if they do not write constantly they starve; and their funeral dirge is always: 'They struggled to make a living and died filled with bitterness and remorse.' I went through a period of acute depression when reviewing the lives of the gifted men who wrote the zarzuelas; so frequent was the statement 'With his four chief works he made millions of pesetas for the managers of the theater, but himself died in poverty' that I suspended my studies. The literary condition in Spain is rather the reverse of that in the States; American writers earn a good living but play no significant role in their society; Spanish writers earn almost nothing, but when dead they are enshrined.

One of the aspects of Spanish intellectual life which struck me repeatedly was the fact, reflected in these pages, that civic leadership so often rested in the hands of medical men. They wrote the best books, made the most daring statements and were revered as the element of society that could be trusted to support good movements. The doctors of Spain formed the stable, liberal cadre and I wondered why this was. I therefore asked a government official if he could arrange for me to meet a typical Spanish doctor who might care to discuss the matter.

I was taken to a huge apartment building, Avenida Generalísimo Franco, 520, whose rickety basketlike elevator crept precariously up a good many floors, opening first on one side then on the other, for it was all doors. It ejected me onto a vast, gloomy ledge with a central well that dropped straight down to where the doorman looked like a midget; it could have been designed by Piranesi. A somber door standing back from the chasm was marked Dr. Arturo Fernández-Cruz, and when the maid opened it I was admitted to the richly decorated apartment of a man of taste. Paintings hung on the walls, which contained many bookcases. Fine rugs and antiques, including what I took to be a valuable Chinese ivory of Confucius and a Thai ceramic of a princess, occupied me until the doctor appeared, and no man could have been better prepared to explain the dynamism of Spanish doctors than he.

He was a cyclonic talker and a man of wide interests. Of medium height, with a head of dark hair that reached down toward his eyes, he wore a mustache which seemed constantly in motion. His eyes were expressive, and his cheeks puckered in when he found delight in some idea which he had begun to offer only tentatively but which had matured into a kind of truth. Because he sat with his back to a solid wall of medical books in varied languages, many of them having been printed in the United States, he gave the impression of being a good medical man, which my friends assured me he was, but it was his reaction to other subjects which captivated me, and I think it wisest if I simply repeat his flood of ideas, for they better than my comments on them will provide a picture of the Spanish medic.

'I suppose I carry a strong strain of the Visigoth in me. I was born in Sevilla, of the middle-class type that they describe as "muy fino y muy frío" [very fine and very cold], but I must have had Germanic inheritance because of the way my mind works. I was a professor at the medical school in Santiago de Compostela, in the heart of Galicia, where a man's character is all-important. "Of course Juan's a good violinist, he comes from such a good family." I prefer it here in Cataluña, where performance is what counts. "Juan claims he's a violinist. Here's a fiddle. Let's hear him play."

'The ideal Catalan, as I study the type in my office, would be Ben Franklin. If you understand his practical nature, you understand Cataluña. No, one more thing would be necessary. He'd also have to be able to sing.

'But you came here to talk about doctors. Remember this. There is no analogy between the role of the doctor in Spain and the doctor in any other country. Our tradition stems from the great Jew Maimonides and the Muslim Averroës. A sick man must be cured, factually. We are not prone to philosophizing about medicine or the good life or the nature of cure. A man is sick, cure him. We set a high pragmatic standard and this gets to be known in the community. From Maimonides and Averroës we also inherit the high position enjoyed by the doctor. This was never a Spanish trait. It was a Jewish and a Muslim trait, and fortunately for us it was adopted by our society.

'Our pragmatic attitude to medicine allows us much mental space for speculation in other fields. No group in Spain reads as much as we do. In all languages. We're the educated ones . . . in medicine and everything else. You see my books. I don't buy them because they have pretty covers, but because I need to know what's going on in the world.

'This means that we come to have the reputation of knowing more than we really do. But we try to know, therefore we are applauded by the people. Oftentimes the doctor is the only educated man a family will know. His opinion is given more weight perhaps than it deserves. But if you look at Spain's position in the world at large, you find that it is only our doctors who stand at the top when judged internationally. We produce good men who do their best to keep up with what's happening in Vienna and Massachusetts General.

'Now, because of our unusual position in Spanish life, we find ourselves constantly invited to lead liberal movements. I suppose doctors the world over incline toward the left in politics, because we see society as a whole. We are driven to become intermediaries because of the trust imposed upon us, and as learned men we must lean toward social justice and a more liberal interpretation of society.

'But let's confine ourselves to Spain. The average family knows only two persons in whom it can trust, the doctor and the priest, and since the priest is obligated to support a certain status quo of which his church is a major component, the family can look only to the doctor for the liberal interpretation toward which it may be groping.

'I've thought about this a great deal, because in Spain, doctors have been foremost champions of advance, as they are everywhere, and I've come to two conclusions. We are able to espouse liberal causes where others would be afraid to do so, because we have a prepared position to which we can retreat. If we are savagely rebuffed in attempting to get better housing, we can still live, because doctors are needed. We can absorb enormous defeats and still live. A priest might be thrown out of the Church. A newspaper editor might be fired and be unable to find work. But we have that prepared position.

'The second factor is that because medicine was for so long the prerogative of Jews and Muslims, children of the best families won't go into it. Only the middle-class families provide medical students. When I was a student in Sevilla we had a young duque in class. He asked me one day what I was going to be, and when I said, "Medico," he said, "My God, I'd rather be a bullfighter." To boys like me medicine was a form of democratic opportunity, the escape from mediocrity, and that's true of all the doctors you see. Middle-class origins, first-class brains. That's a powerful combination. But having come from such backgrounds, we have a natural interest in social betterment, as all doctors should, and I judge that accounts for our favorable position.'

The longer I talked with Dr. Fernández-Cruz the more obvious it became that he felt a personal identification with the Maimonides–Averroës tradition, and like thousands of his associates, was ready to act upon it. One of the most moving things in Spain is the frequency with which one sees in small towns the rude statue to some local doctor who had led the community's fight for social justice. In Badajoz, in Teruel, in a dozen nameless little villages I had seen these evocative monuments: 'To Dr. Teófilo Gómez, predilected son of this village, to whom we are indebted.' It seemed to me that about half the books I read on recondite subjects of Spanish life were written by medical men like Marañón, but my lasting memory is not of their scholarship but of their unfailing championship of liberal causes.

On the other hand, I also noticed that no matter where I went, it was the doctor's house that was the most luxurious, his car the biggest. If he read more books than anyone else in the community, it was partly because he alone had the funds to buy them. I felt sure that the schoolteachers I met would have enjoyed reading more, but their condition was so pitiful that they barely kept ahead of their students; if the condition of the doctors of Spain represents one of the best aspects of the country, that of the schoolteachers represents one of the worst.

There was one publishing company which I particularly wanted to see, much to the astonishment of my Spanish friends, for I thought its operations threw much light on one aspect of life in Spain. To explain, I must detour to a cinema hall on Las Ramblas that carried a banner which I had seen across Spain: 'Marisol: *Cabriola*.' Along with the banner were motion-picture stills showing a delightful blond girl of unascertainable age named Marisol; when supposed to be winsome, she was photographed as

573

thirteen, but when sexy in a refined sort of way, she looked more like nineteen. In either case she was adorable and apparently most of Spain thought so, for her movies were the most popular then being shown. I had intended for some six years to see a Marisol show and there would never be a better opportunity.

All Marisol pictures were alike, I was told, but this one had special features in that it had been written and directed by Mel Ferrer when he was not engaged in various movies that his wife, Audrey Hepburn, was shooting in Europe. And Cabriola was the name of a famous horse ridden in the ring by the Andalusian bullfighter Angel Peralta. Shortly after completing the film, Cabriola had been killed while fighting at Alicante or somewhere in the south, so that the movie was a kind of funeral ceremony for a notable beast.

The theater and all that transpired within was a fairyland. Children were everywhere, waiting for their idol to appear, but there were also many middle-aged women, wondering why their daughters had not turned out as well as Marisol. When the curtain finally opened, after eighteen minutes of advertising slides, a lovely gasp rose from the crowd and a story of complete improbability unfolded.

Marisol, photographed with a skill that I admired, came on screen as a gamin with a beat-up old horse and a cart in which she collected garbage in the slums of Madrid. She lived with her younger brother (this was apparently de rigueur in a Marisol film, since it allowed little girls to imagine how much fun it would be if they could escape parental control) in a makeshift hovel on the edge of the public dump. In addition to the horse that pulled her dump wagon she had another, one of the most beautiful mares ever bred (played by Peralta's Cabriola, a gelding), but how she got her or why was never explained. Through a variety of plot complexities that were winsome if not logical, Marisol trained her horse to fight in the bullring, and with no explanation as to where the money came from, she suddenly appeared with the horse at the ranch of Angel Peralta on the edge of Las Marismas. She was dressed in a whipcord costume that must have cost four hundred dollars.

Now, all this time she was dressed as a boy, and part of the delight the children experienced was in whispering to their friends, 'She's really a girl but the matador doesn't know.' Since Marisol sings, an orchestra had to appear in Las Marismas. Since she dances rather well, a famous flamenco male dancer appeared with her in a dream sequence. I think one would have to be a misogynist not to enjoy such a film if seen in the presence of young girls and middle-aged women, gasping with apprehension when little Marisol found herself by accident in the middle of the bullring facing an enraged animal from whom Angel Peralta would rescue her. And of course there came that electric moment when the matador discovered that she was a girl, so that the film could end with her in another mysteriously provided costume riding behind him in the grand parade of Sevilla's feria.

The publishing company I wanted to visit was called Editorial Felicidad, and there could not have been a happier choice of names, because it published the small hard-bound books which were released in conjunction with each Marisol film. They consisted of the plot of the film, or the major incident of the plot, told in simple words and illustrated with scenes from the picture. The books did a tremendous business not only in Spain but also in Latin America, for Marisol was just as popular in Buenos Aires as in Barcelona.

'We publish an edition of thirty thousand for Spain,' one of the Felicidad people told me. 'For Latin America even larger. With *Cabriola*, because the horse is popular in its own right, we'll probably do better. And you must remember that a serious novel is lucky if it sells three thousand. The books are sold in bookstores. I saw one the other day that had sixteen separate Marisol titles, although there may have been some Rocío Dúrcal ones mixed in.' Rocío is a late rival, a marvelous young lady with a face that is perfectly square and a somewhat better figure than Marisol's.

'Some years ago we published a biography of Marisol. Huge edition. You can't buy a copy anywhere but maybe the president of our company will mail you one to North America. [He never did; no copies available.] She was born in the Calle Refino in Málaga to a middle-class family and her talent was mysterious. At the age of seven she was a professional, and the significant fact about her is that in all the following years she never made one false move. She must have had incredibly good advice. You've seen how careful they are in photographing her. Everything must be just right. A million parents in Spain pray at night, "If we must have a girl, let her be like Marisol." I feel that way myself.

'Boys starting to read will often buy our books, but mostly they sell to little girls and middle-aged women. But we find that even older boys will sometimes peep into the books and whisper to one another, "Well, if all girls were like Marisol it wouldn't be so bad." '

I observed two interesting things about the Marisol fad. The situations in which she finds herself are those which could be especially alluring to girls being brought up in the restrictive customs of the nineteenth century. *Marisol Goes to College. Marisol on TV. Marisol, Girl Reporter. Marisol, Detective. Marisol Learns Ballet. Marisol, Sportswoman.* I doubt that one can present to the young girls of Spain such a standard of freedom without its having some effect.

The other facet of the craze is that in most of her pictures the plot, as we have seen, gives her an excuse to appear in men's dress, and most effectively too, but in this respect her rival Rocío is even more appealing, for she has a figure that seems to blossom when shown in formal men's wear. This is, of course, a carry-over from the tradition we met in the

zarzuela, for when a society aggravates the difference between the sexes, postulating a completely manly man and a womanly woman, the temptation to burlesque the nonsense is great. Unfortunately, this is a low form of art, as proved by that endless flow of abominable English movies in which sailors are given an excuse to dress as women, to the boundless delight of the unsophisticated British audience. In the legitimate theater next to my hotel on Las Ramblas I had an opportunity to see a play I had missed in Pamplona, *La tía de Carlos,* which Spain's fine rubber-faced comedian, Paco Martínez Soria, takes back and forth across Spain, year after year, because audiences love to see him caper as the old lady from Brazil. He does a fine job, featuring long monologues in a crazy cracked voice; his nephew's fiancée asks him if they dance in Brazil, and this is good for a nine-minute explanation of the rhumba, but the significant fact about his popularity is that like Marisol in men's clothes, it is based on the exaggerated difference between the sexes. Also, he is very funny.

In Barcelona books are important, but music is king. My wife and I discovered this when we wanted to attend the opening of the opera at the famous Liceo, which stood just down Las Ramblas from where we were staying. 'We can get you tickets but they'll be dreadfully expensive,' the government official said, and I nodded. Then he frowned. 'But I'm afraid that even if you're willing to pay, it won't do much good, because you norteamericanos don't travel with dress suits.' I said I didn't have one, and he shrugged his shoulders. 'I could get you the tickets, but without a dress suit they wouldn't allow you in.' I explained that we would be happy to sit upstairs in one of the balconies, and he said, 'Apparently you don't understand. This is the opening of the opera. All Cataluña will be there. And the people in the balconies are more meticulous about their dress than those downstairs.' It was impossible for us to enter the building, so we went like peasants to stand in Las Ramblas and watch the limousines arrive with the great of the region, and although we had attended opera in most of the fine houses of the world, and sometimes under rather gala conditions, we had never witnessed anything like this. The dress was impeccable, the excitement intense and there must have been a couple of thousand of us in the street, watching the entry of the Catalans into the Liceo.

Later in the week, when evening dress was not essential in the upper balconies, we were allowed to buy two rather poor seats for $9.40 each to see a performance of *Turandot,* and most of those in the tiers below us and on the main floor were in formal wear. The performance was excellent, and during one of the intermissions, which lasted forty-five minutes each because the Catalans wanted to be seen parading the handsome foyers, I had a chance to study the program for that season, and better than the words of some Catalan enthusiast it demonstrated the musical taste of this city.

Fourteen different conductors from nine different nations, using sing-

arisol.

ers from all parts of the world including Russia and Japan, were presenting twenty-one different operas from eight different nations, including
Russia and Belgium. What impressed me most was the fact that in the
twenty-one operas only nine war-horses like *Aïda* and *Tannhäuser* appeared, but eight that I never had a chance to hear, like the German *Zar
und Zimmermann* by G. A. Lortzing; the French *La Carrosse du Saint
Sacrement* of H. Busser; the Portuguese *Serrana* by A. Keil; and the
Mexican *La Mulata de Córdoba* of J. P. Moncayo. The charge of provincial-
ism that can justly be made against Spanish music in general certainly
does not apply to Barcelona opera, because a season's attendance at the
Liceo would give one a wider purview of what was happening in this genre
than a season in New York or London.

I was advised that this catholic taste, like so much that was commendable in Cataluña's cultural life, stemmed from the French influence
of which Dr. Poal had spoken. A man at the opera told me, 'We have a
mania for knowing what's happening in the world. We read. We have a
constant fear of sinking into the intellectual lethargy you find in . . . well
. . . Andalucía. No norteamericano loves his English heritage the way a
Catalan loves his French. If I thought I would never again read a French
book or hear an opera in French, I think I would wither.'

A man who was listening added, 'We're not French, you understand.
We're Catalans. We don't want a separate state and a seat in the United
Nations. The world should be moving toward larger units, not smaller. And
since we have to be a part of something, it's best to be a part of Spain. But
we are not Spaniards, we are Catalans, and in the future this fact will be
stressed. We want our own language, and our newspapers, and our university. We were on our way to having these things when Civil War overtook
us in 1936. Everything was lost . . . lost. How tragic it was. That damned
war. Now we must begin over again, slowly. But we will be Cataluña. We
will be Catalans.'

I asked numerous residents of the city, 'Do you consider yourself a
Catalan?'

'What else? Did you happen to attend that great performance of
Haydn's *The Seasons* at the Palau de la Música? Notice how the soloists
imported from England and Germany sang in German. But the choir, God
bless it, sang only in Catalan.'

These attitudes naturally arouse in the rest of Spain a suspicion
against Barcelona. Time and again in other parts of Spain intelligent
Castilians or Andalusians queried me as to what I thought of Barcelona,
and when I said, 'I've never been there,' they frowned and said, 'It's a
shame you're saving it for last. It could have an injurious effect.'

Between Madrid and Barcelona there is open war. Forty years ago the
latter city was the industrial leader, with its access to the Mediterranean
and its superior contacts with Europe; the intellectual center too, the

progressive, clean, handsome, well-educated city, and as such it constituted a kind of affront to the rest of the country. Barcelona was both
envied and ridiculed; often I heard the statement, 'Who would want to be a
Catalan? All business and no soul. There's not a man up there who
comprehends pundonor.'

In recent decades, of course, with the central government concentrat-
ing in Madrid and with Barcelona suspect because of its anti-Franco role
in the war, there has been a concerted effort to draw major industry to
Madrid, and it has succeeded. Madrid is now the larger city in population
and much the more important industrially. An Englishman connected with
the business of distributing films explains what's been happening: 'As you
know, the film industry has always centered in Barcelona. Metro-
Goldwyn-Mayer, J. Arthur Rank, Warner Brothers . . . all have their
offices here. For good reasons. In Barcelona you have linguists, typists,
people trained in business. I judge it's three to five times easier to conduct
business here than in Madrid. But starting about 1950 a quiet pressure has
been applied on all us Johnnies, "Move to Madrid. Move to Madrid." And I
wouldn't be surprised to see us frozen out of here before much longer.

'It works this way. You require a piece of paper signed. "Bring it to
Madrid and we'll handle it for you in ten minutes." So you fly to Madrid,
because if you don't, you get no signature. You want to talk about quotas.
"Fly to Madrid." You're interested in a peseta deal. "Fly to Madrid." After
four years of this you get the message. We'll all have to fly to Madrid, but
where we'll find the trained personnel no one can say.'

There used to be newspapers in Catalan, but after the war they were
forbidden. Once church sermons were in Catalan, but they too were forbidden. Catalan resistance was formidable: 'After the war they installed a
Madrileño as editor of our best newspaper *La Vanguardia*. To police us,
and he was a true swine. One morning he happened to be in an out-
of-the-way parish church when the priest, feeling himself secure, gave his
sermon in Catalan. After mass the editor grabbed the priest and said
things like "You dog. You've been warned not to use Catalan. I'm going to
report you to the police." An old woman happened to overhear the threats,
which were much worse than I've said, and she alerted the city. By
nightfall almost every major business had canceled its advertising in
Vanguardia. And kept it canceled. Well, planeloads of people flew up here
from Madrid, and one general kept shouting, "We'll knock the city down."
Enormous pressure was brought on us to reinstate our advertising, but our
leaders were clever. They never mentioned Cataluña or the real problem.
They simply said, "How can we advertise with a man who abuses a
priest?" In the end the government had to give in. The editor was removed.
Word swept through the city, "He's being replaced by a man who respects
priests." And we were very happy.'

Today Barcelona once more has a Catalan newspaper, but it is watched closely by the police. I was in one printing plant when officers from the Guardia Civil swept in, confiscated the entire printing of a calendar and burned it. The proprietor sequestered two copies, which he let me see. At first glance it was innocuous enough, printed in Spanish as such things had to be. But at the bottom of each month appeared in fine print a list of events under the heading *Never forget these days.* I was not allowed to take the calendar or to copy the dates that had made it illegal, but I recall them as something like this: 'On this date Comte Ramón Berenguer el Gran betrayed Catalan hopes. On this date Spanish armies burned Barcelona. On this date brave Catalans defied the forces of King Felipe IV.' On and on went the litany of hopes seduced and infamy rampant; for each month the Catalans had six or seven evil events to remember, and I suppose the official who gave orders to the guardia was prudent in deciding to burn this calendar, for it was inflammatory.

At the same time that I was being inducted into the arcane mysteries of Catalan nationalism, I was walking through the museum quarters of the city and I cannot recall a more pleasant experience. Margarita Tintó, a tall and beautiful archaeologist, led me through the amazing subterranean museum that lies under the Gothic quarter, showing me the columns and viaducts of the Roman city, the remnants of Visigothic times and a few fragile relics of Muslim rule. At one point, as we climbed across a viaduct many feet below the surface, Señorita Tintó said, 'We are now under the nave of the cathedral. See where its roots begin.' I commend this unusual museum, for in no other have I ever been taken into the bowels of a living city in order to witness its birth.

More spectacular is that unparalleled collection of buildings called El Pueblo Español, where behind a stone-for-stone replica of the entrance gate to Avila hides a complete village which could house about eight hundred people. It was erected in 1929 as merely one feature of an international exhibition, but it proved so popular that it was converted to permanent status and is now one of the most enchanting museums in the world. It contains eighty-one major buildings, each faithfully copied from some famous original and so distributed that all regions of Spain are adequately covered. This attractive little house comes from Toro, where King Fernando V offered to duel King Alfonso of Portugal. Every stone in the copy is faithful to the original. These three handsome old houses have been copied from Teruel; this one reproduces a family shield we saw in Santillana del Mar. In addition to the houses, which are strung out along streets duplicating real streets in the various provinces, there is a plaza mayor where concerts are given in summer, half a dozen smaller plazas modeled after real ones, a cathedral and a full-sized monastery with a cloister. There are about eight major streets, and to see everything would require the better part of a day, but for one who has visited most of Spain, a tour through this village is an architectural treat, for at every corner he sees some famous house that he visited a month ago. For the person just beginning his tour of Spain, I could imagine no better introduction to the quality of small-town building than this; the village is a synthesis of all that is most typical in Spain.

It is difficult to describe how tastefully this has been done, or indeed how it was done at all. The village is now nearly forty years old, but it remains clean and fresh. It has deteriorated in no way and looks stable enough to weather another twoscore years. Obviously the eighty-one buildings are merely false fronts, just deep enough to permit a chain of attractive shops to function inside; here one can see the old arts of Spain performed by experts: glass blowing, printing, weaving, candy making. What perplexed me was how the buildings had been put together. Let's begin with this flight of stone stairs duplicating those before the cathedral at Santiago de Compostela. They are real stones on which hundreds of thousands of people have walked, and that wooden balcony over there on the house from Oviedo is real wood upon which people can stand. The cut stones in this arch are also real and have been quarried on the site from which the originals were cut, but imperceptibly the real merges into the unreal, because this wall is clearly stucco only a few inches thick but skillfully etched to represent stone. A builder could spend a profitable morning trying to detect the real and the unreal; I was not able to.

I visited eighteen major museums in Barcelona and the only second-rate one was the newly opened Picasso museum. In appearance, of course, even it was excellent, for it occupied one of the city's old private palaces, which had been remodeled in exquisite taste. Also excellent were the interesting materials on the life of Picasso, which could not, I suppose, be duplicated elsewhere, and these too were well arranged. For example, I here learned for the first time that one of Picasso's chief works, the enigmatic 'Les Demoiselles d'Avignon' of the Museum of Modern Art in New York, got its name not from the papal city of Avignon in France but from a well-known Barcelona house of prostitution bearing that name.

What was depressing about the museum was that it had so few paintings by Picasso! The spacious walls were covered mostly by lithographs which any private collector could duplicate for a few thousand dollars, a few etchings, a couple of drawings and a handful of paintings, rarely of top quality. I can think of fifteen American cities that could throw together an infinitely better exhibition of Picasso's work by showing only those paintings owned by collectors in the city. Picasso is a Spaniard, but Spaniards have never collected his work.

In a mournful way the museum exemplified the intellectual tragedy of contemporary Spain. Her foremost talents have either been destroyed, like García Lorca, or muffled, like Pío Baroja, or they have turned their backs on Spain, like Picasso; Jiménez, the Nobel Prize poet; and Pau (Pablo) Casals, the cellist. To me it is beyond explanation that an event of such magnitude as the Civil War should have produced no artistic synthesis. In Germany, Russia, England and Italy there has been such synthesis, but Spain has stifled hers, both in the field of plastic arts, where a new Goya should have arisen to depict the contemporary horrors of war, and in the drama and novel, where works like those of Günter Grass and Alberto Moravia could easily have been evoked. I can think of no nation of modern times, except Turkey, which has experienced such traumatic shock without its artists' having reacted to it in works of grandeur. This is the severest criticism one can make of the dictatorship and the most pertinent: it has forbidden the artistic statement and has therefore crushed it, for the authentic statement once stifled cannot later be revived.

There is, however, a commendable attempt to catch up now, and the Picasso museum is an example, for Spain is desperately eager to reclaim this man as her son. In one year I must have read fifty articles about Picasso the Spaniard: one referred to him as the jovial Málaga painter. On his eightieth birthday sincere felicitations were extended, and if the Picasso museum in Barcelona is not much good, it is certainly crowded with young people hungry to know what kind of man this fellow Spaniard was. There is also a chance that the Gironella novels may pave the way for an honest evaluation of recent Spanish history, but I doubt it. A professor said, 'It is one thing for Picasso to be brave in the safety of Paris. Hell, you complain about Spaniards having no Picassos. During most of the last twenty-five years I'd have been arrested as a suspicious character if I owned one . . . even supposing I could afford it. But for a writer, who has got to live in Spain, to write the way you're talking about . . . that would be suicide . . . now and for the next twenty-five years. We are a state that is determined to live without ideas.' In fact, twice during my stay in Barcelona I was supposed to meet with professors who were described to me as 'cautious men, middle of the road, but with profound ideas concerning the future of Spain.' In each instance the interview had to be called off because gangs of bullyboys established for the purpose of terrorizing intellectuals had waited outside lecture halls and had beaten the professors unconscious. Their crime? They had dared to discuss serious questions seriously.

This dualism, this seeking on the one hand for French enlightenment and the crushing of it on the other, explains the following letter:

Since you left Barcelona I feel very old and defeated, but also very young and hopeful. The cause of the first is Marisol. Of the second, Gironella. Marisol has announced that she's going to get married! I had thought she was about fourteen but she's in her twenties and it all seems dreadfully wrong and I seem very ancient. But your friend Gironella has given us much courage by daring to discuss openly in the paper the deficiencies of the new constitution we've been promised. You would have been thrilled by his clear-cut, honest statement:

> In my opinion Spain has had for many years two basic problems. One, that of progressive democratization; the other, that of what's going to happen when a vacancy occurs in the Chief of State's office.
>
> I do not believe that the Ley Orgánica [Organic Law] approved with such bewildering speed by the Cortes solves either of these two problems.

Gironella continued with a lucid analysis of what the law should have done . . . The kinds of things you and I talked about so much and he had the extreme guts to end:

> In consequence, then, the new Ley Orgánica appears to me a movement of hope but not a solution.

Occasionally my inquiries into the intellectual life of Barcelona bore unexpected results, as when friends took us to see the old monastery of San Cugat del Vallés, lying some distance from Barcelona in a country region. It was there that I saw one of those plain and powerful Romanesque churches which will play so important a role in the final chapter of this book, and as I was admiring its solid simplicity, my guide said, 'While we're here, let's have lunch at El Rectoret,' which was easier suggested than accomplished, because we drove for some time about the countryside without finding it. Finally a shepherd told us which turns to take and we came upon a dilapidated farmhouse standing completely alone. Only an optimist would have believed that within those flaked and weather-beaten walls he would find food.

In a sense, we didn't. What we found was an adventure in family living in which food was incidental. That it was some of the best food in Spain was beside the point, for El Rectoret could have been called 'Cataluña at Table.' It consisted of eight or nine farm rooms, as beat up as the exterior, jammed with simple tables and chairs. I was invited to inspect the fifteenth-century kitchen, where I stayed for more than half an hour, watching a unique operation. El Rectoret serves only four dishes: sausage, chicken, lamb chops and rabbit, with the last selling about as much as the other three combined. With whatever meat you choose you also get a raw salad, a pitcher of marvelous sangría and a terrifying dessert called for some inexplicable reason 'a pijama,' that is, a large soup plate lined with mixed fruit in heavy syrup around a center of flan, the whole smothered in gobs of vanilla ice cream. Salad, rabbit, sangría, pijama! The farm tables were crowded with hundreds of stalwart Catalans, stubborn rocklike people with a passion for good food and music.

The kitchen was a madhouse of open grills, smoking charcoal and sizzling meat. About sixty cooks and waiters moved in and out, all relatives of one huge family. The grandmother checked salads to be sure they contained onions. One aunt did nothing all day long but cut the tops off huge tins of mixed fruits for the pijamas. Another unmolded flan after flan. One traffic manager stood on a little box and shouted numbers at the women tending the grills: 'I have twenty chickens waiting, fifteen sausages, ten lamb chops and forty rabbits.' At the huge fires one man kept applying charcoal as the women opened enormous flat grills and placed the meat upon them, then closed them and thrust them over the fire, where grease from the cooking sizzled all day.

Fifty years ago the grandmother and her husband had opened their farmhouse kitchen to the mule drivers of that day, and in the intervening years they had not altered the menu. Now, on Sundays, customers might wait for a couple of hours to find a place at one of the tables, but as they stood in line they could see great-grandchildren of the original couple washing vegetables in the yard for use in the salads.

Wherever we went on such excursions we met by accident Catalans who represented the best of their culture. Friends took us to the well-known Los Caracoles restaurant (The Snails) at the foot of Las Ramblas, and at the next table sat Joan Alavedra, an elderly man built square, with a rumbling voice, a wild head of hair and a thick homespun suit. He was a poet whom other Catalans respected for his integrity, and throughout the evening many came to pay their respects. When he heard we were in the room he wanted to tell us of his adventures with President Kennedy. It was a poet's story, roundabout and not to the point, but very moving in its conclusion: 'I am the man whom Pau Casals has honored, for it was my poem "The Manger" that he chose as the basis for his great choral composition. Same name. I was with him in Greece when *The Manger* was sung before the royal family. What a night of splendor. How Europe loves this noble old man. Last summer when he was at Prades over the border in France, conducting his summer festival, sixty members of the Barcelona music fraternity made themselves into a little orchestra and traveled from here all the way to Prades. With their instruments. When they got there they unloaded and stood in the street outside Casals' house and played Wagner's *Siegfried Idyl* as a present for the old man. To let him know we still love him even if he can't come home. Then they packed their instruments back into the cars and drove home to Barcelona, and as they came over the hills and saw Cataluña in the moonlight some of them broke into tears and one said, "How the heart of old Pau must break on a night like this. To be so near to Cataluña. To be so near."

'So when this great honor came to Casals in Puerto Rico he wanted me to share it with him, and I flew there to do so. We were to fly to the White House in Washington to receive in person the gold medal of freedom of the norteamericanos. Old Pau, as you probably know, speaks only Catalan in public. Only Catalan, and I would interpret for him. But the week we were to go your President was assassinated. Old Pau sat in his room, rocking back and forth, saying, "I can't believe it. He was my friend." Mrs. Kennedy invited him to participate in the funeral and I urged him to go. "Play one last piece at the grave of your friend," I said, but he was afraid of the crowds.

'The reason I'm telling you this, Señor Michener, is that when I came back to Barcelona my heart was filled with grief and I wrote a poet's account of my visit to Pau and by extension to the Kennedys. It was called "Carols and Kennedy," but in Catalan, of course, and within two hours of the time word flashed through the city that it was available, every copy was sold and I don't even have one for myself. It now sells for more than five dollars on the black market. Because Pau and your President stand for the same thing in the hearts of the Catalans. They stand for freedom.'

At another time it was Lluis Oncins Ariño, the unpremeditated Catalan painter who had spent the middle years of his life as the Spanish representative of the Reynolds Aluminum Company but who suddenly announced that he would henceforth be a painter. With a brooding palette of only four colors, 'My cuisine,' he calls it, dark purple, a blue that is almost black, a very dark red and a heavy orange, he paints heads representative of Spain's varied regions. He has a curious Goya quality, but if you mention this to him he becomes bitter. 'I am Oncins, metal merchant, with my own vision of a crazy world.' When I pointed out that his best pictures seemed always to contain groups of heads, arranged awkwardly but with force, he said, 'With four heads you can't escape dramatic involvement, which seems to be what you prefer, because it's easy to perceive. The real drama lies in the single head, if you could see it.' When I tried to look again at a canvas I had liked, he growled, 'Don't touch the paintings. The hands of the non-artist corrupt.'

I was somewhat ill at ease with Oncins, because he looked exactly like Hubert Humphrey and I expected him to talk politics; also, in his best work he reminded me much of the American painter Robert Henri, who had come to Spain from Philadelphia and had painted the grandmothers of the models Oncins was using. I started to tell Oncins of this, but he was impatient: 'I'm not interested in other painters. It's a savage job to find out what one wants to say, in one's own way.' In pursuit of this I asked him how he had settled upon his four strange colors, and he growled, 'They settled on me.' I obviously wasn't getting very far with this hard-headed Catalan Hubert Humphrey, so I paid my respects and moved on, but after I had been back home in Pennsylvania for some weeks a traveler from Spain climbed my hill with a large bundle.

'This painter in Barcelona heard I lived in Pennsylvania and he made me bring this to you. He said you were a tough man who asked sensible questions.' And with that my visitor unwrapped a good-sized board on which, in his dark colors, Lluis Oncins had painted me from memory against a background showing stylized elements of the American flag. I looked like a Spaniard, a Catalan to be exact, but the likeness was good, except that he gave me somewhat more hair than nature allowed. How-

ever, the salient characteristic of the portrait was that I was shown with a glowing heart, painted in Oncins' traditional dark orange because, as he had explained to the messenger, 'Michener's love for Cataluña was self-evident.'

With another painter I had a much different experience. Norman Narotzky was an American working in Barcelona, for he was married to a girl of that city, and while I knew him a notable storm developed over a painting of his which synthesized his reflections on Spanish history. A friend told me of the work before I had a chance to see it for myself: 'I'm afraid Norman was ill advised. You see, he's done a pair of portraits of Fernando and Isabel and titled them "The Catholic Kings." ' I said I thought this was appropriate for an American, since it was these kings who had launched the discovery of our country, but my informant said, 'I'm afraid you don't understand. The portraits, which are really very fine, serve only as the kick-off point for what Narotzky really wants to say. Accompanying them are symbols of religious repression through the ages. The swastika, the stake, the crucified Christ wearing robes used by the Inquisition. It's a real beauty! Norman has omitted nothing.'

The two paintings, which I liked so much that I tried to buy them, evoked a scandal. A government official pointed out that since Spain was officially sponsoring a movement to have Isabel declared a saint, the painting was not only offensive to the nation's historical sense but sacrilegious as well. He fulminated that his country did not intend to sit idly by and allow intellectuals to cast aspersions on the grandeur of the Spanish heritage. Others felt that for an American to speak ill of the Inquisition was unfair, unhistoric and probably subversive. Narotzky was investigated; inquiries were made at the American embassy; and the dealer who had exhibited the work was badgered by the police with all sorts of hampering restrictions.

I found it was impossible for the tourist to understand the ins and outs of Spanish censorship. Whenever a newspaper was censored and taken off the streets clandestine copies circulated, and I read them avidly to detect what had offended and almost never was I able to do so; but my Spanish friends would take a quick glance at the paper and almost always spot the article that had caused the trouble. However, even when they told me which article it was, I frequently read it without appreciating why it had been found so offensive. The only insight I uncovered for myself came in a bookstore when I saw William Faulkner's *Requiem for a Nun* published in Spanish as *Réquiem para una mujer* (Woman). When I asked the bookseller why the change, I found that he was a marked agnostic: 'On the face of it the Faulkner heroine could not be a nun because she wasn't a Catholic, so it's not illogical for our censors to deprive the author of his

his Italian painter on Las Ramblas
minds one that European visitors have been more
lcomed in Barcelona than in other Spanish cities.

cheap little play on words. But more important is the fact that we can permit nothing that would cast even oblique reflections on the Church. All of us know that well over seventy percent of priests maintain mistresses, and the general public approves, for it keeps the priests away from our own women, but to speak of this in a book? They'd never permit it.' However, shortly after he spoke, a Barcelona publisher brought out a Catalan translation entitled *Rèquiem per a una monja*.

One Sunday morning as I was walking through the Gothic quarter, of which I never saw enough, for it is not often that one finds in the heart of a modern city an ancient one existing as a kind of soul imprisoned in stone yet mysteriously vital, I heard the lovely sound of rustic pipes and muffled drums. I could have been in a woodland except that the cathedral rose above me, and as I entered its plaza I saw that several hundred people or perhaps even a thousand, all dressed in Sunday clothes, had gathered about two orchestras that were playing a concert while worshipers heading for the cathedral or coming from it after Mass passed by and nodded approvingly, even though the music was not religious.

The orchestras were special. Each was composed of a dozen members whose instruments had been determined centuries ago: one double bass, five country oboes, one trombone, three cornets and two fiscorns, which were small and gave forth piercing sounds. I was surprised to see there were no drummers, for I thought I had heard drums, but when I approached the orchestras I saw that the oboe players had tiny drums, not more than three inches across, strapped to their left forearms, and these they struck from time to time without interrupting their playing on the oboes. One of the fiscorn players had a cymbal even smaller strapped to his wrist, and this he struck with another which he held daintily between his fingers. The music these orchestras produced, one playing while the other rested, was delicate and unlike any I had heard before, the wedding of oboe and cornet being especially pleasing. Naturally, I compared this sardana, for so the music was called, with the oboe music I had heard in Pamplona, and although I much preferred the latter as being more raw and mountainous, I respected the sardana as being more artistic. Since the orchestras played for about four hours, I had ample opportunity to judge their work.

As I was watching the fiscorn players, for I had not before seen this instrument, a strange thing happened all around me. A moment ago the Catalans in the plaza had been listening to the sardana; now, without anyone's having given a signal, large circles had formed, containing men and women of all ages down to eight years old, so that the entire plaza was covered with people silently performing the folk dance that accompanies the sardana. I was astonished at how quietly this had happened, for there were at least eleven of these large circles, some with thirty members, and the dance was vigorous and beautiful, yet how it had started I couldn't say.

The sardana was like the movement of an animated clock that ran in both directions. Slow steps left, slow steps right. Left, right. Left, right, with arms held closely to the side. Then faster steps, with hands slightly raised. Then fast, intricate steps, with hands held high above the head and the body swaying beautifully as the tempo of the music increased. Finally the entire plaza in motion, with worshipers filing in and out of the cathedral and stopping to join the dance if they felt so inspired. Then a tinkling clang of the tiny cymbals, a ruffle on the toy drums, a wail on the oboes and the dance ended. In the flash of a moment the circles disbanded and the plaza was both silent and sedate for Sunday morning. After ten or fifteen minutes' rest the second orchestra began and the dance was under way once more.

I found that if I took my eye away from the plaza for even one moment, I missed the beginning of this strange dance. The fresh orchestra would play for perhaps eight minutes and nothing would happen. Stolid Catalans in dark suits would be looking off into space as if dancing were the most remote intention of their lives, and if at this moment I looked away, I missed the whole thing, because when I looked back, there they would be, in great circles, dancing slowly left and right.

I was determined to see who gave the signal for this dance, so on several occasions I kept my eyes glued to a fixed spot where experience had told me a circle would be formed. One moment, not a sign of dancing. Then a girl, unaccompanied by any boy, sedately placed her purse on the flagstones. Nothing happened. Then a boy carefully took off his jacket, folded it and placed it atop the purse. Within seconds a dozen purses, jackets, walking sticks and coats were piled neatly in that spot, and around them the Catalans, strangers one to the other, began their slow sardana. More than anything else this strange beginning resembled the process by which ice forms across the surface of water; now it is fluid; now it is crystallized; the dance has begun.

Toward one o'clock that afternoon the orchestras combined to play a very slow and mournful sardana and for a long time no circles formed. Then an old man, with tears streaming down his face, solemnly folded his jacket and placed it on the stones. He was joined by others, and some of them were crying too, and soon the plaza was filled with solemn music as a tragic song was repeated over and over by the orchestras. I asked a man sitting on the cathedral steps what was happening, and he said, 'This piece is called "Patética." We play it when some famous person has died.' I asked whom it was memorializing, and he said, 'Yesterday Maestro'—I didn't catch the name—'he died, and he was one of our best composers of sardana music.' I went down to stand with the musicians as they played, because I wanted to see how the music was written. It was written out by hand, 'Patética,' and as the fiscorns shrilled their lament for the dead musician I saw that some of the players had tears in their eyes too, for music is something to be taken with great seriousness in Cataluña.

If I were to choose one man to represent the intellectual curiosity which I found so marked in Barcelona, it would have to be Luis Lassaletta (1921–1959), for although his history was unique, it was also representative. He was a slim, extremely handsome young man whose father had been Spanish manager for the Hispano-Suiza company. At the outbreak of the Civil War, Lassaletta senior was the only man in managerial status brave enough to remain in the city, which was obviously going to fall into the hands of the leftists. He paid for his bravery with his life, shot through the head without trial and for no reason except that he was an employer.

His son Luis, fifteen at the time, was thrown into jail and kept in a hole in which he could neither lie down nor stand up, with water dripping on him and a bright light shining in his eyes. He later reported that it was only through the exercise of will that he avoided going insane. When the war was over and he was released from prison, along with his younger brother José María, he was so dedicated to freedom that he was determined to go to the freest place he knew of, the African jungle. He grabbed a ship out of Barcelona, as young men like him had done through the centuries, and landed in Africa with enough money to sustain him for three months; but once ashore he exhibited skill in trapping wild animals and in training them. 'He spoke to them,' a friend says, 'and they spoke back. With his intense eyes he looked into the hearts of his animals, and although he was known as a "great white hunter" he never shot animals . . . or at least, not for sport.'

The fame of Lassaletta spread over Europe and he was consulted by zoo directors and naturalists. He was offered jobs by many different nations but his love was life in the jungle with his friends, and there he became a legend. In Gabon, in the Ubangi country, along the coastline of Lake Chad, he was the man who appeared suddenly out of the wilderness accompanied by Negroes bearing a live python or a cage containing a gorilla.

Then one day during the Christmas holidays, which he was spending in Guinea, a Gabon viper bit him in the face. 'Luis knew there was no anti-venom serum in the district, so he went to the hospital and told the doctors, "I am going to die. It will be three hours and painful but you mustn't worry, because there is nothing you can do." In the most dreadful agony he died, and the Barcelona papers mourned, "When Luis Lassaletta, who was the friend of all animals, dies from the bite of an animal, the world makes no sense." '

I of course never knew Luis Lassaletta but I did have the good luck to meet his two younger brothers, and with José María, who has inherited Luis' affection for animals, I spent some time. He kept in his back yard a tame hyena that he had captured in Africa, for it is now he who supplies European zoos with wild animals, and for some reason which I cannot explain I became close friends with this hyena; perhaps it was because I was lonely for my two dogs, whom I had not seen for nearly half a year; perhaps it was my fascination with his tremendous jaws which could bite through the thighbone of an ox. At any rate, this ugly beast and I had a great time. He seemed to know that I would play with him, no matter how rough he got, and there were times when he would take my forearm in his mighty jaws and bring his teeth against my skin and grin at me as if to say, 'Can you imagine what I could do if I had a mind for it?' I knew, and with my free hand I would bang him in the snoot, and he would roll over backward with delight.

José María went to Africa to recover his brother's possessions, among which he found a letter in which one of Luis' bearers sought help for the murder of four people:

Douala, French Cameroons
14 July 1955

Dear Sir, Professor of Help,

I have the honour most respectfully to put this humble petition towards your understanding.

My life is very poor and as such I shall be very grateful if master could give me a helping hand towards the battle of life by giving me some money for killing the understated persons as victims. Meanwhile the secret shall only remain the both of us.

Names of Victims

I	John Osungwe	a man
II	Andrew Oruh	a man
III	Sadrack Mbeng	a man
IV	Nkhnge Enota	a woman

All these are the enemies who try to kill me. I would be very grateful master could grant my plea.

Your future customer,
Joseph Ayok

I suppose that most visitors to Barcelona sooner or later make the trip to Montserrat (Serrated Mountain) but, paradoxically, few ever see it. They see the famous monastery, of course, and the shrine beloved of all Catalans, and they take one of the numerous téléphérique rides to the tops of peaks, but the mountain itself, one of the most exquisite in the world, they do not see, for this can be done properly only by going far north of Barcelona to the ancient town of Vich, which is worth a trip in itself if only to see the church decorated in gold murals by José María Sert. From Vich, whose hotel has a restaurant of notable reputation, one drops back south to where Route N-141 cuts off toward the mountains, and as one

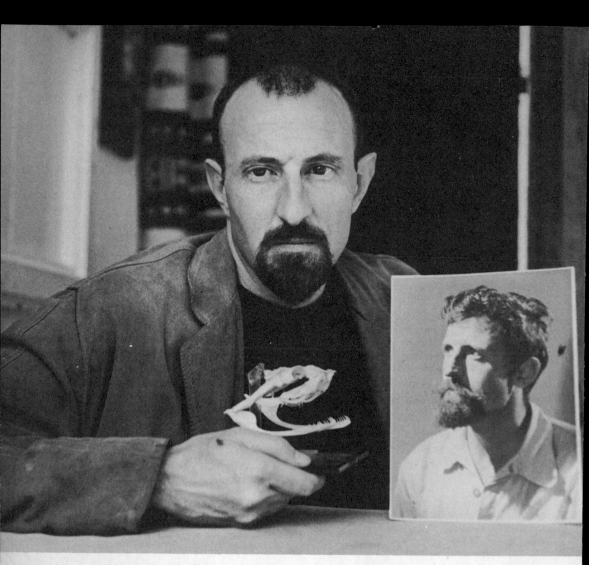

José María Lassaletta holds a photograph of his brother Luis, killed in Africa by a Gabon viper, whose skull Don José holds in his right hand.

drives down this twisting road he comes to a spot from which Montserrat in all its wonder stands forth against the southern sky.

The mountain is prodigious, a chain of sawtooth peaks that resemble the Tetons of Wyoming except that the former are not so tall, only 4072 feet against the Grand Teton's 13,747 (of course, Montserrat starts from sea level, whereas the base of the Tetons is well above it). The peaks of Montserrat are more compact, and if one can use the word in this sense, more artistic. They blaze in the sky like tongues of flame, not one or two peaks but scores of them thrown together to make a jagged pattern. When I saw Montserrat from this ideal vantage point I'd already seen most of the world's famous mountains, but for an assembly of peaks of limited scope I had seen nothing to surpass this group.

The ascent from the north is also more exciting, I think, than the traditional approach from the south, which is how one climbs if he starts from Barcelona, but by either path the narrow road is magnificent and the final turn which throws one onto a small plateau just under the summit of the mountain is surprising, for unexpectedly one finds himself face to face with a series of massive buildings wedged into crevices below the rocky spires that rise above them like a crown. I had expected to end my climb at a shrine; instead I found enough recent buildings to house a small town and was amazed to think that all these rocks and timbers and steel girders had been lugged up this steep mountain.

Obviously, centuries had been required to build this complex. As long ago as the year 700, religious hermits had established themselves in these caves and had launched the legend of pure men hiding in inaccessible mountains. Their isolation ended after the year 880, when shepherds found in one of the caves a beautiful wooden statue of the Virgin, dark of face and majestic in manner; she had been hidden there when Muslims overran Cataluña. A Church commission affirmed that she was the last statue carved by St. Luke. She made the mountain famous; Goethe and Schiller visited the monastery that developed in her honor, as did innumerable kings and cardinals. Throughout Europe, Montserrat became identified with the legendary Monsalvat, the hiding place of the Holy Grail as depicted in Wagner's *Parsifal,* so that pilgrims had a double reason for climbing the mountain; even today the path is crammed with devout travelers who know that if they can complete this journey, some special blessing will be accorded them.

Even if one were not religious, an expedition to Montserrat would be a rewarding experience, for when the buildings are reached the day has only begun; from them téléphériques swing upward to the tips of the highest peaks, from which amazing views of Cataluña can be seen, even as far as Las Islas Baleares (the Balearic Islands). There are also picnic grounds tucked away at high altitudes and trails across the plateaus to needles which can be climbed if one has ropes and crampons.

Montserrat is the shrine of Cataluña; here couples come each day of the year to be married, a custom which became additionally popular during the years when the Catalan language was proscribed, for at Montserrat the wedding service was conducted in Catalan, no matter what the Madrid bureaucrats decreed. As one middle-aged woman told me, 'I wouldn't feel married if the priest had done it in Spanish.'

But Montserrat has always been, and still is, primarily a monastery. In many-tiered buildings, whose multiple windows, set against rocks, reminded me of the Buddhist lamaseries of Tibet, Benedictine monks maintain the old traditions of prayer and work. It is they who occupy this plateau set among spires; they operate the stores and collect the profits from the téléphériques. They live far removed from the problems of

Spain's ordinary life and seek a perfection which not even the average monk living elsewhere could attain. Says the official guide: 'The monks' chief occupation is reciting the Mass, and this they try to perform with the utmost care in every particular, so that it may be effective to the Glory of God and for the good of the Church.'

As I traveled in and out of Barcelona, and especially when I went to high points like El Tibidabo and Montjuich, I became aware of a singular

*Nature forms
in La Sagrada Familia.*

building in the eastern section of the city. From a distance it looked
something like a church, except that it had four main steeples and a covey
of smaller ones. When I asked what it was, a friend said, 'El Templo de la
Sagrada Familia, The Expiatory Temple of the Holy Family. But its real
name should be Gaudí's Folly.' When I asked why, he said, 'Go look. You'll
understand.'

When I told the taxi driver that I wanted to see the Expiatory Temple and so on, he interrupted: 'Gaudí, okay,' and after a short drive, put me down before one of the strangest-looking serious buildings in the world, a huge unfinished cathedral, a gaping wound in the heart of genius. For some minutes I stood in the street, just looking at the fantastic thing. All I could see was a façade terminating in the four spires I had noticed from El Tibidabo. Behind the façade . . . nothing, but off to the right I could see what looked like one spur of the transept topped by the group of lesser spires.

When I say spire I do not mean the traditional church steeple that ends in a cross. I mean something quite different. A French visitor was also in the street, looking through field glasses at the top of one of the spires, and noticing my interest, said, 'One of the true masterpieces of modern art. Regard.' He passed me the glasses, and at first I could not believe what I was seeing through them. First of all, the spires were built in such a way that they resembled pretzel sticks studded with salt crystals, except that at the upper end they narrowed down to points of rock candy, brilliantly colored. The spire was decorated with ceramic bits set in plaster and color was reflected everywhere. 'The sun lives in each part,' the admiring Frenchman said, and since many of the ceramic pieces were finished in gold, the spire seemed to be a finger of the sun.

'Have you studied the tip?' he asked, and how can I explain what I saw when I did? I said it wasn't a cross but I would be hard put to say what it was. I could think only of Angkor Wat and its repeated use of the cobra head with hood extended. Yes, it looked much like a cobra, except that it was angular, off center, totally bizarre and with the hood indicated by a score of ceramic balls that looked as if they had been racked up for a celestial billiard game. There was also something that resembled a four-leaf clover and a series of golden protuberances that looked like either sails or segments of a peeled orange.

'Glorious, eh?' the Frenchman asked.

'What is it supposed to be?'

'Who cares? It's a work of genius. So who cares?' He took back the glasses and passed into the unfinished building, but I remained in the street, studying the lower portions of the façade, for it was here and not in the fantastic towers that the genius of Gaudí had manifested itself. The entire front was a kind of garden rising vertically from the pavement. Vines climbed upward to provide niches in which statues of Biblical figures stood as if resting in some countryside grape arbor. What in a traditional façade would have been a pillar, here became a tree in whose spreading branches perched stone birds. On either side of the main entrance, at eye level, families of realistic chickens scratched, beautifully carved, and wherever human figures appeared, animal life appeared also, for it was obvious that Gaudí had loved nature; his definition of religion encompassed all that lived.

I suppose the outstanding characteristic of the façade was that when seen from where I stood, there was scarcely a square foot that was not covered with ornament in some way. One night, when I saw it illuminated by flares, it cast a million shadows and the spires looked like decorations on a wedding cake. Few lines were straight and some of the windows were wonderfully inventive; the man who designed this façade knew what fun was. It reminded me of two other structures I'd seen, one in Barcelona and the other in Watts, the Negro section of Los Angeles. The first, of course, was the Palau de la Música, and I assumed that Gaudí had also built that, but I was wrong. In Barcelona at the turn of the century there had been a flowering of the Catalan spirit, and a different group of architects had been responsible for the Palau. As for Los Angeles, in Watts in the early years of this century an immigrant Italian tile setter named Simon Rodia decided to build by himself a memorial to his love for the United States, and it took the form of a cluster of huge towers one hundred feet tall and built of iron rods handsomely interwoven. He ornamented them with anything he could salvage from junk yards: broken plates, green and blue soft-drink bottles, chipped cups and saucers, flashy tiles from old bathrooms. From the seashore he collected shells and from garbage dumps odd containers, and all this he set into concrete slabs which formed the sides of his structure. Working pragmatically and alone, he spent thirty-three years on his task, creating what has been called 'the greatest structure ever made by one man.' Today the towers have become an embarrassment to Los Angeles, for they have begun to deteriorate and vandals have worked much damage; it may be that they will have to be torn down, but if they vanish something unique and beautiful will have been lost, as subtle as the skin of a lizard, and committees have been formed to save them, for many world critics judge them to be the one authentic work of art to have been produced by California. At any rate, if one has seen the Watts towers he is prepared for the Gaudí, and vice versa.

I left the street and passed through the façade as if I were entering the church, but inside there was nothing. Not even the walls were up, except at the unfinished transept. 'How long have they been building this?' I asked a caretaker.

'A long time,' he said, pointing to a crane I had not previously seen. Some work was under way, but from the magnitude of the task that lay ahead, I judged it would take a crew of thousands forty or fifty years to finish. 'Are they proceeding with it?' I asked, but the caretaker shrugged his shoulders.

I did find a placard which explained the façade. It was intended to portray events connected with the birth of Christ, and the four spires represented the major symbols of the faith which Christ had founded: the cross, the walking stick of Joseph, the ring and the miter, though what religious significance the last three had I did not know, but I did know that

an architect of noble imagination and vast intention had drafted this memorial to the Holy Family but had somehow run out of energy. The demanding task had staggered to a halt and I saw in the gaping emptiness both wonder and tragedy and was driven to discover what had happened and why.

I asked so many questions about the building that friends arranged for me to meet the one man in Barcelona best equipped to explain. I was taken to an attractive country-style house which now stood well within the city but which must have been in a rural area when built. An old-style fence with the kind of latched gate I knew as a boy surrounded a pleasant yard, and at the door of the house a girl obviously just in from the country bowed and said in Catalan, 'Dr. Bonet will see you shortly.' She led me into a library, where I found, in addition to the ninety volumes of the *Espasa-Calpe,* whole shelves of books about Gaudí. French, Italian, American and especially German writers had compiled an impressive series of essays on Gaudí and photographic studies of his work, and from their titles it was obvious that their authors considered him one of the important men of his generation. But what was his generation? When did he live? I did not feel free to take down the books, but since they all appeared to be of recent publication, for they were largely in the new international format, I judged that he must have died fairly recently.

The door to the library swung open and a slight, old-fashioned gentleman in dark suit and vest, in his late sixties perhaps, came into the room with that air of excitement which marks men who love to talk about work that fascinates them. 'Luis Bonet y Gari,' the man said, extending his hand. 'I am delighted to meet with someone from América del Norte who knows the work of Antoni Gaudí.' I decided not to tell him that I was there because I knew nothing about Gaudí, for it was obvious that he had much to tell. He wore a black bow tie which stood out against the whiteness of his shirt and hair. His eyes were unnaturally bright and he spoke crisply.

'I am, as they told you, the architect of the Sagrada Familia. I was a student of Gaudí's, and although no one can say what his exact plans were for finishing the structure, I am at least in harmony with his general ideas.'

'When did he die?' I asked.

Dr. Bonet was surprised that an expert like me didn't know this fundamental fact about the master, but he said courteously, 'Born 1852 Antoni Gaudí i Cornet in the small Catalan town of Reus. Struck down by an automobile here in Barcelona in 1926. Unrecognized, he was thrown into a pauper's bed in an out-of-the-way hospital, where he died some days later without having regained consciousness.'

'Then the Sagrada Familia dates from the last . . .'

'Another architect had made preliminary plans for a traditional kind of church, but in 1882 Gaudí drew a set of sketches showing how a structure more suited to Cataluña could be evolved from the work then under way. He got the job and the result is history.'

'How did he come upon the ideas he used in the façade?' I asked.

'Ah! Where? As a young man I worked with him and discovered many secrets about building in the new style, but how he conceived that style I never knew. Obviously, he saw architecture as an outgrowth of nature. Obviously, he was inspired by the Mediterranean and all the cultural forces that grew up along its shores. But above all else he was a Catalan, and something of our essence flowered in him. He could have come only from Cataluña.'

I was afraid to ask the next question, for it would betray my ignorance, but I was caught up with the mystery of Gaudí, so I asked, 'Did he do much work in Cataluña?' It turned out to be a good question, because Dr. Bonet pulled down from his shelves a score of books written within the last decade by non-Spanish experts and in their pages showed me pictures of the work Gaudí had done.

'The amusement park here in Barcelona. Oh, don't miss that! It's a child's fairyland built in stone. Then the apartment houses with their shining roofs. And don't forget his beautiful Casa Vicens not far from here.'

What really surprised me was a sketch Dr. Bonet showed me of the church as it had been intended to look, for this showed that the façade I had been looking at was not the main one at all but merely the entrance to the south transept; the main nave had not yet been started, except for the apse, which stood under the cluster of lesser towers. The finished church would have eight more of the giant spires; and the placard I had seen earlier was wrong. The spires did not represent abstract attributes of the church but rather twelve men from the New Testament: the four already standing were those for Barnabas, Jude, Simon and Matthew.

Dr. Bonet reviewed the plan with me and I could see that he visualized the church finished as his master had intended. It would require sixty or seventy years to complete, but the determination to do so was present. 'The four existing spires of the Sagrada Familia have become for Barcelona what the Eiffel Tower is for Paris or the Statue of Liberty for New York. They are the recognized symbol of this city and of Cataluña. It is unthinkable that the remaining eight should not be completed, because the four we have are among the few works of true architecture built in the last century. Throughout the world they are recognized as such.'

But not in Spain. I was to find that among Spaniards familiar with the problem, Gaudí is looked upon as a Catalan crank and his work dismissed as irrelevant. One man in Madrid asked me, 'What can you make of those towers? At their base, Gothic. Midway up, pure Art Nouveau. At the top, Picasso cubist. It's junk architecture and it's lucky for us it was left unfinished. Perhaps a real architect can move in now and bring the mess to some conclusion.'

I heard the same arguments in Barcelona. 'The Sagrada Familia should be turned over to a committee of architects under the age of fifty. Make that forty-five. They should keep what's already up and finish the damned thing off in some kind of ultramodern simplistic style and give us a church that can be used. The four main towers can stand where they are. They're no good, but they do no harm.'

If a plebiscite on this matter were taken throughout Spain, it would be meaningless, for most Spaniards know nothing of the Sagrada Familia. If only those qualified to vote were polled, I suppose the decision would be to finish the job quickly and without regard to Gaudí's imperfectly recorded master plan. If the architects of the outside world were questioned, I believe they would vote for finishing the church with due respect for Gaudí's plan but with modifications dictated by the probable taste of 1990. (This would be my preference.) But to the devoted followers of Antoni Gaudí, the only way to finish this monument is in strict adherence to his wishes. This would require eight more towers, an additional lesser façade depicting the Passion of Christ to balance the existing Infancy, and a gigantic main entrance showing Christ in Glory with a wealth of imaginative detail that I fear only Gaudí himself could have devised. He was a unique genius who carried his plans in his head and I doubt that they could be reconstructed from the inadequate notes he left.

What will be done? No one knows. In fact, no one has even a coherent guess. Men like Dr. Bonet are convinced that sooner or later the people of Barcelona will recognize in this magic shell a Catalan treasure and will insist upon its completion. A committee has been formed to speed the work and collections are taken each year; visitors from other countries often return home and write out checks to further what one correspondent described as 'the most exciting thing I saw in Spain.' But the city fathers, faced with this gaping wound and the prospect of another century before it can be healed, are understandably impatient to get along with the work in some simplified manner. The debate is bitter.

As for Parque Güell, a garden area lying northwest of the church, it is a child's delight and faces the same problems as the church. It was never finished, really, and the dreamlike buildings have become dilapidated; I don't see how they could be properly refurbished without an expenditure of funds that could scarcely be justified. For as long as they last, however, the inventions which Gaudí poured into this park are a joy to the spirit: caves where one can rest and towers that seem made of gingerbread, flights of stairs lined with rocks of all hues and huge flat buildings whose Assyrian-like pillars lean at odd angles. It was in this park that I saw a work of Gaudí's that made my heart skip through sheer pleasure: it was a swinging gate made of wrought iron. Its basic design was a series of large squares onto which were fixed circles fashioned to look like the ribs of a palm branch with the core off center. The solidity of the squares, the beauty of the circles, the unbalanced position of the cores and the airiness of the whole concept represented invention of the highest order, and if I had seen nothing else done by Gaudí, I would have known from this gate that he was first rate.

'This is how he looked,' Dr. Bonet said, handing me a photograph taken in front of the cathedral one Corpus Christi day. Gaudí was a small man, a Catalan to be sure, with white hair and beard, ill at ease in a dark store-made suit and staring intently into space while those around him attended to the formation of the parade in which he would march, carrying a long wax taper. The thing that no one could miss was the way he leaned forward from his ankles, as if there was work to be done or a quest to be followed. He never married; he left no coherent account of his artistic philosophy; only rarely was he able to finish the great works he began; and he must have been a difficult man to deal with. But one glance at his iron gate and you know that he was a poet.

In view of what I shall later be saying about another Catalan, Ramón Llull, I should like to leave Gaudí, who moved me deeply, as described by Dr. Bonet: 'He felt the entire Mediterranean to be at his disposal. Here he used the palm trees of Egypt and the pillars of Karnak. Byzantium was very much on his mind. And the caves of Crete and the temples of Greece. He had deep affinity for the Etruscans, their hard colors and sure touch. Rome was here, the great builders, the men who were not afraid to throw aqueducts across valleys. He looked out to the Mediterranean and was in no way provincial.'

I said, when speaking of Córdoba, that I would not bore the reader with a recital of my disappointments in trying to find a good performance of flamenco, but what happened when I carried my quest to a village near Barcelona could not be termed boring. When friends heard that I was still trying to find authentic flamenco they proposed a dance hall at the waterfront end of Las Ramblas, but when I looked at the program I saw that the music was to be provided by a band called something like Les Greer and his Dixie Wildcats and the dancer was The Flame of Cádiz, and I felt that I could forgo that one; but about this time I met one of Spain's best-publicized playboys, and he said, 'Michener, this country would be humiliated if a serious student like yourself came here and found no decent flamenco, so I've arranged for the best flamenco party in recent times, and you're to be guest of honor.'

I was driven to a finca in the country, an exquisite place overlooking the sea and decorated with animal skins from African safaris. Four professional bartenders served drinks and the audience was glittering: three motion-picture stars of world reputation, several writers whose books were widely known, four Spanish noblemen including a couple of condes, a famous bullfighter retired to honor and a score of similar luminaries. We had convened at midnight and the singing was to last till dawn. All but a few lights were turned off, and before the music began we could hear the whispering of the Mediterranean. This was not one of the legendary gypsy caves of Andalucía, but it was the next best thing, and my host said, without smiling, 'If you don't like this flamenco you don't recognize duende when you see it.'

I should have been warned when I saw the principal singer. Instead of a man trained over many years in the intricacies of the art, a square-built woman of forty appeared, with a voice like a bullfrog, or worse. She was apparently a great favorite of the crowd, for when she gave her deep, throaty 'Adiós, amigos,' one of the condes called something and she yelled back, 'Soy más macho que todos aquí, y tengo un par de cojones así de grande!' which a friend translated as 'I'm more manly than anyone here and I've got the biggest testicles.'

Well, flamenco types are sometimes rather tough and I assumed that this was merely her manner of speaking, and that when the music began she would sing properly, but the appearance of her guitarist gave no assurance of this; he was a kind of comedian, with a rubber face, who could play tricky little passages which went well with her kind of singing, such as it was. I groaned, and then the principal girl dancers came out, tall, willowy, beautiful gypsy girls, I thought, and the evening started. I didn't recognize the first song, but the others did. It was more like a rock-and-roll flamenco than what I had hoped for, but with the savage grunting of the singer and the simplified dancing of the two girls it was acceptable.

It was on about the fifth number that I finally realized that something was more seriously wrong about this evening than the beat of the guitar. I was sitting on a Mongolian-style hassock covered with the skin of a lion which the owner of the finca had shot, when the prettier of the girls came to stand before me and dance a sevillana, for which normally she would have had a partner. After a few steps, which I recognized as something less than top flamenco, she began a slow motion of her shoulders, which I had not seen before in this dance. She continued thus for some minutes and then began to undress, taking off one piece of clothing after another until she stood about a yardstick from me wearing only a burlesque G-string, which she proceeded to throw away while the female singer uttered her guttural nonsense and the guitarist played a music hall number. After some moments of dancing for me, as guest of honor, the young lady asked me to join her, but I did not feel equal to the task, not knowing either the steps of the flamenco or those she was improvising, but one of the condes obliged and the pair did a brief fandango of sorts, after which she picked up her bits of clothing, chucked me under the chin with her G-string and repaired to a corner, where she slowly dressed in view of everyone.

In this style the flamenco continued till dawn. There were breaks, during which casually arranged couples drifted off to nearby rooms, and occasionally one of the guests would take over the singing or even the guitar playing; once or twice there were moments of quiet beauty as the second of the strippers sang folk songs in an appealing voice, once while standing naked by a window. I remember that there was almost a fight, too. A Catalan asked a man from Madrid how he liked Barcelona, and the Madrileño said condescendingly, 'Este pueblo no es mi pueblo,' which in Spanish carries a lilting condescension because of its repetition of words: 'This town ain't my town.' 'What's the matter with this town?' the Catalan demanded. 'It just ain't my town,' the Madrileño said, but neither was drunk enough to fight.

At eight in the morning, when a cab came to drive me back to Las Ramblas, my host finally dropped his pose of seriousness and said, 'Well, you won't see another flamenco like this one in a hurry.' I laughed, and he said, 'The singer's the one who's famous. We all love her.'

On the way back to town I thought of the contradictory reputation Spain has in this matter of sex. The country is advertised abroad as the home of passionate women who click their heels with impatience, but the press, the Church and political leaders always speak of Spain in puritanical terms. The highest moral ideals are preached, yet most men who can afford it maintain mistresses with the tacit approval of the Church, which knows how far to go in these matters. The major cities boast of the absence of prostitutes, yet when a foreign male checks into a hotel alone he is barely in his room before his phone rings and a soft voice says, 'Ello, Señor Brooks of New York. This is Encarnación. Señor Keller asked me to call you.' And on all levels of society there is a circumspect, rather well-behaved circuit of sexual freedom whose operation I had witnessed this night. From what I have seen of Spain in action, it seems to me that they handle the moral problem about as well as any country I've visited . . . if one can dull his ears to the moral preachments, which at times grow downright tedious.

Under normal circumstances the high point of my stay in Barcelona would have been the Sagrada Familia, but because of the agitated political situation the thing I remember most was the aftermath of a chance meeting that had occurred some months before in a remote valley northeast of León where the road from Potes to Riaño crosses the mountain range known as Picos de Europa. There at a well beside the road I had met a Catalan university student whom I shall call Pau Lluis Freg. We had talked politics for some minutes, and after I had answered a chain of his questions, he said, 'When you get to Barcelona, look me up. I have friends who would enjoy talking with you.' I lost his address, but one night in the city, as I was about to deliver a speech to an assembly of students, he appeared suddenly out of a doorway and with conspiratorial manner said, 'I shall call on you at your hotel.'

Through him I was introduced to student life in Barcelona at a time when it was under serious stress, and I must make clear, because people who have never lived under a dictatorship are sometimes confused as to what happens in a country like Spain as compared to Russia, that I shall here report only a fragment of what students told me. We conducted a series of the most frank and open discussions I have ever held with university people; they were no more afraid to speak openly and in open places than I would have been in Pennsylvania, and if in what follows critical points are left untouched, it was only because I didn't raise them or have forgotten what I was told. The muffled hesitancy that I had known in other countries I did not encounter in Spain; yet the Spanish students were afraid in other ways and had good cause to be, for many of their associates were already in jail. If this is a contradiction, it is merely what I experienced.

'The turmoil in our university is much worse than the newspapers have dared admit,' Pau Lluis told me as we walked through the small streets off Las Ramblas. He was an earnest young man of twenty, dressed like a conservative English businessman but with the eyeglasses of a student. 'There have been six riots that I know about and my division is closed down altogether. I don't know what I shall do for an education.'

'What are you doing now?'

'We protest. We meet near the university, but you understand . . . we're locked out. There are no classes.'

'What happened?'

'Riots. We reached the end of our patience. Really, our endurance was used up. So there were riots. I think the administration was with us and could have handled the problem, but the police saw a chance to get even with us and gave us severe beatings. Real trouble in the streets. So it was the government that closed the doors. The police, you might say.'

I was vague as to what had caused the riots, for newspaper accounts had been meager, it being one of those cases in which I learned more from the *New York Times* than from the Spanish papers, which were under severe censorship. 'What are the riots about? Politics?'

Pau Lluis looked at me in astonishment. 'No! We're not radicals or anything like that. We had to strike because we were being treated with contempt. Let me tell you why I finally struck. I had four professors, and three of them were swine. True swine. They came to class about two times in five, and when they did come they stood at the podium and insulted us. Once I asked a question about a difficult passage, and the professor shouted, "I am the professor and I explain when I think it's necessary. Sit down." To show his displeasure he didn't come back to class for three weeks.'

'Who taught the class?'

'Nobody. If a professor becomes angry, there's nothing the students can do.'

'Then how do you learn?'

'You don't. Time of the examination comes and you're not prepared. So you flunk, and there's nothing you can do about it.'

I found this difficult to believe, so Pau Lluis introduced me to an English boy who was studying at the university and he confirmed the story. 'In English universities we were sometimes treated with infuriating condescension, but here we're treated as pigs. The government fears us . . . hates us, really. In Spain the educated man is held in contempt.'

This was a direct contradiction to what I had been told by Dr. Fernández-Cruz, who had emphasized the regard in which doctors were held because they were educated, and I asked about this. Pau Lluis said, 'Both points are correct. The Spanish countryside loves the medical man because he can do something and despises the scholar because he can do nothing but read. Don't forget that Don Quixote was held to be a fool principally because he read books. The idea still exists.' At another time he said in frustration, 'Of all the major countries, Spain has the greatest need for intelligence, and we distrust our universities, which are the only agencies that can provide it. Most of those people out there, even in Barcelona, honestly believe that if the students said their prayers and listened to the police, they wouldn't need the university.'

I asked whether the riots in Barcelona, which had been prolonged and violent, had anything to do with Catalan nationalism, and Pau Lluis laughed. 'Everywhere I went in the north, on that trip when I met you, people asked the same question. In the last four years I haven't once heard Catalan separatism mentioned seriously. We used to talk about it in lower school . . . the poets . . . the bad days of betrayal. But now what sensible man would believe that Cataluña could exist as a separate state? That's what you go to university for. To learn some sense.'

'Do you think of yourself as a Catalan? Or as a Spaniard?'

'As a Catalan. An American who studied with us last year said, "If I hadn't known Texas, I wouldn't have understood Cataluña. They're Texans first and Americans second. You're even worse." He was right, I suppose. But as a Catalan I'm quite satisfied to be part of Spain. It could be good for both of us. As a matter of fact, Spain without Cataluña would be a miserable place.'

'Were the priests who rioted also free of politics?'

'Quite. If you read the stories carefully you saw that the reason the priests marched in defiance of police orders was to show their support for us students. That's all it was. On the other hand, the police had begun to resent the freedom with which young priests were speaking out on social problems, so I suppose you'd call that politics. When the government gave the word "Beat up those damned priests," the police did it with real brutality. I was there, marching behind the priests, and it would have been just as easy for the police to beat us up but they were gunning for the priests and they waded in dreadfully. It was very bad to see. A priest would fall down and the police would jump on him and club him. It was the natural hatred for the priest in black showing itself in a new form.'

'How do the students feel about the Church?'

On that one Pau Lluis bit his cheeks for a long time. 'We were pleased that the priests marched in our defense. It was a ray of hope. Maybe the Church is going to abandon the big families and the army and finally help the people. Certainly the young priests know that this is what it should do.'

'The Church as a whole?'

'I know only Cataluña. Here there's a possibility, but I suppose you know that once again, when our bishopric became vacant, they refused to appoint a Catalan and brought in some fellow from Astorga. I think the Madrid government fears the Catalan church as much as it does the Catalan university.'

In the days when I knew Pau Lluis there was great agitation in the Church. Seminarians marched out on strike, something unheard of before. Junior priests signed manifestoes which they carried in person to newspaper offices, so that even though we were unable to find out what was being protested, we knew that protests of a vital nature were being made. Other priests of high rank circulated petitions demanding that the precepts of Pope John XXIII be followed in reforming the Spanish clergy. And in a small city not far from Barcelona, one priest who was outspoken in his demand for a general reform of the Church was arrested and publicly charged with having had immoral relations with a female parishioner in the back seat of an automobile. No one I met could recall ever before having heard of a public charge of this nature. It seemed to a group of Americans, some of them Catholic, who followed the turmoil, as if 'the young priests had matriculated at Berkeley.'

Pau Lluis was an unusual student in that he spoke no foreign language; we conducted our conversations in Spanish, and when we encountered a subject for which my Spanish did not suffice we sought out translators, and one Saturday afternoon while traveling out into the countryside to visit the lodgings of the student from England, I became involved in an experience which quite startled me. We were riding in one of Spain's good trains and the coach was crowded with a group of schoolgirls heading for a weekend camping trip, accompanied by four young, attractive nuns. After a preliminary half-hour of squealing as we pulled out of Barcelona, the girls subsided into informal group singing. 'My Bonnie Lies Over the Ocean' and 'Old Black Joe' they dedicated to me. I think they next sang 'Cielito Lindo,' which made their first three songs English, American and Mexican, which was properly international for a group of Catalans. Then they began a soft folk song, one of the best ever written; I have often wondered why it has not been introduced to the United States, for it seems to me to have everything a song of this type requires. I could not believe that the girls of this Catholic school were singing it, so I asked one of the nuns, 'What's the song?'

' "Stinki Rass," ' she said.

They were even singing it under its own name; in the United States some school-board member would have insisted that new words be substituted, for this was one of the great revolutionary songs. 'What do the words mean?' I asked.

'It's a song of freedom,' the nun said. 'Stinki Rass was a man who loved freedom.'

The girls were singing a Catalan version of 'Stenka Razin,' the Volga folk song that speaks of the famous revolutionary who defied the tsar and surrendered his head on the public chopping block sometime around 1700. It was an unlikely song for Spain, the apotheosis of revolt against tyranny, and I was not satisfied that the girls knew what they were singing, so I made further inquiry, and the same nun said, 'Stinki Rass fought against the tsar and was beheaded.' When I asked why he was fighting, she said, 'For freedom.'

It was not the first time I had been perplexed by the contradictions of Spanish censorship. A man was arrested for spiriting Protestant Bibles into the country, but this Catholic school was honoring Stenka Razin as freedom's hero. In a Spanish cinema house I saw an Italian motion picture about Benvenuto Cellini in which Pope Paul IV was shown defending the Catholic Church against the infamous troops of Spain, and periodically one character or another reviled Spain and Carlos V; they were the villains and were so specified, but the censor had not objected, yet not long ago an American was thrown in jail for having spoken disrespectfully of Spain.

I remember when I was visited in my hotel room in a northern city by a newspaperman. He wanted to talk with someone from the outside world and spent several hours telling me how censorship operated in his field. 'I have a friend in the French city of Hendaye, and each month he crosses the bridge into Irún and mails me the liberal journals from France.' From a briefcase he produced four or five magazines which were obviously more valuable to him than food. 'I know what's going on in the world. I'm at least as good a writer as you are. I'm a professional, and I could write brilliant articles on what's going to happen in the next ten years, where the government's making mistakes. Michener, I know.' He was close to having tears in his eyes as he translated from the clandestine magazine a series of titles which had attracted him: 'De Gaulle and the Gold Standard.' 'Harold Wilson's Four Major Problems.' 'The Failure of Johnson's Viet Nam Policy.' He tapped the magazines and said, 'That's what a man writes. What do they make me write?'

He handed me a piece of paper on which, having anticipated meeting with me, he had typed out the titles of his last three articles: '¿Existe el hombre abominable de las nieves?' (Does the Abominable Snowman

Exist?), 'El crimen en Chicago' (Crime in Chicago), and '¿Es verdad que los ingleses aman Isabel Segunda?' (Is It True That the English Love Elizabeth II?) He said that more intellectual ability was being wasted in Spain than in any other nation he knew, and he could foresee no end to it.

Pau Lluis and I debarked at a seaside resort well south of Barcelona and walked over sand to a beach house where a group of students waited to pepper me with questions. Like the newspaperman of the north, they were as intelligent as those of similar age in America. For a long time they spoke of nothing but my country, and their knowledge of it was astonishing. They wanted to know what role McNamara was playing in the government and whether Bobby Kennedy would run for President in 1968. They were, like all Europeans, especially interested in the *Report of the Warren Commission* and were unprepared to accept it, but their rejection was not based on personal prejudice; they had read of certain books contesting the *Report* and had been influenced by them.

Finally my turn to ask questions came. I wanted to explore the problem of how far politics intruded into the student riots, and as soon as the subject was broached I found a willingness to talk which quite surprised me. If students in Stalin's Russia, Hitler's Germany or Mussolini's Italy had spoken so openly of their grievances, they would probably have been shot; I suppose that in Franco's Spain if I were to betray the individuals who talked with me, they would also be in some kind of trouble, but of a much lesser degree, because these students showed no hesitancy, which they would have had to do with a stranger if their lives were endangered.

'Pau Lluis is right. This is not a political movement, essentially. It's an attempt to force choices now, before the big changes come at Franco's death.' The speaker was a girl who looked as un-revolutionary as a student could. She was quiet and obviously middle-class, with an interest in social problems. It was her opinion that the students and the young priests were trying to impress the government with the fact that they must be taken into account when the new Spain was formed. 'We can't have the old sloppy university teaching. We won't tolerate it.' To hear her and Pau Lluis one would have thought that Spain's major problem was improvement of the university.

A more radical young man, a would-be engineer, for the students I met were enrolled in practical courses, with no poets or philosophers intermixed, had a different opinion: 'Politics has had no part in launching these student riots. We've spent little time discussing specific steps to be taken when the change comes. I have no interest in politics, but of late I've seen that in the end we shall have to become involved. We will want certain things, just as the young priests do, and in the end the police will bang us over the head, and we'll be in politics.'

I asked what form this participation would take, and he said, 'The students, the young priests, the young businessmen will say, "The New

Along all the beaches of the Mediterranean it is the foreign girl who attracts and perplexes the men of Spain.

Spain must have this kind of freedom," and the Old Spain will say, "Now you be still and we'll make the decisions," and somebody will have to get banged on the head. It'll be us, and in the end we'll have to align with labor and I suppose they'll have to send the army against us, and there we are!'

We pursued this for some minutes and there were those who agreed, up to the point of army intervention. 'There will be no civil war,' students like Pau Lluis believed. The engineer asked, 'But if we are pushed too far?' The students refused to say, 'Then there will be war.' Instead they said, 'No one wants a return of 1936.'

There was agreement, however, that I would see a good deal more student agitation within the next year, and even before I had reached home it had erupted in both Madrid and Barcelona. The students also warned me that labor, having taken heart from the example of the students, would begin to strike, and this too happened as they had predicted. They also said that the government, aware of these pressures, would liberalize the constitution; they had seen reports of this in the *New York*

Times but not in their local newspapers, and again they were right, for shortly after, Generalísimo Franco announced a liberalization of the form of government, although not much relaxation in actual operation. In other words, the students understood rather well what was happening.

There was heated discussion of a point on which I was uninformed and whose intricacies I could not follow: the government in Madrid had promulgated a fake student organization with appointed representatives, 'no better than the labor syndicates,' one of the engineers said, and the students were determined to by-pass it and elect their own representatives. Whereas politics in the abstract did not arouse them, this matter of a union did, and I could anticipate the pragmatic steps whereby they would escalate from university problems to national ones, and I suppose that this was why the Madrid government had cracked down so hard.

At the conclusion of the meeting Pau Lluis surprised me by inviting me to his home, a comfortable apartment in the western end of Barcelona, where his small, attractive mother and businessman father were pleased to entertain me. They were perplexed, as all parents are, at having bred a son who had strong opinions, but they were proud that other young people sought him out as if his opinions were important. 'What should Pau Lluis do about his education?' his mother asked. She seemed no older than forty and must have married young. 'It's disreputable for a boy his age not to be attending classes.' Her husband turned out to be an aficionado of the zarzuela and had a large collection of records; he was relieved when I turned the conversation away from his son, who was in trouble no matter how well behaved he might appear, and spoke of *La revoltosa* and *Gigantes y cabezudos*. The Fregs served a formal tea, much as I might have got in London except that the cakes were sweeter and the tea weaker. Señora Freg came back to her son's education: 'From what you hear, is there any chance that the university will reopen soon?' I told her that in American circles it was believed that classes must reopen soon; it was only logical not to penalize an entire student body. 'But this is Spain,' she said reflectively, as if here it was not illogical to stamp out intelligence that seemed to be developing a mind of its own. Her husband remarked wryly that it was good to know that in California, too, people had trouble with their universities. 'It's not localized.' The Fregs were proud of their studious son and dreadfully apprehensive. They showed this by their reaction to me; Pau Lluis had shown them a clipping about my lecture and they realized that he would not have taken the trouble to make my acquaintance if he were not an exceptional boy, but they also knew that he would not have done so unless he had a kind of radical approach which must ultimately place him in conflict with the police. I wanted to tell them that Pau Lluis was as stable a young fellow as one could expect to meet under the current circumstances, but I lacked the Spanish. However, I mumbled something to that effect and I believe they got the drift.

It was now time to leave Barcelona and I did so with reluctance, for the city had been a revelation to me, and my wife was pleased that I shared the enthusiasm she had developed years earlier. When speaking of Andalucía, I said that if I were a young workman stuck away in some bleak pueblo I would emigrate to Barcelona, and the more I saw of the city the more surprised I was that the influx from the south had not been greater; but it is necessary to complete the analysis. If I were a young Catalan with intellectual promise I think I would leave Barcelona and emigrate to Madrid, and I would do so for two reasons. I am inherently suspicious of separatist movements, whether active or sentimental, political or artistic, and I fear that Catalan nationalism would in the long run weaken me. Also, I would want to be in Madrid because for the next forty or fifty years it is there that the decisions will be made, and as a Catalan intellectual I might play an important role in helping make them. The figure of speech with which I opened this chapter was more relevant than I had supposed: Barcelona has the heady and dangerous quality of champagne and should be taken in moderation.

One of the pleasant aspects of the city is that it serves as the sea terminus for the Baleares, which, with Palma as their capital, have long provided a romantic holiday land for vacationers from northern Europe. Here George Sand and Frédéric Chopin came when there were no hotels on Mallorca; today there is a heavier concentration of tourist facilities than elsewhere in Spain: sixteen hundred hotels, five thousand bars, ten thousand tourist shops and two and a half million visitors a year. Impossible as it seems, in the winter season one can leave Sweden by plane, spend three months in Palma in a top-class hotel with all meals and fly back to Sweden for a total cost of $248. At one hotel the manager told me, 'And because we happen to be outside of town, if you stay with us, we allow you the use of a car at no extra cost.'

My wife and I took a night boat to Palma, and asked the steward to call us an hour before dawn so that we could go on deck to watch the islands rising from the sea. How beautiful Mallorca was! First the mountains showed like a dark mass, sufficiently high to assure us that they would contain valleys, which are among the chief pleasures of the place. Then as dawn brightened, much of the darkness changed to green forests, so that Mallorca was going to be a verdant island. Next we saw lines of white cliffs dropping down to the water's edge and these I had not heard about, so I asked a sailor, 'Does Mallorca have so many cliffs?' He peered into the uncertain light and said, 'Hotels. They're all hotels.'

Now, as the sun approached the horizon, I saw for the first time the fortress on the hill that guards Palma, and before long its round gray towers caught the first direct rays of sunlight. I could imagine how impres-

Spain's ye-ye boys are giving signs
that they refuse to take seriously the leadership
of Church, army and landed families

The harbor of Barcelona is a place of much coming and going.

sive those battlements must have seemed to pirates moving in to sack the place, which happened frequently, or to armies obliged to lay siege to Palma. One part of the Baleares had had a chameleon-like existence; it had been occupied by Phoenicians, Carthaginians, Greeks, Romans, Visigoths, Muslims, and in the age of stability, when it was presumed to be Spanish, by a whole parade of European powers.

As I was reviewing this turbulent history, full sunlight burst over Palma and I saw, standing beside the sea, the great cathedral which since its inception has been the conspicuous symbol of Mallorca. It was a magnificent sight, this poem of stone rising from the waves, and if one complains that in cities like Toledo, Sevilla and Barcelona one can barely see the cathedrals because of encroaching houses and shops, the deficiency is repaired here, where the cathedral stands as free as a lighthouse on a promontory. The full sun was now reflected from the white hotel faces, so that more than ever they resembled cliffs, and my wife said, 'There ought to be sea gulls flying out of them.'

I had made the trip to Mallorca not to see one of Europe's major playgrounds but rather to pay my respects to the greatest Catalan of history, a man of cloudy reputation but grandeur of spirit, a bit of a charlatan but a leader of the Church and one of the most congenial figures in Spanish history, whose fame has always been relished by a few and whose general quality must one day be recognized by the many. In the uncomplicated days of the medieval period when to be Christian was to be Catholic and when, even though heresy might crop out here or there to be speedily exterminated, there was not yet open schism, the five major nations of Europe produced five scholastic philosophers. In the order of appearance the first four were Abélard of France (1079–1142), Albertus Magnus of Germany (1193–1280), Thomas Aquinas of Italy (1225–1274) and Duns Scotus of England (1265–1308). In Spain the comparable figure was the Catalan from Mallorca known throughout Europe as the Doctor Illuminatus, Ramón Llull (1235–1315). In English he is known as Raymond Lull (or sometimes Lully) and in Latin as Raymundo Lulio, but each of these names is deceptive as·far as pronunciation is concerned, for it is Yool.

The date of his birth to a noble family of Mallorca is significant, in that Christians recaptured the island in 1232, only three years before Llull was born, so that in effect he was a child of Muslim–Christian inheritance. For the first thirty years of his life he proved to be an ordinary fellow with certain extraordinary habits. He was a roisterer, married early to Blanca Picany, who seems to have been a stable woman of deep sensibility by whom he had children, including a son to whom he wrote a delightful book about growing up. The first unusual thing about Llull was that he wrote poetry, and very good poetry too, of a high lyrical pitch but not much spiritual content. Mallorca legend says that his life would have gone forward in customary routine, focusing on his good wife and his beloved children, except that one day he conceived a passion for a young unmarried woman of the city. He was driven to confusion by her pale beauty and one day rode his horse into the center of the church during worship so as to impress her with his love. She rebuffed him in various ways and there was talk of calling in her male kinsmen to chastise him, but at this point she chose a more dramatic gesture. She had her duenna arrange an assignation, and when she was alone with Llull she confessed that she was smitten with him but that one thing had deterred her from confessing her love, and having said this, she undressed to the waist and allowed him to see her breast eaten away by cancer and she only weeks from death.

The impact upon Llull was so staggering that he became more or less unhinged. The girl died on schedule, and he began that withdrawal from life which became so pronounced that his wife had to sue the court for the appointment of a custodian for his possessions, and this was done. Henceforth Llull was in effect a penniless friar. After a pilgrimage on foot to Santiago de Compostela, he joined the Franciscan Order; and after a sustained mystical experience in which he beheld Christ five times, he conceived the idea that he had been chosen to convert Islam to Christianity. Later he realized that to accomplish this he must know Arabic; finding that faithful Muslims would not teach him the language when his avowed purpose was to subvert Muhammad, he escaped their boycott by borrowing enough money from his wife to purchase an Arab slave whose only job was to teach him Arabic. When the task was done and Llull could speak the language—he never learned Latin—he tested his powers by conducting a theological disputation with his slave, but the latter must have been a courageous man, for either he bested Llull in the argument, proving that Muhammad was superior to Christ, or he blasphemed Christianity; whatever the case, Llull flew into a rage and killed his slave. His remorse was so great that from this time he lived by only one rule, 'He who loves not, lives not.'

It would be a pleasure to recite the accomplishments of this brilliant man, but recently I came upon a passage from Havelock Ellis' tribute to Llull, written in 1902 when Ellis was among the first writers in English to bring the Catalan philosopher to the attention of Europe, and this sums up the matter:

> The multiplicity of Lull's acquirements remains astonishing. He wrote, as a matter of course, of metaphysics, logic, rhetoric, grammar, dogmatics, ethics; these were within the province of every schoolman. But beyond these, he dealt with geometry, astronomy, physics, chemistry, anthropology, as well as law and statecraft, navigation and warfare and horsemanship. He foresaw the problem of thermo-dynamics, the question of the expenditure of heat in the initiation of movement; he discussed the essential properties of the elements; he was acquainted with the property of iron when touched by the magnet to turn to the north; he endeavored to explain the causes of wind, and rain, and ice; he concerned himself with the problems of generation. He foresaw the Tartar invasion before the coming of the Ottomans, and he firmly believed in the existence of a great continent on the other side of the world centuries before Columbus sailed out into the west. He was not a great scientific discoverer or investigator, he had not the exclusively scientific temperament of another great Franciscan of that day, Roger Bacon; but his keen and penetrating intelligence placed him at the head and even in front of the best available knowledge of his time, and we can but wonder that a man who began life as the gay singer of a remote centre of chivalry, and ended it as a martyr to faith, should have possessed so much cold, intellectual acumen, so much quiet energy, to devote to the interpretation of the visible world.

Ellis' imposing catalogue fails to touch the two facets of Llull's career that attracted me to him. I do not mean his perfection of the astrolabe, whereby travelers were able to ascertain where they were on the ocean, nor his writing of two hundred and twenty-eight treatises on almost every important topic of his age, but rather the fact that it was Ramón Llull who intellectually initiated the cult of the Virgin; his philosophical expositions paved the way for the doctrines of Immaculate Conception, Intercession and Assumption. (The theological underpinning was provided by Duns Scotus.) Therefore, since the cult of the Virgin has become the central fact of Spanish theology and perhaps of Spanish thought in general, Llull must be recognized as one of Spain's prime movers.

The second reason why I regarded him so highly had to do with other matters. Years before, when I was studying Muslim and Jewish thought in the eastern Mediterranean, I came upon an essay whose title and author I have forgotten, because at the time I was not concerned with the problem it discussed; it was called something like 'Raymundo Lulio and the Last Crusade' and was by a Jewish author who took a rather dim view of Llull, because the Franciscan had conceived a scatterbrained idea of converting all Jews and Muslims to Catholicism by means of his rational persuasion alone. It was a brilliant essay, and long after I had read it and apparently forgotten it, the picture of Ramón Llull returned to stand with me at unexpected places. In Cyprus I recalled that Llull had journeyed there in hopes of converting the Tartars, whom he mistakenly believed to have overrun the Holy Land. When I wandered among the barren rocks of Carthage, Llull appeared, and at Tunis he was very much present, for he had gone there to argue with the sultan and to prove deductively the superiority of Christ. In Paris there was Llull; in Rome, where he went so often to plead with the popes for a crusade of the intellect and not of the sword; and in a half dozen other cities of the Mediterranean where he had engaged in disputation with Jews and Muslims, trying to convert them by his logic.

'I see many knights going to the Holy Land beyond the seas,' he reasoned with the Pope, 'and thinking that they can acquire it by force of arms; but in the end all are destroyed before they attain that which they think to have. Whence it seems to me that the conquest of the Holy Land ought not to be attempted except in the way in which Jesus Christ and his apostles acquired it in the first place, namely, by love and prayers and the pouring out of treasure and blood.' He ended all his exhortations with the reminder 'He who loves not, lives not.'

It was with these recollections of a man who had become a brother to me that I watched our ship dock at Palma, where Llull had galloped his legendary horse into church to seek an assignation with his reluctant lady. As soon as the gangplank was lowered I set off for the Basílica de San Francisco, whose three-tiered cloister marked by palm trees is one of the choice sights of Mallorca. There I had the good luck to meet the young Franciscan who directed the monastery attached to the basilica, Father Antonio Riutford, who seemed scarcely old enough for such a job. He was a scholar and well versed in the life of Ramón Llull, of whom he said, 'Fine philosopher. Poor theologian.' To confirm this judgment he led me to the stained-glass window which showed St. Francis and St. Dominic watching with approval as Ramón Llull in purple robes and Duns Scotus in blue announce their doctrine of the Virgin. 'Llull for ideas. Scotus for sanctity,' Father Riutford said. He then took me to a second window overlooking the nave of the church, and here Llull appeared in the brown robes of a Franciscan, preaching to Muslims with more success than he enjoyed in real life; the window is striking in that the unbelievers are not struck dumb by Llull's eloquence. They listen with dignity to the Doctor Illuminatus and some of them have voluntarily moved into the ranks of his converts.

Next Father Riutford showed me a painting which has caused much discussion. It shows Llull twice: first as a bearded old man of eighty preaching on the shores of Africa as an angel brings him a martyr's crown; second as he dies a miserable death supported by his defenders, who are unable to save him from his Muslim executioners. 'A very dubious work,' Father Riutford admitted. 'Had he died so, he would surely have become a saint. The fact seems to be that he went to Africa, preached to the Muslims, accomplished nothing and sailed back to Mallorca. When his ship was in sight of Palma, he died.' Through delicacy, perhaps, Father Riutford did not bore me with the unbecoming struggle that enveloped Llull in death. Franciscans insisted that he had died a martyr and must be made a saint; Dominicans laughed at the claim and charged instead that he was a heretic and should be posthumously excommunicated. Through the centuries one pope inclined toward one interpretation, his successor to the other; as a result Ramón Llull has not even yet been proclaimed a saint.

This Papal ambivalence was duplicated among the citizens of Palma, who could not decide whether Llull was saint or heretic. 'This nave summarizes the story,' Father Riutford says. 'Originally Llull was buried in this chapel over here, but antagonisms between his supporters and his detractors became so vicious, with brawling and the defacing of his grave, that the Franciscans judged it might be wiser to hide his ashes down there, in the ground under the altar. Long after this was done, it was decided that it was a humiliation to a great man, and if he couldn't stand forth in his own church, where could he? So the hidden urn was dug up and Llull was buried anew in this other chapel back in the apse. It's a beautiful tomb, but as you might have expected, it's been left unfinished for these last five hundred years. Those responsible for the church have not yet been able to agree as to what kind of man Llull was.'

It was a strange tomb that Llull's followers erected in the 1450s. Well above the level of the eye rests a stone sarcophagus decorated with the jacent statue of a bearded old man holding a rosary in hands clasped for prayer, but the statue does not occupy a normal position on the lid of the sarcophagus; it is carved on the side facing the viewer. Llull, therefore, does not lie parallel to the floor but sleeps on his elbow and looks as if he might fall off the side at any moment. There were supposed to be two statues flanking his tomb, Philosophy and Theology. Below, so that their heads would have stood at eye level, should have been seven additional statues representing: Grammar, Logic, Rhetoric (the trivium) and Arithmetic, Music, Geometry and Astronomy (the quadrivium). The niches are waiting, set off by Gothic pilasters, and angels stand by with crowns to grace the missing figures, but the statues have not been completed even though sculptors have had five hundred years to do the job.

'Mallorca has never been able to make up its mind,' Father Riutford said, showing me a crypt which had been dug under the altar in 1915, the sixth centenary of Llull's death, with the idea that his body should be identified with the Host and thus to serve as the focus for a cult. The crypt was prepared, even though many graves occupied by friars buried there over past centuries had to be dug up, but when it was finished the old animosities against Llull prevailed and the move was not permitted.

Spain as a whole has not been easy in its attitude toward Llull, who seems to have been more a Frenchman than a Spaniard; his orientation was to Paris and not to Toledo, certainly to Rome rather than to Barcelona. One of the scholars at the Madrid tertulia had told me, 'Llull is a man you can't trust. You think you have him, and he slips out of your fingers.' As the man spoke I recalled the poem Llull had written at the age of sixty-five:

> I am old, poor, unappreciated and without assistance from anyone. I have undertaken superior tasks, insofar as my ability would permit. I have journeyed through a great part of the world. Very fine examples have I given of learning, but nevertheless I am little loved and less known.

(Later, when I returned to the tertulia in Madrid, I asked Martínez López of Texas and Cossío of the Academy their opinion of Llull, and they agreed that he was one of the supreme Spaniards, whose theories have yet to be exhausted.)

I revere Llull because in his day he saw the interlocking nature of the world and was willing to sacrifice his life to help achieve unity. To him the Mediterranean was infinitely larger than the Atlantic and the Pacific are to me, yet he went forth to all the shores, preaching one message, 'He who loves not, lives not.' If the Tartars overran older civilizations, he was ready to talk with the Tartars. If the Muslims held Africa in slavery, he was prepared to walk on foot through Africa and debate with its rulers. If he came upon an island, he said, 'Let's build a university.' If a subject was obscure, he wrote a book about it, explaining its intricacies and relating them to all other known fields. Beaten and expelled from Bugia (today Bougie in Algeria), the Muslim capital on the northern coast of Africa, he blamed no one but himself, reasoning that if his logic had been more persuasive the Muslims would have listened; so after surviving shipwreck on his way to Pisa he retired to perfect his argument, after which he returned to Bugia alone to see the sultan face to face. And in spite of the defeats he met, he remained a poet to the end.

His reputation in the Church has been much damaged by one of those perplexing historical accidents that one can neither explain nor correct. In the eighteenth century a fable circulated to the effect that Ramón Llull, the world's master alchemist, had succeeded in compounding an alkahest that would speed the transmutation of lead to gold. For prudent reasons he had refrained from committing his formula to writing, but if one studied his numerous books on alchemy one could deduce the formula and with it make gold. Understandably, there was a run on Llull's alchemical works and he became famous throughout Europe. What were the names of his books on the subject? He wrote none. Close study of his major work proves that he held alchemy in contempt; certainly he ridiculed the idea of transmuting metals and frequently spoke poorly of those who tried. He was, in effect, his age's principal foe of alchemy; but because he was known to have written on chemistry, and partly, I suppose, because pictures of him showed the long beard of the typical Faustian alchemist, he became the symbol of the movement and it would have been fruitless to deny that he was its leader.

As for the alchemy books attributed to Llull, which do exist and in extraordinary number, they were all forgeries, done mostly in Germany and very late. For a book on alchemy to sell, it almost had to be signed by Raymundo Lulio, and so they proliferated. Even today the few persons who have heard of Ramón Llull are apt to remember him only as Europe's chief alchemist. For a man who founded his intellectual life on rationalism, it is a bitter trick.

I was surprised in Mallorca to find no monument to Llull, as I had been surprised in Córdoba to find none to Averroës, but at lunch I discovered why. A friend in Barcelona had asked a young scholar in Palma to supervise my lunch, and when we were seated I asked him why Llull had been ignored, and he said, 'But he wasn't. In 1915 plans were laid to erect a statue on the waterfront. The site was selected and the base was built. But . . .'

'There were objections?'

'Yes. I'm a great admirer of Llull's. He was probably the best man these islands ever produced, but there are many who consider him a heretic. So the monument was not permitted.'

It so happened that at a nearby table a medical doctor was having his lunch, and when he heard that I was from the United States he introduced himself, Dr. Antonio Bauza Roca from the Mallorcan city of Petra. 'We make many shoes there for shipment to your country, but we are famous for something quite different.' He was a peppery little man with a rim of dark hair about his bald head and a set of very dark eyebrows; he had many interests and spoke with fluency on economics, politics, shipping and literature, but when he handed me his card it was as El Presidente de la Asociación de los Amigos de Fray Junípero Serra. 'He was born in Petra,' Dr. Bauza said proudly, 'but it was in California that he found his immortality. He's buried in Carmel and we've been told he's practically the patron saint of California.'

Then, with his eyes dancing beneath their large brows, he explained why he had wanted to speak with me. 'In 1969 we celebrate the two-hundredth anniversary of Fray Junípero's arrival at San Diego. Festivities here and bigger ones in California. At that time our great project will come to fulfilment . . . the one we've been working on so hard.'

I asked what it was, and he said, 'The rich people of California consider it shameful that in Mallorca there is no fine statue to Fray Junípero, who is the greatest man ever to come from these islands. So they're collecting money and we're going to build a tall statue . . . right over there. Fray Junípero Serra, the patron of Mallorca, rising like a giant and looking across the sea toward California, the land he went to convert.'

I noticed that my luncheon partner did not respond to this news but sat with his hands clenched. When Dr. Bauza, having invited my wife and me to attend the celebrations enshrining Fray Junípero, departed, he cursed and said, 'Can you guess the spot they've chosen for their monument? The very one where the statue to Ramón Llull was to have been built. I wouldn't be surprised if they used the same base. And what did Junípero Serra ever do? He stumbled his way into California. Oh my God!'

Sadness possessed my friend as he reflected on the world's unjustness: 'A man like Ramón Llull can have the foremost mind of his age. Write more than two hundred books that kept intelligence alive. Identify the true nature of the Virgin. He can work to unite the known world, and it all comes to nothing. Even his own Church rejects him . . . his tomb is left unfinished. And all because he worked in the field of the intellect. But let an ignorant friar happen to wander across land where oil is to be discovered . . . and where American millionaires are to flourish. And all the money you would need is made available for erecting a statue to that friar.'

He turned to me in mock bitterness and said, 'You norteamericanos are ruining Spain.' Then like a conspirator he drew close and whispered, 'But if you do put up that statue to Junípero Serra . . . on the site reserved for Ramón Llull. Well, don't be surprised if some dark night the damned thing's dynamited.'

I thought it wisest not to tip my hand at this early stage, but if his plot goes forward, I plan to be in on it.

FOLLOWING PAGE:
This noble animal lost its ears in the arena
in proof of the great fight he gave.

XI

THE BULLS

0 MILES 100
OCEANO
ATLANTICO
Barcelona
SALAMANCA
Madrid
Lisboa
Linares
Córdoba
ANDALUCIA
Sevilla
Jerez de la Frontera
MAR MEDITERRANE

From that first Sunday in Valencia when I watched La-
landa, Ortega and El Estudiante fight six bulls I have been a devotee of the
bullring. Over a period of thirty-five seasons I have seen all the great
matadors in Spain and Mexico save Pepe Luis Vázquez the Spaniard,
although strangely enough I was a good friend of the Mexican matador of
that name. I have traveled with bullfighters in both countries, have read
almost everything in print in both Spanish and English, plus many fine
books in French, and instead of losing interest as the years passed, I have
found my appetite for this art increasing.

I suppose I have seen over 250 fights with full matadors, which is a
far cry from the 750 which a professional bull-follower like Kenneth
Vanderford has seen, or the amazing 114 which the American girl Virginia
Smith saw in one year by dint of driving her Renault like mad back and
forth across Spain during the bullfight season. I have long since stopped
making apologies for my interest in the bulls, but I do believe that the
following observations by a Spaniard who had lived in America will prove
relevant.

American: How can a civilized man like you tolerate bullfighting?

Spaniard: A fair question and one deserving a serious answer. I suggest
that you think of bullfighting in Spain as you would boxing in America.

American: Exactly the point I wanted to make. All decent Americans are
opposed to boxing. Each time after a boxer is killed in the ring, there is
an outcry from our responsible press, questions are asked in Congress
and movements are launched to end this bloody business.

Spaniard: Rightly so, because boxing is much more brutal than bullfighting.
And of course far more men are killed in the boxing ring than in the
bullring. Statistically boxing is more dangerous. Morally it's more
debilitating.

American: I agree. And that's why we're all against it. Why aren't you Spaniards against bullfighting?

Spaniard: To a certain extent we are. Many decent Spaniards oppose bull- fighting on precisely the grounds that decent Americans oppose box- ing. But on the other hand, there are decent Spaniards who rather like bullfighting and feel that the brutality is a small price to pay for so much beauty.

American: That's what we Americans can't understand. How can anyone argue that fleeting beauty, fine as it is, justifies a thing like bullfight- ing?

Spaniard: To understand this I invite you to compare bullfighting not with a rejected American sport like boxing, but with an accepted one like football.

American: (*aggressively*) What do you mean, football?

Spaniard: I've been following your statistics for some years, and each year your American-style football kills more than forty of your finest young men.

American: There's an accident now and then.

Spaniard: Forty men, year after year. And not dead-end kids like boxers. But the best young men of your country, many of them fine scholars. Yet I hear no outcry against football.

American: Well, football's different. Our best colleges play football.

Spaniard: Why is there no public outcry against a sport which kills forty of your best young men each year?

American: Well, football's part of the American way of life. Everybody's for football.

Spaniard: Exactly. Football's part of your way of life. Universities pay for their stadiums with football. Television earns enormous sums from bringing it into your homes. Automobiles and razor blades are sold by means of it. Newspapers, who might be expected to lead the fight against such brutality, earn much of their profits from emphasizing football. It would be ridiculous to attack something that earns every- one so much money.

American: But we don't look at football as a way to earn money. It's a manly sport.

Spaniard: To a European like me, the amazing thing is that while you're killing your forty a year, you have at your disposal a much finer version of football which kills nobody.

American: You mean soccer? The sissy game?

Spaniard: All the rest of the world plays what you call derisively the sissy game and finds it the best team game ever invented for professionals. Millions of people watch it with interest. It sells just as many automo- biles and fills just as many pages of newsprint. And it kills no one.

American: But fundamentally it's a sissy game. And it's not part of the American pattern.

Spaniard: Precisely. Because Americans demand a more brutal game. And if fine young men are killed each year, that's a small price to pay for your entertainment.

American: I've never seen anyone killed.

Spaniard: And the maimed?

American: Well, a broken neck now and then. Or your front teeth knocked out. But boys get over things like that.

Spaniard: And walk with a limp the rest of their lives. The solemn fact, according to fatality statistics, is that your football is some six hundred times more dangerous than our bullfighting. Yet you want me to go out and protest against bullfighting while I am not allowed to demand that you protest football.

American: There's this difference. In football the young man can either play or not play . . . as he wishes. In bullfighting the animal has no choice. And he's killed.

Spaniard: If you want to lament the death of a bull and forget the death of young men, it's your decision. What we might conclude is that bullfighting is a relatively safe brutal sport, and Spaniards like it. Football is a relatively dangerous brutal sport, and Americans like it.

American: Yes, but bullfighting is somehow degrading.

Spaniard: If you say so.

Although I have known most of the great matadors, some fairly well, my major interest has always been with the bull, for I find this noble animal one of the most praiseworthy beasts existing. When left with his fellows he is gentle and can be easily handled; when separated and alone he will fight anything that moves. His stubborn heroism is unmatched, for he has attacked and sometimes conquered automobiles, trains, airplanes, trucks; in organized fights with lions, tigers, elephants, bears and dogs it is seldom he who slinks away. He has a tenacity of purpose not equaled in the animal kingdom; on July 10, 1966, in the plaza at Pamplona a bull raised by César Moreno was pitted against the matador Tinín in third position. He gave a notable fight, was brave as a bull could be and was killed by a good thrust of the sword. I say killed, for the bull was technically dead, but in the waning moments of his life he walked stolidly nearly twice around the entire circumference of the ring, seeking some spot in which he could defend himself in this battleground where he had behaved with such honor. Up and down pumped the mighty hooves, here and there probed the doughty head. If men molested him, he fought them off, conserving his strength and dealing with them as he would with pestering flies. On and on he went, refusing to die, marching like a Roman legion that had been assaulted in the north of Spain, resolute and beaten and magnificent. Men standing beside me had tears in their eyes, and an awe-struck Englishman whispered, 'My God, he's a Winston Churchill of a bull.' Finding no protecting corner in which to make his final stand, he backed against the wall, his feet wide-spread, his horns still dangerous.

Lower and lower dropped the magnificent head, and at last he died. The mules dragged him in a circuit of the ring so that men could shower flowers upon him and hosannahs, but his triumphal tour dead was as nothing to the two he had made alive. It is this kind of animal one sees occasionally in the ring, and he reminds us of the quality that inheres in all animals.

The fighting bull is a special breed, and some of my happiest days in Spain and Mexico have been those long and lazy afternoons spent watching bulls in their native habitat. Dark against the brown fields, they stand in monumental groups, serenely indifferent to the stray men who happen to move upon them. My lasting memory of such days is of a group of Concha y Sierra bulls in Las Marismas, raising their heads at my approach, watching me for a few moments, then returning to their browsing. I have always loved animals and have spent many hours comparing them: the elephant is more majestic than the bull; the lion is more animated; the tiger is certainly more terrifying; but for the inherent nobility of the animal kingdom, a nobility which I have observed in dogs, in horses, in kestrels, in ants, in groundhogs, in antelope and in the three kingly beasts just named, I prefer the bull, as men of a philosophical mind have done since the beginning of time. It is not by accident that the bull marches across the rocks at Altamira and Lascaux; the young nobles of Crete could have tested their skill against lions or bears, but the adversary they chose was the bull; and the mystic rites of Mithras could have been composed around any well-proportioned animal, but it was only the bull that gave power and significance. I respond to the fighting bull of Andalucía exactly as my ancestors responded to his ancestors at Altamira and Crete.

In writing of Pamplona, I pointed out that in 1966 the last day of running with the bulls through the streets was not the last day of the fair, and this requires some explanation. That year San Fermín covered eight days, and on the first seven the running with the bulls occurred each morning as planned, but on the eighth day there was a fight but no running, and for good reason. On the first seven days the bulls to be fought each day all came from a single ranch, and what was more, all from the crop of bulls born four years earlier and raised together since birth; on the final day one bull from each of six different ranches was fought in what was called a concurso. This is a formal competition with two characteristics: a panel of judges awards a prize to the bravest bull, so that the reputation of the competing ranches is at stake; and the public is attracted by the possibility that it can, if some bull proves to be extraordinarily brave, spare that bull's life. I have seen only two concursos, the classic one held each year in Jerez de la Frontera and this one in Pamplona. I have, of course, seen several fights in which six bulls from six different ranches

The calf, bloodstained and wet, struggles to rise from the eart
At the end of his life he will struggle just as valiant
to avoid returning to the sandy earth of the aren

were brought together haphazardly, but these could not be termed concursos because there was no competition for the bravest bull, nor did the public have the right to excuse a bull from death in case he proved unusually brave. In general I have found fights built around bulls from different ranches disappointing; one gets a better sense of the bull if all six come from the same ranch.

To attempt to run the six bulls of the Pamplona concurso through the streets would have proved impossible, for since they came from different ranches and were strangers each to the other, if they were lumped together in the holding corrals at midnight, by dawn five would be dead. Bulls will not tolerate other bulls whose smell they do not know and will duel such intruders to the death. In fact, if from the same ranch a five-year-old bull were to be thrown in with a group of adjusted four-year-olds, the latter would probably kill the former because they would not be accustomed to his smell.

I remember at the Sevilla feria of 1961, when Robert Vavra and I spent about ten hours during visits to the Venta de Antequera corrals, studying two strings of bulls to be fought later. We were fortunate in the bulls we chose to concentrate upon, because one string came from the ranch of Benítez Cubero and were to give the finest six fights I have ever seen a set of six bulls give; in the corrals they were magnificent, relaxed yet quick to respond to anything unaccustomed, and we were able, by dint of careful comparison, to determine fairly well the kind of fight each bull would give and how he would be differentiated from his fellows. Our error was that we consistently underestimated the bulls; I had never seen a finer group, but I did not discover this until the fight unfolded.

The second string was not so fine but in some ways it was more interesting, and to it we gave the bulk of our attention. It was a group of six Miura bulls from the famous ranch whose animals have killed more toreros than any other and against which, at the beginning of this century, a group of matadors went on strike. Even today, when Miuras are fought, the matadors are apt to be the hungry ones of fading reputation who cannot get other fights; well-established matadors consent to fight them only rarely. Part of their evil reputation stems from the fact that the Miura ranch has been in unbroken existence longer than most others and has thus had time to build up its list of fatalities; at any rate, it is the most feared of the existing ranches and along with that of Tulio Vázquez one of the most prestigious. The Miura is noted for a sway-back body, a long neck and a relatively small head. They turn with incredible swiftness and are said to be 'all over the matador in an instant,' so that many matadors refuse to fight them. As we studied these six we began to isolate obvious characteristics: one of the bulls appeared to have homosexual tendencies, which so perplexed him that he was not going to give a good fight, nor did he; another was shy and nervous, apt to jump at unusual phenomena and always away from the source of the surprise, not toward it, but he was a splendid animal and we felt that although he would be dangerous in the first portion of the fight, when he struck the horses and was made to know the seriousness of the battle by the picadors jabbing at the hump of muscle over his neck, he would quieten down and give good combat, which proved to be the case; there were two bulls from which nothing much could be expected, for they simply lacked class, and in the arena some days later they proved to be as poor as we suspected; and there was a powerful red bull who might go either way.

He was a contentious beast and accepted no nonsense from any of the others, but he was far from suave, which a great bull should be. The more we watched him the more complex he became, for although he wanted to fight he was fundamentally unsure of himself. He fascinated us, for he was obviously a beast of much potential, and then on the morning of the fight, before the hour when the bulls are put into the little cells from which they emerge into the sunlight of the arena to give battle, that solemn hour at high noon when the peons of the matadors who are to fight that day assemble at the ring to determine how the bulls can be most fairly matched in pairs and to draw lots to see which man will fight which pair, a sly and tricky negotiation, we saw the big red bull for the last time, and he had become so self-contained, so suave that we knew he was going to be one of the memorable Miuras. He was fought by the matador Limeño from Sanlúcar de Barrameda, and he responded so well to all elements in the fight, charging the first capes, assaulting the horses and ignoring the picadors, following the red muleta at the finish, that all agreed he was the notable bull of the year.

It is by such study that men come to know bulls and to love them for the simple, brave things they are. I remember once in Madrid when Vavra and I went out to the Venta de Batán corrals to see a set of Cobaleda bulls from Salamanca. (For some inexplicable reason bulls from Andalucía are apt to be brave and strong, bulls of Salamanca quite the contrary. Of course, a fine Salamanca bull, and each year there are some, is superior to a poor Andalusian, but in general it is the bulls from the south who give good fight. Several wild guesses have been made on this subject, none of which satisfy me. It is claimed that grass in the south is richer in vitamins and the water in minerals, but analysis does not bear this out; the more even length of day in the south has been suggested, but this makes no sense at all; one argument has been persuasive, that the rocky land of Andalucía develops stronger hooves and leg muscles than the softer soil of Salamanca. Persuasive, that is until one recalls that in the swamps of Las Marismas are grown some of the finest fighting bulls so far produced, and during half of each year these animals walk only on a soft and marshy

FOLLOWING FACING PAGES:
Like members of the Guardia Civil, their weapons poised, the bulls maintain a vigil.

soil. Experts, of course, argue that it is the effort required when the bull drags his feet out of the sucking mud that builds up his muscles.)

Well, these Salamanca bulls at Madrid looked fine. They were big and in the corrals they comported themselves with dignity. But they were very heavy and their fore knees were weak. Even from the barrier Vavra could detect signs of weakness. 'Those knees won't stand up in the fight,' he predicted, and later when these pathetic creatures came into the ring they made one or two charges, as their taurine hearts commanded, but then their knees gave out and they fell into heaps around the ring, too heavy to get back up on their feet. The fight degenerated into a dismal spectacle of one pass, bull down, haul the bull back up, another pass, bull down again. Two of the poor creatures, their hearts still willing but their legs played out, simply lay on the sand and protected themselves by cutting swaths with their horns; to get them to their weakened legs proved most difficult. The afternoon was a travesty, the worst I've ever seen. My only consolation was that long before the fight we had guessed that it would probably be so.

As I explained in the chapter on Badajoz, I am loath to introduce unfamiliar Spanish words which are not essential, and foreigners who write about bulls offend in this respect, peppering their pages with italic instead of information, but for what I wish to say from here on, a limited taurine vocabulary is necessary, with as many of the words as possible kept in English:

Torero includes all men engaged in the fight, whether matador, picador, peon or banderillero.

Cuadrilla (crew) is the team working in support of one matador. It consists of two mounted picadors who ride on horses supplied by the ring, and three peons, who are called banderilleros when engaged in placing the banderillas.

Corrida (a running) is the complete bullfight, customarily consisting of six bulls from the same ranch fought by three matadors. The senior man in point of service fights bulls number one and four; the second, bulls two and five; and the junior, bulls three and six. Since it requires about twenty minutes to fight one bull, the corrida lasts about two hours. In June fights may start as late as seven; in the autumn as early as four. I have often seen acceptable fights on rainy days but never on windy.

Single fight is the action of one matador against one bull. It has been described by earlier writers as a ritualistic drama in three unequal acts, plus prologue and epilogue. One advocate of this interpretation has said, 'The prologue, which consists of the matador's testing the bull with the cape, might be thought of as *A Midsummer Night's Dream*, with its airy joy. The first act with the picadors is heavy like *King Lear*. The relatively unimportant but poetic second act of the banderilleros is *Twelfth Night*. The stupendous third act, heavy with emotion and impending tragedy, when the matador alone faces his destiny, is of course *Hamlet*, while the overpowering epilogue of death can be likened only to Aeschylus.'

634

Don Quixote . . . a wash drawing by Picasso . . . an echo from the Caves of Altamira . . . a bull and picador separated from their forms . . . all these can be seen at certain moments of the corrida.

Cape is the large stiff-fabric cloth, magenta on one side, yellow on the other, used by the matador in the prologue and first two acts and by the peons throughout. The bull will charge either color equally.

Pic is the long steel-tipped pick or lance used by the picador in the first act.

Banderillas are the colorfully decorated short sticks with barbed steel points which are placed in pairs by the banderilleros in the bull's shoulders.

Muleta is the red-flannel cloth, smaller than a cape, used by the matador during the third act and epilogue.

Faena is the vital third act in which the matador exhibits his skill with the muleta. Tradition requires that during the faena he keep his sword in his right hand, which usually also holds the muleta. Experts judge that the excellence of any single fight depends about sixty to seventy percent on the faena, which can excuse poor work elsewhere.

Kill is the tragic epilogue that ends the fight.

Let me make one thing clear. Most corridas are a disappointment. Six bulls are fought, and of them, five are apt to be so difficult that the matador cannot parade his skill. In all the years I've been seeing corridas, only the six Benítez Cubero bulls of which I have spoken gave a uniformly excellent show. No other set has ever provided even as many as four good fights, and the vast majority have provided none. Of a hundred corridas taken at random at least eighty will be bores; ten will be reasonably good; five will be unquestionably good; four will be worth remembering; and one might be superb. Therefore, the mathematical chances of buying a ticket on impulse and seeing a good fight are at least four to one against. At one catastrophic San Isidro feria in Madrid of sixteen fights, fourteen were very poor and the other two barely acceptable.

At the Pamplona feria in 1966, government inspectors found that sixteen of the forty-eight bulls failed to meet legal standards, being either underage, underweight or with the tips of their horns shaved off. Fines of 265,000 pesetas were assessed, and this in a feria which was supposed to emphasize the excellence of the bull. In the two hundred and fifty corridas I've attended my luck has been poor, for I have seen even fewer good fights than the averages would have indicated.

In watching a single fight I have said that it should be considered as a ritual drama, and philosophically this is correct. Occasionally one can receive from this tragic play a catharsis precisely like that described by Aristotle, and that is why so many foreign writers have been attracted to the bullfight. I have found it more practical to see the single fight as a spectacle built up of several identifiable skills, for in this way I can better judge what I am seeing. A really complete single fight would consist of six components, each performed with art, as follows: one, after the bull enters the ring and has been tested by the peons, the matador must initiate his part of the fight with a series of delicate and artistic passes with his large cape; two, the bull must then three times attack with resolute bravery the picador and horse, and the picador must handle his lance properly; three, after each pic the three matadors in proper turn must lead the bull away from the horse and execute artistic and sometimes intricate passes with their large capes; four, three separate pairs of banderillas must be placed correctly and with art; five, the matador with his muleta must build an artistic faena consisting of a series of linked passes that make sense; six, the matador must kill proudly and honorably, going in over the horn and finishing the bull with one thrust.

Well, that makes six components for each bull or a total of thirty-six for an afternoon, and if on a given day you see out of thirty-six as many as four items properly performed, you've not been cheated. On some afternoons you see none. To see all six performed well on a single bull is so rare as to be historic, and to see the six performed well on each bull of the

Matador Fulton with cape.

afternoon would be positively impossible. It has never happened and never will. At the beginning of the Pamplona feria in 1966, I had seen some fifteen hundred bulls fought and had never seen one on which the six components were properly performed, and I did not expect ever to do so.

These doleful facts are summarized in a saying which reports as a permanent truth: 'Si hay toros, no hay toreros; si hay toreros, no hay toros.' (If there are bulls, there are no bullfighters; if there are bullfighters, there are no bulls.) This applies equally to golf, to love-making, to buying stock in the Xerox Corporation and to most other human endeavors: 'When everything looks right, some one thing is bound to go wrong.'

For the uninitiated foreigner, especially one who loves animals, a corrida is usually an unrewarding experience; he sees a confusing spectacle in which the bull appears only as a necessary and fractious evil who, after disrupting everyone's plans, ends ignominiously as a kind of animated pincushion. The animal is without individualized personality; and it is not illogical for the foreigner seeing his first fight to hope that the bull will catch or even kill the matador, for that would introduce into the mysterious rites at least a focal point of comprehension. But when one has attended many corridas and has begun to catch a glimmer of the intricate and subtle construction of a bullfight, he begins to center his attention on the animal, and occasionally he will sense the overtones of the tremendous drama being enacted before him: the confrontation of man and primordial animal. The devotee therefore finds something of interest in every corrida, for this confrontation can take any of various forms and all are challenging.

What have I found in the Spanish bullfight? A flash of beauty, a swift development of the unexpected, a somber recollection of primitive days when men faced bulls as an act of religious faith. In the bulls I have found a symbol of power and grandeur; in the men I have seen a professionalism which is usually honorable if not always triumphant. I have never seen a corrida which did not teach me something or which did not at some point develop unexpectedly, and I am willing to settle for this limited experience. No matter how disastrous the fight, and some of them can be dreadful, there is the ancient drama of hopeful man and savage beast and the mysterious bond that exists between them.

I have stressed the professionalism of the matador because when one enters a plaza, having paid up to twenty-five dollars for the privilege, he can be reasonably assured that if a good bull thunders into the arena, the man facing it has served an apprenticeship which taught him to give a decent fight. Since top matadors earn enormous sums of money, say seven thousand dollars a fight for eighty or ninety fights a year, the competition is grueling, for the bullring is the traditional route by which boys from impoverished families attain bull ranches of their own, and fame, and wealthy wives. It is a matter of endless training, the fighting of imaginary bulls day after day in the public parks of Madrid or Sevilla. One boy grasps a pair of horns, bends over, snorts like a bull and charges into the cape or the muleta held by another boy. Hour after hour they practice, first one boy playing the bull, then another. At home they practice passes before mirrors to attain grace, and always they bum about the countryside seeking invitations to those testing exhibitions in which the young heifers of the bull ranch are thrown against picadors and matadors to see whether they are brave or not. If the heifer charges the horse bravely, and we have seen at Trujillo and Pamplona how these scrawny, awkward beasts attack, driving at any moving object time and again, she is set aside for breeding purposes. If the heifer proves faulty or unwilling to attack when hurt, she is ticketed for beef. (If you think for a moment, you will understand why it

In each bullfight come moments of nightmare intensi
when forms melt together and strange combinations appea

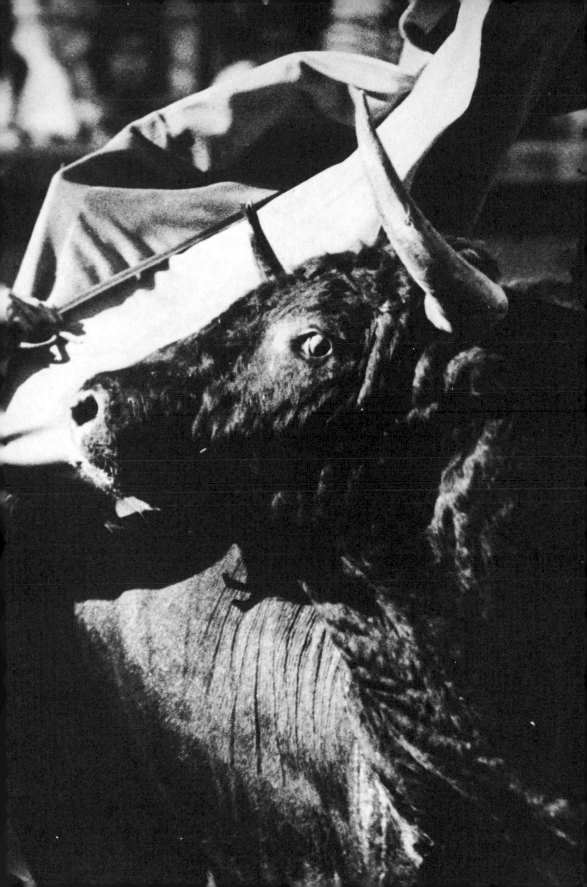

is the heifers who are tested and not the young bulls; these animals learn so quickly that if the males were tested with capes when young they would remember, and when they entered the arena against the matador they would kill him. Since the bravery of a bull is determined primarily by his mother, she must therefore be tested to see if she is brave; the father contributes only the young bull's physical conformation, and a visual inspection tells whether it is satisfactory or not.) At any rate, the would-be matador must seek out these testings to familiarize himself with the bull family and to exhibit the skill he has learned in the parks and before the mirror. Especially he must keep his ear tuned for word of any village festivals in which improvised arenas are set up in the main plaza, with upended carts forming the barriers and boards protecting store windows, for at these rowdy festivals wise old bulls are turned loose on which aspirant matadors can try their skills without killing the animal. The bulls have attended so many festivals they know better than the young fighters how to position themselves and when to react to the passes. 'That bull speaks Latin,' is a customary description. I once heard a young fighter say, 'After I gave him two good passes he tried to borrow money from me.' The Mexicans have a wonderful word for such goings-on. Pachangas, they call them, and the syllables evoke the madness; capeas they're called in Spain, and they do not always end humorously. Each year some aspirant is badly gored by the canny old beasts and sometimes death results. But the competition to become a full matador is so keen that young men must take these chances.

Of a thousand boys who begin at age twelve to learn the bullfighting passes, perhaps a hundred will succeed in fighting one of the old bulls at a capea; far fewer will ever face a heifer at a ranch. Of a hundred who progress to the point where they have actually fought bulls as beginners, only four or five will become full matadors. And of a hundred full matadors, only four or five will become big stars. The adverse odds in this profession are overwhelming.

But since the rewards can be overwhelming, each year the horde of boys at practice remains about the same, and some very moving literature has grown out of this drudgery. Anyone interested in the purely seamy side should read Luis Spota's *The Wounds of Hunger*, which has been translated into English by Barnaby Conrad. It is based on the saying that for a bullfighter the wounds of hunger are more terrifying than the wounds of the horn.

There are several fine recent books on bullfighting, and as in the case of Spain generally, the best are by Englishmen; Kenneth Tynan's perceptive *Bull Fever*, which analyzes the mystique of the art; Angus Macnab's *The Bulls of Iberia*, which has some excellent summaries of individual

e horns, which might be seen in any pueblo
Spain, are those of an old bull.
e face is that of an old man.

fights; and John Marks' *To the Bullfight,* of which Hemingway said, 'the best book on the subject—after mine.' Of recent American books the three best are, perhaps symbolically, compendiums featuring photographs, but they are very good: Peter Buckley's *Bullfight,* which gives a fine account of how matadors cruise back and forth across Spain; Barnaby Conrad's *La Fiesta Brava,* which is well informed; and Robert Daley's *The Swords of Spain,* the classic photograph of which has a heroic tourist running into the arena at Pamplona in sheer terror, full speed and at least three hundred yards ahead of the nearest bull. El Valiente, Daley calls him, and every time I see him bursting into the arena I think of myself.

Of course, the best thing so far written on bullfighting is Ernest Hemingway's *Death in the Afternoon.* As his friend Quintana says, 'It's amazing that a man who spoke no Spanish to begin with could have so quickly caught the spirit of a foreign art.' It remains a masterpiece of insight and persuasion and is as popular today as when it was first published in 1932. Recently an American, John McCormick, aided by a Mexican, Mario Sevilla Mascareñas, has produced an opinionated but highly literate and well-informed philosophical analysis, *The Complete Aficionado.*

The period during which I have seen bullfights may be divided into three epochs, each named after a matador: the Epoch of Belmonte, 1914–1936, the Epoch of Manolete, 1939–1955, even though Manolete himself died in 1947, and the Epoch of El Cordobés, 1955 till today. Of the three, the most varied and rewarding was the first, for then one had normative figures like Belmonte, the peerless Joselito, Chicuelo, the preposterous El Gallo and Marcial Lalanda. The middle period was the most dramatic, with the confrontation of the tragic Manolete and the Mexican Carlos Arruza, ornamented by half a dozen additional figures of first category. The third period, running into the present, has been for me more difficult to categorize. I have found it dull, marked by certain honorable matadors but none of supreme excellence, and while it has given us El Cordobés, the most popular matador of all times and the one who has earned the most money, it has provided neither a classic figure nor a tragic poet. To such judgment authorities like José María Cossío and Vanderford say, 'Nonsense. Antonio Ordóñez has been at least as great as Joselito.'

My favorite in this long procession has been none of the men named but the austere classicist Domingo Ortega. He was so pure a bullfighter that men wrote long books about his art, claiming that he had saved the bullfight from becoming a mere ornamentation. Philosophers invoked him as a reincarnation of Seneca; motion-picture theaters throbbed to the classical emotion which he was able to cram into a few controlled passes; and at the plaza men were alternately perplexed by the rigidity of his style and enchanted by its purity. If I had been a bullfighter I should have wanted to fight like Domingo Ortega, and my memory of him in the ring has had a

Rehearsal for what? Applause, money, the wounds of honor, death? The pain of disillusionment?

profound influence on the way I think and especially in the way I evaluate work in the arts. I would say that he has had an impact on me as great as that of Johannes Brahms.

The quiescent third epoch, in which I have seen most of my fights, did produce the much publicized Domínguín-Ordóñez confrontation, in which the latter excelled, and some, including Hemingway and the experts just cited, have believed that Ordóñez has been the greatest fighter of this century; but as I described in the chapter on Pamplona, I have never seen

643

him good but have seen him when his arrogant contempt for the audience was unbearable. In this period most of my knowledgeable friends have tried to convince me that the great figure is Curro Romero, and I well remember the afternoon I sat in the stands at Pamplona and happened to mention another matador as my favorite. A voluble Spanish gentleman next to me, who had remained unmoved by all my other judgments over a period of six days, exploded with rage, and Vavra caught a series of eight snapshots showing his disgust. 'There is only one matador in Spain worthy of a man's respect,' he shouted. 'All the others are what? Nothing! Poof! To see Romero on one of his fine afternoons is like seeing God Himself descending to supervise a performance. Then the cape stands out like sculptured gold, the muleta is like a thread of silk binding the man and the bull together. It is exquisite, the stuff of dreams, and one feels tears in his eyes, a profound exaltation in his heart. I have seen Curro when he molded fifteen thousand people in the plaza as if he were an angelic child playing with sand. You hear the phrase "he and the bull were one." With Curro it's different. There is no man. There is no bull. There is merely a golden moment, and when it's past you turn to your neighbor as I'm turning to you now and ask, "What was that I saw?" And he explains very humbly, "My friend, you saw a miracle." Therefore, please don't speak to me about so-and-so. At least not in the same plaza where I have mentioned the name Curro Romero.' John Fulton, Orson Welles, Kenneth Vanderford, Robert Vavra and scores of others all felt the same way, although they tended to express themselves more forcefully than did my Spanish friend at Pamplona. To have seen Curro Romero was to have seen the ultimate.

Well, finally I saw him. At Sevilla he came into the arena, a rather pudgy young man of undistinguished height, carriage, feature and bearing. He was a disaster. I saw him four more times in Sevilla, always miserably bad. He seemed to take one look at whatever bull fate had allotted him and to decide, 'This animal is not for me.'

'You mustn't judge him until you've seen him good,' Fulton insisted, paying him the cherished accolade that comes when one matador praises another. 'It's not a question of the bull's being good or bad—he must be right for Curro.' Now, one of the attributes of Domingo Ortega that I remember best was that he could take whatever came out of the chute and give it a majestic fight. If luck gave him a bad bull, he made it good; if his lot was a good bull, he made it great; and on those rare occasions when he received a naturally great bull, he handled it with such noble precision that its head was subsequently mounted. Ortega gave new meaning to the word pundonor.

Curro Romero must have had his own analysis of this word. At Jerez he was abominable because he would not try to accomplish anything with

Last known portrait of Juan Belmonte (not Somerset Maugham
the man who revolutionized bullfightin
taken shortly before he shot himse

average bulls, although his competitors did passably well with theirs. 'You've got to catch him on the right day,' Vavra explained, while Vanderford growled in his beard, 'With Curro you must not use the words pundonor or sinvergüenza. They do not apply. He is honestly terrified of a dangerous bull . . . or of a good one. Lack of courage? Yes. Lack of honor? Never.'

I remember the agonies Orson Welles went through at one San Isidro, for since Curro's first appearance in the ring, Welles has always held that he is the one bright light in the taurine world and he had been warning us not to miss his boy's performance. First day, horrible. Second day, nothing. Third day, deplorable. 'Wait till he gets a good day,' Welles advised.

In Barcelona the bull came out the chute wrong, and Curro quit. At Valencia there was wind, and he attempted nothing. Back in Madrid he screwed up his courage and like Ortega tried to make a good bull great, but in the end he ran in palpitating fright past the bull, jabbed his sword out sideways and punctured a lung. The audience wanted to annihilate him on the spot, and would have done so had pillows been concrete blocks, for they showered him with the former while officers of the Guardia Civil kept them away from the latter. 'This wasn't his day,' Welles said sadly 'But just wait.'

I had now waited through more than twenty fights. I'd seen Curro face forty-odd bulls and never had the magic moment come. Never had the magic moment even been in the same province. I had seen him bad, and I had seen him worse, and I had seen him disastrous. And I no longer hoped. Each of my bullfighting friends had seen him in apotheosis, and apparently he could be something wonderful, running the bull slowly and majestically in passes of impossible beauty. My testifiers were not liars, nor were they combined in a conspiracy to create a White Legend. The agitated poet to my left at Pamplona had not compared notes with Orson Welles or Kenneth Tynan. That was his judgment, founded on fact, but it was a fact I was apparently destined not to see. To me Curro Romero would remain a legend, a reward which good fairies brought to good little boys. Alas, I was bad.

There was, however, in these same years a tall, ungainly, angular and thin young man from the village of Vitigudino near Salamanca who entered the arenas with little fanfare. I was in Madrid on May 13, 1961, when he underwent the ceremonies which confirmed him as a full matador; he took his sword from the hands of Gregorio Sánchez while standing a few feet from me, then strode with austere dignity toward the bull to give battle in the time-honored way. He was El Viti, and in Madrid he was a sensation. In Sevilla he was extraordinary. In Málaga and Jerez and Barcelona he was cold and precise and clothed in honor. Wherever I went I saw this reserved young man with the grave sculptured face and the long thin body fight in a manner I had thought forgotten. He engaged in no heroics and there was nothing of lyric poetry in what he did, but there was a distant echo of the epic. He never allowed himself to be hurried and I doubt if he could perform an arabesque with a cape if he wanted to, and I'm sure he never wanted to. Because he never once smiled in the ring, his detractors called him cold and frigid and rooted. Vavra and Fulton spent hours explaining to me why he failed to excite the crowd. In Pamplona it was my mention of his name that had started the argument with my poetical neighbor. 'Viti's nothing!' he exploded. 'An iceberg!'

Yet day after day this quiet young man with ice-cold manner, this youth who never smiled, who never displayed even the slightest emotion, not even when gored a few feet from where I sat, turned in a beautiful performance and won awards that others missed. He became for me the epitome of what I looked for in the ring, and almost never did he disappoint. I'll correct that judgment: never did he disappoint, for even when the bulls were bad he tried. Like Domingo Ortega before him, he brought new distinction to the word pundonor, for he was composed of this manly virtue.

The finest single component of any fight that I have so far seen was the work with the muleta that El Viti performed one day in Madrid. Luck had given him an evil bull, a little worse than those the other matadors had walked away from in disgust, slaughtering them shamelessly. El Viti took his fractious bull and with masterful low chops began to give it both direction and confidence. Never did the animal have to charge more than a few feet and always its horn was so placed that with a bad toss left or right it could impale El Viti. Slowly, with infinite precision, the fight continued, and bit by bit the matador made of this bull a noble animal that charged with fury and followed the cloth as it should. The process continued long, until El Viti was making all the passes that a matador should make with the cloth, and the ungovernable bull was kept as close to him as I was to the man sitting next to me. It was a culminating performance, so wonderful that people were screaming with admiration of the sheer mastery.

Finally El Viti took his stance before this once most dangerous of bulls and raised his sword for the kill. He waited. The bull would not charge. He waited. He waited some more, what seemed to be an infinity of time. At last the bull charged, the most dangerous moment of the fight, for the man must move forward, go in over the horn and somehow make his escape as the sword plunges home. But this time El Viti did not move. He kept his rigid posture and allowed the bull to bear down upon him; as the animal threw his great weight forward, the man stood fast, lured the bull off to the right with the muleta and directed the tip of the sword toward the lethal spot, where it was driven home by the weight of the charging animal. El Viti had killed recibiendo, that is, receiving the bull while keeping his feet motionless, and you can attend a hundred fights without seeing this done properly, or done at all, or even attempted. But to have done it successfully on such a bull was miraculous.

During this epoch there was a very brave young man who was to give his name to the period, El Cordobés, an illiterate street gamin from a town near Córdoba who electrified the bullfighting world by the animal vitality he exhibited in the plazas. Part vaudevillian, part satyr, part inspired improvisator, he sold enormous numbers of tickets and charmed huge numbers of people but not me. In the remotest towns of Mexico, where impresarios had experienced trouble half filling their bullrings once a season, they could now hold three corridas in three days and cram the ring each day by merely announcing the name of El Cordobés. With a shock of unruly hair, a rock-and-roll manner and a mouthful of unusually handsome teeth, he revitalized bullfighting, but I am not sure that it was any longer an art. It was something else.

I would have to confess, however, that three times I saw him perform a feat that even now seems impossible. Eager to make a good impression in classical Sevilla, he came out to cite his bull from a distance four times as great as the ordinary matador would normally choose, and as the bull charged at him, eleven hundred pounds of furious power, El Cordobés whirled in a tight circle, his small protecting muleta furled tightly about him and he in direct line with the bull's charge. At the last moment he stopped his whirling, dug his feet in and unfurled his muleta, allowing the bull to thunder past a few inches from his chest. It was exciting, but it wasn't bullfighting; it was vaudeville, and after a few performances I lost my taste for it. But not even the young man's severest critic could deny him extraordinary courage and the ability to spread his charisma over an entire nation.

In any discussion of matadors the question arises: 'How good are the Mexicans?' This needs careful analysis. First, Mexican bulls are decidedly inferior to Spanish. They are smaller, more difficult and less likely to give good fight. Therefore, the Mexican faces obvious limitations. Second, whereas in Spain there are scores of bull ranches where a would-be matador can work with heifers, in Mexico there are few, so that the training of Mexicans is apt to be less thorough. Third, in raw bravery nothing can surpass a Mexican matador, and in this department they have no cause to defer to anyone. You will see exhibitions of pundonor in Mexico that you will see nowhere else. Fourth, the Mexican crowd is rowdy, largely uncritical and a joy to be with. Therefore, the Mexican matador can get away with nonsense that would not be permitted in either Madrid or Sevilla. Finally, a good Spanish matador may fight sixty or seventy fights a year; the finest Mexican is lucky if he performs forty times, so that the Spaniard obviously has more chance to perfect his art.

One curious distinction needs to be made. The art of placing banderillas, which can be a graceful and lyric performance if the man doing the job has skill, has declined so badly in Spain that not often does one see a pair placed properly; since 1960 I have seen only four or five pairs done with any style by a Spaniard, whereas in Mexico almost every matador is master

andonor in a rented suit.

of this art and one can see almost any afternoon pairs of banderillas sent home with a delicacy that elicits shouts of admiration from everyone. Spanish bullfighters could do as well, I'm sure, but the public no longer demands that they do so.

In this century there have been three Mexican matadors the equal of anything that Spain has produced. In the Age of Belmonte there was Rodolfo Gaona, a large man with a complete repertory and the personality to support it. At the transition period between Belmonte and Manolete there appeared a string-bean-thin Indian with a style so exquisite that he seemed to float across the sands. Fermín Espinosa is known in history as Armillita, but in accuracy he should be called Armillita Chico, since his older brother Juan, using the name Armillita, became a full matador in 1924 but surrendered the rank in 1933 in order to serve as peon for his more gifted brother. Armillita Chico was, if I understand correctly, the only major matador who fought a lifetime of complete seasons without once having been seriously gored, and he is reputed to have understood the psychology of bulls better than anyone else who ever got into the ring with them. And in the Age of Manolete there was Carlos Arruza, the golden boy of bullfighting who could do everything with diffident grace. He was the equal of Manolete, and the great confrontations between these two constituted one of the highlights of the century; even in their deaths there was a kind of competition: in 1947 Manolete was killed by the Miura bull Islero; in 1966 Arruza was killed in a violent automobile accident.

Many Spaniards refuse to acknowledge these three Mexicans as top caliber. Gaona they denigrate, and the lovely floating pass which he perfected whereby the cape, held behind the body of the fighter, sways first to this side, then that, and which throughout the rest of the world is called a gaonera, is in Spain called de frente por detrás (facing the bull but with the cape behind the body). Armillita they dismiss in silence, for his cold Indian style repelled them and they could not believe he was as good as he was. And Arrruza, whom they cannot deny as one of the great, they embrace by insisting that he was a Spaniard, which his parents indubitably were before they emigrated to Mexico. Arruza considered himself a Mexican.

However, when one drops below the category of Gaona–Armillita–Arruza one finds few Mexicans who equal the middle echelon of Spaniards, and the record books are replete with names of Mexicans who stood at the top of their profession at home but were disasters when they faced the bigger bulls of Spain. Of course, there have also been a few matadors of good reputation in Spain who were found inadequate in Mexico, but not many. Furthermore, in the past twenty years there have been no Mexicans of major reputation, and in this period it would be impossible to claim that Mexican matadors were as good as those in Spain.

Four Americans have become full-fledged matadors. The first, Harper Lee, was born in Isletta, Texas, in 1884, and after drifting about the plazas along the Mexican border, finally took his alternativa in Monterrey in 1910. Lee never fought in Spain but he gave commendable performances throughout Mexico and seems to have been a thoroughly engaging human being. His life has been favorably summarized in *Knight in the Sun,* by Marshall Hail, published in 1962.

Sidney Franklin, a Jewish boy from Brooklyn named Sidney Frumpkin, took his alternativa in Nuevo Laredo, Mexico, in 1932, from the hands of Marcial Lalanda, and confirmed it much later in Madrid in 1945 at the hands of El Estudiante. He fought well both in Mexico and Spain and won commendation from Hemingway. His autobiography, *Bullfighter from Brooklyn,* is a hilarious affair, no single statement of which should be taken too seriously. I once had the pleasure of knowing Franklin and dining with him over an extended period, and never have I met a man whose conversation was more engaging. A group of us used to frequent his company simply to hear what he was going to come up with next, and one of the pleasures of my home in eastern Pennsylvania is that every Saturday night at eleven Sidney Franklin is available on television, broadcasting the fights from Mexico City. His chatter on the air is almost as diverting as it was in person.

In 1966 Robert Ryan, of Los Angeles, took his alternativa in Mexico and performed well in the Tijuana plazas.

John Fulton, the boy from Philadelphia, is the only American ever to have earned his alternativa in Spain. He took it in Sevilla in 1964. His doing so is an epic of determination and I hope that one day he will write his account of how it was done. Since he is also a gifted artist, his black-and-white drawings of what he was talking about would enhance the narrative.

His is a tale of a young man with an idée fixe plus the grim resolve needed to carry it out in one of the cruelest ambientes on earth. For three years Fulton in Sevilla rarely sat down to a meal, eating at most twice a day from a stand-up bar where the bill was a few pesetas less if one did not take up space at a table. Once when money from home enabled him to sit and eat a regular meal, the waiter rushed up and asked, 'Fulton, are you sick?'

Like his idol, Rafael Gómez, called El Gallo, Fulton has a running sequence of sardonic observations on the difficulty of becoming a matador. 'It's as easy for an American to be a bullfighter in Spain as it would be for Cassius Clay to be mayor of Birmingham!' When asked by a lady if he feared the bulls: 'Not half as much as I do the men who manage the bullrings.' On being complimented for speaking idiomatic Spanish: 'I had to learn Spanish. The bulls won't speak English.' Of a famous Sevillian who sponges off matadors: 'That man is well known . . . at lunch.' Of the determination of a young aspirant: 'If he gets one foot in the door, he'll keep it there till gangrene sets in.'

I know of no ambiente more totally corrupt than that of bullfighting.

It is said, and properly so, that in this miserable racket the only honorable figure is the bull, and him they mutilate by shaving down the tips of his horns so that he has difficulty in locating his target. They try to drop sedatives in his drinking water to make him drowsy and sacks of cement on his back to make him weary. On one occasion when the draw for the bulls required a matador to face a particularly tough beast, his brother tried to shoot it in the corral with a rifle.

I suppose one could argue that the management of American boxing is as corrupt as bullfighting, but I doubt it. There must be one or two people in the boxing hierarchy who are comparatively honest; but in the management of bullfighting I have not met any. Symptomatic of the general corruption is the case of the typical newspaperman who reports on bullfighting in the daily press or in the many colorful magazines devoted to the art. With several honorable exceptions he receives no salary from his employer; indeed, he is often required to pay the employer for the privilege of writing in the journal. He must therefore steal his income from the matador, whose future bookings depend on what is said about him in the big-city papers. Suppose a matador has a disastrous afternoon in Sevilla. Everyone in that city who was at the ring will know about it, but there's nothing to be gained by having people in Barcelona and Madrid know about it too, so for six thousand pesetas to each of five strategically placed newspapermen (or one hundred dollars in all), the matador can see to it that in all other cities in Spain the bullfight fan will read on Monday morning that 'Juan Diego had a sensational triumph in Sevilla, with the fans clamoring wildly and carrying him from the ring on their shoulders.' The really bizarre thing about it is that even in Sevilla, the same stories will appear if the matador pays enough, so that a bewildered American or French fan who went to the fight and who can read Spanish begins to wonder if he can trust his own eyes. His eyes are all right. It's the newspaperman that he can't trust.

I once had dramatic proof of this venality. I happened to be in Jerez de la Frontera on Monday, May 10, 1965, for a novice fight in which the youthful sensation of that year was appearing, Sebastián Palomo, called Linares. He came into the ring—an extraordinarily handsome boy of fifteen, very small, very slim and very brave. The afternoon was a complete disaster; the ring was showered with the cushions of disgust, and if the fans could have got hold of Linares they might have lynched him, but the police saw that this did not happen.

I drove the next day to Badajoz, where the newspaper in its edition of May 12 carried a report that I clipped: 'In the brilliant fight held yesterday at Jerez, Sebastián Palomo Linares, fighting large bulls, heard loud applause on the first and an ovation on his second.' This was so blatant that I asked one of the men connected with bullfighting in Badajoz about it, and he said, 'Look, we have a contract with Linares to fight in Mérida. The boy is sensational news. We have to pay him a lot and therefore we have to sell a lot of seats. What does it matter what actually happened in Jerez? Everybody in Badajoz wants to believe that when Linares appears in Mérida they're going to see the new Belmonte.' And he showed me a poster which proclaimed the forthcoming appearance of Linares: 'Destiny Sent Him as Special Envoy to Save the Fiesta Brava. Fresh from his sensational triumph in Jerez.' Looking at the poster, with its gallant young man facing a bull of tremendous size, I began to wonder what I had seen in Jerez, and I realized that the man was right. It didn't really matter.

I was to see Linares twice as a beginner and twice as a full matador, to which he was promoted long before he was ready, and each time he was miserable. In fact, cushions were thrown at him, but I could see that the boy had the figure to be a matador, the courage to face bulls and a charisma that simply radiated. The last was enhanced by the release of a well-calculated motion picture called *First Time in This Plaza,* in which he was both a winsome little boy whom women could love and a brave man whom men could envy. Wherever he was due to fight, his manager scheduled this film in the movie houses, and when I last saw Linares he was besieged by screaming girls wherever he went. Vavra thought he might become the new El Cordobés.

This business of making a motion picture to enhance one's reputation, or even to create it, is amusing, because the plots are so invariable. A poor boy who wants to become a bullfighter has a serenely faithful manager who believes in him and two girls who are competing for him, one blond and good, the other brunette and bad. There is always the testing of heifers at the country ranch, where we see the good girl, and the flamenco party at which the bad girl makes advances. There has got to be one bullfight in which he is, as they phrase it, 'a clamorous success,' and one in which he is not, the latter being used to show his courage under adversity. In recent films a new ingredient has been added after its successful introduction in one of the El Cordobés films: the hero, frightened by his bad afternoon, sleeps fitfully, during which it is obligatory for him to dream in color of his own wounding in the plaza of destiny. Next we see the fatal ring, with him in civilian clothes kicking at the sand and stopping in long-drawn horror when he sees, always unexpectedly although he's been in this ring ten times before, the door marked Enfermería. We now switch to the good girl, who is kneeling before an altar graced by one long, tapering candle. As she prays the candle gutters and goes out, and from the wall behind her a picture of the matador falls mysteriously to the floor. When she picks it up the glass is cracked, at which moment we cut back to the ring, where one hell of a big bull is bearing down on our boy and giving him the works. An operation is required, with dozens of doctors in white and the anguished manager biting his lip, after which the wheels of a Mercedes-Benz squeal and the good girl rushes to the bedside of the dying matador. While she is weeping there an ordinary taxi pulls up and the bad girl dismounts, but she is prevented from entering the infirmary by a kindly priest who explains that now the matador is with the girl who truly loves him. But as the priest leaves, we see the face of the bad girl, and it is bathed in tears and she bites the corner of a handkerchief and slowly climbs back into the taxi, which takes her off into the shadows, leaving the impression that she too, at heart, is a good girl.

Many of the matadors have made films, always to critical acclaim and to the satisfaction of their fans. One of the best was Luis Procuna's Mexican film *Bullfighter*. The most successful was El Cordobés' *Learning to Die;* the most artistic was an Italian film starring the matador Miguelín, *The Moment of Truth;* but the one with the right blend of ambiente and pathos was the one I mentioned earlier, *Afternoon of Bulls,* featuring Domingo Ortega and Antonio Bienvenida. This one I would like to see again. The worst I ever saw was an epic turkey made by handsome Jaime Ostos, and it, too, is worth seeing if only because it is so bad that it evokes memories of the grubby world which it portrayed.

I suppose many readers have been either irritated or perplexed by my insistence that bullfighting is an art and not a sport, but in this I am correct. It is so reported in the Spanish press and is so considered by anyone really concerned in the matter. I was reminded of this one day on an airplane, when I had been absent from the bullring for some years and had forgot the wonderful sleazy world that envelops it. I picked up one of Spain's best newspapers and found it engaged in a public brawl which had been started by an article that spoke disrespectfully of El Cordobés. Within a few weeks the paper received 17,000 letters, of which 15,107 supported the matador, 1624 the journal, while the remainder 'were so confused that we couldn't decide where to place them.'

There was no confusion on the part of the people who defended El Cordobés. In various letters he was compared favorably with Velázquez, Goya, Zuloaga, Picasso and Dali, which should give some indication of whether Spaniards think of their matadors as artists or sportsmen. Many writers referred to 'the crazy month, in which El Cordobés fought thirty-one times, a feat never equaled before.' To accomplish this he had to fight one day in the morning in one town and in the afternoon in another a hundred miles away. One enthusiast let himself go: 'To compare the average bureaucratic bullfighter with the great El Cordobés is to compare one of those elegant white-glove comedies we see on the stage with a great drama like *Oedipus Rex, Medea, Othello,* or *Death of a Salesman.*'

My favorite letter, however, summed it up concisely: 'I have for a long time considered El Cordobés the Johann Sebastian Bach of bullfighters, but after his recent performances I suspect we shall soon have to refer to Johann Sebastian Bach as the El Cordobés of musicians.' I have not quoted the letters which indulged in hyperbole or in which the writer allowed his emotions to get the better of him.

I once had a full day in which to contemplate the sordidness of the bullring, for at eight one morning I reported at the box office in Sevilla to purchase a set of tickets for the feria. I was fourth in line. When the window opened I was fourteenth, men connected with the racket having edged in ahead of me with the connivance of the police. At one o'clock, when the window had been open for five hours, I was twelfth in line, because all morning drifters had sidled up to the window with bribes to the ticket sellers. At one the police announced that the windows would now be closed, but at four we could resume our positions, which would be noted and honored. At four the best I could do was sixteenth.

I was determined to stick it out; in fact, I was enjoying this first-hand experience of what the devotee of the art goes through, and my long vigil was lightened by the fact that a most engaging American wound up behind me in the line, Charles Moore, an ice-cream salesman from El Paso, Texas. 'We'll see if they have the nerve to keep us standing here all day without selling us a ticket,' I suggested.

'Okay by me,' Moore said, and we watched the comedy.

The closest we ever got to the window was eighth. Where the connivers and drifters and the slinky individuals in long coats came from I'll never know, but sometimes an hour would pass without our moving up one slot. A policeman finally came up and said, 'They prefer it if foreigners buy their tickets on the black market. You're expected to.'

'We'll wait.' He shrugged his shoulders and escorted two more characters to the head of the line.

At eight o'clock that night, when they closed the windows, I was fourth in line and Moore was fifth. The men inside, who had seen us all day long, were quite prepared to have the day end this way, but the policeman told them, 'You'd better do something about the norteamericanos. I saw the one with glasses taking notes and he may be a writer.' So at five after eight Moore and I were allowed to buy our tickets. The man at the window couldn't have been more gracious.

John Fulton has a more harrowing story to tell. For an American without friends to arrive in Sevilla determined to become a matador, and for him to buck the prejudices of Spain, where honest men are convinced that no one but a born Spaniard, or at the very least one of Spanish ancestry, can ever truly understand the ambiente, required a courage that few young men could muster. It is interesting to observe that the Spaniards are nearly as reluctant to accept Portuguese as they are Americans, even though I have seen Portuguese like José Julio give fine performances against the big Miuras in Sevilla. Spaniards are convinced that Portuguese and Mexicans and Venezuelans and North Americans never quite catch the hang of this peculiar art.

They were much relieved, therefore, when John Fulton ran into trouble in his presentation in Madrid. In all ways possible they stacked the cards against him, then sat back amused when he failed. 'A fine boy, an intelligent one, too, but not a bullfighter,' they said. 'How could he be? He's a norteamericano.' But when he had a splendid afternoon in Sevilla and was carried from the ring on the shoulders of Spaniards, they said, 'Interesting, but not true bullfighting. How could it be? He's a norteamericano.'

I've seen motion pictures of some of Fulton's good afternoons in Mexico, and they were indeed good. His tall and very graceful body moves well against the dark mass of the bull and he has a repertoire of passes that is wholly professional. If he is no Belmonte or Manolete, few are; he is certainly as competent as the average Spanish matador and better than many, but he is a foreigner, and no Spaniard is eager to sponsor him.

Critics of this insular Spanish attitude point out: 'In American baseball we accept players from any part of the world, especially Spanish parts. Luis Aparicio gets off the plane from Venezuela at the Baltimore airport and ten minutes later he's a full-fledged member of the Orioles. Or Tony Oliva flies in from Cuba to Minneapolis, and next thing you know he's leading the American League in batting. When the Alou brothers arrive from the Dominican Republic it is an invasion. Felipe plays for Atlanta, Matty for Pittsburgh and Jesús for San Francisco. But let someone try to break into Spanish bullfighting and even if he arrived in Madrid on the wings of the Archangel Gabriel accompanied by the ghost of Juan Belmonte, he couldn't make it.' The analogy is not fair to Spaniards. What has been said of their insularity is true insofar as bullfighting is concerned, but it is not true in professional soccer, which is the true parallel to our baseball. When Real Madrid reigned as the best team in the world it employed international stars like Ferenc Puskas of Hungary, Alfredo Di Stefano of Argentina and Raymond Kopa of France. In fact, when I first looked at the roster of Real Madrid in 1961, I found it difficult to believe that it was a Spanish team.

Say the Spanish: 'In the international sport of football we want the best, and to get the best we have to buy in the world market. In the Spanish art of bullfighting we also want the best, and that can be found only in Spain. No one else can master the nuances of this art.'

One of the side attractions of bullfighting is the bizarre gang of fans addicted to the art. Everyone who has followed the bulls has known the epicene from Peru or Chile who drives his Hispano-Suiza back and forth across Spain, enamored of some young man whom he attends slavishly and without regard to the pathetic figure he is cutting before his friends. He doesn't care. He has bull fever interlaced with sex, and few diseases are more virulent.

One also gets to know the American widow of forty-six whose husband left her several hundred thousand dollars and a passport, and with these she travels from feria to feria, passionately in love with some matador who has not yet spoken to her, for he does not know that she exists. If I were to describe faithfully even one of these women, and I have known several dozen, American readers would be incensed and would claim that I was burlesquing the species. 'Such women couldn't exist!' my friends have protested on the few occasions when I have tried to describe them orally, but they do exist and some of them are dear friends whom I regard with affection. They happen to be nutty about bullfighting, and some of my other good friends are nutty about other things.

One hears much of integrity these days, and I have indicated that I prefer El Viti among the current crop of matadors because of his integrity. Once when the crowd had petitioned for, and the judge had awarded, an ear, El Viti turned it back, saying, 'Today I did not deserve an ear.' But no one connected with the art ever exhibited such integrity as an American woman I know who pined for one of the leading matadors. She followed him about Spain as if she were a puppy and he a wise old bulldog. At the arena she showered him with roses; at his hotel she would stand for hours waiting for him to make an appearance; she suffered humiliations by the score; and then one day when she had already paid for a ticket to a good fight in Madrid she heard belatedly that her idol was to fight that afternoon in Aranjuez, some thirty miles to the south.

She thereupon gave away her ticket to the fight in Madrid, paid a scalper's price for a ticket to the new fight, bought an armful of roses for her matador and hired a taxicab to take her to Aranjuez, where she found as she was about to enter the plaza that her beloved, to whom she had so far not spoken a word, had been injured the day before in another town and would not fight this day. His place was being taken by a matador of higher category, so that the fight was probably going to be better than the one scheduled, but to her this was inconsequential; if the object of her passion was not going to perform, the fight was not worth her attendance. She handed her ticket to a young man hanging about the entrance in hopes of just such a miracle, gave her roses to an old woman selling flowers and climbed into her taxi, announcing with a certain grandeur, 'Take me back to Madrid.'

The aficionado from whom I have learned most is Angus Macnab, who has been described as 'the Scotsman's Scotsman.' To hear him explain, in Scottish accents, the merits of a particular fight is to enjoy language and emotion at its best: 'Mind you, I'm not one to question the judgment of Ernest Hemingway, nor of matador John Fulton, but when I hear people assure me that in the great hand-to-hand at the Málaga feria in 1959 Antonio Ordóñez and Dominguín presented between them the fight of the century . . . some even claim the fight of the ages with six bulls killed by six single sword strokes, et cetera. Well, when sensible men tell me this with their smiles on straight and I'm expected to believe them, I keep my mouth shut and ask myself one question: "Has no one bothered to read what Alberto Vera, who wrote under the name of 'Areva,' said about this so-called magisterial fight?" Have you bothered to read it, Michener? No? Then I'll quote: "This afternoon we saw two famous matadors fight six bulls, and each animal had two distinctions. It was barely three years old and was therefore more truly a calf. And what horns it did have were mercilessly shaved." Michener, if you want to select one afternoon as an example of what bullfighting can be, at least choose one in which bulls were fought and not calves with their horns removed.' Even the most trivial of Macnab's ·opinions on matadors and bulls are expressed with similar force. 'Biggest bull I ever saw was at Pamplona one year. A Miura of nearly fifteen hundred pounds. Can you imagine how big that was? Killed two horses just by running into them. But the best man-and-bull together I've ever seen was Domingo Ortega and a runty bull of admirable courage to whom he had given a great fight. At the end he dropped on his knees before the fine animal, then turned his back to the horns and remained so with the bull's right horn in the middle of his spine. Still on his knees he crawled away to pick up a hat that an admirer had thrown in the ring and this he placed on the bull's shoulder. Then, standing back, he sighted with his sword, moved forward and pushed the sword right through the hat and into the proper spot. The bull took one step and dropped dead.'

The addict with whom it is most fun to attend a fight is Kenneth Vanderford, who has a sardonic wit and a dry skepticism concerning everything. At his apartment in Madrid, where all writers interested in the fiesta brava sooner or later converge to check facts, he has a modest library of taurine material, including complete files of most of the bullfight journals for the past eight years. Apart from the nonsense of looking like Hemingway, from which he derives much amusement, Vanderford is unusually erudite, with a Ph.D. in Spanish from the University of Chicago. When I last saw him he was engaged in a newspaper duel with a learned Spaniard who had written an essay lamenting the fact that the Spanish language does not permit words to begin with the letter s followed by a consonant, so that English words like scarp, spume and stupid became in Spanish escarpa, espuma and estúpido. This meant, the essayist had pointed out, that the two radically different English words, eschatology which means the philosophical analysis of ultimate goals, especially those religious, and scatology, which means preoccupation with or study of excrement, had each to be translated by the Spanish escatalogía. Vanderford, a remarkably irreligious man (he calls himself a humanist), humorously proposed that since no intelligent man really believed in the future life any more and since there was not much to be gained by continuing to talk about it, maybe it would be better to drop the first meaning and cling to the second, which is concerned with an inescapable fact of life that is always with us. He continued with the suggestion that on second thought neither meaning need be dropped, since further study of the conflict had revealed an intimate relationship between the two meanings of the word, psychologically if not etymologically. He pointed out that the famous ascetics of history, who have always been interested in eschatology, have also notoriously been interested in scatology, since the French Catholic writer Viscomte Maxime de Montmorand, in his *Psychologie des Mystiques Catholiques Orthodoxes*, holds that nearly all Christian ascetics have been scatophagous. Vanderford holds equally recondite and stubborn views on bullfight matters.

'You say it. Hemingway says it. Tynan says it and Macnab says it, so I suppose I can't fight you all. But to say that at the kill a matador "goes over the horn" is pure nonsense. Let him go in that way and he'll get a horn in the gut every time. What he does is to trick the bull into charging one way while he slides in on a curving trajectory the other way, thus avoiding the horn. Over the horn? Never.'

It is Vanderford's opinion that 'the best-informed and most dedicated foreign bullfight expert of either sex is Alice Hall.' This tall, slim gray-haired spinster was, until her recent retirement, a teacher of Spanish in a fancy private school in Atlanta, Georgia. She came originally to Spain for the laudable purpose of improving her pronunciation, little aware of what was in store. Like any dutiful tourist she went routinely to a bullfight, had the good fortune of seeing César Girón on one of his great days, and promptly surrendered. Year after year she returned during her vacations and applied to bullfighting the tenacious scholarship which had made her a fine teacher. A friend says, 'Alice feels intuitively what the bull and the man are going to do next . . . what they must do . . . and she is in the ring with them when they do it.' 'Each autumn when I go back to Atlanta and face my first class of girls,' she says quietly, 'I feel as if I have been sentenced to exile, that I am in a strange land surrounded by strangers. My heart was left behind in Andalucía.'

My favorite aficionado was a Frenchman. On the afternoon of the first fight at Pamplona, which is quite near to France and therefore attracts many Frenchmen, this doughty little bourgeois, with mustache, close-buttoned black suit and lunch in a briefcase, became so enraptured with the performance of Paco Camino that as the matador took a turn of the plaza he threw his bota of wine into the ring, and Camino drank from it. The crowd applauded. Later my Frenchman did the same for Diego Puerta, and again the crowd cheered.

It was not until the fourth day that I was close enough to see why the crowd kept cheering this modest Frenchman, but on this day, when he tossed his bota at the feet of Miguelín, his section of the plaza rose en masse and accorded him a round of applause usually reserved for generals or generalísimos. Why? Because when this prudent fellow tossed his bota into the ring he kept it attached to a long length of French fishing cord, so that when the matador finished taking his drink, the valuable leather bottle, worth about forty cents, could be reeled back to its owner.

The aficionado who best exemplifies the emotional hold that bullfighting can exert is a man I have not met. George Smith, a retired high school Spanish teacher from Los Angeles, saw his first fight in Mexico and subsequently came to Spain on vacation, developing an intense interest in the bulls. He began to acquire a bullfight library, and with the help of a former matador who in retirement became an expert on old books, has built up what many call the finest library of its kind in the United States. He intends leaving it to the Los Angeles public library. Sudden and protracted illness has prevented him from returning to Spain but he is so infatuated with the ambiente that each spring, during San Isidro, he sends his matador-bibliophile a substantial check in order to assemble in Salvador's taurine restaurant a group of aficionados to partake of the feast that he would like to give in person. In 1967 Nicanor Villalta, one of the finest and bravest of the old-time matadors, attended. Also present was the critic who wears the gold watch that once belonged to Manolete: 'The mother of Manolete to Antonio Bellón, loyal and unselfish friend of her son.' Vanderford was there and several others who appreciate the bulls, and as the meal drew to an end, Vicente Molina, the book dealer, proposed the toast, 'To a man who truly loves our crazy world.'

Some travelers in Spain, seeing the crowds of such tourists at bullfights, conclude that it is only the thrill-seeking foreigner who keeps the art alive, and it is true that along the Mediterranean coast the rings are populated mainly by travelers from northern countries who understand little of what they are seeing. I remember the last fight of the season in Barcelona, when more than two-thirds of the meager audience consisted of white-hatted sailors from the visiting American fleet. In Mallorca foreigners constitute a majority of the audience, and standards have degenerated so badly that a local impresario has rigged up his private plaza and keeps a tame bull therein for tourists to 'fight' at five dollars a throw. For two dollars they rent gaudy matador suits, and for an additional two dollars they can have their photographs taken facing the bull. When they get back into street clothes for another dollar they can purchase from the Plaza Mallorca a colorful poster showing their name printed between that of Manolete and El Cordobés.

'We call that animal El Toro de Oro, the Golden Bull,' Bartolomé Bestard, honorary American consul in Mallorca, told me. 'He's so smart that when he sees a camera he shows the one-day matadors where to stand. But don't laugh! That bull personally has paid for those three apartment houses over there. A fabulous animal.'

As my Spanish friend implied in the dialogue which opens this chapter, many intelligent and progressive Spaniards decry bullfighting as a blemish upon their country's reputation. In 1965 I saw a series of excellent fights on government television, but in 1966, following a disastrous corrida which revolted many people, the broadcasts were quietly eliminated. Word went out that the government had decided that public reveling in bull-fights must stop, at least over television. (In 1967 the programs were resumed.) More significant was what happened on Sunday afternoon, September 18, 1966, when Vanderford and I attended a corrida in Madrid, only to find that without previous warning members of the Guardia Civil had stationed themselves at all entrances and were turning away children under the age of fourteen. Later the government encouraged the rumor that this was henceforth to be the law in all cities. 'They've determined to stamp out bullfighting by driving young people out of the arena and onto the football field,' a matador told me. 'In the end they'll succeed.' (In 1967 this ban was still in force.)

The best-reasoned and most forceful condemnation of bullfighting to have been voiced in recent years is that published in 1962 by Eléna de La Souchère, a Barcelona woman of French descent who fled Spain after the Civil War:

> Beginning in the eighteenth century, the uprooted and somewhat indolent masses who pushed into Madrid and Sevilla conceived a passion for the arena. Bullfights, which until this time had been occasional single combats for the pleasure of the knights-combatant, now were transformed into periodic spectacles; the professionals of the arena reappeared. . . . These games were the response to a deep-rooted psychological need. The people had ceased to participate in public life and the psychologically passive plebeians refused henceforth to take any risk or assume any effort; nonetheless, they craved a chance to demonstrate their aggressive instinct. . . . In Madrid, as formerly in Rome and Byzantium, the people continued to fight and to triumph but through an interpreter—an appointed slayer-of-beasts—with whom they could identify. . . .
>
> The *corrida* in fact completes the destruction of the conditions which gave it birth. The games of the circus are costly, voracious. There is not enough bread—and the wheat fields lie fallow as far as the eye can see, giving graze to the *corrida* bulls. The farmer trudges behind his antique wooden plough: The bullock is a luxury, reserved for the minority of wealthy cultivators. Thousands of bulls are sacrificed each year to the arenas. The circus devours the unsown harvest, the bull unharnessed to plough the scanty soil, the glebe land, which is the raw material of bread and of man's labor.
>
> Each village should awaken from the torpor into which all have fallen. But the *corrida* is an obstacle in the path of necessity which orders man to work. This torpor is born of and nourished by the perpetuation of man's resignation. Every Sunday, the circus games sap his vital energy: the intensity of a prolonged and repeated emotion summons all his energies,

gathers them, strains them to paroxysm, breaks them by an abrupt relaxation, knots them together once again, breaks them once again, to the
rhythm of the bull's charge and retreat, charge and retreat. In this impas-
sioned catharsis, the active energy of a people becomes so many nervous
sparks strewn on the sterile sand of the arena. Becoming accustomed from
an early age to the death-spectacle, the dolorous diversion, destroys the
sensitivity of the human being. Henceforth, he is predisposed to any abuse,
any cruelty. Familiarity with bloody spectacles goes a long way toward
explaining the sadistic abuses which have marked the revolutions and the
civil wars in nineteenth- and twentieth-century Spain. By tolerating the
arena games, by promoting them and allowing children to witness them,
the Church and the public authorities have shown to what extent they
submit to the *terratenientes*, landowners, who raise the bulls; and they
show once again how indifferent they are to their esential task: education
of the masses.

On the other side of the ledger, the idolatry of these circus games has
been condemned by all the great figures of late-nineteenth- and early-twen-
tieth-century liberal Spain, from Blasco Ibáñez to Pío Baroja and Ortega y
Gasset. In that era all of the progressive forces, particularly the liberals and
the anarcho-syndicalists, were alarmed by the psychological effects of the
corrida. Their alarm was all the more pronounced because the ravages of
the arena, physical ravages first of all, are felt most in the lowest classes:
each Sunday during the bullfight season is marred by several accidents. In
a special issue, September-October, 1962, devoted to bullfighting, the
Madrid magazine, *Indice*, published the complete list of Spanish *toreros*
killed in the arena since the end of the eighteenth century. Listed were the
names of some 278 victims between 1900 and 1962; in other words, considering the brevity of the bullfight season (from Easter to the autumn) one
death every six weeks.

But the *corrida* perverts even more than it kills. Its false prestige has
demoralized generations of young workers; in presenting a gilded mirage
and factitious universe it tempts their appetites for luxury, for vainglory,
and instills in them a disdain for useful work. Yet the majority of appren-
tice *toreros* have not even a chance to prove themselves in regular *corridas*.
While casting about for engagements they subsist on shady deals.

A varied fauna buzzes about the walls of the arena . . . these down-
and-outs perhaps were once the hopes of a season; ever suppliant, they
cling to the neighborhood of the plaza in low taverns filled with the stench
of refried oil. The adolescents who hang about the arena in search of work
will join them one day. And others, and still others . . . The arena wins.
It spreads out. It eats into the city, as an ulcer eats into healthy flesh; the
ulcer is devouring the city.

Señorita de La Souchère speaks for many, but her figures on deaths
from bullfighting apply primarily, of course, to a previous condition. One
man altered the trend of those figures, and outside the bullring in Madrid,

The old, who used to dream of becoming bullfight
now hang about the young, who still have ho

matadors have erected a statue to him: 'Dr. Alexander Fleming, discoverer of penicillin.' Four-fifths of bullfight deaths in times past came because horns infected with animal manure produced instant gangrene; most of these men would have lived had penicillin existed in their day. Today Fleming's miracle drug saves literally dozens of bullfighters, and he is properly their patron saint.

In her criticism, Señorita de La Souchère implies that the meat of the fighting bull is wasted; this has never been true. In the old days the carcasses were butchered at the bullring and passed along without charge to hospitals and poorhouses, but today the meat is carted to selected butchershops throughout each city and sold at a slight reduction. At the ring in Pamplona, I came to know Señora Aniceto Oloriz, a small, doughty woman with a marvelous smile and reddish hair who supervised the butchering of the dead bulls as promptly as they were hauled from the arena. About ten minutes after Paco Camino killed a bull, Señora Oloriz had it cut into quarters and early next morning was hawking it at her stall in the Pamplona market.

In recent years bullfighting has been increasing in popularity and probably more people are seeing it now than ever before. New arenas are replacing old in cities like Burgos, Avila, Badajoz and Córdoba, while completely new ones are being erected where none existed before. The number of corridas fought and attendance at them have grown. For every great Spaniard who has opposed the art, one could name two others who have supported it.

Much nonsense is perpetrated when foreigners compare bullfighting with football, especially when they see the huge stadia used by the latter or read that a hundred and ten thousand fans have attended a football game, as compared to a maximum of twenty-four thousand at a bullfight. Also, they see boys all over Spain kicking footballs in the street, and it is not illogical to conclude, 'In Spain football is the rage. It's all that kids play, so bullfighting must be dying.' The first two statements are true. Football has become Spain's lovely madness, as I have shown.

But this does not mean that bullfighting is dying, for the two seem not to be in competition. The truth is that football is a popular sport which commands an enormous following, and bullfighting is an artistic spectacle which retains its traditional adherents. An analogy might be the popular movies in Japan as compared to the classical art of kabuki. One does not eliminate the other, and no football player has attained in Spain the popularity enjoyed by El Cordobés. The status of bullfighting, as of 1966, is summarized in the accompanying table.

These figures require comment. They summarize the season of 1966 in Spain only and do not take into account corridas in Portugal, France, Mexico and South America. Contrary to what some say, the total number of corridas fought each year has been increasing rather than diminishing.

A Typical Year–1966

	Full matadors	Novice matadors
Total corridas	599	480
Number of bulls killed	3647	2836 [1]
Number of matadors eligible to fight	172	8162 [2]
Number of matadors fighting	116	247
Average corridas per matador	5.2	1.9
Median corridas per matador	7	3
Number of matadors fighting only:		
Three times all season	9	29
Two times all season	10	42
One time all season	17	77
Number of promotions to full matador		24
Top pay one matador one corrida	$25,000.	$1,600.
Bottom pay one matador one corrida	−$100.	−$50.
Corridas fought in:		
Madrid	51	43
Barcelona	51	16
Palma de Mallorca	31	1
Sevilla	18	14

TOP MATADORS

Full Matadors	Fights	Novice Matadors	Fights
Paco Camino	95	[4] Flores Blázquez	58
M. Cano 'El Pireo'	78	[4] Pedrín Benjumea	53
M. Benítez 'El Cordobés'	74	[4] J. L. Bernal 'Capillé'	50
Diego Puerta	71	Ricardo de Fabra	48
José Fuentes	70	[4] Paco Ceballos	45
S. Martín 'El Viti'	68	[3] F. Rivera 'Paquirri'	38
[3] J. M. Inchausti 'Tinín'	68	A. García 'Utrerita'	38
[3] S. Palomo 'Linares'	64	Fernando Tortosa	35
Jaime Ostos	53	[4] A. Sánchez Bejarano	35
[5] Fermín Murillo	51	[6] F. Rodríguez 'Almendro'	31

[1] Not counting 193 bulls and 85 novillo bulls killed in France and 4 Spanish bulls fought in Portugal but not killed, since that country forbids the fight to end with the death of the bull.

[2] Men carrying cards issued by the matadors' union.

[3] Novice matadors who were promoted to full matadors during the season; their figures are for the two categories combined.

[4] Novice matadors who were promoted to full matadors during the 1967 season.

[5] Retired from bullfighting at end of the 1966 season.

[6] For purposes of comparison, in 1966 Curro Romero fought 24 times.

*One of the four Córdoba memorials
to Manolete.*

To me, the startling figures are those for the total number of aspirant matadors and the minuscule few who make the grade. Most depressing is the number of established matadors who are able to fight only two or three times a year. These are the proud and gallant men with whom the citizen who follows bullfighting becomes so familiar. In his three fights a year such a full matador down on his luck may earn for himself a total of a thousand dollars, and on this he must support himself, keep his hair cut so that he looks prosperous, his shoes shined and his clothes sharp. And he must frequent the popular bars so as to be seen. Since his professional pay will not permit these things, he must scrounge from his family, his wife or his girl friend; if unusually lucky he will be able to attach himself to some well-heeled businessman who in his youth vaguely wanted to be a matador and who now finds pleasure in supporting a matador so as to feel himself

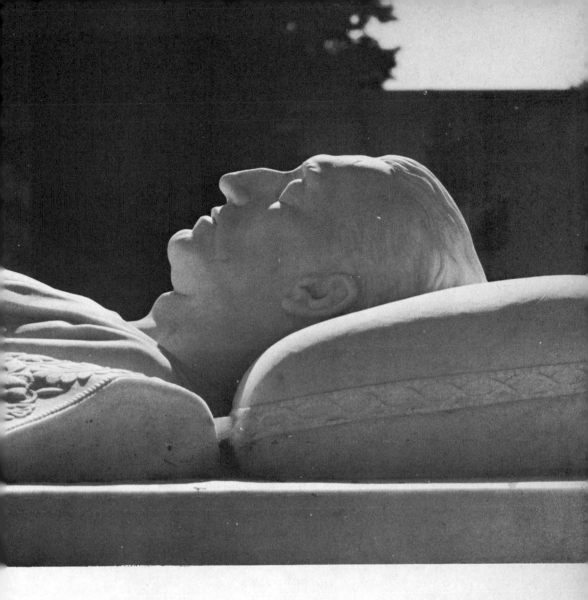

part of the ambiente. It is this situation that accounts for the minus figures at the line 'Bottom pay one matador one corrida,' for many times unscrupulous impresarios will allow a beginner (and not infrequently a full-fledged matador) to fight in a given city if the matador pays for the privilege. If a man has prospects of only one or two fights a year, and if he has a friend who will foot the bill, he will accept and will pay for the privilege of once more appearing in the suit of lights, once more leading the parade as the band plays. As for the number of times full matadors are bullied into fighting for seventeen dollars an afternoon or nothing, these are so common as not to warrant a special line in the statistics.

To understand the lure of bullfighting, one must go, I think, to Córdoba, where the city operates a taurine museum dedicated to the five so-called Caliphs of Córdoba: Lagartijo (1841–1900), Guerrita (1862–

1941), Machaquito (1880–1955), Manolete (1917–1947) and El Cordobés
(1936–   ). The numerous rooms are evocative of these peasant boys
who attained folk immortality, and as one moves among the ancient
costumes and posters and sees the mementos of their dramatic lives he can
catch a glimpse of what bullfighting meant to the underprivileged; but more
can be gleaned, I believe, from walking the streets of Córdoba and seeing
those grandiloquent monuments to Manolete, whose death at the horns of a
Miura bull in Linares stunned the city. Fronting the church of Santa María
in the peasant barrio there is a huge monument; a little farther along, at
the square where his once-impoverished mother lived, there is a second
huge monument which must have cost more money than she has spent in
her life; beyond, there is a plaque in the wall indicating where the great
man was actually born; and in the cemetery there is a monument surpass-
ing them all, showing the matador recumbent. But more impressive to me
than the museum and the monuments, which are, after all, dead recollections, is the Bar San Miguel, not far from where I lived in Córdoba and into
which I stumbled by accident. It is run by a fine-looking man in his
thirties, Manuel Barrera, and it consists of five rooms literally covered
from floor to ceiling with mementos of El Cordobés: three different niches
built into the walls display full-sized plaster statues of the matador; half a
dozen carved heads stand about; and at least five hundred framed photographs hang in rigid order.

Before he became famous El Cordobés used to hang out in this bar,
Barrera says proudly, 'and I was one of the first to recognize his ability.
The world's first Club El Cordobés was launched right here . . . in my bar.
My sister carved the first full-sized statue of him. That one. We make
plaster casts of it and sell them to El Cordobés clubs throughout the world.
He's the greatest man Córdoba ever produced. He's immortal.' In the bar
hangs a framed slate with categories painted on in white enamel with
space for the relevant figures to be added in chalk.

EL CORDOBES

THIS YEAR

CORRIDAS	82
EARS	138
TAILS	28

THIS WEEK

MALLORCA	1 ear

There are many such bars throughout Spain, each dedicated to a
predilected bullfighter, and if the art is on the wane, the habitués of these

One of the statues carved by Barrera's sister.

PLAZA DE TOROS

Among the bronze figures who carry the casket of Joselito, beau ideal of matadors, walks a boy who bears an even graver burden: the gnawing worm of bullfighting.

bars, the members of the numerous clubs and the other fanatics do not know about it.

On the other hand, the perceptive traveler soon discovers that bullfighting is an anachronistic spectacle; if the Republicans had won the Civil War in 1939 I suppose they would have outlawed it in deference to progress, and most progressive Spaniards would have approved. The victory of Generalísimo Franco provided the art with a reprieve, for bullfighting is essentially a reactionary operation dependent upon large areas of uncultivated land and a feudal system; now that a new generation of managers is about to take over responsibility from Franco, men alert to opinion in Berlin and London, it is quite possible that bullfighting will come under serious pressure. It will be interesting to see if its 1967 return to television will become permanent.

Why does one bother with a spectacle so archaic and so often disappointing? On July 13, 1966, when I got up extra early in Pamplona to be with the bulls on the last day of the running, I went to Marcelino's restaurant after the bulls had passed and had a breakfast of bacalao (steamed salted codfish) and then went on the unforgettable picnic at the Pass of Roncesvalles. In the patio de caballos I renewed acquaintance with Domingo Ortega and El Estudiante, and had my picture taken with Antonio Ordóñez, who had been miserable on his first appearance and who wanted to recoup this day. In the plaza I exchanged amiable greetings with the Curro Romero devotee on my left, who took the opportunity to remind me that, by all accounts, Curro had been sensational a few days before in Madrid. 'The kind of matador we dream about,' he said, repeating himself.

The fights this day were ordinary, with here and there a few details, and then the fifth bull, a big red one, came out. Looking back on it, I can scarcely believe that in the early morning this extraordinary bull had passed my doorway with only a few inches separating us, but I had been so excited that I failed to notice. 'A big red bull like that? You didn't even see him?' friends asked afterward. I said, 'He wasn't there,' nor had he been, so far as I was concerned.

But he was certainly there that afternoon. He pertained to Andrés Vázquez, a matador of only ordinary qualifications but who was to prove the truth of what I claimed earlier, that any professional, when he gets the dream bull, will at least have the basic techniques for giving it a great fight. Whether he does so or not is another matter, and much can go wrong in the process of leading a noble bull from the first cape work, to the horses, through the muleta work and on to the moment of death, so that many fine bulls are wasted.

On this day nothing went wrong. The bull entered the arena at a gallop and roared to the center of the ring, where he stopped, motionless, as if posing for a poster. He then charged toward the first cape that showed itself, and as soon as the crowd saw how true he moved, a loud shout rose from the stands, applauding the bull and expressing the hope that at last we were to see a good fight. Vázquez, recognizing the quality of the beast the luck of the draw had thrown him, ran into the ring and took charge, unfolding a series of slow and majestic passes in which the bull followed the cloth as if his nose were pasted to it. I had not seen such passes for some years, nor had the crowd, and the applause grew, with six or seven bands playing at the same time in a kind of super-bedlam. The horses now entered, and for once we saw a powerful bull charge the horses three times, take all that the picadors had to offer, then slide each time off the horse and into the cape of the waiting matador. Vázquez, El Pireo and Ordóñez in turn launched beautiful series of passes in which the bull followed the arabesques of the cape with arabesques of his own, more astonishing in that he used his long and powerful body to execute his passes. It was magnificent and the bands roared with delight.

Now came the highlight of this fight. Vázquez and his banderillero Mario Coelho came into the ring, dismissed the two peons who would normally protect them with capes and the other two matadors who stood by in case of danger, and ran in a series of exquisite ellipses before the bull's nose in such a way that whenever the bull was about to catch Vázquez on his horns, Coelho would mysteriously appear at the apex of his ellipse and lead the animal away to the point at which the red beast was about to catch him, whereupon Vázquez would suddenly appear and the bull's charge would be diverted. In the midst of this chinoiserie, Coelho stopped long enough to place the first pair of banderillas, and it was done so flawlessly that the crowd exploded with joy. Now the brass bands grew silent and allowed the primitive oboes of Pamplona to take over, and a rustic melody from centuries ago filled the arena, as fine music as I have ever heard at a bullfight. Suddenly the running figures converged with the arc being described by the bull's horns, and in some fantastic manner Vázquez placed the second pair, almost as perfectly as the first. The matador now left the ring, and no protecting capes appeared to guard Coelho. Very slim, very quiet, the banderillero took his position close to the red wall of the arena in a spot from which escape would be difficult if he misjudged the bull's charge. Keeping his feet rigidly planted, he cited the bull from a considerable distance, and as the animal started his charge, Coelho moved his body but not his feet to the left and when the bull lowered his head and charged at him there, he swiftly brought his shoulders over to the right and as the bull thundered past, planted two perfect banderillas in his shoulders.

Bands and oboes alike sounded their approval. The fight stopped while Vázquez and Coelho came repeatedly to the center of the ring to acknowledge the tumultuous noise. They were forced to take a turn of the ring, with the music rising to a higher pitch, and gifts were tossed to them in honor of banderillas such as had not been seen in Pamplona for years. On July 8, 1915, the great Mexican Gaona had placed a pair here in a manner which seemed impossible; a camera fortunately caught the moment of impact and even today men looking at that photograph will swear the bull must have caught the man. The event has become historic and is called 'The Pair of Pamplona.' Statues have been made of it and the photograph is remembered as one of the most famous in bullfight history; if there were a fine snapshot of Coelho's performance it might properly be called 'The Second Pair of Pamplona.' The set of three was one of the best

Alone in the blazing center of the ring, in terrain as alien as the craters of the moon, the fighting bull waits for the challenge.

offered in Spain in recent years. This seems to contradict what I said earlier about the mediocre quality of Spanish banderilleros, but it doesn't necessarily, because Mario Coelho is a Portuguese and his performance had the stamp of Portuguese excellence about it.

So far the fight had provided four above-average components, but the major tests were ahead, for a bullfight is judged not so much by early cape work or banderillas as by the faena and the kill. Bullfighters say, 'With the cape a matador wins applause; with the muleta, contracts; and with the sword, money.' Vázquez came forth for his faena, and the audience grew hushed as he started slowly to test the bull with the muleta. Finding the animal as good as ever, he began the first of what would ultimately be seven series of intricately linked passes, each series building in intensity on the one before. Before he was through, Vázquez displayed a good selection of the known muleta passes, executing them with a cool firmness that kept the crowd roaring its approval. He ended with a series of spinning passes, in which as the bull rushed past he whirled about in the direction contrary to its charge, drawing the red cloth away from the bull and wrapping it around his own body, unwinding quickly so as to be ready for the next charge of the animal. They were beautifully done, and the braying of the bands left no doubt that Vázquez had passed with honor the fifth test, but now came the kill, and many a matador had come to a culminating moment like this only to dissipate it with inept sword work. (In the twelfth fight of Madrid's 1967 San Isidro feria El Cordobés accomplished a feat rarely seen. With a splendid Antonio Pérez bull he performed such a dazzling faena that in spite of botching the kill and messing around until two warning signals had to be sounded, the public launched a blizzard of white handkerchiefs and screams, demanding that he be given two ears, and this was done. Previously I had not seen even one ear awarded under such circumstances.)

Silence fell over the plaza again, but the suspense was to be short-lived. Addressing the bull with meticulous care, Vázquez prepared everything as properly as he could, squared the animal so that his two front feet were together, and sighted the fatal spot along the extended sword. Rising on his toes, he started forward with full power, and if at that first moment the bull had raised his head unexpectedly the horn would have caught him full in the chest. On and on he came, his abdomen and groin wholly exposed to the horn, and at the last moment he pressed the point of the sword precisely into the target, and with his stomach almost on the bull's shoulder, drove the steel in up to the hilt, so that his fingers could have touched the bull's back.

Vázquez fell away, miraculously untouched. The bull staggered forward with this new burden of steel in his vitals and after a half-dozen bewildered steps fell in a heap. A great sigh rose from the crowd and for a moment there was unbelieving silence.

Then the arena practically fell apart. Brass bands and oboes, men and women screamed their approval. For once in my life I saw a plaza truly covered with white as practically everyone inside waved a handkerchief to the judge, beseeching him to award honors to Vázquez; normally some time passes after such a petition to allow the judge to study the propriety of the request, but on this day there was none. One ear, two ears, the tail, almost as quickly as that. The grave alguacil in seventeenth-century costume stepped forward to detach the trophies, but before they were handed to the matador the dead bull in grandeur was dragged about the arena and the bands played for him.

When the bull departed through the gates, trailing glory in the dry sands, Vázquez stepped forth to accept the trophies, but when they were handed him he did an unusual thing: he forced Mario Coelho to share the applause with him. He gave one of the ears to the Portuguese whose phenomenal pair had been the emotional highlight of the fight, and the two men made their parade together, two times around the ring, or was it three, gathering roses and women's handbags and cigars and wallets and God knows what.

After some fifteen hundred bulls, the vast majority of which were disappointments, I had at last seen my one complete fight. Of the six components, each had been performed properly, and I never expect to see this again.

I must point out that in this fight no one of the six components was the best of its type that I have seen; it was the conjunction of the six that was so unprecedented. As to opening cape work, I had seen Marcial Lalanda do better. Regarding the picador who fought the bull so cleanly and so well, he did not compare with fat Felipe Mota, whom I had watched in Mexico. The cape work by the three matadors after the pics did not equal what Ordóñez and Dominguín are said to have done one afternoon in their famous series of hand-to-hand confrontations. The banderillas, as I have explained, were wonderful but not to be compared with the things performed by Carlos Arruza at his greatest. The work with the muleta was better than one sees in twenty typical fights but not so good as Domingo Ortega used to offer. And the final kill did not equal the recibiendo of El Viti. But if one records honestly what he has seen happen to one bull alone, I doubt if he could find an instance in which a more complete fight had been given.

I can compare it only to an opera I once saw in which Gigli, Rethberg and Pinza sang, each at the very top of his career, each in flawless voice. A great deal can happen to spoil an opera and does, but once or twice in a lifetime one sees a *Carmen*, a *Lohengrin* or an *Aïda* in which all things blend in due proportion: the horse performs without going to the toilet on stage, the swan floats get past without getting stuck at the outskirts of Antwerp, the tenor is as good as the soprano and the ballet dancers do not bump into one another, and this kind of performance one never forgets.

FOLLOWING PAGE:
Gravedigger.

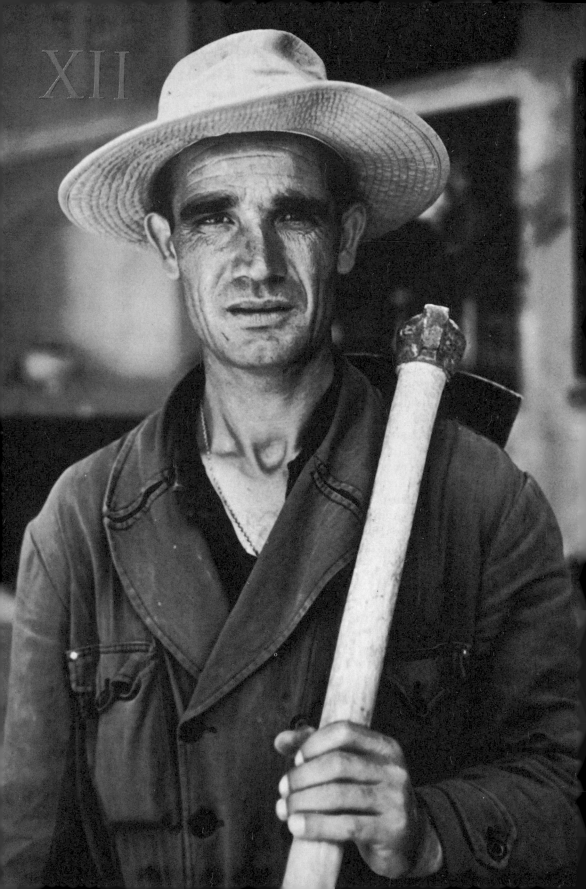

TERUEL

0 MILES 100
OCEANO ATLANTICO
Zaragoza
Barcelona
Albarracín
Teruel
Madrid
Castielfabib
Valencia
Lisboa
Sevilla
MAR MEDITERRANE

I was lost, and I was unhappy about it. I had been heading for Teruel, of all the Spanish cities the one with the most personal meaning for me, and it was late afternoon when I saw ahead of me the dirt road ending in a high solitary peak on whose top perched a little town. It was a heroic sight, one which evoked memories of sieges and a handful of men defending themselves against infidels or Christians, as the fortunes of war had directed. Then, as I progressed down the road, I spotted on the far edge of the peak a remarkable church whose slab-sided, unbroken walls dropped from a great height precipitously into deep gullies, so that it gave the impression of occupying an entire peak. From where I first saw it, the building was totally unapproachable, and the closer I drew the more convinced I became that there was no way by which human beings could get into that church. On all sides it was impregnable, alike to the infidel who might seek to capture it and to the Christian who might want to pray in it.

I studied my map again and concluded that the village ahead could only be Castielfabib, a settlement I had not heard of. I had no intention of ascending that formidable hill, but since the road ended there I had no choice but to plow ahead, and finally I came to a point at which the road turned abruptly left, passed into a tunnel which carried it beneath the lofty town and broke out onto as fair a valley as I had seen in Spain. Hills rolled away in soft battalions and a bubbling river was coaxed into irrigation ditches. Fruit seemed to be growing everywhere and it was obvious that Castielfabib, in spite of its strange location and stranger name, commanded an area of some prosperity.

The road now swung back on itself and began a very steep climb, up and up until the church hung directly overhead, at which point I satisfied myself that my earlier conclusions were right; the preposterous building did occupy every inch of a peak and contained no visible entrance; yet it was so massive that it could obviously house the worshipers of a community many times the size of Castielfabib. Forgetting the church, I entered the village and found myself in a kind of fairyland that history had forgot. After a cursory exploration which showed far vistas in all directions, including a deep canyon that led the river through bright cliffs, I came upon an inn, if such it could be called, where on the very edge of the steepest cliff a small house perched, with one public room containing some thirty low rush-bottomed chairs placed in rows before the town's only television set. The room was miserably lit by one narrow window which cast a pale light on the gloomy interior. The man who grudgingly tended bar seemed embarrassed by my presence and said he did not have any of the first three drinks I suggested. I concluded that Castielfabib had a negative influence on its inhabitants, making them as aloof and lonely as it was.

Then the door banged open to admit a woman of enormous vitality. She was about five feet two inches tall, was not thick through the body but was strong in the shoulders, and owned a face of lively, amused dignity. Like many Spanish women in their late thirties, she was dressed in black, but her face was so animated that she made the dark clothes seem a party dress.

'Ah!' she cried warmly, 'you've come to the loveliest town in Spain. It's older than Valencia, twice as old as Madrid. Have you ever seen anything finer than our little plaza?' She led me to the door to study the Plaza del Caudillo, which my own eyes had dismissed only a few moments before. Now, looking at it with her, I saw a severe lopsided square delineated by a series of ancient buildings with classic façades. Several trees threw congenial shade and in the middle a fine, simply carved granite fountain produced four jets of constant-running water from which village wives, all dressed in black, were filling large clay jars which they carried sideways on their heads, the nozzles so tilted that the water did not run out.

'Beautiful town, eh?' she cried with real love. 'And look at our fortress of a church.'

'How does one get inside?' I asked.

'And up there the ruined walls of the old Moorish fort. Have you ever seen a town more exciting than this?'

She led me back to the bar and ordered me a bottled drink. 'You'll like it more than what you wanted,' she said. Kicking at the low chairs, she said, 'You ought to see this room when there's a good show on television. Forty people. We don't charge admission but we do sell drinks. Forty people can sit here laughing for two hours and not one ever gets thirsty.'

'Husband!' she called. 'Run to Rodríguez and get his book of photographs.'

Village cart.

Her silent husband disappeared, and while he was gone a delightful girl of ten ran in, duplicating her mother's vitality and joy in living in this mountaintop village. The child insisted that I climb to the roof with her, for from there I would see the whole area, and the steep approach was worth the effort, for from the top of the building I could see a miniature presentation of Spain at its best. Hills closed in the valley on all sides, except to the north, where a distant village showed its red roofs. Lush fields of wheat and corn glistened in the sunlight, forming a golden checkerboard in which the darker squares were fields of apple trees and pear and apricot and cherry, with here and there large areas of low-growing grapevines. 'Show him the ruined convent!' her mother called from below, and the child pointed out the gray, weather-beaten relics of a building that must have been impressive in the late seventeenth century, standing as it did at the edge of the red-walled canyon. The little girl also traced out for me the footpaths used by the farmers, and I understood why those who lived in this remote village loved it.

'What do you suppose is under us, as we sit here?' the woman asked

when we had descended to the bar. 'A tunnel, right through the heart of this mountain. And what do you suppose the tunnel was for?' I said I had just driven through the tunnel, whereupon she shouted, 'Not that one. I mean the old one. The big one!'

She launched into a history of Castielfabib. The name, she supposed, was a corruption of Castillo de Habib and referred to an age when the Moors had occupied the fortress at the peak of the mountain, more than a thousand years ago. The area had been rich in silver and copper, and the tunnel had been scooped out for a foundry in which coins and metal objects had been minted for more than a millennium. In this tunnel the bells of the church had been cast . . .

View from Castielfabib.

Her narrative was broken by the return of her husband, bringing Señor Rodríguez's photographs of the town, and with much civic pride she pointed out the features, and as she spoke I reflected on the peculiar fact that around the world generally, Spain is known as a man's country, but the women of Spain seem not to have been informed of this fact. In England the proudest sign that can appear on a shop is 'Henry Thompson and Son,' signifying that the male line of the Thompsons is strong and that Henry's son is prepared to carry on the traditions. The same is true of France, where 'et Fils' is a blazon of commercial nobility. In Spain, however, the proud sign is quite different: 'Viuda de Juan Gómez,' or more often the abbreviation 'Vda. de Juan Gómez.' This means that the widow of

Gómez is carrying on the business and assures her patrons that she will give the same distinguished service she gave while her husband was still alive, except that now she will be relieved of his bumbling interference.

'But how do you get into your church?' I asked again.

'You'll be surprised when you see.' We left the plaza and followed an extremely narrow footpath which appeared to end at the edge of the cliff; however, at the last moment it swung to the right, then ducked swiftly into a tunnel that ran completely beneath the church. At a midway point, as one stood under the huge structure, a door led upward from the tunnel, and it was by means of a very steep flight of stairs that one entered the church. It was indeed a church founded on a rock.

This unplanned excursion to Castielfabib, one of the more rewarding interruptions of my tour, meant that it would be nearly night when I reached Teruel, but this was not a loss, for as I wandered down from the hilltop and picked up the Río Turia, which would lead me in to Teruel, I came upon one of those memorable evenings in Spain when low-hanging clouds provide a darkened sky against which the sunset can reflect from below, so that one seems to move in a sea of color. How beautiful the little villages were as I drove through them. Take Villel, for example, with its enormous tower rising against red hills, streets lined with flower boxes, doorways glistening in blue-and-white tiles, cypresses lining a cemetery. Not many villages in Spain are prettier than those along the Turia. I also saw the imposing sign welcoming travelers to the province of Teruel:

BIENVENIDO   WELCOME

BIENVENU   BENVENUTO

WILLKOMMEN

with the coat of arms that I remembered from my first visit, a ferocious-looking bull over whose head hovered a star.

It was now past eight-thirty but the sun still lingered on the horizon, throwing a blaze of light across the eastern sky; over the earth itself a dull red glow lay like a fog, while at my feet ran the dark Turia, the combination of colors forming a most dramatic entrance to a city. My breath came more quickly when I realized that at some unpredictable moment I would turn a bend in the road and see once more that city which had been so often in my mind and so deeply in my heart. I was actually nervous at the prospect, but then the river turned abruptly and I saw before me, on a hill in the distance, the outlines of Teruel, and I remember thinking, Those buildings to the left and those big apartments to the right. They weren't here when I knew the place. And the more I saw the more I realized that Teruel was not going to be the way it had been thirty-four years ago; the changes were to be of a magnitude that I would sometimes be unable to comprehend.

Teruel today from a bunker of yesterday.

But then, as if to make my return to this mystical city simpler, on my left I came upon a cluster of five once-handsome buildings, now torn and roofless, their yellow bricks crumbling in the night air. They looked as if they must have been there when I was first in Teruel, but some tremendous force had ripped them apart, say an artillery bombardment during the Civil War. What had they been, these handsome structures? And why so many in one group? A convent? A monastery caught in the cross fire of armies? I stopped three passers-by, old men walking home from their work, but they did not know.

In considerable excitement I entered the city, and my first superficial impressions allayed my fears on the road, for Teruel looked pretty much as I had remembered it. The railroad climbing the mountains from Valencia still deposited passengers at the foot of that splendid flight of stairs. The Moorish towers, the finest still standing in Europe, were as handsome as ever in their coats of tile. The public square was still small and poorly designed and congested. And from his Roman tower the bull of Teruel still looked down upon the community of which he was the symbol. As I paid my acknowledgments to the bull, I thought of the strange manner in which this city had been born, because Teruel is one of the few settlements on earth whose moment of birth can be specified.

Teruel is a young city, not much older than Madrid, and it is small. Its birth had been auspicious but there things ended, for it was now the least of Spain's fifty provincial capitals, with less than nineteen thousand population. In October, 1171, when El Cid had been dead for three-quarters of a century, King Alfonso II was endeavoring to establish a defensible frontier between Christian Zaragoza and Moorish Valencia; one evening his troops decided to give battle next morning at a favorable spot marked by a hill; but the Moors offset his advantage by collecting that night a herd of wild bulls and fastening to their horns bundles of firewood which were set ablaze. The maddened bulls stampeded toward the Christian lines, with the Moors following behind. In previous battles this tactic had worked, for in the confusion caused by the fiery animals the mounted Moors had overwhelmed the Christians.

But this time Alfonso's men stood fast, and with catapults which lobbed boulders at the onrushing bulls, with long half-moon lances that severed their hamstrings, with pikemen who formed solid walls of spear points, the onslaught was repulsed. Infidel power was broken in the area and it would now be possible to establish a permanent border between the two forces. It was a crucial victory.

While celebrating, the victorious Christians saw a sight which became the symbol of their triumph: one bull, the only survivor of the stampede, remained on the crest of the hill, shaking his head at the heavens in such a way that the brand still burning miraculously between his horns shone as if it was a star. 'He has been converted to our side!' the Christians shouted, and the hill which the bull had chosen for his last stand became the site of Teruel.

The next thing I did proved symbolic. I got a haircut at the barbershop of Maximiano Gómez, Calle del Mariano, 12, which was an event of no importance except that as soon as Maximiano heard that I was interested in Teruel, he stopped cutting my hair, ran to a friend's house and brought back a pamphlet on the city, which he insisted that I take and for which he would accept no money. 'I want you to have the best visit possible in my city,' he said. 'It's small and during the war it was much abused. But

The bull of Teruel.

now it's fine again.' This meeting with Maximiano set the standard for all that was to happen to me in my chosen city.

On my earlier visit I had stayed at a small hotel; this time a new parador was available, and in its dining room I was introduced to a specialty which I commend. The menu said simply 'Entremeses variados,' which from my attendance at theater I could translate only as 'Theatrical entr'actes varied.'

'What might they be?' I asked the waitress, and she smiled condescendingly as if I were a relative come in from the country.

687

'You don't know what entremeses are?' she said loudly enough for all in the room to hear, and without waiting to determine whether or not I wanted them she hurried into the kitchen and appeared sometime later with an enormous tray, from which she placed on my table, for me alone, twenty-one small saucers, each with a respectable portion of hot or cold food. It was a feast both to the palate and the eye. There were four kinds of fish, three meats including little balls of mutton highly spiced, eggs in aspic, four or five vegetables including the finest fried eggplant, olives, pickles, pimientos, potato salad, potato chips and hot toasted almonds. And it must be remembered that entremeses were merely the first dish of a four-course meal.

Next day my bland good luck continued, for I met Señor Don Francisco Cortel Zuriaga, a native of Teruel and for the past fourteen years its director of publicity. He was a lively man of middle years and height, with a dark mustache and grayish brown hair; his stocky, rugged appearance made me think his ancestors must have come from the mountains of Spain. He could not be considered a literary man, but he possessed an unusual sense of what a writer might like to see, and he would not rest until it had been seen.

'You know the Lovers of Teruel, of course?'

'No, I haven't heard about them.'

His jaw dropped. 'You were in Teruel thirty years ago and you didn't meet the Lovers?'

'That's right.'

This information was so disgusting to Don Francisco, so incredible, to judge from his reaction, that he sent out for a guidebook and sat twirling his thumbs while I read the section on the Lovers. As soon as I had done so, he whisked me out of his office and across the square to a narrow alleyway that led up a small hill. 'No man can know anything about Teruel unless he understands the Lovers.' He took me to a tiny chapel attached to a church and there, as we stood surrounded by the tapestries that enclosed the place, he showed me a pair of marble tombs, one topped by the jacent statue of a handsome young man, the other by a girl of most exquisite beauty.

As I contemplated the tombs, Don Francisco was on his knees with his eyes at floor level. 'See for yourself. Not legends, these two. Real people.'

He invited me to kneel with him, and when I had done so I found that the lower portions of the tombs consisted of slabs of marble carved in an ornate geometrical design; it had many holes through which I could see into the caskets, lit by electricity and containing the mummies of the Lovers, dead for more than seven centuries.

As I knelt there, a bus drew up and thirty or forty tourists from a distant part of Spain filed into the little chapel to pay homage to the only two people who have ever brought fame to Teruel, and I should like to

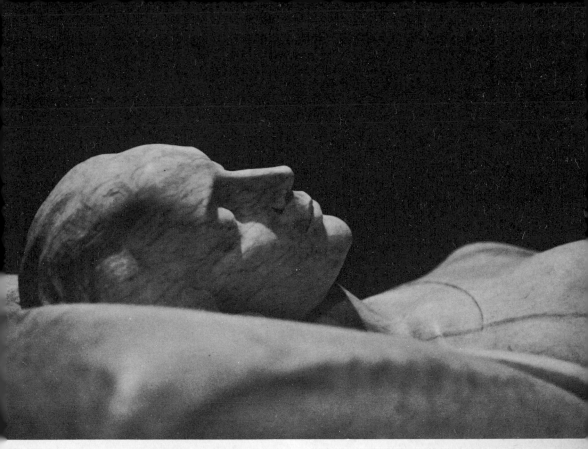

report the history pretty much as the singsong guide recited it to the visiting group.

'The year was 1217, Don Domingo Celada being judge of Teruel. In his city were two noble and influential families, Segura and Marcilla. Daughter of the first was the beautiful Isabel, whom you see here. Son of the second was the brave Diego over there. From the days when they played together as children they loved each other, but Diego's family had fallen on hard times and was poor, wherefore Isabel's father, the richest man in town, forbade their union.

'However, Diego sought and obtained an agreement whereby he would leave Teruel and for five years try to build his fortune in the world, at the end of which time, if he had succeeded, he would return and wed Isabel. With the fire of youth he left the city, and since no one heard from him for the next five years, at the expiration of the term the head of the Segura family forced his daughter to marry the very rich Don Pedro de Azagra of nearby Albarracín, the hill town which we visited this morning.

'The wedding was convened. The couple were married, but as the bells ceased ringing, there was a clatter at the Zaragoza gate and watch-men ran to advise the townspeople that Diego Marcilla had returned from

689

his five years' exile with great riches, ready to marry his beloved. Diego had not counted in his five years' grace that first day on which he had fled Teruel. Isabel's family had.

'The young man ran to Isabel and pleaded with her to marry him, but she pointed out that this was impossible as she already had a husband. Diego then begged her to give him one kiss which he could bear with him as he wandered through the world. This, too, Isabel refused, whereupon, as a book in our archives reports, "Diego was not able to bear the anguish and tension of his enforced departure, and with a sigh died from pain at the feet of her."

'Next day, at this church of San Pedro his funeral services were held, to which Isabel came, dressed in her wedding gown. Silently she walked down the nave and advanced to the bier, where she knelt in order to give Diego the kiss which in life she had denied him, but as she did so, she died, falling prostrate upon the corpse of her beloved.'

The two deaths from love, something never before heard of, so impressed Teruel that the citizens demanded that Isabel and Diego be buried side by side in the church, and it is surprising to find that the religious authorities acceded to this improper demand. Throughout Spain and the medieval world sped the fame of the Lovers of Teruel, and during repairs made to the church in 1560, the graves of the couple were uncovered and their mummies translated to the spot where they now rest.

Naturally, the authenticity of a tale like this was bound to be challenged in later years, especially since the Italian Boccaccio in 1353 told practically the same tale under the title 'Girolamo e Salvestra,' except that he introduced considerable salacious and amusing material. The question thus became: did Boccaccio in 1353 hear reports of an event which actually happened in Teruel in 1217 and adapt it to his pen, or did someone from Teruel in 1400 happen upon the tale of Boccaccio's and adopt it as a local legend? Powerful minds have addressed themselves to this problem, and for some decades at the beginning of this century it was pretty well agreed that the yarn had originated with Boccaccio.

But recently this conclusion has been subjected to serious review, and in 1963 Señor Don Jaime Caruana Gómez de Barreda, cronista of Teruel, summarized all available studies and offered substantial reasons for believing that the tale had originated in real events which occurred in Teruel as stated, in the year 1217, when Don Domingo Celada was judge. (One wonders what might have happened to the cronista's job had he concluded otherwise.) An aspect of the argument that has carried much weight with me is one which I have not seen in print in any books relating to the lovers. I offer it to Professor Caruana for consideration in his next edition: When a story is told in two different versions, only one of which stresses erotic elements, it is likely that the more erotic version came second; specifically, it is difficult to find instances in which popular taste borrowed an erotic tale from a professional writer and retold it with the erotic elements missing. Applying this tentative theory, it is unlikely that the simple folk of Teruel borrowed a naughty tale from Boccaccio and cleaned it up in their retelling; whereas it would be within reason for a sophisticated writer like Boccaccio to borrow a sentimental folk tale emanating from Teruel and to introduce erotic elements in his version. It therefore seems probable that it was Boccaccio who did the borrowing and the 'sexing-up,' as Hollywood terms it. Other curious reasonings supporting the authenticity of the Teruel version can be found in Professor Caruana's book.

In recent years Teruel, aware that it had on its hands one of the top attractions of Spain, enclosed the mummies unearthed in 1560 in a reverent new chapel and engaged the sculptor Juan de Avalos to fashion the two new tombs which we have seen. In doing so, he created a masterpiece of popular art. The caskets are made of grained marble and emblazoned with shields of the Segura and Marcilla families, but it is the lids that draw the crowds. On the Marcilla casket Diego lies, very tall, barefooted, sallow-cheeked and handsome. His hand reaches out across the open space separating the two and almost touches Isabel's, but not quite; religious propriety would not permit him to do so since Isabel was already married. Isabel's figure, draped in a loose-flowing gown, her fair head resting on two pillows, is one of the most charming portraits carved in recent years, and what is surprising, one of the sexiest. Indubitably she is a woman; indubitably she is lovely. As Don Francisco says, 'Whether the Lovers lived or not, I want to believe they did.' And so, apparently, does most of Spain.

There are, of course, dissenters. Schoolchildren herded in to see the mummies sing a blasphemous little jingle:

> Los Amantes de Teruel
> Tonta ella y tonto el.

Reversing the order of the last line so that it conforms to the chronology, this might be translated:

> Ah, the Lovers of Teruel,
> He was a dope and she as well.

Without being aware of what I was letting myself in for, when I returned to the parador I studied the various books Don Francisco had brought me, and in cronista Caruana's essay I came upon the passage in which he tries to explain why the Italian Boccaccio, hundreds of miles away from the scene, had dealt with the strange deaths, whereas no one in Teruel had even so much as mentioned them in writing until a good three hundred years later: 'In Teruel nothing was written during the thirteenth, fourteenth, and fifteenth centuries, nothing that had any literary character, neither a novel, nor a poem, nor any other form or genre of literature . . . Naturally, since Teruel had neither a great poet nor a literary man of any quality, no one sang or conserved the true happenings in the epic or lyric form which such a tradition merited.'

That night I lay awake, pondering the case of a city in which for three hundred years no one wrote anything of merit, and I wondered what the citizens of that city had visualized their major responsibility to be. It would be difficult to find another city of nineteen thousand in which, during three centuries of vast change and heroic impulse, no one had written anything or painted anything or composed anything, especially when one of the most compelling natural incidents in world literature had occurred within the city boundary. It is not difficult to imagine Boccaccio's hearing from some traveler the account of the Lovers of Teruel and starting that night to write his version; it is difficult to imagine the citizens of Teruel living with the story for three hundred years without any inclination to do anything constructive about it, but that seems to have been the case.

I then began to imagine how different the results would have been had Teruel in those days produced one young man like Thomas Hardy or Truman Capote, and my imagination began running wild through the long dark hours as I tried to construct what these talents would have done with this story in medieval terms. It was a game of vast dimension and unexpected twists: it was not difficult to imagine Capote tracking down each nuance of the story and taking delight in depicting the journey of rich Don Pedro de Azagra from Albarracín to Teruel to claim the bride he was to know for only eighteen hours, and I could visualize Hardy working slowly to construct a study of rural passions.

But then the strange affliction of being a writer overtook me, and I was no longer concerned with Thomas Hardy; I was in bed in Teruel, imagining what my responsibility would have been had I been a citizen of this beloved town during the days of its intellectual aridity, and I started to draft my medieval epic on the legend. At first I was perplexed by what had happened to Diego Marcilla during his five years' absence and for a couple of hours I wasted my time devising an explanation for this lacuna; finally I recalled that every writer who had dealt with the legend after Boccaccio had ruined his story through bothering about what the boy had done during these years. Whoever had told the story originally had hit upon an idea that could not be improved: 'After five years' adventuring in the great world, Diego returned to Teruel, entering by the Zaragoza gate.' Take it or leave it; he was absent for five years and he came back.

What was important, I realized, was not the detail but the universal fact that young men leave their villages in search of adventure that will make them famous or success that will make them rich, and the problem for the storyteller was to reflect the permanence of this theme. At about five in the morning, as dawn was breaking, I began to visualize the Zaragoza gate as it must have been in the Middle Ages. Now, when Diego left Teruel on his five years' pilgrimage I could hear the stones of the gate admonishing him, saying that they had watched many young men leave on missions such as his and that the fame they had sought proved meaningless; the riches they had won were unrewarding, for the love they had abandoned would not be recaptured.

Like most men, on the rare occasions when I am kept awake through a night I fall asleep at dawn, but on this long night I didn't, for the dialogue of the stones preoccupied me during several more hours, after which I began pondering how a medieval writer might have depicted the triumphant homecoming, and I was thrown into a Greek-chorus type of passage in which the stones of the Zaragoza gate both welcome him as their long-absent son and comment on his journey, and I was winging away for another two hours. When I finally went down to breakfast the people I was with said, 'Michener, you look all beat up. Where have you been?' I replied, 'If I told you, you wouldn't believe it,' for I had spent my night at the Zaragoza gate.

(Late in the editing of this manuscript friends brought to my attention the fact that an art cinema in Philadelphia was offering a French motion picture titled *The Lovers of Teruel*, which had won a top prize at the Cannes Film Festival of 1962. A Russian–French cast headed by Ludmila Tcherina had been photographed in marvelous color patterns by Claude Renoir, son of the painter, and the result had been highly regarded by critics. I took the long trip and was more than gratified. Poetic and surrealistic, the picture told of a grubby little traveling show which had set up its stage opposite the railroad yards of a small French town in order to present a mime-dance version of the Spanish legend, but the real-life actors were finding their personal lives paralleling those of Diego and Isabel. Scenery, acting, fantasy and movement were exceptional, and a splendid sense of the old legend was achieved, but unfortunately neither in the real-life nor in the inserted play was the overpowering simplicity of the original achieved. Diego died not of love but from the dagger of his rival. Isabel died from the same dagger. Great folk-sentences like 'The year 1217, Don Domingo Celada being judge of Teruel' and 'There was a clatter at the Zaragoza gate' were not caught, and I went away supposing that the legend was so primary that it could not be reproduced in art; but upon reflection I cannot believe this. I therefore draw attention to the legend, trusting that sometime within the next hundred years someone with talent will direct himself to it.)

For a chain of happy days I wandered about the city, nodding to the bull on his pillar, revisiting the places I had known before and talking with groups of men wherever I found them. And then on the third evening as I was standing in the garden of the parador I felt a voice within me saying in an accusatory manner, 'You didn't come to Teruel to feast on entremeses or to wander about looking at bulls and mummies. Get to the main problem.'

What was the main problem? In 1932 I had seen, by merest accident, a Teruel which existed for all practical purposes in the sixteenth century.

Men of Teruel.

It was the most backward of the provincial capitals, and when judged by ordinary cultural indices, had least to commend it. But it had caught my fancy as typical of the problems of Spain, and during the years that followed, I kept it much in memory. This, however, would not alone have accounted for the striking significance of Teruel in my life nor for the fact that when I approached it from the Río Turia my hands were wet with perspiration.

For a brief moment, in the winter of 1937–38, the chances of history

made Teruel the most important city in Europe, where decisions of great moment were in the balance. It became also, for men in all parts of the world, a source of moral anguish and has continued to this day to be a source of moral guilt. I doubt that many men live entire lives without incurring some sense of regret; for many of my generation their regret centered on Teruel, and the guilt which it evoked has never been discharged, not at Anzio nor at Guadalcanal nor at Bastogne.

In 1936, when the Spanish Civil War broke out, I was at an age when it would have been relatively simple for me to have broken loose from my prosaic job of teaching in Colorado and come to Spain to fight in the Abraham Lincoln Brigade, composed of Americans who wanted to help defend the Republic. Some of the men I respected most in American life were so serving, and when I thought of them doing the job that I should have been engaged in, I felt ashamed, for most of them knew nothing of Spain and had no spiritual connection to it, whereas I did know and the ties which bound me were strong indeed. I had watched at close hand the birth of the Republic and had seen its first faltering steps; I had spoken with the president and while he had not impressed me I had applauded many of the changes his party had introduced into Spanish life. I had read the brave words of his lieutenants and had picked out of the Spanish newspapers to which I subscribed the doings of this group of dedicated men. That change was overdue in Spain, I knew better than most, and when an army revolt arose to end that change I was desolate. Of all the young men available in America in those crucial years, I should have volunteered to defend the Republic, for I saw clearly what must ensue in Europe; I was convinced that a world war was upon us and that in the end my country would be involved.

Then why didn't I fight in Spain? For three reasons. First, I was not invited. Recruiting campaigns for the Abraham Lincoln Brigade were conducted mainly in the big cities, and although some of my friends were active, they were in New York and made no approaches to me, for they were seeking a different kind of person. In the absence of a specific opportunity to join, I was never confronted by a hard choice. Why didn't I volunteer? In my life I have rarely volunteered for anything, nor sought anything, even though I have been willing to take unusual risks when they evolved, and I still find this a logical attitude. Second, since I was convinced that America would soon be at war and since I had taught my students that our survival depended upon its successful prosecution, even pinpointing Singapore and the Philippines as the spots where the war would probably begin (one student had asked, 'How about Hawaii?' and I had explained, 'Impossible. The Japanese would never dare'), I was willing to wait until we made our entrance, satisfied that the Spanish Republic could hold out till then. Third, and I believe this was the most important, those men and women engaged in enlisting Americans for the Brigade, even those who were my personal acquaintances, were people whose general judgment in other matters I did not respect. For some years certain of them had been goading me to join the Communist Party, a step which I refused for the good reason that in Europe I had known many Communists and had found them ill-informed on politics, corrupt in personal judgment and ruthless in their attempts to force others into their orbit. In Europe they had posed a difficult problem for me, and now in America they did the same, for although I sympathized with many of their objectives, as did many of my generation who had watched the depression puncture pompous old verities, I was suspicious of their immediate judgment and their long-term intention. I was especially schizophrenic regarding the Communist relationship to Spain; as a sensible man I had to applaud the efforts of this long-misruled nation to achieve a modern government, but the manner in which my Communist friends proposed to dictate to that government disgusted me and I could not find it within myself to support them. Did I, in 1936 and 1937, suspect that they might have a goal beyond the apparent one of defending the Republic? Did I anticipate that their ambitions would quickly escalate to the point where their goal was no longer a Republic but a Communist dictatorship? I did not. Such conclusions would have required greater insight than I possessed. I believed that the Communist commitment was deeper than mine and that it was only this enthusiasm which caused them to say and do things which I considered nonsense. But in the latter months of 1938 I began to read in impartial journals reports which made me wonder if a serious change had not occurred in Republican ranks. The defense of a free democracy had been subordinated to the expanded goal of establishing a Communist government, and the intuitive suspicions that I had entertained in 1936 matured.

One obvious question must be asked. Are the three reasons cited above mere ex post facto rationalizations masking the fact that I was afraid to volunteer? In any sensible man fear of battle will always be a partial motive, and in my case it could have played a decisive role. On the other hand, in World War II, I was exempt from military service because I was a Quaker, but I joined the navy anyway. In Asia, I have seen a good deal of war, more than most, and I cannot recall ever having shied away from battle. I therefore conclude that the reasons cited above are not spurious and did actually govern my behavior.

It was with a sense of doom that I followed the news which began to come out of Teruel in late 1937. We have seen that in 1171 the city was founded because a fortress was needed to stabilize the battle line that existed between the Christians in Zaragoza and the Moors in Valencia. Now, almost eight hundred years later, Teruel found itself serving the same function, except that this time it was General Franco's troops that were in Zaragoza and the Republicans that were in Valencia. It had become the keystone of the Republican line running between Valencia and Barcelona and its retention would determine who would win the war.

In October, Franco's army occupied Teruel and in forays from it began to cut the Republican lines. If the Republic were to survive, it must recapture this city, even though winter was approaching.

Teruel was defended by some ten thousand Franco troops under the command of a colonel bearing a French last name, Rey d'Harcourt, who had ordered the building of defense positions on all slopes leading up to the city. Teruel would be difficult to assault, but for the job the Republicans had assembled a force of a hundred and ten thousand well-trained men, and on December 15 they began the attack.

It coincided with the beginning of one of Teruel's famed winters; for several weeks the thermometer dropped each night to zero degrees Fahrenheit, bringing some ice and much snow, which helped the Franco men inside the city. Nevertheless, the Republicans attacked, only to be repulsed by slanting fire. Again and again the Republicans tried to climb the sloping flanks, but had to retreat, leaving their wounded to die between the lines. Here in this significant city, which I had stumbled upon years ago, developed the most terrible battle of the war; and here the fate of the world, at least for this period, was being decided.

The Republican attack continued for twenty-four gruesome days, during which frightful crimes were perpetrated by both sides. Prisoners were shot. Bystanders were executed. Dead bodies were mutilated. Buildings were wantonly destroyed and vengeance was exacted on any enemy at hand. If the brutality of the two armies was about equal, so was the heroism. To storm the hills of Teruel over ice and snow and then to penetrate the rubbled defenses required courage of an absolute order, and this the Republicans had; to remain inside the city walls, with no water, no food and diminishing supplies of ammunition, while determined assaults came hourly, required of Franco's men a determination which never faltered.

In America, I followed the siege with a sense of tragic despair. The hills I had tramped were the ones under contention and the city streets I had found so meaningful were those where the shellfire struck with such fury. Reports said that several columns of Franco's troops were rushing south to relieve the handful of men inside Teruel, and I prayed that they would not arrive before the Republicans had won the city.

Shortly after January 8, 1938, I read with enormous relief that Colonel Rey d'Harcourt had surrendered Teruel to the Republicans. His men crawled down out of the rubble, looking like emaciated ghosts, and women who had undergone the siege and the bombardment appeared half dead as they begged for water. It was a tremendous Republican victory and aroused hopes throughout the eastern half of Spain. In Fascist capitals like Berlin and Rome, especially the latter, it caused despair, for it seemed the first of what might be many Republican triumphs. In America, I breathed deeply and looked at the new map. The great cities, Madrid, Barcelona and Valencia, remained in Republican hands, and the war had obviously become a contest between the reactionary rural sections and the liberal metropolitan ones, and I could not believe that in an age of technical development rural areas could win a war.

But almost immediately the relief columns which Franco had set in motion toward Teruel began arriving to start a new siege. This time it was the Franco forces who had to attack up the dreadful slopes; it was the Republicans who were trapped inside the city, with inadequate food, water or ammunition. Only the cold remained the same. At first the ice and snow

Wall in Teruel.

exacted more casualties than the bullets, but finally the Franco forces moved heavy Italian batteries into position and these began the systematic destruction of the city. Row after row of houses were pulverized. In early February the Republicans had to evacuate the commanding hill on which the Bull of Teruel had appeared, and it was soon occupied by an Italian battery which fired point-blank into the city.

Throughout the middle weeks of February, in intense cold, the Franco forces inched their way forward, and it was during this fatal time, when the result of the battle was obvious, that the worst atrocities were committed. On February 20, Franco assault troops broke through to the first line of houses and bayoneted all in sight. On February 21 the Franco men swept into the heart of the city, took all the major buildings and began those reprisals which would permanently remove from Teruel any persons with Republican connections.

The battle had lasted sixty-nine days. Twenty thousand Republican troops were dead, ten thousand Franco men. Twenty-eight thousand prisoners had been taken and the number of wounded could not be calculated. Thousands of civilians were dead; on each side thousands had been assassinated under one pretext or another. But at last the battle was over and Teruel, almost totally destroyed, was permanently in Franco's hands. The Republican lifeline from Valencia to Barcelona and to Madrid was threatened if not wholly cut, and the uprising of the rural areas against the cities had succeeded. Germany and Italy had won the first round in the test of arms, and a world war was inevitable. Of course, the war in Spain would struggle along for another year, with the terrible Battle of the Ebro still to unfold and the final siege of Madrid, but after Teruel sensible observers knew that the outcome was determined.

With the death of this mountain city I experienced a spiritual agony that has not diminished through the years. A noble effort of men to govern themselves perished with the collapse of Teruel, and not all the rationalizations of the postwar period can deny that fact. Now it is popular to describe the whole war in terms of white (the victorious forces) and red (the Communist), but when the war began this was not the distinction nor was it the commanding consideration at the Battle of Teruel. When I read, as I do in the book before me, that 'finally the white forces of freedom triumphed over the Russian-led reds,' I feel sick at my stomach. When I see official publications which seek to prove that all Republicans were Communists, that only Republicans slaughtered civilians, that only Republicans were guilty of heinous crimes, my reason balks. The war had begun on different principles, even though I do now admit that it ended in a debacle in which those original concepts were engulfed.

On March 11, 1939, Almería, Murcia and Cartagena surrendered and the long struggle ground to a halt. About 900,000 Spaniards were dead, of whom some 175,000 had been assassinated. More than 170 monasteries and convents were burned and nearly 1900 ravaged to the point where they could not be used. Some 3000 others were wrecked in part. More than 250,000 homes were destroyed, and nearly 400,000 Spaniards preferred exile in countries like Mexico and France to the reprisals that awaited them in Spain. Any rehabilitation of the country was made more difficult by the fact that 8,000,000,000,000 pesetas had been sent out of the country by the Republican government to purchase arms; 1,500,000,000,000 were subsequently recovered by the Franco government, but the remainder stayed abroad, mainly in Russia and Mexico. (The data in this paragraph come principally from Georges-Roux, *La Guerra Civil de España,* translated from the French, 1964.)

As to the number of priests and nuns assassinated in the early days of the war, the figures are uncertain, but at least fifteen thousand perished, including fourteen bishops, not one of whom would commit apostasy in order to escape martyrdom. In one town after another, where for the last two hundred years observers had reported that the citizens were above all else Catholics who loved their priests, one of the first things that happened when war started was the indiscriminate slaughter of clericals, and this occurred even in areas where Communists were not in control. On the other side, events such as those at Málaga, where eighty suspected Masons were garroted, were common.

Today, looking back at such evidence as has so far been made public, I must conclude that the apprehensions which kept me from volunteering in 1936 were sound. I was a better judge than I knew, for the seeds of the final Communist debacle in Spain began to mature fairly early in the fight, even though at the time I was not intelligent enough to identify them. I think that no one can see the photographs of Barcelona, Valencia and Madrid taken in the final winter of 1938–39 without realizing that Communism had pretty well taken charge of the Republic; if the leadership of that time had somehow triumphed, there can be little doubt but that it would have organized a Communist dictatorship. But during the Battle of Teruel, Communism was not inevitable.

But I had not returned to Teruel to exacerbate the feelings of guilt occasioned by its fall. I had quite a different purpose. During the war no city had given Franco's army more trouble than this, and at various points in Spain I was warned not to bother with Teruel: 'The victors are disgusted with it. They hated its stubborn people, and the Franco government would give the city nothing.' Others said, 'If you want to see Spain at its worst, go to Teruel. It's a ghost town.' In a well-produced volume called *The Spain of Each Province,* sponsored in part by the government, native sons write about and illustrate each of the fifty provinces, but apparently Teruel still produces no writers, for its essay is written by a man from Madrid. It is a beautiful thing, an elegy for a dead city, and the painting which illustrates it is a handsome, mournful black gash, recalling barbed wire and broken bottles. Because I had an affinity for Teruel, I wanted to see what had happened to it in defeat, for this would constitute a real test of contemporary Spain: How did the victors treat the vanquished?

First I went out into the country to see if it had changed much. I chose the remote village of San Agustín, on the border of Castellón Province, and there under a perfect July sky I walked for several miles through ripened fields where the reapers were at work according to a division of labor laid down prior to Bible times: a young man swung the large scythe; his strong wife gathered the fallen grain; an old man twisted stalks into a rope and tied the bundles. As I watched them I said, 'The recurring sound of rural life has been the swish of the scythe over stubble and rocks, but no musician has been able to put it into music.' In the fields at least nothing had changed, and the trio at work looked just as poor and just as tired as their predecessors had looked thirty-four years before.

Nor had the village changed. The central square was still unpaved; most of the houses were still unpainted; the dust was omnipresent and the heat still kept people indoors. The meanness of the life continued too: the earthen floors, the sparse furniture, the inadequate clothing, the harsh

The spirit of Teruel.

poverty of Spanish rural life. I recalled that day in Badajoz when our car had taken the injured man to the hospital, and in San Agustín the standard of living was the same. Of all the countries in which I have traveled, only India and Turkey have had a rural poverty as grinding as that in Spain, and the much publicized 'Twenty-five Years of Peace' have brought little to the farmers.

Yet even as I thought this, I became aware of the improvement. Out beyond the village I could see electricity wires which had not been there a generation ago; in what once had been barren fields I could see where millions of young trees had been planted, as they have been throughout Spain. The roads were better and the village even had an automobile and two television aerials. The farmers looked poor, but nowhere did I see any in rags, nor did any look underfed. On balance I would say that in the country things were a little better than they had been before; but when one considered what had been accomplished in rural areas in Germany, Denmark and Britain, the comparison was disadvantageous. On the other hand, Spain had accomplished more than Turkey and much more than India.

On my return to Teruel, I picked up, along the road, a fine-looking young man in clerical garb who said he was hitchhiking home from his studies at the seminary in Valencia, and his pleasant chatter was so charming that I shall repeat it without interruption: 'I'm twenty-two years old and entered seminary training at eleven. I was an orphan, you see, and was stuck away in an orphanage and this was the only way that I could see of getting out. I wasn't a real orphan, I suppose, because my mother and three sisters were living, but my father died and we could scarcely live on what my mother earned, so it was decided that I should go to the orphanage, and I made up my own mind to go to the seminary. We have no students there from the upper class and none from the lower class, so today all priests come from the middle class. I suppose when I become a priest I'll be sent to some small village like the one you've been visiting, and I'll bring my mother to live with me and I'll find jobs in the village for my three sisters, who will live with me until they're married. I've noticed a priest can usually find jobs of some kind for his relatives. You mention the novels of Pío Baroja, but we're not allowed to read them. He's much too anti-clerical, but the disappointing thing is that the Spanish novels we are allowed to read are so pro-clerical they aren't much fun. But I understand the Church's problem and obey its suggestions. I saw your motion picture *Sayonara*. All of us at the seminary did. It's about two soldiers and two Japanese girls. Japan must be a wonderful country and I wouldn't be unhappy to be sent there when I'm graduated, but I suppose I'm destined for Spain. This is a great country and there's much work to be done.'

When the seminarian left me in Teruel, I was assaulted, there can be no other word for it, by noise such as I had not heard for some years. At first I couldn't identify it or its direction, but as I drove toward the center of the city I heard the rhythmic roar of motors off to the west and decided that Teruel must be holding some kind of auto race, and I set out to find it. I was wrong. It was a motorcycle race around a circular course that ran through a handsome new section of Teruel which had grown up in recent years on the other side of the ravine down which the Saracen bulls had charged the Christians in 1171. Before the war this area had contained no houses or even any barns. I took my place behind some bales of straw that marked a turn in the course and decided simply to look at what was on display in this new Teruel. The thirty or forty motorcycles which kept roaring past were the best that Europe built, and each driver wore an expensive leather suit with goggles to match. The competition was keen. Number 1, in green, drove at a sensational speed and could not be overtaken, but a real battle developed between 11 in red and 15 in the same color. The latter tried to drive 11 into the wall at the turns, and when 11 protested, rowdy 15 yelled the Spanish equivalent of 'Up your bucket.' The

CASA-CUARTEL DE LA GUARDIA CIVIL

TODO POR LA PATRIA

noise was unbelievable, for not only did the motorcycles thunder with their mufflers open, but as usual three huge loudspeakers suspended from public buildings kept up a constant chatter, while a Coca-Cola truck below played records over its public address system. The streets along which the race careened were wide, well paved and finely planted with trees. The houses, all of recent construction, were about what one would find in southern California, except that since Teruel has bitterly cold winters, said to be the worst in Spain, its houses had more provision for heating than California's would have had.

It was the people, however, who were most impressive. To watch the race cost about twenty-five cents, but the course was jammed, and I saw no one poorly dressed; their clothes would have fitted in without comment in Chicago or Edinburgh. It was a well-fed, well-groomed audience, and as the motorcycles roared around the walls of the bullring for their dash right at the bales of straw where I stood, I saw at least as many pretty girls wearing make-up as I would have seen in a similar American city. Their dresses were about as short, and if they were accompanied by young men, they walked hand in hand as they would have in a small English city. In fact, except for a rather heavy concentration of men in clerical garb, I could see nothing that would indicate I was in Spain.

In this cautious manner I checked each experience I was having in Teruel and could find no evidence that this was the city on which Franco's forces had broken their teeth in the Civil War. The visible scars were healed. If in the sieges of 1937–38 the city had been mainly destroyed, it has now been well rebuilt. Not even in the ancient Jewish quarter, with its crowded streets, were there evidences of the war, but I did see set into the wall of a house built in 1400 one sign which startled me: 'This building is insured against fire by the Great American Insurance Company of New York.' If the Franco government has rebuilt Teruel in a spirit of forgiveness, no matter how grudging, then the outward bitterness of the Civil War has subsided. In the new suburb where the motorcycle race took place I saw much evidence of new construction sponsored by the government: new schools, new homes, even a new bullring, and a handsome new sports center where for fifteen pesetas (about twenty-five cents) a month young men can enjoy a swimming pool, a large gymnasium and a basketball court as good as that in any American city of comparable size. A sign said that the sports hall had been erected with funds from the Youth Front, so I suppose that only those boys whose families support the government can participate. I saw the tennis courts on an emotional morning: the day before, Manuel Santana had won the world's tennis title at Wimbledon, Spain's first title of the kind in history, and Teruel was celebrating.

Today, even though the sore of Teruel has not healed in my heart nor will it ever, I can accept most of the statement which the Franco govern-

uardia Civil headquarters.

ment has recently drafted in English for inclusion in any tourist publication where reference to the war cannot be avoided.

> For a century and a half Spaniards had tried to live in peace according to the formulas laid down by the French Revolution—generally speaking under a Monarchy, though twice under a Republic. It was impossible to implant a purely liberal policy in a country without a middle class, and with an almost feudal structure. And so we spent a century and a half hitting each other over the head, familiarizing the world with the spectacle of civil war, and introducing the word *'pronunciamiento'* into most languages. The nation was filled with hatreds, and those hatreds provided a fruitful field of action for ideas and political groups which ended up by dominating the rest— Anarchism and Communism. And this was the outcome of a policy full of liberal phrases!
>
> One day, in 1936, those hatreds exploded. The world still remembers that three-year war to which the Catholic Church gave the name of Crusade. We don't pretend that all the goodies were on one side, and all the baddies on the other; for one thing, goodness and badness are always mixed. But what we can and do claim is that the war was won by that section of the people who preferred a Spanish Spain to a Spain turned into a satellite of Russia.

And then, when my opinion about modern Teruel had about crystallized, I stumbled upon an extraordinary building, a modern hospital built on the skyscraper design, with an elegant reception floor topped by tiers of rooms bursting with every modern medical device. I was shown around the building by the administrator, Don José Callado Ruiz, who had been born in nearby Cuenca and educated in Madrid. He was indistinguishable from hospital administrators in England or Holland, efficient, knowledgeable and proud of his institution. Where the ordinary hospital might have one iron lung, his had two, and incubators for premature babies, and gleaming trays of all the latest medical tools from Solingen in Germany, and x-rays galore and a splendid medical library. It was the kind of hospital that put the ones I knew in America to shame.

It had one fault, however. It had almost no patients. There were, I believe, four women on one floor awaiting childbirth; the rest of the gleaming installation was unused and had never been used. I tried to pierce the secret of this amazing building, for I had recently been in a hospital in America, and judging by the overcrowding there, this Teruel installation had space for about four hundred patients, and certainly in the villages I had been visiting there were candidates who could have profited from admission. Then, as I waited in the foyer, I understood a little better, for on the far wall, gazing balefully at whoever entered the hospital, was the frightening portrait of a fleshy young man in an open shirt. I had seen this hypnotic portrait before in many public buildings, this all-seeing, all-knowing young god of modern Spain, and his counte-

José Antoni

Aqui Yace
ESTEBAN PEREZ MORA
(BRIGADA DE INGENIEROS) † EN EL FRENTE DE TERUEL
EL DIA 18 DE DICBRE DE 1937
A LA EDAD DE 24 AÑOS
SUS PADRES Y H... LE DEDICAN ESTE RECUERDO

nance was the only thing that had ever frightened me in the country. He was José Antonio, son of the tough dictator Miguel Primo de Rivera, Marqués de Estella. Born in 1903, José Antonio had organized the Falange at the age of thirty and had been the bullyboy of the street-rioting that had helped discredit the Republic. His adherents roamed the streets in trucks, machine-gunning their opponents, and most Spaniards believe that if José Antonio had lived he would have challenged Franco for the leadership of Spain and might have become the country's Fascist dictator, but shortly before the outbreak of war he was arrested by the Republicans and some months after the beginning of hostilities was tried, condemned and shot. Alive, he was a danger to Franco's claim to leadership; dead, he became a patron saint, and at the end of the war his body was carried on shoulders from Alicante in the south to El Escorial, where he was temporarily buried among the ancient rulers of Spain. Later his corpse was translated to the newly built basilica of the Valley of the Fallen, where it lies in enormous solemnity before the high altar. I say that the visage of José Antonio is frightening because he looks exactly like a younger Hermann Goering, and had he lived and triumphed he would each year have resembled Goering more. He would now be only sixty-three and good for another fifteen years' rule, which is a frightening thought.

At any rate, the hospital he now supervised in absentia, the finest I had visited in a dozen years, was reserved for those who, like himself, were dedicated to a certain way of life. For members, the rates of the hospital were low and the service provided by the medical head, Dr. Antonio Moreno Monforte from the college in Zaragoza, was, I am sure, excellent. In England such a hospital would be crawling with patients and overworked nurses and grumbling doctors, for members of the Labor and Conservative parties alike would be eligible, and one had to sense the difference.

On the last day of my sentimental return to Teruel, Señor Cortel Zuriaga, the man who had shown me the tomb of the Lovers, took me to a high point overlooking the city, and with the cemetery at our backs, explained how the fortunes of the great battle for Teruel had fluctuated, and he spoke with decent respect for each side: 'If the Republicans were to win the war, they had to capture this city. They did so, and then General Franco knew that he must retake it. It was as simple as that.' And he pointed out the routes used by Franco's rescue columns as they brought pressure to bear on the city then held by the Republicans. 'For anyone in Teruel it was a terrible war,' he said. 'It was a blessing when it ended.' Then he said something about the bull that stood in the plaza, representing the city, and in these words summarized the spiritual significance of Teruel: 'We saw the other day that the symbol of Teruel is a bull. But which particular bull? A Saracen bull sent against the Christians as an

Here lies Esteban Pérez Moral. Brigade of Engineers.
Died on the front Teruel the 18th day of December 1937
at the age of 24 years. His father and
brothers dedicated this remembrance. R.I.P.

The survivor.

enemy. It came to destroy us, but we converted it. If the Spaniards in 1171
were able to accept such a bull as the symbol of their city, then other
Spaniards in 1939 should have been able to accept their recent enemies.'
Apparently, after the first long year of revenge, that is what has
happened.

    As I stood looking down upon the city that has meant so much to me,
I asked myself the question which perplexes many people who wish to visit
Spain: 'If I was once so committed to a Republican victory, how can I bear

to visit Spain now?' I have often wondered, for after the destruction of the Republicans, I went through a period of bitterness in which I did not care ever again to see Spain, and I would schedule my trips through Europe so as to avoid it. Then two things happened. One day, while talking to a group of Spanish exiles in Mexico, I asked myself, 'Why should I allow Franco to deprive me of a land which is almost as much mine as his?' More important, as I studied the world I came to the conclusion that each nation, at the end of a cycle of about twenty-five years, starts anew. What went before is historically important and probably sets a limit to what the newborn nation can become, but the fact is that the past is past and a new nation is in being, with fresh possibilities for success or failure. That is why General de Gaulle has been so right in France; he is governing an entirely new country not bound by the debacle of 1941. That is why the young Germans are so right in disclaiming responsibility for 1935–1945; they're a new nation, almost as if they had been discovered on the moon, and they are correct in insisting that they be so treated. It is obviously true of China, though most of us have been reluctant to admit it. And one of these days it will be true even of Russia, and we had better be prepared to admit that, too.

It also applies to the United States, though we fight against it and blind our eye and conscience to the fact. The median age of our population is lower now. We are more overcrowded, more urban, and whether we like it or not, a permanently mixed nation racially. We are in the midst of swift change in education, technology, labor relations and religion. We are evolving a new morality, a new posture in world politics. Yet we refuse to understand that the advent of such change signifies also the advent of a new nation. The people of Spain seem more prepared to accept their new nation than we are to accept ours, and it may be this reluctance to accept the new that will destroy us.

As a matter of fact, I suspect that the rebirth of each nation occurs about every seventeen or eighteen years, but only the rare social scientist can recognize the change as it occurs. I usually seem to be about seven years tardy. America's present cycle will end sometime around 1970, and if we try to govern our new nation by 1920 policies we shall be truly doomed. Spain's last cycle ended about 1964, and it is the opportunity to watch a new nation coming into being that makes a visit to Spain so instructive and rewarding.

FOLLOWING PAGE:
Stoned roadway.

SANTIAGO DE COMPOSTELA

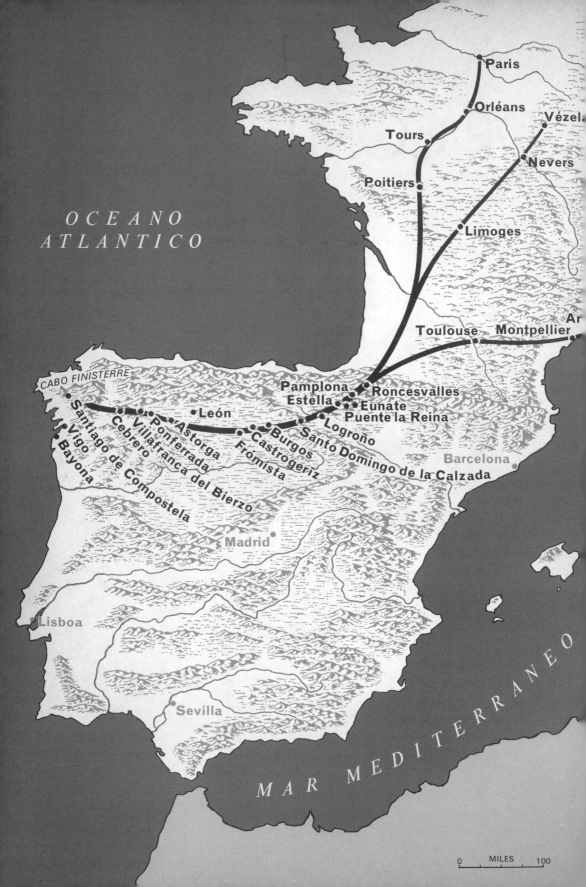

OCEANO
ATLANTICO

Paris

Orléans

Vézela

Tours

Nevers

Poitiers

Limoges

Toulouse   Ar
Montpellier

CABO FINISTERRE

Pamplona   Roncesvalles
Estella   Eunate
León   Puente la Reina
Astorga   Logroño
Santiago de Compostela   Villafranca del Bierzo   Cebrero   Ponferrada   Burgos   Santo Domingo de la Calzada
Vigo   Castrogeriz
Bayona   Frómista

Barcelona

Madrid

Lisboa

Sevilla

MAR MEDITERRANEO

0   MILES   100

Any reader who has come with me so far through the Iberian peninsula should be prepared for a pilgrimage across northern Spain to the sanctuary at Santiago de Compostela, the finest journey in Spain and one of the two or three best in the world. It is a twofold pilgrimage to a long-dead form of art and to a living religious shrine. To understand the latter, certain things must be known.

Fact. Two of the earliest disciples chosen by Jesus were the brothers James and John, sons of the Galilee fisherman Zebedee and his wife Salome. So energetic in their support of the new religion were the brothers that Jesus gave them the honorary second name of Boanerges, the Sons of Thunder. Salome, sister of the Virgin Mary, which meant that her sons were cousins of Jesus, appears to have been a woman of some wealth, for she underwrote many of the expenses of the group and may have paid the tavern bill for the Last Supper. At any rate, both Mark and Matthew, in their gospels, relate the story of how Salome, hoping to gain some return for the money she had spent, requested that Jesus give her sons the positions on his right and left hand in heaven, but he rebuked her, saying, 'Ye know not what ye ask. Are ye able to drink of the cup that I shall drink of, and to be baptized with the baptism that I am baptized with? . . . to sit on my right hand, and on my left, is not mine to give, but it shall be given to them for whom it is prepared of my Father.' In A.D. 29 the brothers were present at the Crucifixion, and in 44, James, having persisted in his energetic propagation of the faith, was beheaded, perhaps at Caesarea, by order of King Herod Agrippa, thus becoming the first of the followers of Jesus to attain martyrdom.

Tradition. In the Book of Acts it is suggested that after the death of Jesus and before the martyrdom of James, the disciples scattered to different portions of the world and proselytized for the new religion, without specifying as to who went where and with what results. Tradition, unsupported by documentation but strong in folk persistence, claims that while Matthew went to Ethiopia, Thomas to India, Jude to Persia, Simon to India and Bartholomew to Armenia, James Boanerges came to Spain, where after extensive labors he succeeded in converting nine Iberians to Christianity and was rewarded by the supreme gift of being visited at Zaragoza by the Virgin Mary, who was still living at the time. This tradition is popular in Spain but textual and historical critics in other countries find it difficult to accept. It should be noted, however, that the tradition specifically states that after this missionary effort in Spain, James returned to the Holy Land, where he suffered martyrdom.

Legend. Late in history a beautiful legend developed in Europe to the effect that following the decapitation in Jerusalem and burial in Caesarea of St. James, his body was mysteriously disinterred and found to have its head once more intact. Into the port of Jaffa, where shipping for Jerusalem customarily landed, came a ship made of stone and manned by knights; the body of James was rescued and brought in seven days to the harbor of Iria Flavia (now Padrón) on the west coast of Spain in the region now called Galicia. Here a willful pagan queen denied burial to the cargo of the stone ship, but miracles awakened her to a Christian understanding, and she allowed the saintly body to be taken inland to an unlikely spot where a Roman burial ground had long existed; here St. James was buried, sometime around the year A.D. 44. It was nearly eight hundred years later, in 812 (some say 814), that a hermit happened to see in the heavens a bright star hovering over a vacant field, a phenomenon with which we are familiar, and when he reported this fact to his religious superiors, excavations were begun and the body of St. James was brought to light, uncorrupted by the passage of time. As a saint descended from heaven, he assumed personal leadership of the Christian remnant who were battling the superior Muslims who had overrun Spain, and at the crucial but legendary Battle of Clavijo in 844, was clearly seen by the Spanish Christians, riding before them on a white horse, swinging a great sword and killing Moors by the thousands, from which he gained the name by which he would henceforth be known in Spain, Santiago Matamoros. It was under his banner that Christianity reconquered Spain; it was following his white horse that Spaniards expelled the Moors, drove out the Jews and conquered the Americas. St. James became the patron saint of Spain, as well he deserved, and his burial place became the most sacred spot in Spain, Santiago de Compostela, the last word of which could have been derived from either the Spanish Campo de la estrella (in Latin, Campus Stellae, meaning Countryside where the Star Shone) or the latin Compost Terra (from compostum, burying ground). In Spain the name James appears in a variety of forms. In Latin it was, of course, Jacobus, so that the pilgrims' road we are about to follow has always been known as the Jacobean route; in Old Spanish it was Iago and evolved into Jacóme and Jaime, the latter of which is still preferred along the eastern Mediterranean coast; as the name of our saint it became the composite form Santiago, which is the prevailing Spanish form today; through a false division this produced Diego; and in nearby France it became, of course, Jacques. In some years all these names could have been heard along the way.

History. We have seen, during our visit to Córdoba, that the Moors of southern Spain kept in a vault in that city a relic of considerable emotional significance in their wars against the Christians: the visible arm of the Prophet Muhammad, and there are historians who believe that much of the advantage which the Moors enjoyed in their triumphant sweep across Spain derived from their belief that they were invincible as long as the arm of the Prophet led them into battle. The Christians, on the other hand, were supported by no comparable relic from their New Testament, and we know from documents that a kind of fatality overcame them when without heavenly assistance they had to face Muslims who had such assistance. I think it neither ungenerous nor unlikely to suggest that the body of Santiago was found not by a hermit following a star but by hard-pressed soldiers who needed a rallying point; certainly it arrived on the scene when some kind of counterbalance to the Prophetic arm was needed, and over the centuries this heavenly figure riding his white horse, sword in hand, proved more potent and of farther-reaching significance, if we consider his role in helping conquer the New World, than the arm of the Prophet.

At any rate, we can be certain that after the year 812 Christian fortunes took an upward swing, but not all the miracles connected with Santiago were military. A bridegroom riding his horse along the sands to his wedding was swept into the waves and drowned, but his bride appealed to Santiago and from the sea rose the groom, his garments covered with white cockleshells, after which this beautiful symbol of the shell shaped like human hands extending alms became the mark of all who fought the infidel and the badge of those who made the pilgrimage to Compostela.

It is not surprising that at the scene of such miracles a series of churches should have risen to mark the grave, culminating in the early 1100s in a cathedral of majestic proportions, much of which can be seen today. It was to this ancient site that pilgrims from all over Europe made their way for more than eleven hundred years.

It is difficult to describe, in a scientific age, the spiritual hold that pilgrimage had on citizens of the Middle Ages. There was, of course, in those days but one Church, and so far as the Christian world was concerned, it was truly universal. Existence outside the membership of this religion was unthinkable, and the three physical locations upon which the

imagery of the Church depended were Jerusalem, where Christ was crucified; Rome, where Peter founded the organization of the Church; and
Compostela, from which point Europe had been evangelized. Any Christian who made a pilgrimage to one of these places was assured of extraordinary blessing, but a man who had journeyed to all three had a right to
consider himself in an almost heavenly state. Those who went to Jerusalem were called palmers, since they returned with palm branches; those
who went to Rome were romeros; it was only those who made the terribly
hazardous trip to Compostela who were entitled to be called pilgrims, and
no devout man in that age bothered to estimate which of the three
journeys was most important, for in sanctity they were equal.

The Way of St. James, as it is customarily referred to in English, was
primarily a French road, and I suppose that in its years of maximum
greatness some eighty out of every hundred pilgrims who traveled it were
from outside of Spain, and of these the bulk came from France, although
the road was also popular with Englishmen and Germans. In the famous
monasteries we shall see, French was spoken, and in the cathedrals French
priests officiated. Indeed, the road started at that curious tower in the
middle of Paris which still stands to excite the imagination of the visitor,
the Tour St. Jacques on the right bank of the Seine not far from Notre
Dame. Here, in all ages, pilgrims from various parts of Europe used to
convene to form bands for the long march to Compostela, some nine
hundred miles away. Kings and beggars, queens and cutthroats, butchers
and knights, poets and philosophers all met here, and for a wild variety of
reasons.

To appreciate those reasons, let us gather with the crowd that clusters
around the Tour St. Jacques one spring morning in the Middle Ages.
Some two hundred pilgrims have assembled from Germany, England,
France and the Low Countries. A few have even drifted down from
Norway and Sweden, and all are divided into seven fairly well understood
groups. First are the devout Christian laymen who seek salvation at the
tomb of the saint; since many are advanced in years, there will be frequent
deaths en route. Second are knights who in battle vowed to make the
journey if they survived; they ride horses and take their ladies with them.
Third are the monks and priests, and sometimes even cardinals, who have
dreamed for years of visiting Santiago as a crown to their life within the
Church.

Fourth are those criminals who were told by their judges, 'Five years
in jail or pilgrimage to the tomb of St. James, whichever.' These criminals,
if it is proper to term them such, for many of their offenses were petty, are
required to get a certificate at Compostela proving that they have completed the pilgrimage, and in Spanish border cities like Pamplona a lively

Give me my scallop-shell of quiet,
My staff of faith to walk upon,
My scrip of joy, immortal diet,
My bottle of salvation,

My gown of glory, hope's true g
And thus I'll take my pilgrima
—Sir Walter Rale

trade operates in these 'Compostelas,' for venturesome businessmen make the journey frequently, collect their certificates and sell them to those who do not wish to undergo the hazards of western Spain. The criminal, having laid out good money for the 'Compostela,' stuffs it in his pocket, has a high time in Spanish inns and returns seven months later to submit his proof to the sentencing judge. Fifth are the beggars, forgers, thieves, robbers and others who hope to make financial gain from the journey, and of this unsavory group some move backward and forward along the endless pilgrims' road, living off the devout for years at a time. Sixth are the merchants, the architects, the itinerant painters, the weavers and that horde of people who use the road as a marketplace. Finally, there is a fairly constant movement back and forth of government agents who keep watch on what is happening in northern Spain, for this is an unquiet land coveted by France and England, by Austrian adventurers and Italian, and among these watchful persons are those French clerics who are inspired more by colonialism than by religion. The buildings they erect are outwardly monasteries and churches, but inwardly they are intended as stepping stones for the French king.

But all groups this morning have one thing in common. All wear the same uniform, famous throughout Europe: a heavy cape which will serve as raincoat, comforter and nightly blanket; an eight-foot stave with gourd attached at one end for carrying water; the heaviest kind of sandal for hiking the nine hundred miles to Santiago; and a curious kind of broad-rimmed felt hat, turned up in front and marked with three or four bright cockleshells.

'I shall take the cockleshell,' becomes the pilgrims' cry throughout Europe, and already a famous dish has been invented, scallops in wine sauce served in a cockleshell and known as coquille St. Jacques.

On this medieval day, as we wait under the chestnut trees of Paris, officials move out from the great buildings that cluster about the Tour St. Jacques. Priests bless the throng, musicians lead the pilgrims to the outskirts of Paris, and a detachment of cavalry rides along to provide protection during the first days of the journey.

Through the most beautiful river valleys of France moves the sprawling army at the rate of nine or ten miles a day. Sandals wear out and new ones are bought. At crossroad shrines the faithful pray, and in each cathedral town the marchers crowd into sanctuaries to offer thanks to local saints. Food is never plentiful, and villagers guard their stores with pikes and dogs. However, each community has designated a small body of Christians whose duty it is to bury those pilgrims who die within its gates.

And so our great, inchoate mass drifts southward through France: Orléans, Tours, Poitiers mark one well-traveled road; Vézelay, Nevers, Limoges define another; Arles, Montpellier, Toulouse are on the famous southern route. And finally there are the Pyrenees leading to Roncesvalles and Pamplona, where Spain begins.

We can speak with accuracy of this vast movement of people—the incredible number of more than half a million moved along the road each year—because in 1130 what is generally held to be the world's first travel guide was written, describing the glories and hardships of this route. It was written at the request of the Church, which hoped thereby to encourage pilgrimages, by a French priest, Aymery de Picaud, who lived along one of the pilgrim routes and set the pattern for future travel writers: things near at home he praised, those farther away he questioned, while those distant he condemned. Of the Poitevins, who lived near at hand, he says: 'They are vigorous and fine warriors, courageous at the battlefront, elegant in their fashions of dress, handsome in appearance, spiritual, very generous and easy in their hospitality.'

Of the Gascons, who lived suspiciously close to Spain, he writes: 'They are nimble with words, great babblers, mockers. They are debauched, drunkards, gluttons, dressed in tatters, and destitute of money. They are not ashamed to sleep all together on one narrow bed of rotten straw, the servants beside the masters.'

But when he reaches the peasants of Navarra, whom he does not consider Frenchmen at all, he says with scorn: 'These people are badly dressed. They eat poorly and drink worse. Using no spoons, they plunge their hands into the common pot and drink from the same goblet. When one sees them feed, one thinks he is seeing pigs in their gluttony; and when one hears them speak, he thinks of dogs baying. They are perverse, perfidious, disloyal, corrupted, voluptuous, expert in every violence, cruel and quarrelsome, and anyone of them would murder a Frenchman for one sou. Shamefully they have sex with animals.'

This ancient book can still be read with interest, for it evokes the dangers faced by the pilgrims: the water in most of the rivers is contaminated and brings certain death; in many regions food is almost impossible to come by; hospitals are infrequent; and rogues lie in wait to ambush and murder.

In one group of twenty-five, all but two will perish because they drink from the rivers. Of another, half will be slain by brigands. One morning in Spain we wake to find all our animals stolen. But still we push on, the pilgrims of the cockleshell, en route to salvation.

To understand the magnificence of this road, consider a few of the pilgrims we might have met upon it:

778   Charlemagne, legend says, but tomb not discovered till 812
813   King Alfonso II, to see what has happened at Compostela
1064   El Cid Campeador, about to make his dramatic moves
1130   Aymery de Picaud, author of the French travel guide

1154   Louis VII of France
1214   St. Francis of Assisi
1495   Hermann Künig, author of a German guide
1719   James III, of Scotland and England
1939   Marshal Pétain, of France
1957   Giovanni Roncalli, later Pope John XXIII

In the blazing summer of 1966 my pilgrimage along the Way of St. James began at a spot south of Pamplona, on a bare and lonely plain marked only by dusty weeds, where the various routes converge for the long westward thrust to Compostela. On this plain I came to the forsaken church of Eunate, surrounded only by haunting emptiness, and I could not have found a more appropriate introduction to the dead art form that was to dominate my pilgrimage. The architecture of this church is Romanesque—that is, it dates from sometime after the beginning of the eleventh century, that transition period when the ancient Roman style of architecture had not yet been replaced by the Gothic. Rome had almost nothing to do with Romanesque; it developed principally from northern sources, but before we try to define what the new style was, or where it came from, let us see how it looks in the church at Eunate.

The principal characteristic of the church is its low, sturdy weight. It is a church that relates to the soil: its arches are low and rounded, as if they preferred to cling to the earth; its pillars are heavy and rooted in the earth; it does not provide enormous Gothic perspectives. It is solid, well proportioned, weighty with the judgment of intellect. The capitals of its pillars are simple and straightforward: walls are neither adorned nor soaring; windows are small and interior vistas are intimate; there is an impression of almost Scandinavian modernity. It has a tower, but not a tall one; it is built with eight sides, for some reason that no one now remembers, and is surrounded by a curious unroofed cloister of austerely beautiful construction.

The church remains a mystery. To what organization was it attached? What priests served here, what peasants formed its congregation? Who built it and when? Is there truth in the local tradition that it once pertained to the Knights Templars, that tragic order whose memorials we shall see again on this pilgrimage? Was it, as some think, a kind of Valhalla for knights who died fighting the Muslims? There it stands, a simple, lovely Romanesque construction in weathered brown stone, a forgotten memorial to the millions of pilgrims who passed it during its eight or nine hundred years of existence.

The Romanesque style, which is the master design of northern Spain, was introduced from France, but once it crossed the Pyrenees it was subjected to Visigothic and Moorish influences, so that it became something new and peculiarly Spanish, especially in the sculpture that came to festoon the semicircular arches that topped the massive doorways. Of all the beautiful things I have seen in Spain, I suppose I liked best the Romanesque churches of the north. To me they were a form of poetry both epic and elegaic; the rows of human beings carved in the doorways were people I have known; the use of space and simple forms produced an impression as modern as tomorrow; and if on my various trips to Spain I had found only these quiet and monumental buildings, I would have been amply rewarded.

Technically, I suppose one should think of the Spanish portion of the Way of St. James as beginning a little farther to the west, where that remarkable six-arched bridge at Puente la Reina unites the main roads leading down from France. It is one of the most beautiful bridges I know, exactly right for the little town that supported it in pilgrim days. It has two sets of arches, large ones over the river and smaller ones set into the pillars, so that rising waters can pass through in time of flood. The resultant design is so pleasing that I, like many others, have often been content to sit and study its perfection. Thus, at the start of the route we have two handsome structures to serve as a kind of foretaste of what we are to enjoy on this pilgrimage.

I had been gone from the famous bridge only a short time when I saw ahead of me a small town which has always excited both my imagination and my pleasure. It is the only town in Spain where women are permitted to fight bulls, and because its ancient buildings have been so well preserved it is better able than most to evoke a sense of what life was like in the apex years of pilgrimage. It is the little Navarrese town of Estella, and if I were to live anywhere in Spain, I suppose it would have to be here.

Prior to 1966 I had made two other pilgrimages to Santiago de Compostela and on one of them had met the distinguished scholar who now greeted me at the edge of town, Don Francisco Beruete Calleja, president of the Center of Jacobean Studies and leading authority on the Way of St. James. Each year he convenes a seminar of scholars from European and American universities and for two weeks conducts discussions on life along the pilgrims' route.

This year the following lectures were to be offered:

The Cult of the Bull in Navarra, in Spanish
St. James and Charlemagne in Legend, in French
The Way of St. James in Italian Culture, in Italian
Islamic Eschatology in the Sculpture at Compostela, in Spanish
The Way of St. James in Portugal, by Dr. José Filgueira-Valverde, alcalde
of Pontevedra, whom we shall meet later

On this bright morning Don Francisco took me to the high plateau of El Puy, where on the night of May 25, 1085, occurred once more the familiar miracle: two shepherds saw a group of lights which formed themselves into a star. They said nothing, but on successive nights the star reappeared; so they warned the authorities, who as usual dug at the indicated spot, this time coming up with a delectable wide-eyed statue of the Virgin. The archaic and highly pleasing statue is now enshrined in one of the most beautiful churches in Spain, a silken web of a building constructed of slim stone pillars and wood in 1930 to replace an older one and to show how the Gothic style can be adapted to modern tastes. As one might guess, stars of various size dominate the interior: on the backs of benches, in the chandeliers, on the candlesticks, in the cupola over the ancient statue of the Virgin and in the wooden ceiling. The Virgin of El Puy, as she is called, has always been an object of extreme veneration and in her bright new home, is more so.

But this morning we did not talk about this old pilgrim shrine, because Señor Beruete had other things on his mind. 'Is there a more exciting spot in Spain than this?' he asked. 'Below us the little city with its great wealth of monuments which the pilgrims knew. Around us the rim of hills and small mountains which have always been the protection of Estella. And everywhere the echoing march of pilgrims' feet, by the thousands and thousands, as they came into this important stopping point.'

'If I had to choose one year which represented Estella at its height,' I asked, 'which would you suggest?'

Señor Beruete is a congenial man whose love for the old days shimmers in his eyes, and now he grew excited as he talked. 'Imagine you are approaching the city in the year 1262, when pilgrimage was at its height. Last night you slept at Puente la Reina and early this morning you crossed the bridge. Now as you enter Estella you pass a circle of stout walls and find fourteen separate hospitals and dormitories awaiting you. If you should be Jewish, as many of the business travelers were, you'd find over in that quarter a fine synagogue. It's a church now, Santa María Jus del Castillo, but in 1262 it was the center of a Jewish quarter which occupied much of the city. But I suppose you'd be a Christian, so you'd walk down the Street of the Pilgrims, which still stands, and ask at the plaza, which today looks exactly as it did then, for the best place to stay. If you were a Frenchman, you'd be sure to halt before the carving on the Palace of the Kings of Navarra showing Roland jousting with Moor Ferragut. Oldest representation of Roland in the world. And as you stood staring at it, some fellow Frenchman would take you in charge.

'What did you look like in 1262? You wore very heavy shoes and would probably wear out two pairs walking to Santiago. You wore a linen undershirt with a heavy woolen robe over it. And you displayed the four essentials. Long staff. Gourd. Big hat and cockleshells.'

'How many pilgrims a year might have reached Estella in those days?'

'We had, as I say, fourteen separate establishments for them within the city, and outside the walls a series of large monasteries. On some days a thousand arrived, on others less than a hundred. Who can estimate the total? Perhaps a hundred and fifty thousand, year in and year out. We do know that in 1965, which was a special holy year for Compostela, two and a half million pilgrims appeared at Compostela, but of course they didn't all pass through Estella. Eight hundred thousand, perhaps.'

He led me down into the town and to the church of San Miguel, built around 1200, and there I was to see a carving which captivated me. The door of San Miguel presents the typical Romanesque arch composed of five receding semicircles, each containing a wealth of carving and a chain of human figures. Some critics have called it Spain's major Romanesque work, but I prefer the portico we shall be visiting at Compostela. Here the door is guarded by a large stone panel depicting the Three Marys at the tomb of Jesus. The stone drapery of these figures is extraordinary and the gestures of the women so real that many critics consider this plaque the masterpiece of the doorway, but it was a less conspicuous part that attracted me.

The pillars which support the semicircles are topped by capitals adorned with scenes from the life of Christ. The one which appealed to me was the scene showing King Herod at the moment when his scribes are endeavoring to unravel the significance of the birth of Jesus. It is a tableau so brilliant, so handsomely preserved and so psychologically sound that it seems a marvel. The capital has two faces at right angles to each other, and on the left-hand face a worried soldier reports what has happened at Bethlehem. On the right-hand face two excellently differentiated scribes consult the omens, while on the corner where the two faces meet, a worried King Herod ponders the news. The face of Herod is as fine as anything I have seen in stone, a masterful presentation of a bewildered and anxious king.

Some years earlier, in preparation for a work in hand, I had read almost everything in print about this ugly and fascinating king, and I suppose I then knew him as well as a layman could; but nothing I encountered gave me a better understanding of Herod than I acquired from this statue in Estella. The variation between the two faces of the stone, the penetrating quality of the human countenances and the subtle arrangement of the tense bodies make this one of the finest statuary groups I have seen, and for me it surpasses even the Three Marys.

Estella is so rich in such monuments that one could spend days here, tracing the secrets which have come down to us from the Middle Ages, but at lunch a stray question of mine catapulted us out of the pilgrim days and into the present. The lunch itself was commendable: savory snails in garlic sauce, followed by lima beans cooked with quail. The latter was so good that I would have been content to accept it as hors d'oeuvres, main dish and dessert in one; the squab was flavored with strong country herbs and the beans were so tasty and mellow that they seemed a different breed from the unsavory ones I had known elsewhere, but the meal ended with trout Navarrese, a large firm fish sautéed with bits of very salty ham. When I had finished I asked, 'Am I confused about this? I seem to remember that Primo de Rivera, the dictator of the 1920s, bore the title Marqués de Estella. Did he come from this town?'

I had asked the right question. 'How astonishing!' Señor Beruete cried, his eyes alight with excitement. 'It was my grandfather, defending the city of Estella in 1876, who had the ugly task of confronting General Primo de Rivera. Same name but uncle of the dictator. The government forces were bent upon destroying Estella, which had given Madrid much trouble, but my grandfather worked out a plan whereby the city was surrendered without too much destruction. Because of his victory Primo de Rivera was made Marqués de Estella, a title which passed on to his nephew. José Antonio inherited the title and was Marqués de Estella when he was executed by the Republicans.'

'What was the war about?'

'Carlists,' Señor Beruete said, and that was all.

It was a touchy subject, for Estella had been the capital of Carlist agitations in Spain and on several occasions had led in civil wars against Madrid. The trouble was deep-rooted and began in this way. In 1700, when the Habsburg line died out in the person of Carlos the Bewitched, Europe agreed to the installation of the Borbón, in the person of Felipe V, but only if it was understood that the Spanish and French thrones must never be united under one ruler. To give effect to this undertaking, Felipe V in 1813, as part of the Treaty of Utrecht, which we met earlier when discussing Gibraltar, took public steps to abrogate ancient Spanish custom whereby women like the great Isabel had ruled, and to substitute therefor the French Salic law, which excluded females from the inheritance. So that his intentions could not later be misconstrued, Felipe announced, 'I ask the formation of a new law to govern the inheritance of this monarchy by the male line rather than the female, preferring that the most remote male, descendant of a male, be always put before the closest female and her descendants.' As an additional safeguard against the French it was decreed that to be eligible, any heir must have been born in Spain.

In 1788, when the danger of French meddling had receded, Carlos IV was allowed to take the throne, even though he had been born in Naples, but to be on the safe side he asked the Cortes to annul the Salic law without announcing this fact to the general public, and this was done by the step known as the Pragmatic Sanction of 1789. Spain, although not aware of it at the time, was once more governed by its own ancient customs and a female could inherit the throne.

So things continued until 1808, when Carlos IV abdicated, leaving behind two sons, Fernando, who became king, and Carlos, who had to be content with the insignificant role usually accorded royal younger sons.

Fernando married three times without producing an heir, so it was understood that when he died his brother Carlos would become king; but Fernando, although decrepit and debauched, took a fourth wife who astonished Spain by quickly producing a daughter. Now who was entitled to the throne when Fernando died, his brother Carlos in conformity to Salic law, or his daughter Isabel in accordance with old Spanish custom?

Fernando had compounded the confusion by first announcing, when it seemed likely that he would have no heir, that the inheritance should be governed by Salic law; but when his young wife became pregnant with her unborn child, who might well turn out to be a daughter, he changed his mind and informed the public of the existence of the secret Pragmatic Sanction of 1789, which restored the old Spanish tradition and thus legalized the succession of his daughter. Before his death he changed his mind several more times, back and forth until no one could say where the law rested, and a real uncertainty gripped Spain; but at his death the partisans of his three-year-old daughter were in positions of command and were able to install the child as Queen Isabel II, with effective control resting in a regency. Such a theft of the throne the followers of Carlos could not tolerate, so the fuse of the Carlist rebellion was lighted.

I have dealt in some detail with this matter of the technical succession to the throne as a cause of Carlism, and of course the rebellion was legally rooted there, but many historians feel that this was merely a cover for what was in fact a revolution to the right in Spanish politics. Fernando VII was about as absolutist as a king could be—one British historian calls him 'the most contemptible monarch ever to occupy the throne of Spain'—but even he was not reactionary enough to satisfy the social and religious fanatics of the north, who had developed a four-pronged mystique: dedication to the principle of legitimacy as interpreted by the Salic law; a profound commitment to Catholicism as the one basic principle on which Spain existed; a preference for an absolutist and theocratic form of government (when Fernando assumed the throne they had shouted, 'Death to liberty and long live the absolutist Fernando'); and a determination to force the reinstitution of the Inquisition, which they described as 'that most august tribune, brought down by angels from heaven to earth.'

By a curious accident of history, this religious movement coincided with the separatist movements of regions like Cataluña, Navarra and the Basque lands, so that many strands were tangled in the Carlist flag and no one could be sure of what a given group stood for. The bulk of Spain was moving along lines directly opposed to the Carlists, except for the plank of fidelity to the Catholic Church, so it is not surprising that the Carlists lost their wars. But during the progress of the fight they did create a northern militia, the Requetés, who wore red berets and who were probably the best troops Spain had produced since the 1500s.

The outnumbered Requetés lost their uprisings in 1833–1840 and

1870–1876, but in 1936, when they found that General Franco and his rebellious generals had views close to theirs, it was the Requetés who stormed to Franco's aid, defeating the Republicans in one crucial battle after another. Indeed, without these shock troops trained originally as Carlists, Franco might not have won, so in a real sense Carlist ideals did eventually triumph. Ironically, they seem to have helped their bitter enemies, the non-Carlist side of the royal family, back to the throne, for it is the legitimate descendants of Fernando VII and Isabel II, the daughter whom the Carlists opposed, who appear to be in line for the crown, although which of the descendants will get it no one knows. Prince Juan de Borbón, born in 1913 as the son of Alfonso XIII, now lives, as we have seen, in exile in Estoril, near Lisboa. During World War II, while Franco inclined toward the Germany–Italy–Japan Axis, Juan openly backed the Allies, thus surrendering much of the support he could have had in the present regime. His handsome but weak-willed son, Prince Juan Carlos, was born in 1938 and has since been a virtual prisoner of Franco in Madrid. He is generally understood to be Franco's choice for the throne, although a secret vote among top army officers showed that they preferred the young man's father, Prince Juan. The Carlists seem further removed from the throne than they were in 1833. The direct descendants of the original Carlos lived in exile in France and Austria until 1936, when the last of the line was struck by a police van while crossing a street in Vienna. He died childless, but a few months before, he had issued a document which designated a nephew, Xavier de Bourbon Parma, as his legitimate heir, and this man's son, Hugo Carlos, who recently made news by marrying Princess Irene of Holland, is now the Carlist claimant. Thus Juan Carlos and his Greek wife Sophia have the inside track for the throne, but the hopes of Hugo Carlos and his Dutch bride are kept tenuously alive.

Each year on the mountains back of Estella, the Carlists of northern Spain convene in almost Druidic rites of dedication to the cause of placing their contender on the throne, and it has perplexed many as to why Franco has allowed these demonstrations. Some claim that like a canny emperor he allows first one potential successor and then another to grow strong. As we saw in Madrid, he appears to prefer Juan Carlos and Sophia of Greece but is said to be impressed by the Carlist plank: 'Old-fashioned respect for established principles rather than adherence to so-called new legislation.' But he must be alienated by the Carlists' final plank: 'The various distinct regions with their traditional laws and liberties to exist in a federation.' This is northern separatism under a new name, and Franco will have none of it.

This is the kind of anachronism that flourishes in Estella, and normally I would be opposed, but I found that I liked Estella precisely because it had always been such an ornery little town. If you read the history of this part of Spain, it becomes a repetitious account of how people who were against the government holed up in Estella and fought it out when all others had surrendered. When Fernando and Isabel decreed the expulsion of Jews from Spain, Estella refused to abide by the edict and gave them refuge. When Navarra was subordinated to central authority, it was Estella that led the banner of revolt. King after king broke his front teeth on this stubborn principality, and not even the Moors were able to destroy it. 'For two hundred years the Muslims occupied that mountain over there,' Señor Beruete says proudly, 'and we remained Christian in this valley, and never were they able to cross the river and subdue us.' How many sieges did the walls of Estella repulse? It must have been in the dozens. How many times did it resist overwhelming moral pressures? Ten at least. How many times did it go down to defeat still fighting? A good many. One king hauled his cannon right to the top of a nearby hill and fired point-blank into the city for a week, knocking down churches and cloisters, but still the people of Estella defied him. I can admire such a city, even if I do not share its chauvinism.

Of Logroño, I have only the vaguest recollections, but they are most amiable. My ignorance can be blamed only on my friend, Don Luis Morenés, Marqués de Bassecourt, whom we have already seen hunting in Las Marismas and working in the government at Madrid. On my first pilgrimage to Compostela I had been accompanied by Don Luis, and to travel through Spain with him is an experience for anyone who might have believed that Spaniards were indolent.

Don Luis had us up at seven, offered us a standard Spanish breakfast of one roll and tea, then started us off to the next halting place on the pilgrims' route. All morning we explored the secrets of this dusty and historic path; rarely did we hold to paved roads and rarely have I worked so hard. Since I took no breakfast, I preferred to lunch, but then we were usually in the midst of work, which would continue till about three in the afternoon.

At this time we would head for the nearest large town, where a deputation of scholars would be awaiting us, and for an hour or so we would discuss what we had seen that morning. At four we would sit down to lunch, but the first hour would be occupied with drinks and further talk about the Way of St. James. At five we would eat, remaining at the table till seven, when Don Luis would shepherd us to a further series of towns whose scholars waited in the dark. At eleven we would reach our halting place for the night, and our dinner would be served about midnight, with more drinks and more fine conversation. At two we would retire, and at seven Don Luis would be waiting in the breakfast room with that cold roll and lukewarm tea. I doubt if any of the twelfth-century pilgrims worked as hard as I did under the lash of the marqués, and I am sure none could have seen so much of the road.

Well, at Logroño, which I am told is a fine-looking city, the lunch was

The pilgrims walked, they rode horseback, they used mule carts, but always they passed through landscapes of exquisite beauty.

long delayed but the wait was worth it, for in the interim I was introduced to one of the glories of Spain, the red wine of Rioja. It takes its name from a geographical district bordering a river, but of only one thing am I sure: the grapes that grow in this district have received a special dispensation which enables them to produce as fine an ordinary wine as any I have ever tasted. I liked it as much as the great Châteauneuf du Pape, which I came upon years ago in Avignon and which I have cherished ever since, discovering bottles in strange and out-of-the-way places, for Châteauneuf is widely valued by those who have encountered it.

It was now past five in the afternoon and I had eaten nothing for seventeen hours, when the alcalde of Logroño said, 'You must try our Rioja. We're very proud of it.' It was good.

One of the alcalde's assistants said, 'That bottle came from central

Rioja. Have you ever tasted one from lower Rioja?' I hadn't, but it too was good.

A patriot from upper Rioja now proposed, 'Our wine is the one that travels well, and when you're in a foreign country and want a breath of Spain, order a bottle from our region.' I found it to be extremely good.

There were, I seem to remember, four or five other districts with outstanding qualifications, none of which disappointed me, and after I had done impartial justice to all I was introduced to a delightful newspaperman, Don José Vidal Iborra, who handed me a small book of eclogues that his friend José María Lope Toledo had composed in honor of Rioja wine, the titles of the chapters indicating the somewhat reserved praise that was here sung of this rare wine:

    II   Hallelujah
    IV   One More Time
    V   Rioja and Nymphs
    XV   A Poet Meets Rioja Head-on

I was a novelist who had met Rioja head-on, but when I had studied through somewhat wavering eyes this book of prose lyrics I felt that the honor of American letters was at stake, and with my cup overflowing with Rioja, and I use the word overflowing not symbolically (I was holding my cup at a decided angle), I proposed a toast to Rioja and explained in what satisfied me as fluent Spanish that the first thing I had ever written in my life, so far as I could remember, was a translation into English verse of that memorable passage in Calderón de la Barca's *Life Is a Dream* in which a shoeless man complains of his bitter lot until he meets another with no feet, and I proceeded to recite both the Spanish original and my sturdy rendition into English. At the end I contrived a nebulous connection between Calderón and Rioja wine, and although I fear I did not make myself wholly clear, I was roundly applauded, except that Señor Vidal muttered, 'He's got the wrong play.'

I have only the kindest memories of Logroño, and if I cannot remember a single monument in the city or any public works, in Rioja wine I found a friend whose dark red countenance and crisp syllables evoke for me the spirit of pilgrimage wherever I encounter him.

We entered the next town, Santo Domingo de la Calzada, at about nine at night, and I had the good luck to visit the church before I became entangled with the bibulous members of its confraternity, for thus I was relatively sober and was able to see the famous hen and rooster who account for this town's fame. Santo Domingo was a real man who had lived nearby and had attained sainthood in one of the most attractive ways listed in the hagiographies. He was born sometime between 1010 and 1030 and died between 1090 and 1109, but where he came from is most uncertain. Spaniards claim him as a local lad; tradition says he probably came from either Italy or the French part of the Basque lands. At any rate, he felt himself drawn to a religious life and tried to enter various monasteries, but the examining monks found him too stupid. Accordingly, he built himself a small house by the pilgrims' route and from this served the travelers, never seeing them in person, for he considered himself too dull for the great ones to bother with. Where roads were bad, he paved them, and is today honored as the patron saint of all who work on roads. Where rivers were high, he built bridges, and some that he built still stand. Where food was bad, he provided kitchens. And where the sick accumulated, he built refuges. He was as saintly a man as Spain has produced, and toward the end of his life, I believe, one of the monasteries which had rejected him was proud to accept him as a brother.

Often as he worked he must have contemplated that delightful incident which had taken place to the east in the French city of Toulouse around the year 1080, when a German pilgrim and his son were much abused, only to be saved in the end by the miraculous intercession of Santiago. Word of the miracle flashed across Europe and was referred to in many documents from the last decade of the eleventh century, and it so typified the spirit of the Way of St. James that it became in time the Golden Legend.

Three centuries after Santo Domingo's death the good people of his village borrowed the miracle of Santiago at Toulouse and transformed it into the miracle of Domingo at Calzada. Today the story is told in this way:

> A German couple and their handsome young son, from near Cologne, stopped on their way to Santiago de Compostela at one of the shelters built by Santo Domingo de la Calzada. The innkeeper's daughter became enamored of the young man and (in one of my favorite versions of the legend) 'wolde have had hym to medyll with her carnally,' but he resisted her advances. Next morning the family resumed its pilgrimage, but the girl, her love now turned to hate, denounced the son for having stolen a silver cup, which she had secreted in his knapsack. Constables were dispatched to overtake him and he was dragged back to the town and hanged for the crime, but Santo Domingo, aware of the lad's innocence and chastity, kept his hands under the young man's feet and prevented him from strangling. When the parents saw that their son remained alive on the gibbet they went to the justice to ask that he be cut down and set free. The justice, who had at that moment seated himself before a banquet of two roasted chickens, one a cock and the other a hen, replied, 'Your son is no more alive than these chickens,' whereupon the chickens sprang to life refledged and flew off the table. Astounded, the justice restored the young man to his family, none the worse for his experience, and they resumed their march to Compostela.

To this day, on one of the pillars of the church of Santo Domingo de la Calzada chicken coops are maintained; they are decorated with life-size ceramic figures of a cock and hen, but inside, real chickens are kept to crow or cackle during services, and one of the prized mementos that a pilgrim can carry with him from his journey to Compostela is a white feather from one of these living chickens as a reminder of the fowl whose return from the dead proved that Santo Domingo had really saved the hanging boy.

The confraternity of Santo Domingo, whose members look after the church and the chickens, meets in a marvelous old monastery which, since the time of my visit, has been converted into a government parador. I was led to the six-hundred-year-old cavern, which served as the meeting room, by certain members who had heard I was in town, and they launched the evening with some bottles of Rioja wine from a district near their town. I found nothing to complain of, so we tried a different kind and it too was satisfactory. In fact, we tried quite a few samples and they were all good, and I recited again and the evening grew so congenial that the confraternity elected me a full-fledged member; I have the certificate still, proving me to be the only Quaker in history obligated to watch over chickens used in the ceremonies of a Catholic church. For the patrons who will occupy the new hostel I can only wish that they have as much fun in the new rooms as I did in the old.

Of Burgos I remember little. When we arrived at the reception which Don Luis had arranged, we were ridiculously late; it was around midnight, I think, but the hosts had thoughtfully arranged some bottles of Rioja, which was as good as ever. I believe that somewhere in the city there is a statue of El Cid Campeador, who came from these parts. From below, at three in the morning, it looks enormous.

And then the next day, in the mysterious manner in which such things happen to pilgrims, I came upon four solemn events which stunned me with their power to evoke the past. The day started routinely with a cold roll and a cup of tea, neither of which could I touch. Then came an inconsequential thing but one which I remarked at the time as a good omen: we visited the famous Royal Abbey of Las Huelgas (The Leisure Times) whose mothers superior were so powerful that it was said, 'If the Pope had to take a wife, only the abbess of Las Huelgas would be eligible.' I roamed the place with double fascination, for it held an articulated statue of Jesus, which reminded me of Alvaro de Luna's statue in Toledo, and it was to this abbey that Doña Ana de Austria finally came as abbess after her long imprisonment because of her love affair with the demon pastry cook of Madrigal. She seemed very real to me as I studied the stones which had once known the passage of her feet, and I thought how rewarding it was to travel when one had such chances to meet old friends and to review old conditions.

When we left Las Huelgas, Don Luis said, 'I think you'd enjoy it if we got off the paved roads and used the ancient routes followed by the

733

pilgrims,' so we departed from the highway and went through much dust, which I did not enjoy, until we saw looming ahead a small mountain which carried on its crest the walled town of Castrogeriz, which was to be the scene of the day's first adventure. It was an echo of a town, really, a set of near-ruins that had once been great in majesty but which were now occupied by shadows and old people; where thousands had once lived in a busy luxury, a few score now eked out a gray existence. We left our car because we wished to walk into Castrogeriz as pilgrims had done a thousand years ago, and as we marched across the flat and dusty land the city became a shining target. How pleased the hungry pilgrims must have been to see such a magnificent settlement rising in the sky before them! The ancient road climbed the hill, entered the walls and led down a very narrow street. Only a few shops were still in existence; the huge hostel that had once provided accommodations for hundreds each night was shuttered; the mammoth church, once glorious and filled with incense, now seemed close to falling down, and its sacristan was irritable, complaining of the trouble I was causing in wanting to see the gloomy interior.

It was this voice that did it! As I heard the whining I was overcome by the most compelling sense of what it must have been like to be a pilgrim in those days. 'They said its name is Castrogeriz. On a hill. I wonder if they'll let us through the walls? See the townspeople protecting themselves behind their shutters. No food from them. That shopkeeper would cut your throat for an empty gourd. Even the church is closed. But look. That's where they said it would be. The hostel's open.' And into the cavernous building the pilgrims poured, assured of hot soup and a place to sleep for one night . . . if they behaved themselves. As the guidebooks of the time said: 'At Castrogeriz good bread.'

Why should a complaining voice in this inconsequential town have had such power to evoke a sense of pilgrimage? I don't know. Once I had walked sixty miles through this peninsula, carrying a pilgrim's staff eight feet long, and as it swung methodically through the air (the point coming down every eight steps when I was walking fast, every twelve steps when I was tired) I had discovered what it must have been like physically to lug such a heavy staff across Spain; the kinesthetic sense of the staff swinging ever onward had drawn me forward with it. But not even the staff and the long walk had told me much about how the pilgrim had felt inwardly, but here in Castrogeriz, as I swung along the road and into the town, I became a pilgrim in reality as well as in imagination, and from that moment on I was to have a sense of what these distant hordes of people experienced as they picked their way from town to town across an inhospitable land, finding occasionally at some monastery or hospital a friendship so warm as to reward them for all the hours of isolation.

My second adventure that day came in the equally small town of

Frómista, where the serene little church of San Martín, built in 1066, is considered by many to be the finest complete piece of Romanesque architecture on the route. It is so pure and unblemished as to be something of a miracle, and its apse is so cleverly constructed of three interlocking semicircles of white stone as to constitute a triumph of the ordinary. Anyone who believes that stone, to be impressive, has to be ornate Gothic or delicate Corinthian should visit Frómista, whose simple church could profitably occupy a dozen pages of this report, except that in just a few hours I was to savor the essence of Romanesque elsewhere; my more lasting memory of Frómista is of something quite different.

It was, as I recall, a very hot day when I studied this sturdy old church and I did not know where we were going to eat, for I had put my foot down and warned the marqués that I couldn't undertake many more lunches at five o'clock, especially when they were preceded by an hour's investigation of Rioja. Don Luis accepted my caveat with grace, canceled a luncheon in some nearby town and set out to arrange a picnic which we would hold at some convenient spot along the pilgrims' road. I considered this appropriate, since in the old days most pilgrims must have eaten along the way, but as we were standing in the doorway of the church, wondering where to spread our picnic, we were hailed by a singular man. 'If you're going to eat anyway, why not do so in my garden?' he shouted.

It was Father Miguel Bustillo Pérez, parish priest of Frómista, a tall, sixty-year-old man of rugged proportions. He had an impressive manner and a booming voice and looked more like a successful bricklayer than a priest. He led us to his small parish house, in back of which he had a lovely garden with trees and benches, and there we spread our picnic. He supplied the wine and much of the conversation; speaking of the old days in Frómista he reminded me of a friar who might have wandered out of the pages of Chaucer, and as he spoke, so fast that I often lost the thread of what he was saying, I saw in him a revenant of all the hard-working and hospitable friars who had helped pilgrims along this way. When he called to us he had known none of us and was certainly not obligated to extend any courtesies, but his inherent conviviality had made him do so. What was more important, it had made his powerful old church come alive and underlined the significance of my experience a few hours earlier at Castrogeriz. It was a fine, lingering afternoon we spent with Father Bustillo, in his garden, one of our better Spanish picnics.

The day's third meaningful experience started with one of the best things that can happen on a journey: I met an old friend. On an earlier visit to León I had been instructed in its history by a witty scholar-priest, Don Antonio Viñayo González, who looked like a figure from Giotto. He now had the pleasure of informing me that his guidebook to León had just been published; he did not think much of it, but I was to find it one of the best because of its erudition. He said that he wanted me to spend my time in the handsome old church and museum of San Isidoro because of its choice twelfth-century frescoes, well regarded by all historians of the Romanesque style. In one dome I found the best representation I had so far seen of that mysterious religious symbol, the tetramorph, in which the four evangelists are represented, for reasons which I did not then know, by human figures with heads of animals: Mark the Lion, Luke the Bull, Matthew the Man and John the Eagle. Among them Christ sits in starry glory, in robe of faded blue and gold and shawl of brick-red. The frescoes are very medieval, and their state of preservation is extraordinary, this crypt having always been cool and dry.

Father Viñayo pointed out one aspect of the vaulting I had not read about: along one set of ribs the twelve months of the year are represented by peasants performing the chores appropriate for each season: March prunes the vineyards; July is a handsome young man reaping wheat; September makes wine; and October fattens his pigs on acorns. February, alas, which is my month, was a hunchbacked peasant of ugly mien, accomplishing nothing as he warmed his hands at a meager fire.

I was about to leave, well content with what I had seen, when Father Viñayo, with that sixth sense which men who love inanimate things sometimes have, said, 'I think you might appreciate the cloisters,' and he led me away from the vaulting and into as drab a cloister as I have ever seen. It had been built, I judged, in the eighteenth century of a gray stucco and was totally undistinguished. Indeed, I doubt if I could find in all Spain another so unpleasing as this, and I wondered what had gotten into the slim priest that he would think me interested in this mediocre thing.

'It is this side,' he said quietly, directing my attention to the fourth side of the cloister, the one nearest the mausoleum. And there I saw what had happened. San Isidoro had originally been joined to what must have been one of Spain's most grand and somber cloisters, built in the earliest days of Romanesque art, but wars and other catastrophes had destroyed three of the sides, and at some point in the eighteenth century, as I had guessed, a local nobleman had paid to have a new cloister built. Three new walls were put up and plastered in a drab and conformist pattern, whereupon the original remaining side had also been hidden in plaster to bring it into harmony with the others. Thus, without appreciating what he was doing, the eighteenth-century renovator had preserved in a plaster cocoon one of the treasures of Romanesque art. It had been less than ten years ago, Father Viñayo said, that a workman had uncovered the original.

It is difficult to explain what now stood exposed in crystal purity, its stones as clean and white as when they were laid down. It is simply a cloister wall, with four or five arches, I don't remember which, each low, unadorned, tremendously powerful and right, and each different in size and structure from its neighbors. It is a plain wall dating back to the early 1100s, but to me it was the soul of the Romanesque spirit, the secret of what I found beautiful along this pilgrim route. I would rather see these arches than the chapel at Eunate, handsome though it is on its barren plain, or the gemlike church at Frómista, or even the portico of San Miguel in Estella with its marvelous carvings, for those are all the externalization of the Romanesque spirit; at San Isidoro in León one sees the spirit itself, laid bare after years of encrustation.

Why do I like Romanesque buildings so much? Why do I prefer them to Gothic? Or baroque? Or Corinthian? I can't say, but I suppose it's for the same reason that I prefer Brahms to Schubert or Keats to Shelley. When I see a fine example of Romanesque, I feel that I am in the presence of the very best that an age could accomplish, and it was an age that accomplished much. I am at the wellsprings of art, those solid beginnings without which no later art could have achieved much. I am standing with stonemasons who saw things simply and who resisted the temptation of flying off at strange tangents. There is something perpetually clean and honorable about the best Romanesque, and when I see it my whole being responds, as if the artisans who perfected this style were working for me alone. I hear voices singing in plainsong, or the oboes of Pamplona playing without harmony. I am in a different age, with a different set of values, and I find its simplicity exactly to my taste. The separatism of Martin Luther, which is to come, does not yet assault me or confuse. From those first days in northern Spain when I saw Romanesque at its best, I have known that this was an architecture put aside and saved until I should come along; in a strange city I can almost smell on the evening breeze those quarters of the town that house great monuments in this style; but never have I seen any that have seemed more beautiful to me than the recently uncovered cloisters of San Isidoro.

Yet how strange travel can be. Even as I formulated these judgments, which in a sense constitute a condemnation of the Gothic, which I have never appreciated or understood, I was about to be shown this style at its most exquisite, and to have had these two experiences side by side, in a city where I had least expected either, still overwhelms me.

It was a surprise that Father Viñayo had arranged. We dined extremely late, I remember, and it must have been toward two in the morning, when I was about to go to bed, that the marqués said, 'Father Viñayo has a little surprise for us. Are you game?' I would have been ashamed to back down at such a moment, so I accompanied the learned priest into the summer night and walked some distance to León's cathedral. There was a partial moon, and in the looming darkness we began gradually to make out the spires of what Father Viñayo said was Spain's purest and simplest Gothic building. In the night it looked like an ordinary Gothic church, plain yet soaring, controlled but with a certain flamboyance. Its two towers were well proportioned and its transept was prominent enough to be a little cathedral in itself. If one appreciated an unornate Gothic, León's cathedral would be above average but no more.

But as I studied the building in the starry night, with León sleeping around me, one of Father Viñayo's assistants inside the cathedral threw a switch, and from different vantage points around the square, large flood-lights came on, and the sudden transition from shadowy gray to brilliant whiteness was startling, and I saw for the first time the feature that makes León unique among the world's cathedrals: more than half its exterior surface is composed of glass. It is a symphony of windows, and where the ordinary cathedral might have six, León has one hundred and twenty-five, plus fifty-seven circular ones and three gigantic roses. At first sight it seems impossible that a massive stone building could contain so much glass and still stand.

Father Viñayo led us inside, and as we looked up we saw, illuminated from outside, the famous stained-glass windows, one atop the other, then others on top of them. I am not speaking of small windows, but of full-sized ones twenty and thirty feet high, each composed of myriads of pieces of colored glass. The apse was a true miracle. It was when he saw this cascade of windows that the future Pope John XXIII exclaimed, 'León has more glass than stone and more faith than glass.'

As I stood in the silence of the night and the vastness of this huge building, I recalled my conclusions at San Isidoro, and while I did not retract any of my love for the Romanesque, I had to soften my criticism of its descendant. We left the cathedral, and when we were in the street Father Viñayo's helper turned off the spotlights and the great pile of glass and flying stone resumed its posture in the night. If one had to have Gothic, I thought, this isn't too bad, and I turned to thank Father Viñayo for having shown me the windows.

'Ah, but you haven't seen them yet!' he said.

'The surprise is about to begin,' Don Luis assured me, and I wondered what he meant.

Then, as we stood there toward three in the morning, with the soaring cathedral above us in the darkness, the helper inside threw another set of switches, and this time it was from within the cathedral that a battery of powerful lights flashed on, so that from the street we saw what men had never seen before, until a few years ago: a vast cathedral composed mostly of glass illuminated from within, so that all the stones that supported the cathedral were invisible and only the windows could be seen, each one an incandescent jewel of the most intense color and variation.

The Spanish have a saying that sums up their attitude toward religion: 'To appreciate the cathedral you must at least go inside.' Now this was reversed, for to appreciate León one must stand off in the darkness and see with fresh eye the miracle as an ordinary building springs suddenly to life, and with such brilliance that no previous experience with light and glass and stone could possibly compare. We stood in the street,

The eight windows abo
are reflections onl

awe-struck by the beauty of the walls above us. We walked three times around the huge edifice, or as far as the streets would permit, and finally we agreed that it was at the apse, with its incredible windows, tier upon tier shining like suns, and its forest of flying buttresses—which explain how the curved space with so little stone remains upright—that León's cathedral looked its best. It is a rare sight, and if I were in Madrid and someone proposed, 'Let's drive up to León to see the cathedral lit from within,' I would not hesitate to make the journey, for to see this thing is to see something so different as to illuminate a lifetime of travel.

I have seen most of the fine sights of the world and know how exciting Angkor Wat can be at midnight with tiers of Cambodian dancers, or the Acropolis at dusk, or Borobudur in a jungle storm, but so far as sheer visual pleasure is concerned, I have seen nothing to excel León's cathedral at three in the morning, lighted from within, and I say this as a man who likes neither stained-glass windows nor Gothic.

On my earliest trip to León, I had had the pleasure of meeting an inventive architect, Alfredo de Ramón-Laca, who had been given the job of renovating a crumbling Renaissance hostel at the edge of town and converting it into a modern hotel to be called the Hostal de San Marcos. 'It'll be the finest in Europe,' he promised me, and we spent a day climbing over the ruins as he explained each step. 'We're putting steel ribs right through the heart of the old building, and when we're through, all the original beauty will remain, but in addition we'll have three hundred bright new rooms.' He was especially pleased that a functioning church, which formed the left wing of the building, would be retained. 'It will be this church which gives the place character.' 'I don't think anybody can make much of this,' I said. 'Come back in eight months and see,' he said.

This year I was able to stay in the hotel that Señor Ramón-Laca had built, and his earlier enthusiasm proved justified, for he had done what he promised: taken a classic building dating back to the early 1500s and preserved its magnificent façade, converting the whole into what is probably the finest hotel in Europe. At least it's one of the most reasonably priced.

I asked the manager to show me his prize suite, and he said, 'We have one reserved for heads of states.' I told him I wanted to see one reserved for the heads of a Buick agency in Tulsa, Oklahoma, so he showed me the Condestable Suite on the third floor, overlooking both a plaza outside and a patio inside. It consisted of two bedrooms, sleeping four people, with seventeenth-century brocaded baldacchinos over the beds, a large living room, all kinds of foyers and two baths. Each piece of furniture, especially the heavy antique tables and the cowhide chairs, was a work of art. The east wall of the suite consisted of the original stone wall of the fifteenth century, gray-beige in color and magnificent in appearance, and all colors used in the rooms harmonized with this wall. The spacious corridors connecting the rooms were once cloisters, and a special feature which attracted me was that the suite connected directly with the choir of Señor Ramón-Laca's church, so that one had what amounted to a magnificent fifteenth-century carved hall as a private chapel, with services taking place some sixty feet below at the main altar. Private to this suite was a spiral stone tower leading to a dungeon, plus a high-fidelity system for playing either popular or classical music twenty-four hours a day, should one desire. The cost of what must be one of the choice suites in Europe was ten dollars a day per person, or somewhat less than the cost of a Spanish-type motel in Tulsa. And to remind one that pilgrims actually used these quarters, along one wall was scratched:

STANISLA° OZEN

KOWSKI. 1,585

The financing of such a hotel is interesting. A National Institute of Industry was established some years ago, using partly governmental funds, partly private. It has three main responsibilities: to provide tourist facilities, and this function is financed one hundred percent by the government; to produce the Seat motorcar on franchise from the Fiat people of Italy, and this is only fifty-one percent government financed; and to build autobuses, which are so important to Spain, and this is financed twenty-five percent by Leylands of England, ten percent privately and sixty-five percent by the government. So far the ventures of the institute have prospered.

One of the pleasures of traveling as I do is that when it is known that I am interested in any esoteric aspect of society, people introduce me to the cronistas and other experts, and now, at lunch in León, I found myself sitting opposite a man who could well serve as an epitome of the scholar in Latin lands, where men of learning find it difficult to make a living when young but find themselves honored sages when old. In America it is the other way around.

The cronista, Don Angel Suárez Ema, was in his late sixties, a big man with a fine expressive face that lit up when he talked, which was most of the time. His sole topic, at least on this day, was the glory of León, for he was also the poet laureate of the city and its cronista. When he spoke he had the capacity to project himself into whatever past age he was dealing with, so that in turn he was a Roman commanding a legion, an impoverished king trying to bind up the remnants of the kingdom, or a princess unjustly treated. To listen to Don Angel for some hours was an exhilarating experience, something like a whiz-bang ride on a historical loop-the-loop. Spain is filled with such cronistas, learned old men who have studied all their lives and who love to share what they have learned.

I already knew a good deal of what Don Angel told me, but one of his stories was new and reflected the spirit that animated the pilgrims' road.

The narrative began with an innocuous question, thrown off by Don Angel in confidence that I would answer it affirmatively. 'Of course you've stopped at Río Orbigo to pay homage to Suero de Quiñones?'

For some unfortunate reason I thought that Quiñones were something to eat and replied that I hadn't tasted them yet, whereupon Don Angel slapped the table with his big right hand, stared at me in disbelief and cried, 'My God, man! You don't know Quiñones?'

'No.'

'The knight-errant sans reproche, except that he was crazy?'

'I haven't heard of him.'

'And yet you make a pilgrimage along his road!'

I asked the cronista to tell me of Suero, the knight-ideal who was a little cracked, and he looked at me with a sort of scholarly love, thanking me for an opportunity to speak about a character who obviously attracted him. 'You understand that in the old days many evil men, especially from Germany and France, infested this road, so that bands of knights were required to patrol it, protecting the innocent. It was for this reason that the Order of Santiago was established, composed of Spaniards. But fine knights from foreign countries formed their own order to protect pilgrims, too, so that along the way there grew up a congenial fraternity. It had, however, one weakness. A garrulous knight, say at Estella, could sit in the tavern, knowing that any competition might be miles away in León, and shout, "I am the strongest and bravest knight on the Way of St. James," and get away with it, while another knight here in León could bellow, "I am well known as the strongest and bravest knight on the Way." In the early 1400s this kind of thing had become common, so one day Suero de Quiñones from a village not far from here decided single-handedly to put an end to the nonsense. He announced, with the king's approval, that he was going to stand for thirty days at a bridge over the Río Orbigo and fight every knight who approached from either direction, which could mean thirty or forty fights a day, until it was made clear who was the champion of the Way of St. James. This was in the year 1434.

'Now, I'm not claiming that Suero de Quiñones was a normal man of the period. For some years he had spent each Thursday wearing about his neck an iron collar which must have caused him much discomfort but which he offered as proof that he would undergo any hardship to prove his love for a lady who did not return it. In fact, the nature of the challenge which he threw down at the bridge was that no knight could pass until he acknowledged that Suero's lady was more beautiful than the knight's lady. He expounded other ideas that were equally heroic.

'As I said, he made the challenge alone, but after he had done so he was joined by nine fellow Spaniards who wished to test the foreigners, and for thirty days these men stood at the bridge and fought all comers. Some chroniclers say that seven hundred jousts were held, which seems a large number, but we do know that Claramont of Aragón died in his fight with

Quiñones, but not because our knight was vengeful. Claramont's horse shied and his own lance snapped and passed through his eye. Where to bury the dead knight? The Dominicans of León wouldn't accept the body, because it had been slain in a jousting unapproved by the Church. And the Bishop of Astorga refused burial for the same reason. So Quiñones himself bought a piece of land next to a chapel burial ground, and we believe that when no one was looking he may have slipped the body underground into the holy burial place.

'At any rate, it was a splendid thirty days, with music and dancing and banquets every night after the fighting was over. Quiñones seems to have won every joust he entered, and it was some years along this road before any loud-mouthed knight dared to announce that he was the most powerful, for all knew Quiñones was.'

Next day, after we had paid our respects to the ancient Roman bridge at which Quiñones had defied Europe, we came to a hill from which we could see the modest but very old city of Astorga, and if Don Luis had at that moment told me that down there I would have the best meal I was to encounter in Spain, I would have derided the suggestion, because Astorga did not look like a place that would have good restaurants. Nor did it. Don Luis said, 'There is, however, this little place owned by a woman whose husband helps her, and it will have something acceptable.' He led us to the Restaurante La Peseta in one of Astorga's little streets, and as I entered and saw one small room and a crowded old-fashioned kitchen, I had only modest expectations. But before we sat down to eat we happened to look into the kitchen and there we found some six or seven elderly women tending a collection of pots which bubbled in a very businesslike way.

'You looking for some real Spanish food?' one of the old women asked me.

'Yes,' I said tentatively, and she took me to her part of the kitchen where she worked at a table positively cluttered with slabs of raw meat, herbs, vegetables and shellfish.

'What would you like?' she asked. It was a hot day and I doubted that I wanted heavy food, but she whispered in confidence, 'Take the lomo de cerdo adobado.' I signified my ignorance and she pointed to a long square chunk of dark meat and to myself I translated the name she repeated: 'Loin of pork adobado.' But what was adobado?

'Is it good?' I asked, for it certainly did not look so, and loin of pork was scarcely something that I would normally order from a menu, especially in midsummer.

'When I finish cooking it,' she began, abruptly stopping and sort of shouting at me, 'Garbanzos, too.'

'Garbanzos?' These are the heavy, tasteless chickpeas which spoil so much Spanish cooking. Garbanzos I did not want, but she took me firmly by the arm and led me to the pot for which she seemed to be specially responsible.

'You have never tasted garbanzos,' she said sternly. 'Now sit down and order some Rioja wine.'

Don Luis asked what I had ordered, and when I said, 'Lomo de cerdo adobado' his face brightened, and while we waited, tasting the Rioja, he said, 'In the old days when I was a boy many families butchered one or two hogs, and when the loins were cut out, long slabs of meat squared on the sides, they were marinated five or six months in a mixture of parsley, garlic, onion, oregano, salt, pepper, oil and vinegar. Then they were smoked until they became one of the best-tasting meats on earth. Michener, you've stumbled into a gastronomical gold mine.'

'But it's being served with garbanzos,' I said, and his face fell. 'With garbanzos you can't do much,' he said.

Finally the dishes arrived. The regular waiter brought the ordinary ones for Don Luis and the rest of the party, but the old woman brought mine, a huge country plate with five slices of pork neatly arranged on one side, plus a heap of garbanzos on the other. As I took my fork, the woman grabbed my wrist and whispered benevolently, 'What you're about to do you won't forget.'

It was not hyperbole. The meat was something unique into which all of rural life had somehow been compressed, for it was both savory and smoky; it was firm to the knife but succulent to the tooth; it had no trace of fat, but the forests of northern Spain seemed to have crept into it, and I have never tasted a better smoked meat. It was, however, the garbanzos that astonished me, and the others too, for when I said how good they were, everyone nibbled from my plate and we called the old cook to bring us additional dishes. She put them on the table and smiled approvingly as we dug in. Softly she said, 'My garbanzos are soaked for two days in cold salt water. They are cooked slowly, and when they are sure of themselves I throw in some salty ham, three different kinds of hot sausages, some potatoes and cabbage, and they stew for eight hours. If you're a workman with little money, you eat garbanzos as your only dish, with meat and vegetables thrown in. If you're wealthy like a norteamericano, you can afford the garbanzos plain. Because I charge you as much as if you'd taken the meat too.'

As the excellent meal was about to end we were visited by the alcalde of Astorga, who said, thinking that I was British, 'We are pleased to have you among us . . . in spite of what happened.' When he had gone I asked Don Luis what had happened, and he replied, 'He was referring to those unhappy days at the beginning of the last century when Napoleon besieged the city and knocked down many of the walls, the time when Sir John Moore allowed his troops to sack the place.'

'Sir John Moore?' I asked, surprised by such an accusation against my old friend.

'Yes. He may be a hero to the British . . .'

'He is to me. To everyone,' and I recited the opening lines:

'Not a drum was heard, not a funeral note,
As his corse to the rampart we hurried . . .'

'Actually, he was a miserably poor general who made a botch of the whole matter. He came to protect Spain from the French but ended by destroying more than the French ever did.'

'Are you talking about the great hero who died at La Coruña?'

'I would advise you not to speak of him that way in a public restaurant in Astorga. Here we remember him as the general who abandoned his Spanish allies, the people of Astorga and the wives and children of his own British troops. Unlike other armies of the time, the English army still encouraged its men to bring their families along, and Moore sacrificed the lot.' He then referred to a book he had recently read, the memoirs of General Baron de Marbot, aide-de-camp of Marshals Murat and Masséna and personal courier of Napoleon. 'Marbot claims that Napoleon lost his world campaign in Spain, and his Spanish campaign in Astorga.'

'But I thought you said Moore was defeated here.'

'The point Marbot was making was sardonic. In the days following the victory at Astorga, Napoleon made three fatal mistakes that ensured his ultimate defeat. He took prisoner the Spanish royal family, which gave us something to rally around. He sorely underestimated the patriotism of the Spanish people, who were not going to be supine like the Italian and German collaborators he had met elsewhere. And worst mistake of all, at La Coruña he killed Sir John Moore, who was the most ineffectual general he faced, thus making way for Wellington, who was the best.'

The purpose of the alcalde's visit had been to extend an invitation to see Astorga's cathedral, but this I did not see, for as we were approaching it my eye was taken by a black-and-white structure so far removed from normal experience that I cried, 'The Brothers Grimm must have built it,' for what I saw was a delightful fairy-tale castle, the epitome of all the towers and moats one has imagined as a child. Yet it was very real and four stories tall. I was about to ask what it was when some detail of its construction caught my eye, an inspired portal that reminded me of Barcelona, and I cried, 'Don't tell me. It's Gaudí!' Don Luis nodded. Only the elfin architect of the unfinished church in Barcelona could have built such a fantasy. 'How did he get to Astorga?' I asked.

And Don Luis explained, 'In 1887 Astorga's bishop was a Catalan, the inspired Juan Bautista Grau Vallespinos, and as you already know, Catalans are cliquish, so when the tempter Gaudí came whispering to the bishop, the latter was inclined to listen. It was from this conspiracy that the grandiose plan developed for building near the cathedral of Astorga a supermagnificent bishop's palace.' The two Catalans dreamed up a building which was not an ordinary religious edifice but the grandest episcopal palace built since the days of the Piccolomini in Siena.

It would be Gothic in basic design, but a grander Gothic than men had seen before. It would have spires and turrets to tease the eye, donjons and mighty winged angels and drawbridges and battlements galore. There would be no flat walls, for each would be broken by arbitrary round towers; only pure white stones would be used, so that the building could be seen from afar, but between them a black cement would be laid so as to emphasize horizontal lines.

Inside, the palace would be as luxurious as the nineteenth century could produce, with ornate halls, complete chapels, audience rooms that would have delighted a Medici, dining salons that would seat scores of prelates, and lesser rooms by the dozen, each its own work of art. The finest contemporary painters, sculptors and tapestry weavers would provide ornament for the palace, and every window would be a masterpiece in stained glass.

Grandiose as the dream was, it came true. When I first saw the result, as lovely as the two inspired Catalans had intended it to be, I liked it, and the more I saw the more I liked it. From top to bottom there is not a false note, on either the outside or the in. The two men who contrived this building were men of vision and joy, but I shall not try to describe in detail the perfection of their construction: the beauty of arch ribs made of red brick with lines of white cement, the manner in which the afternoon sun comes through the tesselated windows, the Moorish arches on one floor, as lovely as anything in Córdoba, the Gothic arches on the floor above, the grandeur of the paintings, and the sweeping splendor of the circular staircases. What I should like to point out, however, is that even in the basement the excellence of Gaudí's inspiration is visible; in fact, it is more apparent there than elsewhere because one least expects it. The pillars are so varied that they have a kind of orchestral beauty, yet each with a function that proves Gaudí to have been well trained in classic architecture. One of the most impressive modern sights I was to see in Spain was this simple yet magnificent basement.

I spent profitable hours studying the place and concluded that it was a monument to the expensive relationship between any architect and his client, for I could hear Antoni Gaudí assuring his bishop, perhaps in the Restaurante La Peseta over a dish of marinated pork and garbanzos, 'Look, Bautista, you're already in up to your neck. Why not find a little more money somewhere and we'll dig a moat around the whole thing.' The moat is there, deep and wide and paved.

Unfortunately, Bishop Grau died in 1893, when construction had been under way only six years, and work was halted. Gaudí was fired as architect and the unfinished palace stood as a Church scandal. A poor district like Astorga had no excuse for having such an edifice and for years it stood empty. When in 1905–1909 it was brought to grudging completion, subsequent bishops were ashamed to occupy it, but in the 1960s Bishop Marcelo Gonzáles Martín, who many believe may one day be the primate of Spain, cut the Gordian knot and decreed, 'The palace will be a museum dedicated to showing life along the Way of St. James in the Middle Ages.' At last the dreamlike building has a function, which it performs well.

I cannot join in the chorus of abuse which has been heaped upon both the palace and the bishop who authorized it. It is not something that I as bishop would have constructed for a city like Astorga, nor is it a building I would have planned had I been the architect. It is about as unfunctional a structure as one could imagine, and yet, of all the buildings erected along the Way of St. James in the last three hundred years, it and the new church at Estella are the only ones that capture the spiritual grandeur of the pilgrims' way. I believe that the millions who trod these stones in ages past would approve, in a contrary sort of way, of what the two crazy Catalans did, for in its flamboyant yet dedicated style, this bizarre palace represents the continuity of the spirit which animated the pilgrims. A church ought to be big enough to absorb unique personalities like that of Gaudí and Bishop Grau. I for one was totally delighted with their majestic nonsense.

At Ponferrada, on the other hand, I came upon a structure which elicited no delight. There, on a high hill overlooking a network of valleys, which because of the gold and silver they contained have throughout history been of strategic importance, a massive castle was erected in the early eleventh century. Manned by the Knights Templars, it played a major role in policing one of the wilder parts of Spain, but today the empty old building sleeps quietly on its hill, one of the best-preserved ruins of its age in Europe.

Why does the old fortress provoke mournful connotations? Not because of what I know took place here but because of what I can imagine. In the Crusades the Knights Templars played an honorable role, even though they sometimes found it necessary to reject kingly and Papal leadership and go their own way. During a report I once made on the siege of Acre in 1291, the final Christian defeat in the Crusades, I found occasion to study the Knights Templars in some detail as they evacuated the Holy Land in retreat to Cyprus, where they set about establishing that kind of semi-autonomous kingdom which had marked their occupancy of Jerusalem. In the Holy Land they had been too powerful for kings to discipline; they disciplined kings. But now they had come on evil days, so in 1306 the King of France, Philip IV, and his Francophile Pope, Clement V, decided that the time was at hand to exterminate these fractious knights.

Accordingly, in 1307, in what has always seemed to historians one of the worst connivances in history, brutal charges were brought against the

Templars, and dissident members were produced to testify that when they had joined the Templars they had been forced to submit to sodomy, that the rulers of the order expropriated funds rightfully belonging to either Pope or king, and worst of all, that at initiation ceremonies the Mass was said backward and made a mockery.

In hideous manner with fire and torture the leaders were executed. Lesser members were hanged. The rank and file were scourged from their castles and turned loose to wander across the countryside, and by 1312 this once-great order was eradicated, its holdings absorbed by Church and king. Looking at the Templars' castle in Ponferrada, I could not help speculating upon the terror which must have overtaken this mighty fortress when word reached Spain that the King of France and the Pope had found the order heretical and had ordered it dissolved at whatever cost. Which disgruntled underlings, thirsting for revenge, lied about their superiors in this fortress? Which addlepated young men swore that their seniors had forced sodomy upon them or had profaned the host in ceremonial mock Mass? Sitting within the stormy old fortress, I wondered what the death agonies of the last master must have been. Was he one who abjured the order in forced confession or was he one of those Templars who endured all manner of torture to die at the stake in flame and silence?

In my report on Acre, I wrote some fairly harsh words about the Templars, their selfishness and lust for power; but never did I find them cowardly or deficient in honor, and the manner in which they vanished, leaving their embattled castles behind, seems one of the most poignant historical tragedies, and I know of no spot more appropriate for brooding upon this matter than Ponferrada, because in this same region, in 1476, Fernando and Isabel, and more particularly the latter, faced a similar problem and solved it in a more humane way. The Catholic Kings decided that the powerful Order of Santiago, the Templars of their age, had served its purpose; it had defended the weak pilgrims and brought security to the Way of St. James. Now it had become a mighty force generating its own power and direction, and like the Templars, it had to be suppressed; but the Catholic monarchs, unlike the French, brought no shattering charges against the knights of Santiago. Isabel simply maneuvered so that her husband was elected head of the order, from which position he quietly disbanded the knights, and anyone who has seen Henry de Montherlant's moving drama *The Master of Santiago*, dealing with the last legitimate master, knows with what dignity Spain eliminated its equivalent to the Templars.

At unexpected spots along the Way of St. James the traveler finds a crucifix or a shrine reminding him that he is passing through a religious country, or he hears an old legend which recalls the age of faith. Few

To the Spaniard a crucifix is a remin
of the central emotional event of his

surpass that of Noriberto, the citizen of Luxembourg, who in the year 1080 joined five other knights for a pilgrimage to Compostela. They composed an oath of fealty, whereby each man volunteered to protect to the death each other, and five swore, but Noriberto, aware that he was not a courageous man, said that he could not. Nevertheless, as a secondary member of the six he was allowed to tag along, and when Felix, the originator of the oath, fell ill in Spain, the others, each eager to be first at the cathedral, forged on ahead, but Noriberto stayed behind to nurse the sick man. Through his agonies Felix called for help, and always Noriberto was there, but in spite of all that he did, Felix died and Noriberto abused himself for his failure. 'I knew I was not worthy,' he mumbled. But when the faithless four reached Compostela they found that Noriberto had preceded them, borne on a white charger by Santiago himself.

At the little town of Villafranca del Bierzo, I was to have two experiences, and since neither was due to planning on my part, they were doubly rewarding. At a roadside café I was accosted by a man I did not know, an English traveler heading in the opposite direction, and he handed me a book which he had finished, saying, 'You might like it, seeing that you're headed west.' It was *Corunna*, written by Christopher Hibbert and published in London in 1961. I was happy to get a copy, for Corunna is the English name for La Coruña; this was an account of Sir John Moore's disastrous retreat through Villafranca and his death in La Coruña on January 6, 1809. For the next hours I was immersed in this mournful history, marking on the map the battlegrounds through which I had just passed; over this terrain Moore had led his disintegrating army, deserted by his disillusioned Spanish allies and harried by Marshal Soult, and the behavior of the English had become so barbarous that I began to understand why Don Luis had spoken so harshly of Moore, for in the retreat, and particularly in the events centering on Villafranca, one saw a rare thing: the degeneration of a British army and the ineffectual efforts of General Moore to hold his remnant together and to maintain them in some kind of decent discipline. The true tragedy of Moore was not the incompetence about which Don Luis had joked nor the burial about which the poet sang, but that he allowed the spiritual control of his army to slip out of his hands.

By the time the English reached Villafranca, discipline had vanished. English soldiers abandoned the English women who had accompanied them; when one woman stumbled into a swamp the men following did not try to help out but used her head as a stepping stone to their own safety. Food depots belonging to the English were looted and those established by the Spanish army were expropriated with no regard for the native troops. Monasteries were sacked; homes were ripped apart; castles were assaulted as if the Spanish were the enemy and not the French. There was murder and pillage and insubordination, and never in the long account of British arms did an army behave worse. Whatever discipline did appear in the ranks seemed to come from German mercenaries serving with the British; what personal courage and good spirits, from the Irish.

A handful of stern-willed English officers did try to maintain some kind of order: floggings were administered, a looter was shot, rapists were ordered to be hanged. But nothing substantial was accomplished, and when even greater tribulations overtook them on leaving Villafranca, the army came close to actual rebellion.

I was interested in what memories Villafranca retained of this debacle, and in making inquiries I encountered a second bit of good luck. I met a distinguished gentleman whose ancestors had owned the castle of Villafranca during that terrible winter of 1808–1809. The Condes de Peña Ramiro occupy one of the surprising castles of Spain, a low-roofed, round-towered structure that looks rather more like an enclosed Norman farm than a castle; but it is so definitely a part of the peculiar terrain of this region that it has an ingratiating charm. It looks, for once, like a castle in which somebody really lives.

The Condesa de Peña Ramiro is a handsome, hard-fibered woman in her middle years, with a face that reminded me of two things: some of the paintings by Velázquez, and those strong-featured Quaker women of Philadelphia who use no make-up except a flawless complexion and a radiant inner beauty. When I presented myself at the garden gate that gives access to the castle grounds, she led me to a cool, tree-shaded part of the lawn, where we sat on old stone benches and discussed many things before we got around to Sir John Moore and the catastrophe of Villafranca. She said, 'I trust you've stopped by our beautiful Romanesque church of Santiago and seen the Puerta de Pardón. It was very necessary in the old days, that gate, because the road from here on to Compostela is terribly difficult. The old and sick who reached this far often knew they couldn't survive the last hundred miles. So we established this door in our church which anyone of faint spirit could enter and receive thereby all the indulgences he would have gained had he persevered to Compostela itself.'

Later she showed me the door, a stolid, heavy thing consisting of five recessed semicircular arches displaying figures in pairs. It was a simple yet very effective portal, with a prudent, peasant-like roof projecting out from the church wall to protect the sculptures from rain. Standing before it, I could imagine the spiritual relief attained by those pilgrims whose strength had permitted them to come this far but no farther; for them the long pilgrimage was over; they had been excused from the final drudgery by a very real pardon.

'What happened to places like this when Napoleon was chasing the English out of Spain?' I asked, and the condesa summoned a young man of the town who understood these matters, and he sat with us through a long afternoon and said, 'For a hundred years the peasants remembered that winter. They looked on the English and the French alike as the enemy, and there was no jubilation when either entered the town. Burning, looting and hunger. When I was a boy old men said that of the two the English were worse, but technically it was the French who were the enemy. It was all very confusing.'

I look back upon the time spent with the Condesa de Peña Ramiro as one of the most gracious experiences I was to know in Spain. The woman was so simple in her manner, yet so profound in her concern about the things that interested me, that to share her information was a privilege. On her dining-room wall hung a portrait of King Alfonso XIII inscribed to the conde; in a corner stood the framed commission of an uncle who had governed the Philippines; old photographs told of old glories that had come to the distinguished family in the nineteenth century, but it was not a family which lived in the past, for the conversation was alive with present references, and I wondered how the conde and his condesa managed this. At the end of our long discussion I asked the condesa, 'From what part of Spain do you come?'

'From Galicia, of course.'

Then her unusual quality became explicable; she was one of those granite-hard Galicians whom I like so much. She came from the part of Spain I was about to enter, a part I had remembered, in absence, as one of the best segments of the Spanish scene; and she was an ideal representative of that region.

But before I reached Galicia I was required to follow the final agony of Sir John Moore's collapsing army as it left Villafranca to try to reach the evacuation ships waiting at La Coruña, forerunners of those later ships that would wait for another defeated British army a hundred and thirty-one years later at Dunkirk.

It was in their approach to Cebrero, the highest point on the old pilgrims' route and surely the most desolate, that the British army suffered its Gehenna. All through the preceding year the army had been pleading with both the English and Spanish governments for money to speed the war, and at last they had got some, but now on the dreadful cliff-lined pass to Cebrero the paymasters had to back their wagons to the edge of the precipice and throw away their funds, a hundred and twenty-five thousand dollars in gold coins, too heavy to carry any longer, and starving foot soldiers had to listen impotently as the worthless gold clinked down the mountainside. It was January, 1809, the coldest part of the winter, and men froze to death in the heavy snow. Women died of starvation and their bodies lay covered with ice beside the road. Horses had to be killed by the hundreds; to save ammunition they were herded to some precipice and forced to jump to their own screaming deaths. At every Spanish village, houses were looted and soldiers would lie down in the ditch, a bottle of wine to their lips, knowing that if they got drunk they would not rise again, but they drank on and hundreds made the noiseless transition from drunkenness to death.

Now, as I stood in this miserable pass, a summer sun radiated from the rocks where low shrubs flowered and it was difficult to visualize the vast debacle that had overwhelmed the British army, one of the worst in its history, but I did take a perverse pleasure from the fact that it was under these circumstances that my hero, Sir John Moore, did finally bring his rebellious troops under control, did lead them on to La Coruña, did stand off a constant series of attacks by Soult, did preserve his men for embarkation upon the ships as planned, and did save for General Wellington's later use in Spain a hardened cadre of men and officers who would ultimately whip both Soult and Napoleon. He, of course, was dead before even the embarkation took place, killed on the field of battle by a French cannonball which carried away most of his left shoulder, exposing the heart and lung. He had lost eight thousand men and himself, but he had saved what he had set out to save: the mobility of the British Army.

During one of my earlier pilgrimages to Santiago I had traversed Cebrero pass in the snow of winter and had experienced some of the misery that had afflicted pilgrims who passed this way. It was night and I was accompanied by Don Luis, who had said, 'It's dark and it's snowing but I'm sure you'll want to see the amazing village perched up there. I doubt if it could be equaled in all Europe.' We left our car at the highest point of the pass and climbed on foot a rather steep hill, at the top of which I saw two flickering lights glimmering through the snow, and it required no imagination on my part to see myself a pilgrim struggling to find a night's lodging. We came upon an extraordinary village, a hilltop cluster of very low thatch-roofed houses unmodified since the days of the earliest Celts. Open fires burned in the middle of the floor and no chimneys allowed the smoke to escape. Wind howled over the place all winter and clouds obscured it much of the time, as they did now. It is maintained in the midst of modern Spain as a memorial to the manner in which hill Spaniards used to live, a huddle of eight or ten houses centering about a low, rugged stone sanctuary which looked in the darkness of night as if it had been built of pinkish stone without the use of mortar. It was unoccupied and unutterably lonely, a rough thing that must have dated far back before the beginning of Romanesque or Gothic. Possibly it was of Celtic origin.

At any rate, in this rude spot I somehow lost Don Luis, and in the snow I spent the better part of a half-hour shouting, 'Halooo, Don Luis!' but I could find neither him nor the footpath leading down to our car. So there I was, as many a pilgrim must have been in the old days, lost on the mountain that had destroyed an army and had caused the despair of millions of pilgrims. It was really a rather bad experience, for the low houses, with no lights or chimneys showing sparks, hid from me and I wandered back and forth in the stormy darkness.

An old shepherd finally heard me and showed me how to open the door of the desolate sanctuary, and there I waited in the dank night till Don Luis should find me. I was standing in shadowy darkness, for there was only one candle guttering behind a pillar, when I heard the shepherd speak from his share of the darkness. He had white hair which showed beneath his cap, and no teeth, but he told a strange story of Cebrero.

'It was during a winter like this,' he said, 'with wind and storm and snow and frozen sheep. A monk was left here to say Holy Mass for any pilgrims who appeared at the sanctuary, but no one ever came except an old shepherd like me. Juan Santín his name, and each day in the storm he would present himself before this altar to hear Mass, so the grudging monk would have to leave his fire and come to this cold place to celebrate the mystery.

'One special night, when the storm was worse than ever before, the monk aspired to stay by his fire, but Juan Santín appeared for evening Mass. It was his only pleasure in life besides caring for his sheep, so the grumbling monk had to leave his fire once more. "Poor me, persecuted me! That I should be driven through the storm just because this idiot of a shepherd comes to hear how I pronounce a few words of Latin before this bit of bread and drop of wine."

'And as he spoke, a clap of thunder roared through the storm, and a great flash of light filled this sanctuary, and on that altar the bread turned into the Body of Christ itself, and the wine in that very chalice which you see tonight, became His blood. And the voice of Jesus Christ said to the monk, "I too have come to hear Mass said this night, for I too am a shepherd." '

The miracle of Cebrero echoed through Spain and France and the shrine became one of the most sacred on the Way of St. James. Queen Isabel was especially moved by it and donated some of the treasures to be seen here now; to me as a writer the old man's story had special meaning, because of all the pilgrim legends told along this road, this seemed the one that applied most closely to the life of the artist. Just as the grumbling monk read his Mass day after day, practically alone, never knowing when he would entertain an audience, so the beginning writer sits alone through many months putting down words which he himself doubts the meaning of, and he wonders if anyone will ever bother to read them. Then, long after they are finished and even forgotten, he may receive a letter from a strange part of the world saying, 'Tonight I was in the sanctuary of Cebrero as I read your words.'

Don Luis finally found me and led me back to the car. In storm we crossed the lonely hills of Galicia and at midnight came to that last small rivulet separating us from Compostela. Here in past centuries guards had been posted to ensure that all pilgrims disrobed for an obligatory bath. Priests claimed, 'It's to clean ourselves before we kneel before St. James.' But wise men knew it was to wash away the lice.

As we climbed the hill beyond the rivulet I knew that from the next high spot the lights of Compostela would be seen, but I was not prepared

Father Jesús Precedo Lafuente

for what Don Luis did as we rode through the night. 'Mountjoy!' he suddenly cried. 'I am king.' He had revived the most ancient rule of the pilgrims' road, that whoever should first spy the towers of the cathedral would call out in French, 'Mon Joie,' and he would be recognized as king of that group. It is amusing to think that most people in the world with family names like King, König, Leroy or Rex obtained their names because some keen-eyed forebear had been first in his pack to see Compostela.

In the summer of 1966 I was in the city only a few minutes before I received a phone call from a valued friend, Father Jesús Precedo Lafuente, a youngish priest then serving as canon of the cathedral and a man of whom much was expected in the future. He had started his studies at Rome with the Gregorians and had finished them in Jerusalem with the Franciscans. He was a Galician from La Coruña and the best kind of clerical intellectual in that he wrote with professional skill and argued with facility on all matters regarding the Church. As he spoke on the phone I could visualize him as I had last seen him: late thirties, a dark handsome man with Galician features and a disarming smile, the kind of priest on whom the Church in Spain has been depending more and more in recent years.

His message characterized the man. 'Tomorrow's Sunday, and I know you aren't Catholic. This being the shrine of Spain, it's understandable that we have no Protestant church here for you to attend, but there's a good one not far away, and if you'd like, I'll send a car around for you in the morning.'

I replied, 'From the canon of the cathedral, that's more than generous and I appreciate it, but I'd rather spend the time revisiting the cathedral with you.' So early the next morning we set out together to explore again one of Spain's most sacred monuments, and much of what I have to report about Compostela comes from what Father Precedo has said or written about his cathedral.

It is unique in Spain in that it can be seen from four different sides, each set off by its own plaza, all of which are architectural treasures. At first glance, of course, it is the western facade that dominates, not only because it is extremely ornate, topped by two soaring and poetic towers, but also because the plaza in front is the second finest in Spain, ranking only slightly behind that gem in Salamanca. It is a huge plaza, and one night I saw many thousands of people occupy it without crowding. Four handsome buildings delineate it, each with its distinctive style of architecture, so that poets have said that at night one can hear a whispered colloquy among the architectural styles that have made Spain beautiful: Romanesque at the religious college, plateresque at the Hostal de los Reyes Católicos, eighteenth-century neoclassical in the city hall, and the wildly ornate baroque of the cathedral.

If one were to see only the western façade of the cathedral he would have to conclude that it was an eighteenth-century work, built upon the site where a series of older churches had stood; but move around to the southern façade and you will see what might be called the true cathedral. The Plaza de las Platerías (Silversmiths) is a delightful, closed-in, antique little square dominated by the huge bell tower of the cathedral and by this southern façade, which is a pure and stately Romanesque. I could very happily devote much of my time to this beautiful wall, but I have something even more compelling drawing me on, so I shall merely say that to see the cathedral pretty much as it originally was, one must come to this Plaza de las Platerías, where the statue of an insouciant King David playing his fiddle on the left doorjamb is a joyous work, probably the cathedral's best-known piece of sculpture.

The next plaza, the eastern, is my favorite, for from this vantage point, especially from the top of the steps at the extreme right, one can see the great cathedral to advantage. The plaza itself is nothing more than a huge empty square hemmed in by the bleak wall of a convent, some low arcades and the beautiful Romanesque wall of the cathedral, into whose face has been let one of the finest things in Compostela, the Puerta Santa (Holy Door), which is opened only during the years of special pilgrimage and is a sculptural masterpiece. The door is protected on each side by twelve finely carved figures of apostles and prophets and along the top by larger figures of St. Athanasius on the left, St. Theodore on the right, and in the middle the best-known representation of Santiago in pilgrim's attire, with wide-brimmed hat, gourd and cockleshell. When I think of Santiago, I think of this notable figure carved in 1694 by the Portuguese artist Pedro do Campo. The twenty-four figures which guard the Holy Door are active in the life of Compostela. Who stole the widow's cow? 'One of the twenty-four.' Who ran off with the municipal funds? 'One of the twenty-four.' Not long ago, when the university administered an especially difficult examination, one of the students responded, 'For the answer to this question you'll have to consult the twenty-four.' And there they stand, twenty-four wonderful figures from the Romanesque age, clothed in massive simplicity, topped by the three plateresque figures of Pedro do Campo. For a dusty pilgrim to have entered through this beautiful door to the cathedral which had lured him on for nine hundred miles must have been a culminating spiritual experience.

The remaining north plaza, known as the Plaza de la Azabachería (The Place Where Trinkets of Jet Are Sold), would be world-famous if it were located, say, in Toledo, whose cathedral cannot be seen from any vantage point, but in Compostela, where it must compete with three finer plazas, it seems ordinary, for the façade which faces it is a dull baroque affair of jumble and confusion. However, from the steps of the monastery

FOLLOWING FACING PAGES:
The twenty-four figures guard the Holy Door,
which is opened only during the Holy Years.

across the way one obtains a good view of the cathedral as a whole, with its varied towers and turrets, and one can begin to unravel the complexity of this strange monument. The earliest church must have been a wooden affair built shortly after the discovery of the body of St. James in 812, and we know from excavations that it was built upon the ruins of an extremely ancient Roman cemetery which dated back to before the time of Christ. This wooden church was quickly replaced by the stone church of Alfonso II, which was in turn rebuilt by Alfonso III at the end of the ninth century. The Muslim al-Mansur al Allah (Victor by the Grace of Allah) destroyed everything in his invasion of 997. A temporary replacement was erected in the early 1000s, but in 1075 Alfonso VI authorized the building of the Romanesque church which has ever since formed the core of this magnificent edifice. In the early 1100s Alfonso VII and his cantankerous Archbishop Gelmírez completed a cathedral which in outline must have looked pretty much as it does today. To this permanent nucleus was then added one feature after another, the last major change being the erection in 1738–1750 of the tempestuous baroque main façade by Fernando de Casas y Novoa.

All this, one can decipher from the supposedly uninteresting northern plaza, but one can see a great deal more. When I looked up at the pile of figures topping the neoclassical monastery facing the cathedral, I asked a guide, 'Who's the man on horseback?' 'Santiago,' he said without hesitating. But as I studied the figure I saw that the rider was cutting his cloak in two with a long sword and I realized that I was looking not at Santiago but at one of the most popular saints of the medieval period, the jovial Hungarian known as St. Martin of Tours, patron of roustabouts, tavern brawlers and reformed drunkards. And this reminded me that I was standing in what for centuries had been the powerful French section of Compostela and the financial capital of this part of Spain. Just as Medina del Campo had determined the value of international coinages in the Renaissance, so the Azabachería had determined it in the Middle Ages, and through this plaza every pilgrim from northern lands was required to pass when he entered the cathedral. This was where the journey from Paris and Brussels and Stockholm ended. This was the French town within the Spanish town, and to reach the Plaza de la Azabachería and to know that you were again within the protection of French power must have been reassuring.

To see the work of art for which this cathedral is famous you must go back to the main plaza, climb the long flight of stairs to the entrance and pass through one of the doors of the façade. Immediately inside, and before you enter the cathedral itself, you find yourself in the enclosed Pórtico de la Gloria, fifty-one feet long, thirteen feet wide and some sixty feet high, one of the major glories of world art which a week of visits will not exhaust. On the floor there is nothing and on the ceiling only routine carving on the ribs of the vaulting. On the two small end walls, nothing, and on the western wall, which is, of course, the back of the baroque façade, merely a set of sculptured Biblical figures and angels: Mark stands by himself in the left corner; then Luke and John the Baptist together; Esther and Judith; and off by himself, Job. The angels aloft are not noteworthy; those who play trumpets direct the bells of their instruments down toward the observer.

So for five-sixths of this portico there is not much to comment about, but the remaining wall, through which one enters the cathedral, contains such a wealth of sculpture and of such stunning quality that I am perplexed as to why it is not better known. It is a masterwork of Romanesque art, an enticing summary of medieval thought, yet as modern in execution as a painting by Picasso. Psychologically it is profound; humanistically it is one of the most delightful works ever composed; artistically it is of the first order; and religiously it recapitulates the faith of an epoch. But having said this I have still missed the essential quality of this masterpiece. It is fun. It has a throbbing sense of real human beings. It depicts laughter, not tears. It contains hundreds of separate figures and a huge proportion of them are having a good time. The oppressive heaviness of much medieval art is here missing and a kind of jollity suffuses the figures. Even Jesus himself is staring wide-eyed at the world about him and finding it good. The Pórtico de la Gloria is not only one of the world's supreme artistic creations; it is also one of the most human, alive and joyous.

The massive wall is broken by three large arches which give entrance to the nave and aisles of the cathedral. This means that from left to right as one faces the wall he sees, in this order, a corner column, the left doorway over which is a large curved area, then a large composite pillar, then the central doorway and it, too, has a very large curved area above it, then a second composite pillar, then the right doorway with curved area above, and at the far right-hand end, a final column. It is in the harmonious utilization of these seven separated areas—four columns, three arched spaces—that this wall is so superior artistically. Actually, there is a fifth column, because the span of the central doorway is so great that it requires this column for support, and there is no better point at which to start enjoying the portico than here. Observe that I say enjoying and not studying, for this is a wall to be chuckled over, and pedantry would kill it.

The slender central column is, like all the others, built up from separate pillars, in this case five plain ones plus one highly carved. Its base is noteworthy in that it depicts the defeat of Hercules, representing old religions, by Christianity. Two lions who accompany the fallen hero have their mouths wide open for the purpose of admitting light into the vaults below. The carved pillar is extremely lovely. It shows the Tree of Jesse,

from which Jesus sprang, and by itself would be a memorable work. Some time after it appeared at the gateway to the cathedral a pilgrim whose name is unknown discovered that among the vines and leaves of Jesse's tree were five indentations, perhaps put there intentionally by the artist, into which a thumb and four fingers would fit, and it became the custom for newcomers to the church to stand before this column and insert their fingers into the spaces and pray. Now, eight hundred years later, the weightless force of these hundreds of millions of fingers has worn deep indentions into the marble, so that the dead Tree of Jesse seems to have acquired a kind of life.

Sitting on a platform atop the tree is a benevolent statue of Santiago, and with him we begin to discover the characteristics of this massive work, for he is calm, his robes are at rest and are not exaggerated, his hands are big and capable and his feet are the ordinary feet of a workman. His face is almost beautiful in its repose and his cheeks are ruddy, for from the beginning the statues were polychromed, and in 1651 their faces were repainted; now they exude only a faded glow.

With this tender and human carving of Santiago the pillar itself ends. Its capital, extremely well carved, depicts the divine origins of Jesus. Atop the capital, and therefore in the main body of the work, sits Jesus enthroned, showing his wounds and surrounded by angels. This, too, is a remarkably human statue of a patient and loving man, as unpretentious as the Galician farmer or fisherman who probably posed for it.

We were now in the central tympanum, a work bewilderingly rich in images and joy. About the figure of Christ rest the four evangelists in the animal evocations we saw earlier in the tetramorph at San Isidoro's in León and which I could not then decipher. Father Precedo now explains that this tradition stemmed from an apocalyptic passage in the first chapter of the Book of Ezekiel, in which the prophet sees a fire: 'Out of the midst thereof came the likeness of four living creatures. . . . As for the likeness of their faces, they four had the face of a man, and the face of a lion, on the right side: and they four had the face of an ox on the left side; they four also had the face of an eagle.'

Another Church historian told me later that the identification of the four figures came from the recension of the above passage in Revelation, in which John beholds the throne of God: '. . . and round about the throne, were four beasts full of eyes before and behind. And the first beast was like a lion, and the second beast like a calf, and the third beast had a face as a man, and the fourth beast was like a flying eagle.' It was the early Church fathers who conceived these animals to be allegorical representations of the evangelists, but they found no key as to which symbol applied to which evangelist. St. Jerome made the definitive application on the basis of the way in which each Gospel opened. Matthew was assigned the man since his account begins with the human genealogy of Jesus; Mark, the lion, because he opens with the loud voice of John the Baptist crying in the wilderness; Luke, the bull, for the sacrifice of Zacharias; and John, the eagle, for the high-soaring flight of his thought in the prologue.

Outward from Jesus and the evangelists stand eight wonderful figures, four on each side. These are the angels who bear the instruments of the Crucifixion, on the left the column to which Jesus was tied, the cross, and the crown of thorns; on the right the nails and lance, the parchment of the verdict, the jug of water with which Pilate washed his hands, the lash, and the lance with the sponge which carried vinegar to the dying Christ. In spite of the lugubrious mission of the eight angels, they are themselves gentle and in repose. The anguish is past and they hold the cruel instruments in loving remembrance rather than in passion or resentment. In this respect they typify the recurrent theme of this wall, that Jesus has ascended to glory and the world rejoices.

Skipping over the multitude of angels who hover above the Lord, singing and rejoicing, each face a separate identity and all of them delightful, one comes to a unique feature of the work and one of the best loved. It is an outer semicircle depicting the twenty-four elders of the Apocalypse: 'And round about the throne were four and twenty seats: and upon the seats I saw four and twenty elders sitting, clothed in white raiment; and they had on their heads crowns of gold . . . four and twenty elders fell down before the Lamb, having every one of them harps, and golden vials full of odours, which are the prayers of saints. And they sung a new song.' In accordance with this passage, the twenty-four are shown with musical instruments, providing us with a portrait of medieval music: fourteen zithers, four psalteries, two harps, two lutes, plus a surprising device I shall speak of in a moment. They are grouped two by two, not ostentatiously but with rare subtlety, and according to the text they should be singing, but it seemed to me as if they were talking amiably among themselves. My two favorites are the fifth and sixth in from the right. The fifth plucks a lute or some such stringed instrument and the sixth has a harp. They talk together as if they had played in many different bands, and I wish I could overhear the conversation, for the harpist seems much pleased with himself as his fingers strum the strings. If I had to choose two figures who best established the serene atmosphere of this great work, I would take these, for whenever I look at them I chuckle.

If the sculptor had disposed his twenty-four musicians into twelve facing pairs, the top of the semicircle, that is, the point immediately above the head of Christ, would be empty, for the two musicians who bordered that spot would be looking away from each other, and this would be artistically displeasing. The artist obviated this by taking the four top figures in the semicircle and arranging them in this way: the two outer figures have no partners but look toward the center, while the two central figures share across their knees a strange contraption called a zanfoña, the left half of which looks like a large guitar while the right half consists of a series of cranks. It is the world's first instrument for cranking out automatic tunes, or more precisely, semi-automatic tunes, because I suppose the man on the left had to finger the strings in order to insure that the man on the right cranked out the correct notes. At any rate, these four central figures, so disposed and with the zanfoña across the knees, bind the massive composition together in a manner that is positively pleasing.

Of the two lesser arches, the left is a construction of quiet poetry suffused with mystical implications. It is built up from three concentric and receding semicircles, each of which is tied together by luxuriant foliage. The inner circle consists of eight crowned figures accompanying a nude Adam and Eve and a benign Jesus. The middle circle contains eleven patriarchal figures seated behind what could be a stylized table but which is more probably a representation of a massive rope symbolizing the continuity of life. The impression one gets from this beautiful arch is order, dignity and a mass of men living together within the boundaries of nature. An undocumented tradition claims that this arch represents the Jewish concept of life as it flourished before the coming of Christ and is a fantasy lifted from the apocryphal Book of Enoch. If so, it contains one of the gentlest commentaries on Judaism ever constructed by a Christian artist, in that the whole archway of Judaism is linked to the central archway of Christianity by a simple, symbolic device. What do you suppose it is? Two little children holding a long parchment indicating the New Testament, which the Jews merely have to accept to be saved.

The right archway is a much different matter. Here the artist is dealing not with alien Jews whom he hopes to conciliate but with Christians who ought to know how to behave within the body of the Church. The right half of this arch is a terrifying depiction of those condemned at the Last Judgment. In the quaint English which is apparently obligatory for all guidebooks in Spain: 'To the right, small reptiles and horrible big monsters harass and tear off the flesh of men, slaves of vice, with their claws and fauces. It is surprising the Dantesque expressiveness of this composition.' The left portion, that is, on the right hand of God as He and His son sit in judgment, are the saved, and they are a happy lot. I have studied this great arch for many hours, finding in it always something new and compelling, but in the end I think the excellence of the work can be reported in two facts: here paradise seems really more to be preferred than hell, which is not always the case in medieval and Renaissance art; and the conspicuous aspect of this work, an aspect not before commented on by writers but one surely planned with much care by the artist, is that we see both hell and heaven through the eyes of little children who share the torment and the glory with their guilty or saved parents. The children shown in this panel are among the finest ever portrayed in art, and I cannot praise them highly enough. In hell they perish in dreadful agony, and in heaven they rejoice with parents who love them, making each aspect more psychologically believable. Spanish religion features this involvement of children in the faith, and one of the most fearful aspects of the Inquisition was that it insisted upon the display in the parish church of a condemned man's sanbenito for at least ten generations with his name clearly upon it, the purpose being to condemn that man's children throughout those same ten generations. It could well be that this harshest of the Inquisitional laws stemmed from this right-hand arch at Compostela; at least, it was an extension of the majestic idea here represented, that heaven and hell are more meaningful when seen through the eyes of children.

Again, just as the Jews were offered salvation through the intervention of two small children, so in this panel the saved are led into paradise by two other children who show the way into the central archway.

We have now seen the six walls of this remarkable portico and more than a hundred and eighty-five different figures, but we have not yet come to the feature which has always been its chief claim to artistic fame. About the four principal columns are ranged, their feet resting at about the eye-level of the viewer as he studies them, sixteen life-sized statues of men in robes, and no matter how much one enjoys the twenty-four bearded musicians or the children of the Last Judgment, he must finally admit that this parade of splendid men is the highlight of the wall.

They are unbelievably well carved, tall, bending slightly forward, extremely human in aspect and mobile of face. Tradition says that each was modeled after a specific man who lived in Compostela at the time, and I find this easy to accept, for this gallery of men could not have happened by either accident or imagination. They are so real they could speak, yet so artistically contrived that in their silence they sing, and to have seen them intimately, day after day and in all lights is to have shaken hands with the Middle Ages.

Meet them. On the left-most pillar, below the world of the Jews, stand long-bearded Joel and quizzical Abdias. ('What name do we know Abdias by?' I ask Father Precedo. 'Abdias,' he replies. 'Everybody knows him by that name.' Back in America I would learn that he was Obadiah of the King James Bible, Abdias of the Douay.)

On the left-hand edge of the first main column stand Hosea, who had such a miserable time with his wife, and Amos. The remaining portion of this column contains the most famous of the sixteen. Jeremiah is properly grave and heavy, but Daniel is a young, beardless man with one of the most ingratiating smiles in the history of art. Standing on one leg with the other playfully crooked at the knee, he seems like a schoolboy about to play some mischievous trick, and he is by far the most popular of the figures in the procession. Since his roguish grin is directed across the portico to the enchanting figure of Queen Esther, who faces him on the opposite wall, tradition says that one of the self-righteous kings of northern Spain directed that Esther be made to appear less attractive, for she was disturbing the propriety of the cathedral, whereupon the artist shortened her nose and made other alterations, without much success, for Daniel still gives her the merry eye.

Next to Daniel comes my favorite figure, an old, smiling Isaiah, heavy with beard and marked by a golden cap, which none of the others wear. To me it seems no great accomplishment for a young man like Daniel to smile; but it is reassuring when old Isaiah with his burden of prophecy should still be able to raise a muffled laugh. Beside him stands Moses with the tablets, and his burden of law is so heavy that he cannot smile.

On the comparable portion of the main right-hand pillar stand Peter with his massive keys, Paul with a book, James the brother of Jesus, and John the Divine, also beardless and with a face of heavenly purity. He seems wide-eyed with surprise that revelation should have been accorded him, but he is not ponderous about it. On the smaller portion of this column, and facing the arch of the Last Judgment, stand solemn Matthew and conversational Andrew, while in the corner, on the last of the pillars, stand heavily bearded Thomas and preaching Bartholomew.

It is a magnificent parade from which Judas Iscariot is missing. The Middle Ages found it objectionable to picture him in such scenes, so he is often omitted. But the others march in a grandeur which seems the more impressive because of its compelling simplicity. With their appearance we leave the Pórtico de la Gloria, but not before we notice one small detail.

I spoke earlier of the angels who appear on the west wall of the portico and of how the two bearing trumpets direct them down as if playing for the delight of the observer. At each end of the opposite wall, which contains the Gloria, appears an additional angel so placed as to form part of both the Gloria and the end wall, constituting a harmonic link between the two unequal halves of the composition. They, too, point their trumpets below, and if you look at these four figures, who form a kind of thematic material for the whole composition, you realize that they are trumpeters announcing the day of resurrection, and they are summoning you to that paradise where music and joy and laughter and winking saints and beautiful queens and the benevolence of children abound, and you may well recall the John Donne sonnet on this theme:

> At the round earth's imagined corners blow
> Your trumpets, angels, and arise, arise
> From death, you numberless infinities
> Of souls, and to your scattered bodies go,
> All whom the flood did, and fire shall o'erthrow . . .

What of the cathedral itself? Could any church be worthy of such an entrance? At Compostela the interior is about what it should be, if one thinks of this building as the spiritual center of a religious nation. It is beautifully Romanesque and cluttered with just enough paraphernalia to remind one that this is Spain. In spirit it is very warm, in aspect majestic, and in its operating manifestations devout. The first thing one encounters inside the church itself is a statue to the man who carved the portico, for the intricate work which I have just described appears to have been accomplished by one man whose name is known: Maestro Mateo (in Galician, Mestre Mateu), a Spaniard who worked in northern Spain during the last third of the twelfth century. Documentary records state that he finished the portico in 1188 and it is supposed that it occupied him for about twenty-five years. His statue, which he may have carved himself, is a properly jaunty thing whose head is covered with lively stone curls, and through the centuries it has been the custom for all who visit Maestro Mateo's supreme work to bow before the kneeling statue and to touch one's head against his in hopes that some of his genius may rub off. O Santo d'os Croques, he is known in Galician, the Saint of the Bumps, and I, like many others, have touched my head against his, hopefully. When I reflect that this great artist is generally unknown, while much lesser figures of the Italian Renaissance are treasured as geniuses, I wonder at the unfairness of history, for to compare Maestro Mateo with those lesser but more famous artists is like comparing the Himalayas with the Poconos of my home district. The Poconos are lovely, for sure, but to mistake them for the Himalayas is an error.

I was fortunate in reaching Compostela at the precise point in the year when I could best witness the significance of the town and its cathedral in Spanish life, for El día de Santiago (The Day of St. James) occurs each year on July 25 and is the occasion for a religious celebration of great dimension. Toward midnight on the evening of the twenty-fourth it seemed as if everyone in the city had crowded into the plaza before the cathedral, where for two days workmen had been hiding the façade behind a huge wooden imitation featuring a panel with the words 'Al Patrón de España.' Now, at eleven, two large rockets were sent aloft to explode with a force so strong that my coat was lashed by the following blast of air. Then to constant applause one rocket after another lifted into the air for about half an hour. I had noticed earlier that this display, which had been publicized during the preceding week, was to be in the hands of a firm from La Coruña, and since the best fireworks are generally considered to come from Valencia, I expected little, and during the first half-hour saw nothing to make Valencia worry.

But after the regulation rockets had been fired, those that exploded in shimmering white or red, the good men of La Coruña let go. On a series of wagon wheels stuck on poles about the plaza they set loose some contraptions that were dazzling, each consisting of at least eight radically different sequences timed to explode one after the other over a period of at least two minutes, so that one wondered how the first charges could ignite without detonating the others. While the crowd was marveling at this, the La Coruña men produced their specialty: a large rocket which climbed in a zigzag pattern to about a hundred yards in the air, then stopped, dashed off parallel to the earth for a hundred yards, where it died in a soft hissing sound, but when it had almost reached the earth it gave forth a huge burst of flame, another rocket fired, and the whole thing went back into a giant orbit that took it higher than before, ending in a loud explosion and a blaze of multicolored lights. It was quite a rocket, much more complex than anything Valencia had shown, and the crowd cheered.

But there was still more! On a distant building far across the plaza a brilliant ball of light began to blaze, and on a thin wire that none of us had noticed before, it sped in wild flight some two hundred yards and crashed directly into the false façade of the cathedral, after which it sped back up the wire to the point at which it had begun; but few saw its journey end, because when it struck the cathedral the entire false front burst into flame and for at least four minutes we saw such a popping of lights, such a rain of rockets and such a confusion of colors that no eye could possibly have followed all that was happening. The whole cathedral seemed to be ablaze, and at the end some sixty standing rockets were automatically ignited and these went off in all directions, filling the sky with flaming color.

Apparently the residents of Compostela are more accustomed to fireworks than I, because next day the local newspapers reported that 'the traditional illumination of the façade went off as usual with nothing special to report.'

At dawn on the twenty-fifth, large black limousines begin to arrive at the Hostal de los Reyes Católicos. In the early 1500s this had been the foremost hospital in the world, a center of medical learning reputed to be without equal, for it had been established by Queen Isabel and King Fernando as a refuge for those many pilgrims who reached Compostela in a state of exhaustion after negotiating the pass at Cebrero and the bitter mountains of Galicia. Now the majestic building, constructed around four different courts, each an architectural masterpiece, serves as a luxury hotel, and in its spacious lounges the early-morning visitors munch cakes and fruit with their coffee.

They are politicians from Madrid and officers from the naval base at El Ferrol del Caudillo, the Galician birthplace of Generalísimo Franco at the northwest tip of Spain. Spaniards say that if Franco had been born one step farther west, he'd have been a norteamericano.

By midmorning the plaza is filled with army units in brown uniforms, accompanied by a competent brass band which plays marches. A small cannon booms out a nineteen-gun salute to Santiago, a military greeting to a military saint, which is not surprising in a land where in 1962 the mummified left arm of Santa Teresa, during a grand tour of the nation, was officially received in Madrid with the military honors due to a 'captain-general in active command of troops.' Additional dignitaries appear in full morning dress, and soon one portion of the plaza is filled with handsome-looking men in various costumes, all prepared to pay homage to the great saint who had led the nation to victory over the Moors, over the Incas and Aztecs and over most of the armies of Europe.

At ten a large parade forms, composed of military units, the civil officials, red-caped priests and green-clad members of the Guardia Civil. These march about the plaza in a show of national solidarity before heading for the cathedral, where at the Pórtico de la Gloria a mitered bishop in red waits to grant permission to enter, and all bow to kiss his hand.

I have not previously mentioned the extraordinary size of the cathedral, but this parade of several hundred led by a brass band will be absorbed in the vast expanse of pillar and chapel without causing much stir. On this day the interior is redolent of past glories: enormous throngs of worshipers crowd the aisles while the massive organ thunders out Bach's Toccata and Fugue in D Minor. Prior to the entrance of the parade a tall priest leads four men clothed in red in a procession that moves along all aisles and transepts of the church. They bear on their shoulders an ornate reliquary containing a statue and memorials of St. James the Less, and on his statue one sees a highly decorated silver collar which has a most curious history: it was given to the cathedral in 1435 by that same Suero de Quiñones who held the bridge over the Orbigo for thirty days. And as this strange gift makes its slow way through the cathedral, it passes the chapel in which hangs the bejeweled pendant delivered later by an equally famous Spaniard of the heroic age, Don Juan de Austria, who came here on pilgrimage after his crucial victory at Lepanto. In the left transept the relics pass the little chapel of St. Andrew, where a niche was recently let into the wall to house a sickly-sweet modern statue of the Virgin dressed in robes of pale blue and white and framed by a bouquet of asters and white lilies. A halo of small electric lights illuminates the head of this very popular statue, for even now with the procession in full swing a group of women prays before the shrine. Before each woman kneels she takes from beside the Virgin a printed slip of paper, and with a pencil hanging from a cord ticks off the subjects in which she is most interested, depositing the marked slip in the prayer box:

9. Peace in the family.
10. A termination to a bad love affair.
16. Success in studies.
23. Peace in the world.
25. For the unity of all Christians.
29. Reconciliation of a married couple.

The niche in the wall has a special appeal to women because the statue of the extremely beautiful Virgin was given by Evita Perón.

Now the procession from outside the cathedral has completed its entrance, and as it moves down the right aisle the organ produces a new song, and eight men in red robes move into action, ready for an exhibition seen in no other cathedral in the world.

Two bear on their shoulders a massive pole from which hangs an iron censer about three feet high. Silver-plated and of a handsome design, it was made in 1850 by the silversmith Losada and is the most recent of a long line of Botafumeiros (Smoke-Throwers) to have been used in this cathedral.

The other red-clad men are busy with another detail. From one of the nearby pillars they have released a very stout hempen rope possibly three inches in diameter and a couple of hundred feet long. This rope reaches up to the highest part of the cathedral, where it passes over a complicated system of pulleys, dropping down so that the Botafumeiro can be attached to its loose end, which is passed through a huge iron ring at the top of the censer and securely lashed. The eight men then grab the other end of the rope and slowly pull the huge object a few feet in the air.

A priest now opens the top of the contraption and pours inside a large bucketful of charcoal and incense and gives the censer an initial swing to start it moving. What happens next I do not understand, but by a series of skillfully timed pulls on their end of the rope, the eight men succeed in getting the great silver chalice to swing in ever-growing arcs until at last, in an unbelievable surge of power, the enormous thing is flying right up to the ceiling of the cathedral some ninety feet away, hesitating there a moment, then roaring down with sickening speed, skimming over the heads of watchers, only to be held in restraint by the rope and swung up to the ceiling on the other side. And as the huge thing flies through the air, perforations admit a flow of air and set the charcoal ablaze, so that sparks fly out in the swift descent and incense fills the cathedral. It is a most extraordinary sight, a thrilling display of motion, power, fire and mystery.

I ask Father Precedo what all this signifies, and he says, 'The people like to believe that the custom started in the Middle Ages when thousands of pilgrims slept in the cathedral and smelled up the place. The incense was supposed to be a germ killer. Actually, the custom may have started in the time of our great Archbishop Gelmírez, who did everything possible to maintain the credentials of Santiago de Compostela on a par with those of Rome. He probably invented the huge censer as a gesture of Compostela's uniqueness within the Church.'

The men who pull the ropes are employed as caretakers by the cathedral, and their origin, according to legend, antecedes that of the present building. When Alfonso III was king of the north, Bishop Adaulfo of Compostela was accused by three men of the village, Isadón, Cadón and Ensión, of 'nefarious vices too ugly to be announced.' The king's judgment ordered Adaulfo to be thrown before a wild bull, but when this was done the animal, knowing that the bishop was blameless, came and placed his

Elaborate rituals are maintained in the smaller chapels of the cathedral for the sanctification of pilgrims who come from parts as far away as Denmark and Turkey.

head in the good man's hands, whereupon the king thundered, 'Isadón, Cadón and Ensión and all their offspring are sentenced to perpetual servitude at the cathedral which they have shamed.' It is their descendants who pull the ropes.

Now they stop, for if they continued they'd send the censer banging into the ceiling and then down into the crowd, as happened in 1499 when ill-fated Catalina, youngest daughter of Fernando and Isabel, stopped here on her way to London to marry Arthur, Prince of Wales. Again in 1622 the Botafumeiro fell, landing in the middle of a large crowd without injuring anyone.

It is now time for the solemn high Mass celebrating Santiago as patron protector of Spain, and what happens next is so strange to Americans reared on a theory of separation between Church and state that I had better translate a portion of the speech which Admiral Francisco Núñez Rodríguez makes to the massive stone statue of Santiago, addressing him personally as if he were present in his role of Matamoros:

> Glorious Apostle of Spain, Señor Santiago, in obedience to the most honorable responsibility given me by the Chief of State, I come here to present you with the traditional offering whereby our people wish to testify to their gratefulness for the protection and aid which they continue to receive from you.
>
> Spain will never forget that she received the Light of Faith and the Doctrine of Christ from your lips nor that you selected these marvelous lands of Galicia for the repose of your glorious remains. Every year on this day we come to hear your message of apostolic impatience, which is like a sunrise testimony which reaches into our blood and fills it with fidelity and missionary zeal.
>
> It was in continuance of your example, O Glorious Apostle, that in the past we sanctified our power and sublimated our ambition, orienting them toward difficult enterprises like the recovery inch by inch of our national heritage and the evangelization of half the globe. A new world we brought you, and later an eighth part of the earth.
>
> We will never permit either error or false doctrine to snatch away our great treasure of Religious Unity, the foundation of our political and social unity, which, thanks to you, O Glorious Apostle, we have enjoyed during these past thirty years.

Mighty and tall in his red robes and biretta, Cardinal Fernando Quiroga Palacios, primate of Santiago, and because of the advanced age of the Cardinal of Toledo, president of the council of cardinals governing the Church in Spain, replies on behalf of Santiago, accepting the homage of Spain and promising that as long as the nation is faithful it shall prosper. At this moment the pealing of the organ, signifying the majesty of government, is joined by the sound of bagpipes marching into the cathedral on the shoulders of the common people. All Spain appears united under a single banner, that of Santiago, and dedicated to a single ideal, that of the Catholic Church.

At this point it is appropriate to consider the role of the Church in modern Spain, and I shall be drawing only upon conversations conducted outside of Compostela. The central fact of Spanish history in the past five hundred years has been the country's willingness to sacrifice for the welfare of Catholicism, and if one doubts the sincerity under which Isabel, Cisneros, Carlos V and Felipe II did so, there is no chance for him to understand Spain. The cost in gold, in armies, in commerce and in freedom has been stupendous; the rewards have been a sense of mission and the building of a nation committed to one Church. Most Spaniards deem the bargain to have been a good one and the cost not excessive. In various parts of Spain I was told what I believe to be true: 'Eighty percent of the men of Spain, as contrasted to the women, inwardly ridicule the involved ritual of the Church, but of those who scoff, eighty percent would take arms to fight anyone who tried to change our religion to something else.' One fatal miscalculation of the Republic in 1936 was its underestimation of the number of Spaniards who would defend Catholicism if it were threatened.

The next point is difficult to explain, for although Spain has been the chief defender of the faith, it has often given popes a bad time. Fernando and Isabel were not loath to rebuke the Pope when he issued edicts they didn't like. Stout Gelmírez, Archbishop of Compostela, openly opposed the popes of his day. Many a law promulgated by Rome was denied proclamation in Spain, for Spaniards have usually done pretty much as they like in governing their Church. Even today the Pope has a more difficult time appointing a bishop in Spain than in any other country where the Church is recognized, for the government, in consultation with the Papal Nuncio, draws up a panel of six acceptable names. These are submitted to the Pope, who designates the three who are most acceptable to him, and from this list the Spanish government selects its new bishop. In many parts of Spain, as we have seen, the memory of Pope John XXIII is poorly regarded and his more revolutionary ideas of ecumenism are opposed by at least half the clergy. It is common to hear a Spanish priest say, 'It is now the role of the Spanish Church to save Rome from itself.' What percentage of the ecumenical reform of the past decade will operate in Spain remains to be seen.

The extent to which the Church dominates civil life is often surprising to visitors. Marriage, family life, education, publishing, health and motion pictures are only a few of the areas in which religious control is supreme. The Church is vigorously supported by the other members of the ruling triumvirate, the army and the landed families, and by the Guardia Civil and the police as well. A citizen is ill advised to tangle with any agency of this group, for the others will jump on him. A man I know was visiting Valencia when a religious procession passed and he alone of the bystanders refused to rise and doff his cap as the Virgin went by. He was arrested and asked by the police, 'What are you, some kind of a radical or something, not paying homage to the Virgin?' He escaped serious trouble only by claiming that his knee had been damaged in an automobile accident. He was warned that in the future he must be more worshipful.

This kind of interlocking directorate between the right-wing politicians and the Church has existed for two centuries and explains why, at recurring intervals, the people of Spain, judging the Church to be indifferent to their needs, have risen blindly to slay their priests and burn their churches. This has happened so often and in such identical patterns that one must consider the killings and burnings following the outbreak of the Civil War in 1936 as merely the latest in a doleful sequence. It is misleading for the Franco government to place marble tablets in churches proclaiming that it was Marxists who killed the priests. Most of these atrocities occurred months before Marxists were in control and should more accurately be considered a typical explosion of Spanish resentment. One incident not related to the war typifies those that were. In July, 1834, a cholera epidemic threatened Madrid, and when a rumor spread that Jesuits and friars had been poisoning wells, a mob swarmed into the Puerta del Sol and fanned out to burn churches and slaughter more than eighty friars and monks. In 1835 similar burnings and killings broke out, almost as if by prearrangement, in all the major Spanish towns.

During the Civil War it was natural and necessary for the Church to ally itself with the army and the landholders, but the continued alliance for more than thirty years has encouraged the lower classes to believe that the nineteenth century is being repeated and that the Church continues to be their enemy. This is why many younger priests and possibly half the seminarians want to create a Church which is divorced from the army and landholders. In Barcelona, as we have seen, priests agitating for social liberalism were clubbed publicly by the police and won much sympathy from the public. In Sevilla sixty seminarians struck for a more liberal interpretation of Church law. In Madrid priests wanted to know what was being done to implement the decisions of the Ecumenical Council, and petitions were circulated within the Church. I never knew, when I began talking with Spanish priests, what unpredictable thing they might say, and among them I found a wider spectrum of opinion than I do among my neighbors at home. Older men seemed determined to keep Spain as it has always been and to defend the country against what they regard as the recent errors of Rome; some of the younger men were surprisingly outspoken liberals.

The recent ruling which permits a degree of freedom for non-Catholics is more significant than would at first appear, and frankly I did not expect such liberalization so soon. Only a few years ago a Protestant chaplain at an American military base was arrested when he held a Sunday School picnic in an open park, for this was held to be in violation of the law forbidding any religion other than Catholicism to conduct ceremonies or meetings for worship in public, yet I have explained that when I arrived at Santiago de Compostela, the very heart of the Church in Spain, the Church itself offered to facilitate my attendance at a Protestant chapel. And when I was last in Madrid the newspapers carried long illustrated accounts of the ordination of a native-born Protestant bishop, but with the caption 'Married and with two children.'

Spain will remain Catholic, more completely so than either France or Italy; newspapers will continue to report ecclesiastical developments as headline news; and the Church will continue to be a major force in the land. But a lively argument within the Church will determine the social and political course it will take. For example, during my last trip Spanish newspapers were giving an inordinate amount of coverage to discussions in the Italian parliament of a limited divorce law. I asked, 'Why this sudden interest in Italian politics?' and a newspaperman told me, 'We don't give a damn about Italy. But we're much interested in the attempt of a Catholic country to get a workable divorce law. We're forbidden to discuss a Spanish law. So we write about Italy as if it were Spain. Everyone understands.'

As for the grandiloquent exhibition at Santiago de Compostela on El día de Santiago, the outside observer has the suspicion that whereas the oligarchy want desperately to believe that the present system will prevail permanently, they have not convinced the general population. When Admiral Núñez thunders, 'We will never permit either error or false doctrine to snatch away our great treasure of Religious Unity,' he is voicing more a hope than a fact. If religious unity continues only as it is, the handmaiden of those who rule, it must eventually be challenged; but if under the pressure of younger priests it can change and adjust itself to the spirit of Pope John XXIII, there could be real hope that in the next time of change the churches and the monasteries will not be burned.

It is rewarding to visit Compostela at any time, but in Holy Years—that is, any year in which July 25 falls on a Sunday—there are additional inducements, for then northern Spain holds continual festival in honor of Santiago. The Holy Years fall in an endless sequence of 6-5-6-11, and since the last occurred in 1965, the next will fall in 1971 and 1976. I asked Father Precedo specifically, 'Are non-Catholics welcomed here during a Holy Year?' and he gave me a document which showed that during the preceding celebration the senior government official in Galicia had been Mohammed ben Mezian bel Kasem, a Muslim from Spanish Morocco. 'If we can tolerate a Muslim at the spot where Santiago went forth to battle the Moors, we can surely welcome Protestants.'

There were long periods when Holy Years meant little at Compostela. In the early 1600s, after more than seven hundred years as the spiritual center of northern Europe, it fell on bad times because of an English pirate and a French king. In 1589 Sir Francis Drake put together a large fleet with fourteen thousand soldiers, with the announced intention of destroying Santiago, 'that center of pernicious superstition.' As his armada approached the Galician coast, priests hid the bones of Santiago, and when Drake retired, the location of the once-famous grave was forgotten.

In 1681 King Louis XIV declared that thieves and pickpockets and false priests were so brazen in their robbery of pilgrims that no Frenchmen would henceforth be allowed to make the journey. Cynics suggested that what Louis was really trying to do was to cut off the flow of money and trade goods into Spain, and he succeeded.

For the next two hundred years the Way of St. James was largely deserted, and then in 1879 devout priests rediscovered his grave. From Rome special investigators arrived to check the authenticity of the find, and after scientific studies by medical men and archaeologists, declared this to be the ancient grave of Santiago. The flood of pilgrims resumed, and a wise priest who worked at Santiago wrote, 'These remains, be what they may, have revived the spirit of pilgrimage.' Today that spirit continues as powerful as ever.

There are within the region of Compostela four additional pilgrimages worth taking which I had always felt constrained to make. Two lie within the city itself and two outside, so it was to the former that I now moved. On a bright sunny afternoon, when giant figures on stilts paraded to the delight of children, an enormous Moor proving especially popular, to judge from the squeals he provoked, I walked through a chain of medieval alleys to find myself at last on the edge of the city at a spot where the small Río Sar became visible, and there, along its banks, I came upon one of the most remarkable churches in existence, a structure so bizarre that I find difficulty in believing that it still stands in this century.

As I approached the small stone building a band of children gathered about me, singing sentences from a popular song, with one enterprising boy of eleven shouting as the others sang, 'Ten pesetas, Englishman. Your only chance in this world to hear songs in true Galician.' I told him I doubted if he knew a word of Galician, whereupon he joined the others in hideous wailing, none of whose words I could understand. 'That's not Galician,' I replied, and instead of arguing with me he halted his choir and said solemnly, 'All right, you want me to take you to the church that's falling down?'

I told him that I wouldn't require his services; the church lay directly ahead of me and I couldn't miss it if I wanted to, whereupon a devilish smile came over his childish features, and he watched with growing pleasure as I approached the church and found the door tightly barred. 'You found it,' he said with evil glee, 'but you can't get in.'

'Can you get me in?'

'Yes.'

'For how much?'

'The same ten pesetas.'

I handed him the money and with a benign smile he led me to the woman sacristan, who had been on her way to open the church from the moment I had first seen it. 'You will like it,' the boy said. 'It's the only church in Spain that's always falling down.'

A short distance from the cathedral an ingratiating barker shouts to the pilgrims, 'Step this way, ladies and gentlemen. Try your skill. You too can win a bottle of wine or a kewpie doll.'

He was correct. It was the only church in Spain or elsewhere, so far as I know, that is always falling down, and I did like it. The Colegiata de Santa María la Real de Sar was built in Romanesque style in the early years of the twelfth century and had a rugged cloister attributed to Maestro Mateo of the Pórtico de la Gloria. What makes the church unique, however, and a center for pilgrimages by those who love architecture, is the fact that its two lines of heavy interior columns are not perpendicular, like those of a self-respecting church, but are cocked outward from the central nave to such an extreme degree that they seem about to topple over into the aisles.

The effect of this unnatural pitch is such as to induce vertigo. You are reluctant to believe that anyone would build a church like this on purpose, and your first impression is, 'I must be dizzy.' Then, when your senses have adjusted to this weird visual sensation, you begin to argue with what you are seeing. 'They couldn't lean so far over and not fall down.' But they do, and when the sacristan shows you the spot from which the pillars exert their maximum effect, some leaning this way and others that, your eye jumps back and forth between the extremes, unwilling to accept what stands before it.

'What happened?' I asked the sacristan.

'The builder intended to show the majesty of God,' she replied. 'Even though the pillars are falling down, He can sustain them.' She then took me outside to show me the massive flying buttresses that had obviously been added at some later time. 'When the great earthquake struck Lisboa in 1755 the effects rumbled right across Galicia and we lost many buildings. When the quake stopped, people ran out to see if the church was still standing. It was, but the walls were weakened. So these buttresses were needed to reinforce the pillars at the top.'

Later I asked Father Precedo about the bewildering little church, and he said, 'We believe that the architect originally planned it to look somewhat as it does today. For some reason we can't comprehend, he wanted to show what could be done with pillars off the perpendicular. But when the church was up, an underground river was found to be eating away the foundations and for that reason the flying buttresses had to be added, probably long before the earthquake.'

Whatever the genesis of this strange church, it is worth a visit. It defies reason and abuses the senses, but it is a rugged building that has been in the process of falling down for the last eight hundred years, and barring further earthquakes and wandering subterranean rivers, it looks good for the next eight hundred.

The second personal pilgrimage which I took in Compostela required only a few steps from the cathedral, for the far side of the Plaza de la Quintana, the austere one which contains the Puerta Santa with the twenty-four, is delineated by the wall of the Monasterio de San Payo, now a Benedictine convent, deeply engraved with that ever-present rubric: JOSE ANTONIO. I have seen so many of these fearful signs on churches across Spain, and without anyone's ever commenting upon them, I suspect that Spaniards may be just a little embarrassed by the whole-hearted manner in which their bully-boy has been identified with their religion. Had Germany and Italy won World War II and had beefy men like Hermann Goering and Count Ciano been forced down the world's throat as authentic gods, then surely José Antonio would have been their Spanish counterpart; but the ideals represented by these three deities did not prevail, and today when one sees the name of the Spanish Fascist cut into the walls of so many churches, one feels a sense of anachronism.

At the end of the blank wall so emblazoned, one comes to the inconspicuous church of the convent which contains an altar so baroque, so outrageously gingerbread, that it serves as a corrective to Romanesque austerity. Even the purist needs a touch of the bizarre; any man who loves the cold asperity of El Viti ought to relax now and then in the sunny warmth of Curro Romero's arabesques, and for me such relaxation is found in this convent church.

Two very large pillars, flattened out to provide space for decoration, flank the approach to the main altar, and from the moment one sees these warning sentinels he prepares himself for an orgy of gilt and exaggeration, for the pillars are twisting Solomonic columns in which foliage intertwines with plaster angels, with horsemen whose mounts are rearing furiously, with wreaths, whole landscapes, bas-relief scenes from the lives of saints, and with a host of odds and ends thrown helter-skelter in hopes that some might stick. Most did.

The two pillars are a mere warming-up for the main altar, forty feet across and seventy high, which stands well to the rear. Every inch of this huge construction is plastered not only with gold leaf but also with figures of saints unnumbered, niches carved deep with flowers, propitiatory tablets set off in high relief, life-sized horsemen galloping forth at strange angles, good men ascending to heaven and other good men being beheaded by pirates. Here the smaller pillars which outline the altar are covered with so many golden vines, shields and flying angels that they seem to be crawling, while over everything there is such a wealth of glitter and gold, of precious stones and violent movement, that the eye is not permitted a moment of repose. Yet the altar and its two forward pillars are so harmonious in their relationship that the overall effect is pleasing.

The two excursions outside Compostela take me through the countryside of Galicia, which hardy English travelers have considered the best region in Spain. I like it very much, a hard, cold, dour land resembling Scotland, where I took my graduate education. The food is heavy, like Scottish food; the dress is colorful, like Scottish dress; like Scots, the Galicians have to be cautious if they are to subsist on their harsh land; the bawdy sense of humor of the two peoples is alike; and the music of Galicia comes from the bagpipe, an instrument almost identical in construction and sound to that made famous by the Highlanders of Scotland. Of course, when I compare the sturdy Galicians with the Scots I knew in my youth I am not, God forbid, referring to the pasty Lowlanders of Robert Burns and Walter Scott but to the honest Highlanders of Ross and Skye and the Outer Isles.

Even a few miles' travel into the countryside of Galicia shows the observant traveler the secret of this land: the granite rock which is both the glory and the curse of the region. From deep quarries, which seem to abound, the Galician digs out a gray-and-white-flecked granite which he uses for everything. A farmer wants a barn? He builds it of granite. He wants a corncrib to protect his grain from rats? He builds one of solid granite. Garages, lean-tos, small homes and large are all built of this fine stone, and nowhere else in Europe could one find so many skilled stonemasons. This sounds ridiculous, but in the fields even fences, which in other parts of the world would be built of wood, are here built of granite: long thin slabs, beautifully cut and stood on end to form stony palisades. Galicia is the granite land.

But this prevalence of stone is also the curse of the region, for land is inherited not by the eldest son alone but by all, so that fields are divided and subdivided so often in the course of a hundred years that the resulting areas are scarcely big enough to support a family. What makes it worse is that each canny Galician insists upon outlining his new field, however small, with granite walls, until the area absorbed by stone equals about thirty percent of the tillable land. And with each death, the fields grow smaller and the fences bigger.

The results: During the last sixty-six years Galicians have been going into voluntary exile across the world, so that the voluntary depopulation of Galicia in this century equals the involuntary depopulation suffered by the Scottish Highlanders in the last century, and that was one of the most notorious land scandals of history. The difference is this. In Scotland peasants were expelled by greedy landlords. In northern Spain the crime against land was perpetrated by the farmers themselves.

Galicians are said to have many superstitions, but these often resemble the monitory yet enticing belief which one of them described: 'Like all country people, we have a mania about protecting our girls until they are safely married. Now, where does a country girl run the greatest risk of being seduced? At the village well, of course, to which she must go daily and without chaperones. In any village one can see girls swinging their way provocatively to the well, hoping, one might say, to be propositioned. So ages ago we created the water rat. Each well has one and sometimes more of these fearful creatures. A water rat can look at a man and nothing happens. But if he looks at any girl, she dies. Then and there. So you can be sure our girls watch carefully and behave themselves when they're near the well. But we're also Galicians, as well as parents, so the myth doesn't stop there. For although the water rat does kill instantly, the death is very sweet. So our girls aren't too careful.'

The glory of Galicia is its chain of rías, those fjord-like indentions of the sea that reach far inland with a burden of fish and salt air and noble landscape. In some places the rías run between meadowlands to create pastoral scenes of deep loveliness; at other times they cut through low hills to produce islands, and I have often picnicked beside them; here a sandy beach for swimming, a forest reaching down to the water; there a ruined castle on the hill; on that headland a long-forgotten church; and each day a golden sun, the smell of salt, the unannounced appearance of a low-sweeping fog and then the sun once more, with everywhere the soft, sweet motion of the sea wandering inland. Galicia has about a dozen of these rías, nicely differentiated, and tourists in general seem not to have discovered them.

But when I headed for the southern rías it was not to go picnicking; I sought the small city of Pontevedra, near the border of Portugal, through which a branch of the pilgrims' route had led up the coast from the seaports of Lisboa, Porto and Vigo. English pilgrims in particular liked to come by boat to Vigo so as to have a relatively short trip overland to Compostela. But Portuguese also followed the route in large numbers and their movement made Pontevedra a center of some importance.

The reader has probably noticed that the Way of St. James lacked one thing to make it an almost perfect pilgrims' route: nowhere was the cult of the Virgin Mary exploited, so that a good half of the mystical wonder of the Catholic Church was unprovided for. At Oviedo, north of the main route, one could detour to see relics of Christ himself, while international saints like Martin of Tours, Nicholas of Bari and James of Compostela could be known familiarly; but the Virgin Mary was not much in evidence, and with her increasing importance in the Church, this lack was felt.

It fell to the little town of Pontevedra to correct this. There, in the years when pilgrimage to Compostela had diminished to a trickle, a new cult grew up around a legend claiming that the Virgin Mary had been the first pilgrim to the tomb of Santiago, who had given his life for her son.

I went to a delightful little gingerbread sanctuary built in 1778 in the form of a combined cross and scallop shell, inside which in a place of high honor I found a most saucy religious statue. It was the Pilgrim Virgin, representing her as a primly dressed eighteenth-century traveling lady in stiff German brocade, a comfortable shawl with tassels, long black Restoration curls, bejeweled staff and gourd, and a positively enchanting Jesus dressed like a child's doll. Atop the Virgin's head stood a jaunty cockaded hat festooned with cockleshells. To be accompanied on one's way by such a delightful lady must have been enjoyable, but the true pilgrim, remembering the dangerous adventures of preceding generations, must have longed for the harsher reality of Santiago with his heavy road-worn shoes and staff. At a kiosk near the sanctuary I bought a portrait of Santiago, and he too had become a sickly-sweet cardboard figure; the granite-hard Matamoros who had led Spain to victory, who had incited whole armies and who had sustained pilgrims on their foot-weary march of nine hundred miles had degenerated into a sentimental nineteen-year-old high school senior with a premature beard. Thus did the impetus of pilgrimage diminish.

It was in this gloomy frame of mind that I met José Filgueira-Valverde, alcalde of Pontevedra and my favorite Galician. A very tall and robust man, he thundered onto the scene, crying, 'Michener! How fine to see you back in Pontevedra.' Before I had a chance to speak he had laid out the day for me. 'A few minutes to see what we've been doing with the museum, a short tour of the city to see how we're saving the old buildings, then a drive to Bayona, where I have a little surprise for you.' The mayor is so dynamic as to be exhausting, yet his delight in what he is doing is so obvious that one keeps up. The museum, for example!

'I told the government, "It's foolish to have all the museums in Madrid," so we determined to have one here,' he explained. I had seen it some years before as a small building exemplifying what one energetic man could accomplish, for even then the museum was well known. Through the generosity of a local benefactor it had acquired an excellent collection of prehistoric goldware. It displayed whole cases of stone axes, Roman pottery and Greek coins. Filgueira-Valverde had also encouraged the Pontevedrans to do certain unusual things: 'This is a Galician city, so I said, "Let's have a room which shows what a Galician kitchen is like. Women would love it." We're also a seaport, very important in Spanish history. So we found the shipboard cabin of one of our sons who became admiral of the Spanish navy. We rebuilt it board by board so our children can see what their heritage is.'

In those days the museum was a positive delight, rambling as it did over two old buildings joined together by a kind of drawbridge. I liked especially two very old life-sized statues of Biblical figures. When I first saw them I thought they were familiar; I had seen them or their brothers somewhere before. Now Mayor Filgueira-Valverde told me what these rare pieces were. When Maestro Mateo's Pórtico de la Gloria was originally installed in 1188 it was an open-faced porch giving onto the public square, but in 1738 when the new façade was added, making what had been an open portico into an inside room, some eight statues no longer fitted; they were removed and kept in a stable for nearly two centuries. In 1906 their Compostela owner concluded a deal whereby they were to be sold en bloc to a museum in America, where they would have formed one of the Romanesque glories of our museum world, but the Spanish government interceded and offered them at the same price to Spanish museums, and these two masterworks wound up in Pontevedra.

For what Mayor Filgueira-Valverde showed me next I was unprepared: a new statuary wing as big as most ordinary museums. He had just presided at the opening ceremonies of what I judged to be a memorial to his own energy, for how such a granite edifice had been paid for out of a small community budget I could not guess. I would recommend this museum to everyone, for it has been done with taste. 'And pull,' a Spanish friend whispered. What this signified I was not to learn till lunch.

At breakneck speed the mayor bundled me out of Pontevedra and down to Vigo, which he passed with a merry tattoo of praise for that famous seaport. His objective, however, lay beyond at the ocean port of Bayona, a town I had not heard of before that day, situated near the Portuguese border, and there he showed me something I could scarcely believe. On a high peninsula which juts out into the Atlantic Ocean the Spanish government acquired an abandoned castle completely surrounded by handsome walls which overlook the sea from a considerable height. The castle has been rebuilt to serve as a parador where rooms have one of two exposures: the choice ones look out upon a series of colorful bays, spotted with islands and marked by half a score of distant headlands against which the Atlantic breaks in silvery splendor, forming one of the most exciting vistas I have ever seen from a hotel; the poor rooms merely look down upon eighty miles of the surging Atlantic, one island and not more than four fine headlands, reaching into Portugal. I doubt if there is any hotel with a setting to equal this, yet the best accommodations cost only eight dollars a day for a double room, while a four-course dinner can be chosen from some fifty dishes for only two dollars and sixty-five cents. Not many Americans will revel in this luxury, because as soon as the parador was announced, Monte Real it is called, the English reserved it for almost a year ahead, having learned from experience that one of the finest places in Europe in which to vacation is this Portuguese–Spanish coast.

At lunch the mayor introduced me to an adventure which I could have done without: he plopped before me a plate of the ugliest food that the human being is capable of eating. They were percebes, a kind of barnacle, which attach themselves to rocks standing at the point where breakers crash in from the Atlantic, and much of the excitement to be found in eating percebes stems from the fact that each year men lose their lives gathering the repulsive things. When served, they look like a plateful of miniature rotting turkey legs with the skin on the leg turned black and flabby and the nails on the toes become coarse. But when the skin has somehow been torn away, beneath lies a stem of delicious, chewy meat somewhat like octopus, while the hideous toes, if properly gouged, can be tricked into giving up morsels of solid meat that is much like the best crab. I enjoyed the repulsive things, the more so later when I heard one morning a lusty old fisherwoman shouting in a quiet street in Pontevedra, 'Buy my percebes! Buy my percebes! They are firm and thick like a fisherman's penis.'

The surprise that the mayor had prepared for me, however, had nothing to do with seafood. Across from me sat one of the most reserved and courtly Spaniards I was to meet, a man in his early sixties, tall, aloof, gray in both dress and manner. He was Francisco Javier Sánchez Cantón, the director of the Prado Museum, whom I had tried in vain to see in Madrid. Introductions were made, and then ensued another of those rare and memorable luncheons which can take place only in Spain. It was about three-thirty in the afternoon when we sat down to eat. It was after six when we finished, and in the interval we talked of only two things: first of the Prado, and I surprised the director by saying that one of my favorite pictures in his care was Correggio's 'Noli Me Tangere.' Filgueira-Valverde, with explosive enthusiasm, interrupted to say that he had eyes only for Spanish painting, and he expatiated on how vibrant the Spanish school had always been, from the earliest primitives through Zurbarán and Velázquez and down to Goya. For him there could be only one school, the Spanish, but when forced to state which of the Prado paintings pleased

784

him most he said quietly, 'Roger van der Weyden's "Deposition from the Cross." There can be nothing better than that.' Dr. Sánchez Cantón, as custodian of all the paintings, refused at first to nominate a preference but did grudgingly admit that Velázquez was good, and he told two stories about his favorite painter. 'An American woman who loved painting walked into the Velázquez room with me one morning, saw that forest of masterpieces and cried, "Impossible! It's a trick of the Spanish government." And then the English woman looked at the beggar and shook her head, "A poor man like this without a peseta to be painted by the most expensive artist in the world!" '

I proposed a toast, saying, 'For three weeks I vainly tracked you through Madrid, and now I find you in a fish restaurant in Bayona,' to which he replied in a soft voice, 'I suppose if one had to pick a single picture it would be Velázquez's "Medici Gardens in Moonlight." '

The second topic concerned a strange, tormented Galician woman about whom Filgueira-Valverde was one of the world's leading authorities, having written several books about her. It was late in the afternoon, with the sun dipping toward the surface of the Atlantic and only husks of percebes on our plates, when the mayor said, 'The older I become, the greater I believe Rosalía de Castro to have been. It has been a great source of pleasure to me to watch Spanish and French critics come around to the view that she was one of the fine poets of the last century. I am additionally proud because of the fact that she wrote her best poems in Galician.' Dr. Sánchez Cantón left off being director of the Prado and became again a Galician from Pontevedra, his home town, and as the two men spoke with animation of the great Rosalía, I understood why the little museum of Pontevedra had such a good collection of master paintings. When you get two Galician cronies like Sánchez Cantón and Filgueira-Valverde, one in charge of the Prado, the other of the museum in their home town, something has got to happen. Galicians are like that.

'She was the soul of our people,' the mayor continued, and as he spoke I reflected that he must be the only mayor in the world who was both a museum director and an expert on imagist poetry. 'She had a tortured and miserable life, but she sublimated it in her poetry.'

Rosalía of the Castros, a name which in her case had special meaning, was born in Santiago de Compostela in 1837, the child of an unmarried daughter of one of the region's important families. She was reared by suspicious relatives who did not hide from her the fact that her father, who continued to live in Compostela, could not marry her mother or acknowledge himself to be her father for a reason so final as to permit no discussion: he had been ordained a priest. Rosalía knew him and followed his career until he died, an inconspicuous padre in Padrón, the port at which the body of St. James had landed eighteen hundred years before.

Rosalía was a heavy, awkward girl who lived her poetry before she wrote it. 'I believe she had an exceptionally wide field of consciousness,' Filgueira-Valverde said. 'She was always interested in thoughts, affections, intimateness, sentiment and the cultivation of one's self and one's philosophical analysis.' She married a dwarf who was equally tortured, a writer who existed only on the fringe of movements without ever directing or understanding them, and the two had an unhappy life, although they did produce six children who shared their anxieties and accomplishments. At forty-eight Rosalía was dead, but she left behind three books of poetry, *Galician Songs,* published in 1863; *New Leaves,* published in 1880 when she was forty-three; and *On the Banks of the Sar,* which appeared in 1884, the year before her death, and it is these poems on which her reputation is founded.

She reminds me of Emily Dickinson, more acquainted with the world than Emily but like her the creator of a personal world which she described with passionate conviction. Her poems are disturbingly simple in construction, depending upon unexpected rhymes and rhythms.

> Dig it with all speed, dig it,
> Thought, you gigantic digger.
> Dig a very deep hole, where we can bury
> Remembrance of what's over.

Rosalía had an intense identification with her natural surroundings and seems always a captive of them.

> Give me your perfumes, loveliest of roses.
> Oh, quench the burning of my thirst, clear fountains,
> For it is scorching me. Clouds made of gossamer
> Like veils of lightest lace now cover over
> The bright beams of the sun at its most burning.
> And you, you temperate and loving breezes,
> Make a beginning of mysterious concerts
> Among the oak trees of the shaded farmland
> Through which the Sar passes with a light murmur.

I, like many pilgrims to Compostela, like especially her poems dedicated to the cathedral or the pilgrim spirit. They have been translated recently, under the direction of Filgueira-Valverde, by the American poet Charles David Ley, who has wisely not attempted to reproduce the almost accidental rhymes which Rosalía sometimes uses. Of the Pórtico de la Gloria she says:

> In highest heaven
> The band of musicians is starting.
> Those who play the concert in Glory
> Are tuning their instruments happily.
> Are they alive? How can those faces

> Which look so genuine be merely stone ones?
> How could stone make those marvelous tunics,
> Those eyes which speak of the life within them?
> You who chiseled them with God to help you,
> Master Mateo, your name's immortal.
> Since you remain kneeling there so humbly,
> Speak to me now and tell me about it.
> With your curly locks around you, you're silent.
> 'Saint they bump their heads against,' I'm praying.

But in Galicia this strange woman is loved primarily for her skill in catching the life of the countryside, and in a series of poems that are at once completely feminine yet hard as the granite of Galicia, she speaks of the most ordinary experiences:

> What's the lad up to?
> What can it be?
> Now he looks at me with a face like winter.
> Up at the mill, he wants me to dance with him
> And won't talk to me down in the village.
> What's the lad up to?
> What can it be?

Occasionally, when she sings of the small incidents of Galician life, she gives her words an unexpected twist which throws them into a universal aspect; she has transmuted Galicia into the whole world, and the expansive horizons of which the mayor speaks when referring to his favorite poet become apparent, as in the longer poem in which she sings of the Feast of the Rock, held beside the sea in one of the Galician rías:

> The quiet little tickles, the humorous tussles,
> The shouts and the leaping, and good-natured tales,
> Everyone tipsy and everyone quite merry
> *And Our Lady is stood there behind the cask.*

As my affection for Galicia has increased, so my interest in this heavy and almost ugly woman has grown. To a newspaperman to whom she refused to give a photograph of herself she said, 'Women such as I, who have not received the splendid gifts of physical beauty from nature, must be excused from exposing their faces to public view.' And now, as the long afternoon waned, I asked Mayor Filgueira-Valverde and Dr. Sánchez Cantón a question which had concerned me for some time: 'I've been studying the lives of your two most famous Galician writers, both women, Rosalía de Castro and the Condesa Emilia Pardo Bazán, whom I read years ago as a student, and I find numerous references to the fact that these two women, both residents of Compostela at one time or another, engaged in a long feud. Some claim that the condesa, who had all good fortune on her side with a great name and a better education, treated Rosalía very shabbily.'

I might have dropped a bomb with less impact than this literary question produced. At first they were astonished that an American wandering through Galicia had come upon this ancient female feud; then they were disgusted that such rumors had persisted; finally they were eager to clear up the matter. It was, of course, the ebullient mayor who led off with a fiery speech which reminded me of how seriously Spaniards take these literary brawls.

'Michener, I give you my solemn word, knowing much about each of these great women, that it was not a feud. Rosalía must be seen as a romantic, a solitary, one who broods incessantly, whose life consists of this tiny corner of Galicia into which she digs with an intensity that most human beings never know.' He spoke of the dead poet with tears in his voice and deep love, but then his voice changed and he became a resonant orator: 'Pardo Bazán, on the other hand, was a complete woman, very intelligent, of suave temperament, sensual, an activist, extremely realistic, a critic of world literature, the translator of Voltaire, but above all a grand aristocrat. She was most erudite, and educated herself a second time in Paris in revolutionary ideals. Remember one fact when you think of the two women. Pardo Bazán never wrote in Galician. Rosalía did.'

'You have explained away the fight,' I said, 'but you speak with such fury that I'm sure one existed. What was it about?'

The mayor placed his large hand on my arm and said, 'As one literary man to another I must tell the truth. It was the age-old case of a husband in a secondary position who fought the whole world in his wife's name, not because he wanted to protect his wife but because he wanted to insult the world which had ignored him. He fought my father. He fought Pardo Bazán. He fought everyone. You can say of him that he was an archivist who filed his fights in neat order, a historian who kept good records of his triumphs and defeats. He survived his wife by thirty-eight years, during which his embattled defense of her became his life's mission.'

'But was there a feud between the two women?' I persisted.

'The family of Emilia Pardo Bazán had a castle in Cambados. They had many castles. Why would their daughter want to fight with a poor countrywoman who had no father? Why? Tell me why?'

I had hoped that these two scholars would tell me why, but like granite-hewn Galicians they hovered protectively over the ghosts of these two fine women, and from them I would learn no more of the passions which once agitated this region. I was haunted, however, by a picture which had somehow been built up in my mind, I do not know how or with what authority: I see the great Condesa Pardo Bazán, rich with honors as one of Spain's leading novelists, sought after by publishers in both Madrid and Paris, a regal and handsome woman somewhat austere in manner. She is attending a dinner being given in her honor and somehow she is brought face to face with a countrywoman, big-boned and awkward and unlovely, fifteen years older than herself, to whom she refuses either a place at table or the ordinary civilities. The novelist is wealthy from her books; the poet so far as we know never gained a peseta from her poems, and between them as I see them in this persistent portrait there is a gulf that life did not permit to be bridged.

I do not invent such things. Obviously I could not have known either Emilia Pardo Bazán or Rosalía de Castro, and so far as I know have never read a complete life of either, but somewhere years ago in my wanderings I picked up this strange story of the feud between the two women and I wish I knew what the facts were.

On my last day in Galicia I did what millions of pilgrims before me had done. I went to land's end at Finisterre, that wild and distant point of rock which had been my introduction to Spain so many years before, and there at the foot of the lighthouse, on a headland looking westward to the New World with which Spain had been so deeply involved, I tried to summarize what I had learned of this contradictory nation in the years that I had known it. So much of what I had wanted to accomplish in Spain had ended in failure. I, who love music so much, had never once since that first night in Valencia witnessed a complete flamenco, and the failure was not in my trying; it is simply that flamenco cannot be ordered; one must be at the right place at the right time when duende is upon all present. The duende I had missed. Nor had I heard one note of Pedrell's music, though I had traveled far to do so.

I had never once, in all my years in Spain, eaten a good paella, even though my wife and I love rice and seek it out in restaurants around the world. At Eliot Elisofon's home in New York I'd had a fine paella, and at a Greenwich Village restaurant I'd had one, but never in Spain. As with flamenco, one must be at the right table at the right moment, for otherwise he is fed dreadful stuff which the cook has the gall to name paella.

Nor had I seen Curro Romero, he of the burning legend, perform even halfway decently. I'd seen him patiently in more than twenty corridas, that is, with forty-odd different bulls, but never once acceptable. At Finisterre, Vavra and Fulton consoled me: 'Come back next year, and go to the feria at Sevilla and then to San Isidro in Madrid and to San Fermín at Pamplona and on to Valencia and Málaga and Vitoria and Bilbao and Barcelona and wind up in Zaragoza, and maybe some afternoon you'll see him good.' The schedule they proposed would require me to attend some eighty corridas on the remote possibility that I might see one acceptable, four hundred and eighty bulls to see the great Curro Romero good in one.

'The odds are against me,' I pointed out.

'Ah, but if you see him great . . . just once . . .'

Much of Spain is like that. If one is willing to come back four hundred and eighty times, he may see something which will forever haunt him, and to those who have seen these things the odds are not excessive, for when duende is upon this land it offers an illumination that cannot be found elsewhere. And of course, the proposal made by my two companions, that I trek back and forth across Spain for months in search of that golden moment, would yield compensations other than the discovery of the moment itself, and this I knew. The search, the renewal of acquaintances with this land and people, would be worthwhile. I am convinced that in Spain I shall never hear good flamenco, nor eat a decent paella, nor see Curro Romero good, but I would always be eager to return for the effort, because we seek duende not to find it but to be assured that it exists at certain times in certain men.

Strangely, it was not until I returned to New York that I appreciated the gracia of the Curro Romero story, for there I met once more Conrad Janis, who had told me of Romero in the first place, and he said, 'I was present in Madrid when something happened regarding Curro which would interest you. His manager told him at the end of 1965 . . . Now understand, this was Curro's greatest season. Fights everywhere. So his manager reports, "Curro, we've had to spend so much money buying off the critics . . . to prevent them from writing the truth about your bad days . . . Well, there's to be no profit this year." Curro asked, "You mean all those fights, all that travel back and forth and nothing left at the end of the year?" The manager said, "Well, we've lived well and you did have that one great afternoon that everyone's still talking about." Tears came into Romero's eyes. I can vouch for this. I was there. And he said, "To think that with the terrible fear I have each time I face the bull . . . the agony . . . the disasters. To face that all year. And at the end to have nothing." '

In the spring of 1967 I returned to Madrid to work with Vanderford on the translations from Spanish used in this book and happened to be in the city when Curro Romero was scheduled to appear on two successive afternoons. On May 25 his first bull looked at him askance; he grew visibly gray with fear; the fight was a disaster. Vanderford, sitting next to me, growled, 'Curro has just enough bravery to dress in the matador's suit. Anything that happens thereafter is immaterial.' His second bull was by any standards a vicious animal, but the president refused to have it returned to the corrals, whereupon Curro did something never before seen in Madrid. He simply refused to fight. The president would not budge. Curro would not budge. So the bull was allowed to chase wildly about the empty ring for the allotted number of minutes, after which the three warnings were sounded on the trumpet and the bull was led off to slaughter and Curro to jail. He was fined twenty-five thousand pesetas, and Madrid was caught up in a frenzy of rumor. Would he be allowed out of jail to fight the second day? Even if he did get out, would the management let him fight? As he left jail next morning Curro made an announcement which seems sure of a place in bullfight history: 'This day I shall be carried from the ring, either on shoulders through the great gate or into the infirmary.'

He was released in time to participate in what has become known as one of the great days in recent Madrid history. Critics were uniformly ecstatic and termed it 'de apoteosis y de antología' (one for the books). It began with a fine performance by Diego Puerta, crisp and magisterial, and continued with a dazzling exhibition by Paco Camino, who fought as if inspired. The plaza was in delirium, and what was most unusual, for the second time in my life I saw a string of six well-matched bulls, each of which gave serious fight, and by curious chance they were from the ranch of Benítez Cubero, who had provided the earlier string of which I have spoken.

And what of Curro Romero? Did he leave the arena through the great gate or through the infirmary? For a moment it looked as if it would be the latter, for the black bull Bastardo, aptly named and twelve hundred pounds of energy, hooked his right horn into Curro's left leg, tore away his uniform and tossed him high in the air. Normally a serious accident like this would have finished Curro for the day, and he would have been forgiven, but on this afternoon something strange happened. He lay flat on the ground while the bull lunged at him several times, just missing his head and chest. Then he leaped up, tied his torn costume about his damaged leg, grabbed his sword and cloth and proceeded to work wonders. He was brave; he was artistic; he was gallant; and in a way which tore at the emotions of the crowd, he was heroic. When the afternoon ended, the three matadors left the arena as Curro had predicted he would, on shoulders through the great gate. Vanderford and my other friends in the stands gathered about me to gloat. 'We told you that one day you'd see him great. Have you ever seen better?' I surrendered. I had seen Curro good, and he was all that Orson Welles and the others had promised. In fact, the experience has given me courage to keep on trying with flamenco and paella.

Throughout this chapter I have spoken of being on a pilgrimage, and now, as I return from Finisterre to Compostela, I think it not inappropriate to speak of this pilgrimage, which was a most real thing. Walter Starkie, in his fine book *The Road to Santiago* when speaking of the four pilgrimages he made between the years 1924 and 1954, offers this cryptic sentence: 'My 1954 pilgrimage bore for me a deep significance, for it marked the time of my retirement from official life, and I wished to perform religiously all the rituals, in order to prepare myself for making my examination of conscience.' This statement perplexed me and I asked various people what it signified; Don Luis Morenés told me, 'After the Spanish Civil War, countries like America and England were studious to send us Catholics as their representatives, and in this spirit England in 1940 sent us as their first director of the new British Institute, the fiddle-playing Irish-Catholic

Starkie. He stayed in Spain during World War II, helping to organize and operate an escape route for British airmen shot down over France. That was his contribution to the grand alliance against Hitler.' An English informant told me, 'After the war Starkie was looked upon with diminished favor by the British but with real love by the Spanish. In 1954 he was retired from his official position, somewhat prematurely, I felt, and Spain lost one of the truest friends it ever had.' It was at this impasse, when he knew nothing of his future—ultimately he landed a good university position in America—that the gypsy-loving Irishman had set out upon his final walk to Compostela.

In one sense my reason for pilgrimage was less dramatic; in another, more so. In early September, 1965, I was stricken with a sizable heart attack, and as I lay in that fitful slumber which is not sleep I thought of the good days I had known in northern Spain with Don Luis, and of the approaches to Santiago de Compostela and of how we had strained to see who would be first to spot those splendid towers rising in the moonlight, and of that portico which I had studied with affection but not carefully. And I thought then that if I ever were to leave that restricted room, which I sometimes doubted, for it seemed unlikely that I would regain sufficient strength to travel, I should like to see Compostela again.

I was lucky in that my doctor was a student of Paul Dudley White, the notable specialist of Boston, whom I had known in Russia. As a courtesy Dr. White flew down from Boston and recited his now-famous theory: 'If a man with a heart attack tries to do anything at all before the passage of three months, he's an idiot; but if at the end of three months he doesn't at least try to do all he did before, he's an even greater one.'

When I returned to Spain my capacity to travel and work was unknown. If I have spoken in this book with a certain regard for the trivial hill city of Teruel it is partly because it was to Teruel that I first went on my return journey, and each step I took in that pregnant place was a test to see whether I could stand the sun, whether I could climb hills, and whether my mind could focus on a specific problem for some hours. Teruel, where I had first seen the true Spain more than three decades ago . . . Teruel, where I had lived and died with the Spanish Republic . . . Teruel, which had been a magnet for years, now became important in another way, and when I discovered that I could negotiate those hilly streets I decided that I was ready for the feria at Pamplona and the long trip across northern Spain.

When I entered the cathedral of Santiago de Compostela for the last time the national celebration of which I spoke earlier was in progress. The great botafumeiro was in full swing, its massive cargo of silver and incense descending perilously toward my head as I slipped through the crowded nave to a point behind the main altar, where the organ seemed to be exploding. There I found the small and narrow flight of stairs which took me upward to a hiding point behind the great stone statue of Santiago Matamoros which occupies the center of the altar. Only the rear of his head and shoulders was visible to me, the latter encased in a metal robe encrusted with jewels, but beyond the saint I could look through the peephole in the altar and out into the vast cathedral where the censer was coming to a halt, where Father Precedo Lafuente was sitting in his red robes, where Admiral Núñez Rodríguez in white uniform was preparing to make his rededication of Spain to the apostle, and where Cardinal Quiroga Palacios waited to make his speech of acknowledgment. It was a dazzling moment, as rich in pageantry and as filled with the spirit of Spain as any that I had witnessed, and there I hid in the darkness as if an interloper with no proper role in the ceremonial except that I had completed my vow of pilgrimage and stood at last with my arm about the stone-cold shoulder of Santiago, my patron saint and Spain's.

THE RULERS

Spanish Kings

For 700 years the Christian areas of Spain were governed by a multitude of minor Spanish kings operating in various regions, but by the end of the fifteenth century these strands had coalesced as follows:

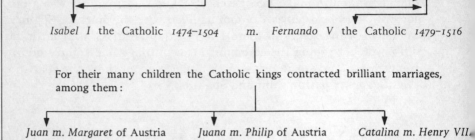

Castilla   *León*   *Navarra*   *Mallorca*   *Aragón*

Isabel I the Catholic *1474–1504*   m.   *Fernando V* the Catholic *1479–1516*

For their many children the Catholic kings contracted brilliant marriages, among them:

Juan m. Margaret of Austria   *Juana m. Philip* of Austria   *Catalina m. Henry VII.*

Habsburg Dynasty of Austria

Margaret and Philip of Austria were the children of the Holy Roman Emperor Maximilian, head of the Habsburg family. When Don Juan died, his insane sister legally inherited the throne but since she was unable to reign, her son did, thus bringing the Habsburgs into Spain.

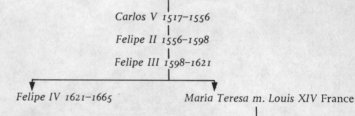

Carlos V 1517–1556

Felipe II 1556–1598

Felipe III 1598–1621

Felipe IV 1621–1665   *María Teresa m. Louis XIV* France

Carlos II 1665–1700

Borbón Dynasty of France

When Carlos II, having been stricken by the Habsburg strain of insanity inherited from Juana, died childless, the throne passed to a grandson of Louis XIV, and in this manner the Borbón dynasty entered Spain.

Felipe V 1700–1746

(Louis I 1724) interregnum

Fernando VI 1746–1759

Carlos III 1759–1788

Carlos IV 1788–1808

Fernando VII 1808 deposed by Napoleon

French Napoleonists

Joseph Bonaparte 1808–1814

Borbón Restoration

Fernando VII 1814–1833 restored

Carlos IV and his wife Maria Luisa Teresa of Parma had many children, among them Fernando VII and his brother Carlos. When Fernando died without a son, Carlos claimed the throne. However, Fernando's last wife had borne a daughter, and over protests she inherited the throne.

Carlist Claims

Isabel II 1833–1868 abdicated

On September 18, 1868, a revolutionary movement overthrew the Borbón dynasty to proclaim a Republic, whereupon the queen abdicated.

First Republic

The Republic having proved itself incapable of pacifying Spain, the citizens indicated a preference for monarchical rule. The throne was offered to a strange succession of individuals, including Spaniards, Portuguese and Germans, all of whom declined. The Carlist claimant was not acceptable, but the committee finally uncovered an Italian prince who agreed to rule, but he succeeded only briefly.

Italian Savoyards

Amadeo 1870–1873 abdicated

Alfonso XII 1874–1885 m. María Cristina regent 1885–1902

Borbón Restoration

Alfonso XIII 1886–1931

In 1923 General Primo de Rivera established himself as head of the Directory, which ruled Spain until 1930, Alfonso XIII being retained as king.

First Dictatorship

In 1931 a popular revolution ended monarchical rule and Alfonso XIII went voluntarily into exile.

Second Republic

Alcalá Zamora, President 1931–1936

Revolutionary tribunal 1936–1939

Nationalist insurgency 1936–1939

Generalísimo Francisco Franco 1939–

Second Dictatorship

The Future

THE BORBON CLAIMANTS	THE CARLIST CLAIMANTS
Alfonso XIII (died 1941)	*Carlos María (died 1909)*
Juan (born 1913)	*Jaime (died 1931)*
Juan Carlos (born 1938) m. Sophia of Greece	*Alfonso (died 1936)* (brother of *Carlos María*)
	Xavier of Bourbon Parma (born 1889)
	Hugo Carlos (born 1930) m. *Irene* of Holland

Index